BLACK MIAMI IN THE TWENTIETH CENTURY

Florida History and Culture Series

BLACK MIAMI

in the Twentieth Century

Marvin Dunn

University Press of Florida

Gainesville Tallahassee Tampa Boca Raton
Pensacola Orlando Miami Jacksonville

Works in the Florida History and Culture Series are devoted to understanding Florida's rich history and cultural diversity. Accessible and attractively designed, the books will focus on topics of historical interest such as the environment, politics, literature, material culture, and cultural studies.

The Florida History and Culture Series
Al Burt, *Al Burt's Florida* (1997)
Marvin Dunn, *Black Miami in the Twentieth Century* (1997)

02 01 00 99 98 97 6 5 4 3 2 1

Library of Congress Cataloging-in-Publication Data
Dunn, Marvin, 1940-
Black Miami in the twentieth century / Marvin Dunn.
p. cm.—(Florida history and culture series)
Includes bibliographical references and index.
ISBN 0-8130-1530-8 (alk. paper)
1. Afro-Americans—Florida—Miami—History—20th century.
2. Miami (Fla.)—Race relations. I. Title. II. Series.
F319.M6D86   1997
975.9'38100496073—dc21   97-20262

The University Press of Florida is the scholarly publishing agency for the State University System of Florida, comprised of Florida A & M University, Florida Atlantic University, Florida International University, Florida State University, University of Central Florida, University of Florida, University of North Florida, University of South Florida, and University of West Florida.

University Press of Florida
15 Northwest 15th Street
Gainesville, FL 32611
http://nersp.nerdc.ufl.edu/~upf

To my wonderful parents,
James C. Dunn and Corine Williams Dunn,
without whom I would have accomplished nothing.

CONTENTS

FIGURES

TABLES

FOREWORD

Marvin Dunn's *Black Miami in the Twentieth Century* represents the second volume of a new series devoted to the study of Florida history and culture. During the past half century, the burgeoning population and increased national and international visibility of Florida have sparked a great deal of popular interest in the state's past, present, and future. As the favorite destination of countless tourists and as the new home for millions of retirees and other migrants, modern Florida has become a demographic, political, and cultural bellwether. But, unfortunately, the quantity and quality of the literature on Florida's distinctive heritage and character have not kept pace with the Sunshine State's enhanced status. In an effort to remedy this situation—to provide an accessible and attractive format for the publication of Florida-related books—the University Press of Florida has established the Florida History and Culture series. As coeditors of the series, we are committed to the creation of an eclectic but carefully crafted set of books that will provide the field of Florida studies with a new focus and that will encourage Florida researchers and writers to consider the broader implications and context of their work. The series will include standard academic monographs, works of synthesis, memoirs, and anthologies. And, while the series will feature books of historical interest, we encourage authors researching Florida's environment, politics, literature, and popular or material culture to submit their manuscripts for inclusion in the series. We want each book to retain a distinct "personality" and voice, but at the same time we hope to foster a sense of community and collaboration among Florida scholars.

Published in the wake of the 1996 centennial celebration of the incorporation of Miami, Marvin Dunn's *Black Miami* is a welcome addition to the historiography of this important city. During the last half century, Miami has attracted the attention of some exceptional writers and scholars, including Helen Muir (*Miami U.S.A.,* 1953), Joan Didion (*Miami,* 1987), David Rieff (*Going to Miami,* 1987), and T. D. Allman (*Miami: City of the Future,* 1987). More recently, Alejandro Portes and Alex Stepick (*City on the Edge,* 1993) and Maria Christina

Garcia (*Havana, U.S.A.,* 1996) have explored the ethnic cauldron of modern south Florida. However, prior to the present volume, no book-length work on Miami has done full justice to the local African-American experience. As Dunn ably demonstrates, Miami's African Americans have had a long and complex history. Tracing various migrations from the American South and Caribbean to southern Florida, he destroys the myth of a monolithic "black community" in Dade County. *Black Miami* reconstructs the remarkable saga of how great forces (the decline of the plantation South, crises in the Caribbean, and World War II) and local and regional events (the Great Freeze of 1894–95 and the coming of the railroad) encouraged the migration and resettlement of thousands of African Americans.

In Dunn's dramatic account, African Americans are active agents in the unfolding of events. When the first vote to establish the City of Miami was taken in 1896, African Americans accounted for 162 of the community's 367 voters. Blacks had resided in Coconut Grove for decades, but with the emergence of Miami came a new neighborhood known as Colored Town. The extraordinary history of this enclave dominates the book. Dunn traces the evolution of Colored Town to Overtown, a community that sustained numerous organizations and an emerging middle class that included a sizable Bahamian minority. Drawing upon a wealth of primary research, he offers a richly textured analysis of how Overtown residents organized their lives around churches, schools, and fraternal societies, and of how they endured and resisted the ravages of economic hardship, white racism, and police brutality. In later chapters, he describes the growth of Liberty City, the scene of a major racial disturbance in 1980; and he pays special attention to the modern civil rights movement and the struggle for racial justice in Miami and other parts of Dade County. The result is an eye-opening book, a work of sophisticated scholarship that promises to reshape our understanding of the history and culture of African Americans in southern Florida.

Raymond Arsenault
Gary R. Mormino
Series Editors

ACKNOWLEDGMENTS

The inspiration for this book came from my former student and friend Robert Loring, who prodded me to write the book and introduced me to computers and the technology I needed to get the project done. He also did much of the preliminary work on the bibliography. I owe a great debt to Dr. Heidi Allespach-Stanley, another former student, whose flawless work produced the substance of the segment on the heyday of Colored Town—in my opinion, one of the book's highlights. In researching this topic, she interviewed the Sawyers, Eunice Liberty, and Garth Reeves. Mildred Slocum, my secretary during most of the time I worked on the book, assisted with the early typing of the manuscript and countless other tasks. During the final year of the project, Sergio Campos, another former student and my research assistant, did much of the data collection and research necessary to bring the work to completion. I am grateful to Florida International University, its Department of Psychology, College of Arts and Sciences, and the African-New World Studies Program for providing necessary support in completing the book. Art Herriott, dean of the College of Arts and Sciences, contributed greatly to the research and photographic acquisition process which allowed me to include so many excellent photographs. I am indebted to Dr. Brian Peterson of the Department of History at Florida International University and to his students for their papers on local black history. I am especially grateful to my friend and editor, Nancy Murphy of Atlanta, whose tireless hours of painstaking work, fastidious attention to detail, and insistence on getting it right helped me immeasurably.

I offer my thanks to the following individuals and organizations for their assistance and support in acquiring photographs for the book: Derek T. Davis of the Black Archives, History and Research Foundation of South Florida; Dawn Q. Hugh, Historical Museum of Southern Florida; Sam Boldrick, who supervises the Florida collection for the Miami-Dade Public Library; the *Miami Herald,* particularly Lissette Nabut, photograph publication sales manager; Joanna Norman of the Florida State Archives; Seth H. Branson, Miami memorabilia collector; and many individual contributors.

Finally, I must gratefully acknowledge my many students who conducted much of the research that went into this book; without them, it might never have been written. The following students of the Department of Psychology contributed to the process: Jacquelyne Agassi, Deanne B. Aguilera, Annie M. Almeida, Heidi Allespach, Estrella Alvarez, Graciela Alvarez, Rick Arango, Dawn Arida, Margo Armstrong, Keisha I. Arnold, Lynne Bannatyne, Isandy Basilio, Julia Berrios, James Bertram, Sally Blanco, Jodi Brown, Raul Calderoni, Alexander Candocia, Esther Casajuana, Jaime A. Castano, Deborah Castellano, Marina Chatoo, Yamilet Collazo, James M. Cordle, Teresa P. Cruz, Sharon Damsky, Elizabeth Daretti, Carla De La Mora, Carla De La Rosa, Elizabeth De La Rosa, Ana Del Rio, Maria Delgado, Lourdez Diaz, Maite Dumenigo, Lia Dunbar, Christine Fadil, William Fayling, Alfonso Fernandez, Iris Fleitas, Marie P. Fleites, Melissa Frank, Erica Frater, Liliana Galindo, Diana Garcia, Waleska M. Garcia, Deborah Goehner, Ileana Gonzalez, Vicky Gonzalez, Kenny Hartley, Diana A. Ho-Yen, Lilian Hunter, Linda Hunter, Maria J. Irvin, Angela Ittel, Sharon Jackowitz, Mary Jaramillo, Jena K. Jenkins, Christine Kalap, Susan Kressevich, Sonia Lagos, Maribel Lam, Jeanease Leslie, Jennifer Leuzinger, Maria F. Lopez, Lazara Lorenzo, Gunn Loyd, Lynn Lunn, Elsie Q. Marchini, Marilyn Martinez, Lupie Mauricio, Michael McCarthy, Ramon Menendez, Laurie Merlens, Lisette M. Mignano, Marisa Mir, Rainiero Miranda, Jean Morris, Nicole Newsholme, Ana O'Byrne, Elsa Orlandini, Beatriz Pacheco, Hector Perez, Ileana Perez, Lillian Ramirez, Marla I. Reis, Eric Reznick, Traci E. Rhone, Amerrette Robertson, Belkis Rodriguez, Maritza Rodriguez, Silvia M. Rodriguez, Yamire Rodriguez, Edward M. Rogowski, Diane Rosenberg, Barbara Rucki, Angela M. Sabares, Hiver Salley, Lynn Sanchez, Cora Sepic, Guy M. Shir, Jodi Strauss, Amy Tobman, Mercedez M. Valdez, Wade Vernon, Claire Villate, Pam Webber, and Pamela Winton.

Currently there are many shades of black in Miami: ethnic shades, economic shades, religious shades, and political shades, among others. There is, therefore, no such thing as *the* black community of Dade County; there are many black communities in Dade County. Indeed, we comprise groups with quite different historical experiences, priorities, and perceptions. Now, after a century on Biscayne Bay, blacks in Dade County face a watershed. In the search for answers to what lies ahead, a look back might be helpful—perhaps even inspiring.

Four historical events brought black people to Miami. The first, in the early 1880s, was the collapse of the Bahamian economy, which forced thousands of black workers to leave their homeland in search of employment. Some came to the Florida Keys, particularly to Key West. By the 1890s, the migration had extended north up the chain of islands to Biscayne Bay. There the emigrants found seasonal work on the scattered, white-owned farms that existed in the area before the city of Miami was established in 1896. A few settled permanently in a small farming community called Lemon City, north of the Miami River. By the early 1890s many had also settled in Coconut Grove, which maintains a distinctly Bahamian flavor even today.

The second historical event that brought blacks to Miami was the Great Freeze which struck the southeastern United States, particularly Florida, in the winter of 1894–1895. Temperatures plunged to fourteen degrees in Jacksonville for four days. Virtually all crops north of Lake Worth were destroyed; the Florida citrus industry, then in its infancy, was decimated. In the aftermath of the freeze, thousands of white farmers and black field workers headed south from north and central Florida and from southern states such as Georgia and South Carolina, hoping to capitalize on the expansion of agriculture in Florida. By the turn of the century, thousands of blacks had settled in Miami and in small farming communities to the south, such as South Miami, Goulds, Homestead, and Florida City.

The third historical event was the arrival of Henry M. Flagler's Florida East Coast Railroad at Biscayne Bay in July 1896. This railroad had been chiefly responsible for the expansion of agriculture and tourism in Florida as far south as West Palm Beach by the time of the Great Freeze of 1894–1895. Flagler had no definite plans to extend his system further south, but the urging of a white woman named Julia Tuttle (later recognized as the mother of Miami) caused Flagler to agree to bring the railroad to the bay in 1896. The city of Miami was established in that year. The building of the railroad and the city required hard physical labor, and thousands of blacks were glad to get the work. Thus, Miami has been populated by a significant number of blacks from its very beginning. Indeed, when the vote to establish the city of Miami was taken, 162 of the 367 voters were black.

The fourth and most recent factor influencing the presence of blacks in Dade County has been the economic and political turmoil in Haiti and Cuba. This unrest has resulted in the arrival of untold numbers of immigrants, legal and otherwise, in south Florida since the 1970s. Many of these newcomers are black.

Massive immigration has caused some African Americans to feel increasingly isolated and angry because they believe the immigrants from Haiti and Cuba have displaced them in the job market. Many blacks also feel that immigration has negatively impacted public facilities such as hospitals and schools. Consequently, among the African-American, Cuban, and Haitian communities exist low-level tension and strong competition for dwindling public resources.

Ethnic tensions in Miami extend beyond the immigration issue. Like most big cities, Miami has not solved its policing problem. The result has been a decade of deadly race riots which have shaken the city to its core and earned Miami the title of the most ethnically divided city in America. Today, multiethnic black Miami has slowly climbed into the mainstream with help from many people in the white and Hispanic communities. From the city's earliest days, there were whites who spoke out against injustices committed upon blacks; whites were a key element in Miami's civil rights struggle. More recently, Hispanics have begun to offer blacks access to the opportunities created by the phenomenal growth of the Latino community.

This book is not intended to be a comprehensive history of black people in Dade County. Nor is it intended to describe every significant event and individual in Miami's one hundred years of black history. Rather, the book represents a look back at Miami's first century through black eyes. It tells the story of black Miami through events in the lives of some of the black people who lived through that century of struggle and triumph. If these pages reveal cause for both agony and celebration, it is because blacks in Miami have had ample reason for both. Personally, I see triumph more than anything else. As this book reveals, blacks ultimately prevailed over the wilderness itself and over those who oppressed them.

PART 1

THE PRE-FLAGLER ERA

From the infamous pirate Black Caesar's arrival on Biscayne Bay (probably in the late 1600s), to the coming of the Stirrups and Dorseys centuries later, blacks have had an influence on south Florida history and development. With the settlement of the Bahama Islands in the late eighteenth century, blacks were but a day's sailing from the crystal-blue waters of Biscayne Bay. Farm workers from the Bahamas were moving up the Florida Keys in considerable numbers by the mid–1900s as the economy of the Bahamas collapsed.

During this time before the birth of Miami, blacks and Seminole Indians in Florida formed an alliance that lasted nearly a century. In 1804 the first black slaves were brought to Key Biscayne. Later others would be brought to plantations built on the site of present-day downtown Miami. In post–Civil War Dade County black settlements sprang up in Lemon City, a few miles north of what would become Miami and in Coconut Grove to the south. All this, before the arrival of the railroad and the founding of Miami in 1896.

Black Pirates on Biscayne Bay

The first black presence on Biscayne Bay was probably a pirate. According to the legend, before the establishment of Miami, Coconut Grove, or Lemon City—indeed, over a century before the Cape Florida lighthouse was built on Key Biscayne in 1825—a black pirate called Black Caesar took a toll on ships sailing off the Great Florida Reef near present-day Miami. His presence on the bay is mired in tales of violence, enforced prostitution, ingenious feats of seamanship, and still-undiscovered treasure beneath the white sands of south Florida.

There are several conflicting accounts of Black Caesar and his murderous henchmen, leading to the conclusion there were probably two Black Caesars, with more than a century separating their exploits. The tales that persist may be more myth than truth.

According to one version, in the late seventeenth century a ship laden with hundreds of slaves was fatally driven against the Great Florida Reef. A giant black man, having reached dry land alive and alone, set himself adrift in the Gulf Stream in a tiny open boat that had washed ashore. A sloop spotted the small craft and rescued the exhausted traveler. Once aboard, however, the huge slave attacked the captain and disposed of the crew members who refused to join him. In the next few years he brazenly parlayed this sloop into larger craft and became known as Black Caesar. His lair was Elliot Key, the first large island south of Key Biscayne; a channel there still bears the name Caesar's Creek.[1]

The area around Cape Florida was ideal for Black Caesar. The Florida Straits provided an unending parade of prizes, and when necessary, the bay granted a magnificent avenue of escape. Biscayne Bay's tricky mud flats and shoals were deadly to the uninitiated, and beyond the bay were mangroves and blind-mouthed channels known only to Caesar. On those rare occasions when he was closely pursued, Caesar headed for the maze of mangrove channels where condominiums stand today. He would quickly disappear in the marshy swamp, dismast his vessel, and sink it in shallow water. With his ship thus underwater and his men hidden, Caesar could vanish from the most determined enemy.

Another tactic Black Caesar favored was the use of a large metal ring imbedded deeply in a rock on a particular small island, possibly near Caesar's Creek. With a sturdy line through the ring, Caesar could heel his ship (tilt the vessel onto its side) and hide its mast from pass-

1. Black Caesar, a huge African slave who, according to one legend, alone survived a shipwreck off the coast of Florida. It is believed that he later pirated ships near Biscayne Bay in the late 1600s. Courtesy Leslye Nagle.

ing vessels. When a prize came within striking distance, a lookout signaled, the ship was quickly righted, and Caesar soon appeared on the forecastle of his startled prey.

According to Florida historian Jim Woodman, as Black Caesar became infamous throughout the region, fantastic tales were told of him. These old yarns form the current legends. Most versions agree that Black Caesar was exceptionally cruel and that he had a lust for jewels along with a passion for luxury. One report claims that at one time he held more than one hundred white women captive at a prison camp on Elliot Key. He incarcerated his prisoners in stone huts, leaving them to starve when he abandoned the camp. Reportedly, a few small children escaped the death camp and survived to wander about the key, subsisting on berries and shellfish and, in time, developing a primitive language of their own. This may account for the Seminole legend that the key was haunted.

In the early 1700s Black Caesar left Biscayne Bay to join the arch-pirate Captain Edward Teach, alias Blackbeard, who was operating from the west coast of Florida near Tampa. Black Caesar became Black Beard's trusted lieutenant; together in the forty-gun *Queen Anne's Revenge,* they plagued the American coast. Their partnership ended abruptly when the British navy killed Teach off the coast of North Carolina in 1718. Black Caesar was reportedly captured, taken to Virginia for trial, and hanged the same year in Williamsburg.

Nearly a century after the death of the first Black Caesar, there were reports of another black pirate operating in the Biscayne Bay area. This pirate was an American-born slave who had an African mother and a Scottish father. He learned the local channels and was attacking ships in the Florida Straits in the early 1800s. This second black pirate soon adopted his predecessor's name, also becoming known as Black Caesar.

The new Black Caesar ventured far into the Caribbean. He was said to have captured a treasure ship eight hundred miles east of Cuba, carrying twenty-six tons of silver. The pirate sailed the galleon to Biscayne Bay, where it is believed he unloaded his prize. What he did with his mountainous fortune remains a mystery.

By 1828 this Black Caesar had become such a nuisance to shipping that President Andrew Jackson's new administration organized a naval expedition to end the buccaneer's Biscayne Bay operations. Black

Caesar temporarily eluded the navy and, like his predecessor, escaped to Florida's west coast where he met his death. There are two versions of what happened. Some say he was killed by a woman while boarding a vessel in the Gulf of Mexico. A second version asserts that he was finally captured by the navy and taken to Key West, where he was tied to a tree and burned to death. The fatal fire was said to have been lighted by the widow of a Baltimore preacher whose eyes Caesar had burned out.

Did either Black Caesar actually exist? Most Miami historians leave the question open, but there is evidence that pirates may have operated in the Biscayne Bay area prior to the arrival of English-speaking whites. According to Woodman, "In the early 1900s, before a concrete breakwater protected Cape Florida, the seas washed away the shoreline and uncovered ancient arms, pirate bar-shot, and a skeleton in a crude cypress coffin. Gold coins have been found on Virginia and Elliot Keys. A captain's chest and silver coins have been uncovered in the mangroves near Cutler Ridge."

Coconut Grove pioneer Commodore Ralph Munroe arrived at the foot of Biscayne Bay by way of Caesar's Creek in 1877. An acknowledgment that pirates operated on Biscayne Bay long before his arrival is contained in his memoirs:

> We entered Biscayne Bay through Caesar's Creek, a long and winding channel, running first through a submerged bank three miles wide, then between a number of beautifully wooded islands, and finally branching into several entrances to the foot of the Bay. Here we were again invested with the spirit of piracy, for this was the stronghold of Black Caesar, a giant negro, who took toll from passing vessels along the reef. . . . Caesar's Rock, a small island about the middle of the creek, was reputed to be the dwelling place and shipyard of the pirate. It was afterwards bought by my friends the Hines, and we explored it on many occasions, looking for buried treasure, but finding nothing more than rusty iron.[2]

Blacks on Early Key Biscayne (1804–1893)

The first sustained presence of blacks in what is now Dade County dates back to 1804, at which time Florida was still under Spanish control. The Spanish government was awarding tracts of land to Spanish citizens, particularly those living in St. Augustine, to settle on an island on the lower east coast of Florida which they called Key Buskin. One hundred acres were granted to each head of household, fifty for each child, and twenty-five for each slave.

In 1790, less than a decade after the American Revolution, a Spaniard named Pedro Fornills applied for a tract containing 175 acres on uninhabited Key Biscayne. In 1804, Fornills left St. Augustine in a newly purchased schooner to settle the island. He was accompanied by his family, two Spanish companions, and several slaves. With his slaves, Fornills brought his tract of land on Key Biscayne under cultivation, but his involvement in the venture was short lived. Being far from the protection of Spanish guns at St. Augustine, he faced raids by marauding English and French ships. In 1805 Fornills returned to St. Augustine, where he soon died. However, in his departure he left behind some of his slaves, who had escaped into the nearby swamp. One of Fornills' companions, a man known only as Vincent, also stayed on the island with some of the slaves and successfully grew crops of guinea corn and coffee.

In his book about the early settlement of the island, Jim Woodman documents the fact that Fornills' slaves remained there for several seasons; however, their ultimate fate is a mystery. The slaves left behind by Fornills and Vincent may well have been the first blacks to settle permanently in what is now Dade County. Woodman observes that after the failure of the Fornills venture, "There were no white settlers in the next few years, instead hundreds of Indians and negroes swarmed over the island."

In the twenty years between the departure of Fornills and the building of the Cape Florida lighthouse in 1825, Key Biscayne was frequented by gulls, sea turtles, Indians, and escaped slaves from Georgia and other southern states. Cape Florida, at the tip of Key Biscayne, was the departure point for runaways en route to the Bahamas and freedom. It was a well-chosen point. Key Biscayne stands nearer to the world's mightiest ocean current, the Gulf Stream, than any other piece of land. Andros Island and several other Bahama Islands were ultimately settled by escaped slaves from the United States who launched their trip to freedom from Key Biscayne, long before English-speaking whites settled the island. According to Woodman, in 1821 more than a hundred slaves and Indians were on the island in search of subsistence. "These hunted 'Black Indians' could feel the slave catchers' foot-steps nearby as they waited for boats to take them across the straits to the Bahamas."[3]

Spain ceded Florida to the United States in 1821. Mary Ann Davis, the wife of the U.S. marshal in St. Augustine, purchased the Fornills tract from Pedro Fornills's son, who was living in St. Augustine with his widowed mother. The Davis family moved to Key Biscayne in the early 1820s. When Davis learned that the federal government was in-terested in building a lighthouse on the island, he deeded the govern-ment three acres at the southernmost tip.

The lighthouse was built in 1825 using English bricks brought in by sea by its Boston builder. The first lighthouse keeper, John De Bose, arrived on May 7, 1825, to assume his duties. In the 1830s the light-

2. The Cape Florida light-house on Key Biscayne, where the slave Aaron Carter was killed during an Indian attack in 1836. During the 1800s countless black escaped slaves, primarily from Georgia and the Carolinas, used this tiny island as their departure point for the Bahama Islands and freedom. Courtesy Historical Museum of Southern Florida.

house served mainland white settlers as a refuge from Indian attacks during the Third Seminole Indian War.

One of the most dramatic events to occur on Key Biscayne took place in July 1836. It involved the lighthouse keeper, J. B. Thompson, a slave named Aaron Carter, and dozens of hostile Indians who held the lighthouse under siege. Thompson and Carter defended the lighthouse for several days as they waited for help to arrive. Carter was killed in the fierce fighting and was buried on the island near the lighthouse. According to Joan Gill Blank, "When they brought down Carter's body, they dug a grave and buried him beside the lighthouse, the only person ever killed in defense of a U.S. lighthouse attacked by Indians. If Aaron Carter was a slave, he was free at last."[4]

As a result of the Indian attacks on Key Biscayne, in 1838 the military established a small fort on the key, called Fort Bankhead. It became the major staging area for United States troops engaged in Indian warfare in south Florida. In addition to the federal personnel on the island, a few white civilian settlers were attracted to the key, and the town of Key Biscayne was platted in 1838. Later the army moved its operations to the north side of the Miami River. There they established Fort Dallas.

The Migration of Bahamian Blacks to the Florida Keys (1646–1896)

In 1646 an Englishman, Captain William Sayle, reported that the British government had granted him of one of the Bahama Islands. Although no record of such a claim has ever been found, it is known that a company called the Eleutheran Adventurers was founded in London in that year for the purpose of establishing a colony in the New World. Sayle led a group of English settlers to the Bahamian island that Columbus had named Segatoo, and he changed its name to Eleuthera.

Probably no colony was ever established with broader or more anarchic concepts of freedom. The whites who were attracted to the colony at Eleuthera were different from other settlers arriving in the New World. Most wanted more religious freedom than was granted in England at the time. Among them were religious zealots and, later, revolutionaries seeking refuge, who contributed to the laissez-faire propensities of the colonists.

Most of the adventurers were cockney fisherfolk. Once ensconced in the Bahamas, their fishing and turtling expeditions carried them to the islands of the West Indies and along the Florida coast and keys. They sold their catches in Key West and in Havana. These people became known as Conchs, named after a shellfish found abundantly in the Caribbean and Florida Keys and eaten heartily by these seafaring people. Some of the Conchs migrated from the Bahama Islands to Key West and up the Florida Keys.

Many of the blacks on Eleuthera were runaway slaves from West Indian plantations. Others were dropped there after British sailors liberated slave ships on the high seas when England abolished slavery in 1807. The descendants of these former slaves moved through the Florida Keys with the Conchs in their various enterprises. Consequently, many black Bahamians became accomplished at fishing and sailing the waters off the Florida coast.

In addition to fishing, the islands' economy and lifestyle were built around wrecking. Whenever there was a shipwreck, white and black wreckers would drop what they were doing and head for the site; whatever they salvaged they either could sell or use themselves.

Many of the black Bahamian men worked on steamers, and some were even ship captains. The abundant cedar and other fine woods on the banks of many of the islands drew other black Bahamian families into shipbuilding.

There were also good jobs to be had in agriculture, sponging, and turtling. Turtling provided food as well as income. Bahamians cultivated pineapples, limes, and sapodillas (which they called sours and dillies). The fragrant, half-wild Mexican limes grown in the islands were in demand as a scurvy preventive on sailing vessels, which accounts for the name "lime-juicers" being given to ships from the Bahamas.

Some of the Conchs and blacks drifted to the Florida Keys to grow pineapples, which turned out to be a remarkable commercial venture. They cut down the virgin mahogany and dogwood forests of the upper Keys to plant large tracts of pineapples. By the late 1890s these plantations had attracted a considerable number of Bahamian blacks as laborers. The main fields, on Elliot Key and Key Largo, were soon producing firm, juicy pineapples of superior flavor, which were transported to the New York, Baltimore, and Boston markets on a Conch-owned fleet of fast sloops. Excitement ran high when the pineapple fleet prepared to sail; black workers, balancing huge baskets of pineapples on their heads, loaded the waiting ships. The sloops then sailed north past Cape Florida, racing one another as well as the ripening fruit. A perfectly timed arrival was highly lucrative, but a late one meant a worthless cargo of spoiled pineapples. By 1875 the upper Keys annually shipped a million crates to northern markets. Blacks made up the bulk of the labor force in this lucrative industry as more and more of them migrated from the Bahamas to the Florida Keys.

Then, suddenly, it all ended. The pineapples stopped growing and the young plants turned brown. The Conchs called it the brown wilt. Actually, the thin layer of rich soil, a product of centuries of decomposing tropical vegetation, had finally given out. As the nineteenth century drew to a close, black workers in the Florida Keys were looking north for new jobs.

A book written in 1889 gives a clear image of black Bahamian family life at the close of the nineteenth century. L. D. Poules was a circuit justice from England who traveled to many of the small Bahamian islands, keeping a journal of daily Bahamian life as he saw it. By his account, meat was imported from the United States, as were peaches,

3. Early black settlers on Plantation Key, circa 1895. Blacks from the Bahama Islands settled in the Florida Keys following the collapse of the Bahamian economy in the late 1800s. Courtesy Historical Museum of Southern Florida.

apples, and pears. Bananas, watermelon, potatoes, and onions were abundant. Fish, grits, sugar cane, and oranges were also plentiful and became an essential part of the Bahamian diet. In spite of the abundance of food, according to Poules, many black Bahamian families were near starvation as the economy of the country collapsed.[5]

Many blacks felt the urge to leave the Bahamas due to the racial discrimination and economic exploitation they experienced in the islands. The so-called truck system of farming, similar to the sharecropping system of the southern United States following the Civil War, sucked the economic life out of black families, who were paid with such goods as flour or other commodities rather than with cash. The desire for cash led many Bahamians to Key West, where work was rewarded with money.

The economic and social deprivation that blacks suffered in the Bahamas sent many of them to the Florida Keys. Very little has been written about the ethnic background and history of these early black immigrants to the Keys, but it is believed that black wreckers from the Bahamas and Key West visited the Biscayne Bay area even before the tip of the Florida peninsula was settled by the first white English-speaking families.

As white farmers began to trickle down to the wilderness on Biscayne Bay in the 1870s, black Bahamians, seeking to escape the economic decline in the Bahamas, migrated seasonally to the south Florida area to find farm work. By the time the city of Miami was founded, there was a growing Bahamian population permanently settled in various parts of Dade County. There were Bahamian enclaves in Lemon City, Coconut Grove, and Cutler in far south Dade County. When Miami was established in 1896 more than 40 percent of its black population was Bahamian.

The Bahamians brought their African-derived customs and traditions to South Florida. The most notable among those that survive in present-day black Miami are the Jonkonnu and Goombay celebrations.

The Jonkonnu is a street festival of African derivation which probably emerged first in Jamaica. It is celebrated around Christmas in the Caribbean and Miami's black Coconut Grove community. The most elaborate eighteenth-century description of the Jamaican festivals may be found in the narrative of Edward Long, an English planter/politician and author of *The History of Jamaica*, published in 1774. Long's history documents elaborate street performances which he undoubt-edly observed during his residence on the island in the 1750s and 1760s. These street performances included masked characters performing in mime as well as troupes of players acting out scenes from English theatrical plays.

Other chroniclers of the time also refer to black dancers wearing strange face masks and horned headdresses. Contemporary descrip-tions, especially Long's, strongly suggest two separate groups perform-ing independently and representing two different traditions of art and theater. One of these traditions was distinctly African, and the other was derived from English folk theater. Long not only describes the performers and their costumes—especially the cow tails, cow horns, and swords—but also notes that the principal dancer wore a visor-type mask with a mouth section supported by boar tusks. He called this central character John Connu. According to one account of the origins of the Jonkonnu, both the parade and the main dancer are an honorable memorial to John Conny, a successful black merchant near Axim on the Guinea Coast around 1720.

According to Basil Smith and Gene Tinnie, experts on the Bahamian influence in Miami, "Junkanoo was first celebrated centuries ago by Africans brought to the New World as slaves. Originally known as John Connu or John Canoe, the festival's name is believed to be the anglicized form of Jananin Canno. The name is said to be a combina-tion of the West African Quojas tribe's deity Canno and the dead, or the Janni, who were regarded as patrons of the tribe."[6]

The other big annual celebration in the black section of Coconut Grove is the Goombay Festival, also a tradition now rooted in South Florida. It is also observed in Bermuda, where the Christmas dancers and their celebration are known as Goombey. These gaily costumed street dancers have performed since at least the early 1800s, although the style of their costumes and the festival's formal structure have changed considerably. In an account of the event from 1829, the cel-ebration was observed near Christmas and was performed on the lawn of an estate in Bermuda. The participants were described as singing special songs and covering their clothing with scarlet cloth decorated with colored ribbons. Some of the dancers also used paint on their bodies. The musicians wore neat white uniforms with scarlet facings.

Nineteenth-century documentation on the festival's form and cos-tumes is sketchy as individual groups of black Bermudans staged local performances in their own distinct manner. One element, however, seems to have been consistent among the various performances: the use of a particular headdress, a house worn on the head. Theodore Godet reports a Christmas parade whose participants sang songs of ridicule and derision. The chief instrument was a small barrel drum called a gomby. The participants wore masks, fantastic costumes, and a chateaux (castle) on their heads:

> The goombay parade is usually held on Christmas Eve, between 11 p.m. and 2 a.m. Perhaps it has been transferred to the holiday season because greater leisure is enjoyed, and it is a time of general merrymaking. At this time groups of men and boys (women seldom take part) parade about the country, going from house to house singing, dancing, and playing on crude musical instruments, among which the triangle and tambourine are prominent, penny whistles and concertinas being also called to their aid. The men wear their ordinary garments, but are masked, bearing on their heads the heads and horns of hideous looking beasts (formidable only to an uncultured mind), as well as beautifully made imitations of houses and ships, both lighted by candles.[7]

According to Smith and Tinnie, the name "Goombay" refers to the indigenous music of the Bahamas. The compulsive, percussive rhythm of this music and the witty, often satirical lyrics played an important role in the day-to-day lives of the island communities. Although knowledge of the actual origin of the word is vague, it is believed by some to have its origin in a West African dialect spoken by the slaves who were brought to the Bahamas over three hundred years ago. Others believe the word is a verbal rendition of the sound made when a goatskin drum of the type used in the music is struck first in the center and then at the edge. This technique results in a sound like "goom-ba" which has come to be pronounced "goombay" over the years.

Smith and Tinnie assert that whatever the origin of the term may be, it is a fact that the music is a unique by-product of the meeting of African and European cultures in the New World. In their view, Goombay developed from the same musical pulse which surfaced in Haiti as the merengue, in Jamaica as the mento, and in Trinidad as the calypso.

In the Black Grove community the Goombay street celebration is held annually in June. The event is attended by tens of thousands of people from various ethnic groups, although most celebrants are black.

Traditionally, a band from the Bahamas is brought over to perform for the event. The festival is known for its wide offerings of Bahamian, Caribbean, and black American dishes from vendors who line the streets.

Rebecca Gibson Johnson, born in the Black Grove in 1903, gave this description of the event in the early 1900s: "The first Goombay festival I remember was held at the Odd Fellows Hall, a long time before I was old enough to take part. Everybody would join in, looking for a good time."[8]

The Alliance of Blacks and Seminoles (1750–1840)

In the early 1800s it was the policy of the new American government, having won its own freedom, to remove all Native Americans from east of the Mississippi River to the territory that later would become the states of Arkansas and Oklahoma. The young government used the Indian Removal Act to clear the way for white settlement on Indian lands in the eastern and southern portions of the United States. This act was signed in 1830 by President Andrew Jackson.

The Lower Creeks occupied land adjacent to Spanish Florida in what later would become Georgia and Alabama. They and the powerful Cherokee nation were the largest of the southern tribes. In 1750 Chief Seacoffee and some of his followers broke away from the Creeks. These Indians became known as Seminoles, or runaways. The belligerent Seminoles resented the attempt to remove them to the West, and in the early 1800s they migrated in earnest into Spanish Florida. Blacks were also moving into the area at about that time in order to escape slavery.

As the Seminoles settled into Florida and developed their own towns and farms, they acquired a considerable number of black slaves, although it is not clear why. They may have done so as a way of imitating whites, among whom the owning of black slaves appeared to be a symbol of power and influence. However, Seminole slavery was a relatively benign system in which the slaves tilled the land, kept a portion of the annual profit (if any) for themselves, and gave the balance to the Seminole landowner.

The laxity with which the Indians treated their blacks worried many white slaveholders in Florida and Georgia, who insisted that their slaves were running away in order to join the Indian-owned slaves. The black Seminoles, as they were sometimes called, lived in the same way as

4. John Horse ("Gopher John"), counselor and interpreter for Seminole chief Micanopy during the Second Seminole War between 1835 and 1842. Blacks often fought alongside the Seminoles, fearing that the army would capture them and return them to slavery. Courtesy Historical Museum of Southern Florida.

their Indian owners and allies. They dressed like them and hunted and fished as the Indians did.

When Seminoles were removed from Florida between 1838 and 1843, nearly five hundred persons of African descent accompanied them. Some of the blacks had only recently joined the Seminoles through purchase, theft, or escape from nearby plantations. Several black families, however, had lived among the Indians as slaves or free blacks for fifty years or more and were part of an alliance of Africans and Seminoles which began about the time the Seminoles were first being recognized as a tribe separate from the Creeks.

In times of conflict with whites, such as when the government attempted to remove the Indians and return blacks to slave plantations, the blacks often cast their lot with the Indians. The Indians repaid them with their loyalty and respect. They also grew more dependent upon the blacks as interpreters in their dealings with whites. There was some intermarriage between the two groups, but their primary bond was their mutual need to survive in the Florida wilderness against the ever-increasing threat of the United States Army. The impact of the conflict with the army was experienced throughout the Florida Territory as, ultimately, full-scale war erupted. The important role of blacks in this conflict generally has not been recognized. Florida's three Seminole wars were essentially about black people. The Seminoles simply refused to surrender to the slavers' chains the blacks upon whom they had come to rely.

Some of the blacks who moved south with the Seminoles became distinguished leaders among the Indians and occasionally even led them into battle against the military forces of the United States and in raids on white settlements. But their most indispensable function was language interpretation.

The most noted among the black interpreters was a former slave called Negro Abraham who had escaped from Georgia and embarked

5. "Negro Abraham," best known of the black Seminoles, shown standing, third from left. He was an interpreter for the Indians in their dealings with whites. He was described by army officers who knew him as being very influential, articulate, shrewd, and almost "French-like" in his bearing. Also shown are Seminole chiefs Billy Bowlegs (seated far left) and John Jumper (seated third from right). Courtesy Historical Museum of Southern Florida.

upon a new life with the Seminoles, marrying an Indian woman. He was characterized by the army's commanding general in the field as "a negro chief and the most cunning and intelligent negro we have here." On March 28, 1833, with Abraham as their interpreter, the Seminoles signed what they thought was a preliminary set of conditions for their eventual move to the West. They were embittered when the government informed them that they had in fact signed a binding treaty requiring them to vacate their lands immediately. The matter soured Abraham, who was accused by some of selling out the Indians. Maintaining his innocence, he never again lent his name in treaty negotiations.

Blacks were present and participated when Seminoles massacred more than one hundred white soldiers marching between Tampa and Ocala in the winter of 1834. Their commander was Brevet Major Francis Langhorne Dade, the man after whom Dade County is named.

On December 28, 1834, a cold and rainy day, blacks joined forces with the Indians at the Great Wahoo Swamp. Together they attacked Dade, who was marching with two companies and a six-pound cannon from Fort Brooke, now called Tampa, to Fort King, near present-day Ocala. As the major tried to cheer the men on from horseback at the head of the column, his troops slushed their way along the little trail called the Fort King Road. Dozens of Indians suddenly rose from palmetto bushes and from behind pine trees, firing at point-blank range. A bullet ripped into Dade's heart, killing him before he hit the ground. Half of his men, more than fifty, fell at the first volley. Satisfied with their swift victory, the Seminoles withdrew.

The battle might have ended then except for an astonishing development. Instead of dispersing and taking cover in the pine woods, Dade's decimated forces chopped down small pine trees and hastily arranged them in a triangular fortification. The Indians, dumbfounded, watched from a distance as the soldiers boxed themselves in, presenting an opportunity that the chiefs could not ignore. In a final deadly assault, the Indians stormed the small fortification and overwhelmed the surviving soldiers. They left no one standing, then retired from the field. An expert on the Dade massacre gives this account of what happened next:

> In a little while the weapons had been gathered and the Indians left
> the silent enclosure, passing back through the woods toward the

west, taking their three dead with them. . . . Nearly fifty Negroes, runaway slaves and confederates of the Seminoles, reined in and slid to the ground from saddleless horses. White eyes rolling in dark faces, they leaned on the barricade and saw for the first time, white masters at their mercy. Escaped from brutal owners and stripped of everything but hate, they heard with pleasure the sounds of dying white men. Taking up the fallen axes of the work crew and drawing the assorted knives they carried they scrambled into the pen, cutting and hacking their way from man to man. Every throat that moaned was cut, and every heart that beat was stabbed. . . . In the cold blue sky, the first vulture circled slowly.[9]

The bodies remained unburied for more than fifty days. On the morning of February 20, nearly two months after the battle, an army

6. Fort King Road as it meanders through the Dade battlefield near Bushnell, Florida. On December 28, 1834, Major Francis L. Dade, the man after whom Dade County is named, fell just a few feet from this spot. Black allies of the Indians were present during the attack. Courtesy Andrea Loring.

of eleven hundred men reached the battleground. "Gracious God what a sight!" wrote Lieutenant James Duncan. "The vultures rose in clouds as the approach of the column drove them from their prey. The very breastwork was black with them. Some hovered over us as we looked upon the scene before us whilst others settled upon the adjoining trees waiting for our departure."[10]

On the day of the battle, Major Dade had a black guide named Luis Fatio, also called Louis Pacheco. Dade used him to scout ahead of his troops. It has been asserted that Pacheco disclosed the troop's movements to the Seminoles, but this is almost certainly not true. The Indians had been watching the Dade column virtually since it left Tampa. The only route the troops could have taken was the Fort King Road; the Seminoles did not need Pacheco to tell them that.

For a time it was assumed that the former slave and guide was buried with the rest of Dade's command, but the slave had survived the attack. In the early summer of 1837 he returned to Fort Brooke, the embarkation point of the Dade command.

The first volley on that fateful morning had missed Pacheco, but with great presence of mind he had dropped immediately to the ground and played dead. With Major Dade and the advance guard lying dead in front of him and the Seminoles approaching during the first attack, he had risen to his feet and pleaded for his life, explaining that he was a slave accompanying the command against his will. A Seminole chief named Jumper ordered his life spared, and Pacheco became Jumper's property thereafter. Chief Jumper accompanied Pacheco on his return to Fort Brooke, and the military authorities accepted his story. So instead of being executed as a spy, Pacheco was sent west with a group of Seminoles to the Oklahoma Territory where, although technically a slave, he lived on an equal footing with the Indians. Later he was sold again and taken to Austin, Texas, where he lived for forty years. Presumably, he gained his freedom, though little is known of his life in Texas.

The Dade massacre was big news all over America. Nothing like it had ever happened. This Indian victory in the Florida pine woods would be surpassed in American history only by the slaughter of General George Armstrong Custer and his men at the battle of Little Big Horn in southeast Montana several decades later.

Following the Dade massacre, General Thomas Sidney Jesup was charged with rounding up and removing all the Seminoles and escaped slaves in Florida. He deployed an army of eight thousand men, the most formidable ever assembled in the territory up to that time. The debilitating effects of warfare waged by this overwhelming force marked the beginning of the decline of black influence among the Seminoles. Gradually, blacks surrendered, tiring of the unending conflict. Some told dreadful stories of the hardships involved in living closely with the Indians under war conditions. The remaining Indians and a handful of blacks who stayed with them were forced further south on the peninsula toward the newly established Dade County.

In the mid–1800s a small band of Cuban maroons or Spanish-Negroes—a mixture of Cuban, black, and Indian ancestry—already resided on the southern tip of the Florida peninsula. This band, which may have included escaped slaves from the failed Fornills expedition to Key Biscayne, remained neutral until August 7, 1840, when they participated in an attack on Indian Key. That attack resulted in the death of Dr. Henry Perrine, a well-known botanist who was the first man to plant mangoes in Florida and after whom a section of south Dade County was later named.

Although the old ties between blacks and Seminoles may not be known generally by people in south Florida today, they are common knowledge among the Seminoles. "We had a lot of blacks that spoke well in the Creek language, my mother used to say," explained Mabel Jumper in an interview in 1990. "The colored people spoke the Indian language and they spoke English, so they would tell the Indians what the white people were doing," Jumper said. She noted that her great-great grandfather owned and kept slaves in the typical Seminole way.[11]

Intermarriage between blacks and Seminoles was not encouraged since Seminoles generally looked upon blacks as being inferior to themselves. Still, Indians interviewed for this work could describe Indian children within their various family groups today who are dark-skinned and have "nappy hair" as living testimony to the Seminole-black alliance.

The Seminole view of blacks is revealed in the following legend. As is apparent, the Indians viewed neither blacks nor whites as their equals:

The Master of Life said, we will make man. Man was made, but when he stood up before his maker, he was white! The Great Spirit was sorry; he saw that the being he had made was pale and weak; he took pity on him, and therefore did not unmake him, but let him live. He tried again, for he was determined to make a perfect man, but in his endeavor to avoid making another white man, he went into the opposite extreme, but when the second being rose up, and stood before him, he was black! The Great Spirit liked the black man less than the white, and he shoved him aside to make room for another trial. Then it was that he made the red man; and the red man pleased him.

In this way the Great Spirit made the white, the black, and the red man, when he put them upon the earth. Here they were—but they were very poor. They had no lodges nor horses, no tools to work with, no traps, nor anything with which to kill game. All at once, these three men, looking up, saw three large boxes coming down from the sky. . . . The Great Spirit . . . said, "White Man, you are pale and weak, but I made you first, and will give you the first choice; go to the boxes, open them and look in, and choose which you will take for your portion." The white man . . . said, "I will take this." [The box] was filled with pens, and ink, and paper, and compasses, and such things. . . . The Great Spirit spoke again and said, "Black man, I made you next, but I do not like you. You may stand aside. The Red man is my favorite, he shall come forward and take the next choice." . . . The red man stepped boldly up and chose a box filled with tomahawks, knives, war clubs, traps, and such things as are useful in war and hunting. The Great Spirit laughed when he saw how well his red son knew how to choose. Then he said to the negro, "You may have what is left, the third box is for you." That was filled with axes and hoes, with buckets to carry water in, and long whips for driving oxen, which meant that the negro must work for both the red man and the white man, and it has been so ever since.

Still, the blacks' only real bondage was ignorance. Blacks, like any men or women with no skill to offer, only their hands, their brain could do nothing but manual labor. But being men and women, they learned. They put themselves under the protection of one chief or another and called him master, "and to whom, for this consideration, they render a tribute of one-third of the produce of the land, and one-third of the horses, cattle, and fowls they may raise. Otherwise they are free to come and go at their pleasure, and in some cases are elevated to the position of equality with their masters."[12]

Folktales and legends reflect the peoples and cultures from which they spring. It is apparent from this old Indian myth that racism is the domain of no single group.

Slavery in Dade County: The Post–Civil War Period (1835–1895)

At the beginning of the Second Seminole War (1835–1842), the United States military abandoned Fort Bankhead on Key Biscayne. Instead, the navy occupied a site on the south side of the pristine Miami River where it emptied into Biscayne Bay. A naval presence was deemed necessary to prevent the Indians from receiving weapons from nations hostile to the United States, such as Spain, or from Bahamian gunrunners. Before the fort was built, Indians brazenly canoed between the mouth of the river and the Everglades. The stockade, constructed on the south side of the river, was named Fort Dallas after Commodore Alexander James Dallas, commander of U.S. naval forces in the West Indies.

In 1838 the army took over this small camp to launch its operations against the Seminoles in the Everglades. The army moved it to the north side of the river near the present site of the James L. Knight Center in downtown Miami. There they cleared a wide area of hammock and built a blockhouse and stockade of pine logs. After the military vacated the site, it was purchased by Colonel Richard R. Fitzpatrick, a white farmer from South Carolina.

In the late 1820s Fitzpatrick was one of the largest slaveholders in South Carolina. Beset by personal problems, he left his fortune and property to travel. When he arrived in Key West, he became an auctioneer, handling scavenged goods brought to him by wreckers. Blacks served the wreckers as divers, searching the sunken ships by diving for up to two minutes at a time, unaided by diving armor or compressed air, which were rare at the time.

As Fitzpatrick recovered financially, he established plantations near present-day Fort Lauderdale and on his newly acquired property on the Miami River. He dreamed of being the first man to develop south Florida and was ruthless in his attempt to make slavery work on his south Florida plantations. Known for his extreme prejudice against blacks, Fitzpatrick wanted another Atlanta to flower on Biscayne Bay.

When Fitzpatrick came to Dade County, the available work force was made up primarily of Bahamian blacks. Of course, slavery had been abolished in the English-controlled islands decades earlier, and the Bahamian blacks saw themselves as protected subjects of the British Crown just as whites did. These independent-minded black Englishmen did not suit Fitzpatrick's need for laborers; he needed slaves. He solved his problem by purchasing sixty slaves from his sister, Harriet English, and bringing them from South Carolina to Biscayne Bay. He intended to grow sugar, cotton, and tobacco. With slave labor, he built a plantation that stretched from what is now the MacArthur Causeway to Mercy Hospital.

Fitzpatrick and the other Florida slaveholders reacted to the Nat Turner rebellion in 1831 by pressing the state legislature to restrict the growth of the free black population in Florida, hoping to escape the effects of their influence on the slaves. Fitzpatrick and his fellow planters were pleased when the state legislature passed a law in 1832 prohibiting the migration of free blacks into the state. The law made it illegal for "any free negro or mulatto to migrate, or be brought into this Territory from any state or Territory within the United States, or elsewhere."

Fitzpatrick, serving as a justice of the peace in Key West, interpreted the new law overzealously. His decisions were so extreme that Florida judges overturned at least three of his key rulings. In one instance, Fitzpatrick concluded that no evidence was needed that a free black person had been brought into the state illegally. He wrote, "The Court will observe that the Law does not *require* any proof upon oath that a free negroe or mulattoe has been brought here contrary to law, any information of any kind is sufficient, or a citizen or officer can take hold of a free negroe or mulattoe *without* a warrant and bring him before a magistrate."

In another case Fitzpatrick had convicted several blacks of entering Key West illegally when in fact they lived in Key West but had returned briefly to the Bahamas on business or personal matters. In Fitzpatrick's view, once a free black left Florida, he or she could not return. A reviewing judge released those blacks, saying,

> The Legislature could not have intended to say, that a free person of colour in travelling from New York to Louisiana, shall not pass along the publick roads of Florida, or if he did, should be taken up and confined in jail until it was convenient to the arresting officer to

send him out of the Territory; nor could they have intended to say that a vessel passing on a voyage from New York to New Orleans, with a crew of free colour'd persons on board shall not stop at Key West or St. Marks to repair damages after a gale of wind, without incurring the liability of having the whole crew seized and sent to jail, there to remain until the Sheriff thought proper to send them out of the Territory.[13]

Seminole attacks forced Fitzpatrick to abandon his Miami River project. Like Fornills before him, Fitzpatrick had trouble getting all of his slaves to leave with him when they realized that they could join the Seminoles and live in relative freedom in the south Florida swamps. Sending back to South Carolina those of his slaves who could be forced or persuaded to go, Fitzpatrick joined the fighting between the white settlers and the Seminoles with their black allies. Fitzpatrick traveled to Cuba and brought back bloodhounds to track Seminoles and blacks in the Everglades. This caused an outcry in northern newspapers, which viewed the use of dogs as inhumane. However, the dogs were not particularly successful, having been trained to track runaway slaves in Cuba rather than Indians and blacks in the Florida Everglades.

After the war, Fitzpatrick tried to sue the government for damages to his plantation and for the use of his property as army quarters. In 1842, he finally gave up on the idea and sold the plantation to his nephew, William English, who also had a vision of creating a southern aristocracy on Biscayne Bay.

From Charleston, English brought a schoonerload of building supplies and a number of slaves, including some who were skilled in construction. He had his slaves reclear the land and plant limes and lemons, which were still in wide demand for the treatment of scurvy aboard ships. The slaves built two stone houses using native lime rock. One was a two-story residence for English and his family; the other, a ninety-seven-foot-long, seventeen-foot-wide, single-story building, was meant to serve as living quarters for his slaves. But before this building was completed, English heard about the discovery of gold in California in 1849. He sailed away with his family and slaves and never returned to south Florida. It is likely that some of his slaves remained in the south Florida wilderness living near or among the Indians.

The military again occupied the Miami River site in 1855 at the outbreak of the third and last Seminole war. The army completed the

7. The old slave quarters at Fort Dallas, built by the slaves of William English in 1842. The building later housed soldiers during the Third Seminole War. It has been moved to Lummus Park near downtown Miami. Courtesy Historical Museum of Southern Florida.

buildings English had started, adding a piazza to the two-story residence. They used the slave quarters to house troops. The military again departed the site, this time in late 1858, leaving a rather comfortable dwelling which would later be purchased by Julia Tuttle, the woman who is recognized as the mother of Miami. The old slave quarters have now been moved from the Fort Dallas site to nearby Lummus Park, where the building is being restored.

The Post–Civil War Period: Blacks in Lemon City (1865–1895)

The American Civil War did not directly impact remote south Florida. The southernmost settlement in the area after the war was Lemon City, also called Motto, located about four miles north of what later would become Miami.

Late in 1865 Colonel Thomas W. Osborn was the appointed head of the Freedmen's Bureau in Florida. This Reconstruction-era federal bureaucracy was the arm of the national government responsible for matters relating to the newly freed slaves. Osborn sent out five teams to report on economic and social conditions of blacks in Florida. Only the report covering south Florida has been found.

Colonel George T. Thompson was accompanied by William H. Gleason, a special agent of the bureau, and they visited Hillsborough, Polk, Manatee, Monroe, Dade, Brevard, Orange, and Volusia counties. They conferred with civil and military leaders and concluded that blacks were faring well. In Dade County they found only three blacks in need of bureau assistance. At this time Florida was still a frontier state and south Florida virtually an untouched wilderness.[14]

During the Reconstruction era, the Freedmen's Bureau devised a plan to relocate fifty thousand former slaves to Dade County, which included all or most of what is now Broward, Palm Beach, and Collier counties. The plan was killed by Gleason, who returned to Dade County as a carpetbagger with his own plans for the area. Broadly speaking, carpetbaggers were northerners who were appointed to civil positions in the South following the Civil War. The name refers to the bags made of material similar to carpeting in which many carried their belongings en route from the North. Carpetbaggers were generally resented by white southerners, including those in Dade County. Carpetbaggers were seen by southern whites as "nigger-lovers" who would have black people rule whites in the defeated South. Gleason did nothing to discourage this impression of carpetbaggers in Dade County; indeed, he encouraged it by his own actions.

Gleason became a legend in south Florida in his ruthless grab for power. Notably, he associated with two freed slaves, Andrew Price and Octavius Aimar, who had settled in Lemon City after the war. After Gleason managed to become lieutenant governor in 1868, he arranged to have Aimar appointed school board chairman and Price appointed as both a county commissioner and a member of the school board. Price is believed to have been illiterate. According to the late Miami historian Thelma Peters, Aimar was a mulatto from Sullivan's Island, South Carolina, and Peters believes that Price was the first black person to hold public office in Dade County.[15] The carpetbagger appointments were made before there was any organized government in Dade County, probably as a political ploy by Gleason rather than as a serious attempt to empower blacks.

A significant number of the earliest Lemon City pioneers, black and white, came from South Carolina. The black pioneers of Lemon City often lived as squatters in shacks in the citrus groves being cultivated by white farmers. According to Peters, "Many black families did not live in communities but were scattered . . . sometimes living on farms or groves belonging to white owners where they were assured of a house to live in and at least seasonal work. Home was a shack—some better than others—for which the rent was usually one dollar a week and paid for by work."[16] By 1890 there were also a few black farmhands from the Bahamas living permanently in Lemon City.

South Florida's main drawback, in addition to its isolation, was that there was no promise of commercial development. For Lemon City pioneers and other white settlers in south Florida in the mid-nineteenth century, the dank wilderness offered no commercial opportunity except to dig for coontie, a wild plant of the cycad family which grew abundantly on the floor of the pine woods. Coontie root could

8. The Hurst starch mill in Lemon City, circa early 1900s. Here coontie root was processed into raw starch and shipped, primarily to Key West. Almost every pioneer family, white and black, dug the roots for their own use or for sale. The root once grew plentifully in the pine woods but was harvested to extinction in south Florida. Courtesy Historical Museum of Southern Florida.

be boiled, converted into starch, and taken by boat to Key West for sale. The root was also edible, and it became a food staple for early settlers, white and black.

Peters reports that in early Dade County every man, woman, and child, black or white, dug for coontie. In 1910 Lemon City's Hurst family opened a starch mill, creating a large and steady demand for the roots, which were eventually harvested to extinction in south Florida.

The most common tasks of laboring blacks were digging coontie and clearing land, called grubbing. However, blacks also found work in the lumber industry, which flourished because most structures of the day were built of the strong pine that thrived in the area. Knight's sawmill was located near the bay at Lemon City and operated from 1894 to 1906. A number of blacks worked there and lived nearby on Sawmill Road, later to become Northeast Sixty-second Street and now called Martin Luther King Boulevard.

> Grubbing was the hand-clearing of the pine woods—usually after the larger trees had been timbered off—the removal of the vegetation, and the breakup of the surface rock by means of a short-handled, heavy, deep-bladed grub hoe with the help of an ax. The tough fibrous palmetto roots so penetrated the whorls and crevices of the limestone as to resist toughly any assault by man. Grubbing was backbreaking work, yet before bulldozers, or some of the earlier mechanical devices that preceded them, it was the only way land could be cleared. Grubbing was assigned and paid for by the "task," which was an area forty feet by forty feet. Clearing a "task" also included piling up the roots and brush for later burning and making a rick of the rocks. A "task" was sometimes a full day's work, and the pay was from $1.00 to $1.50 per task. The *Tropical Sun,* September 13, 1894, reported that black labor in Lemon City was usually paid $1 a day.[17]

As black road gangs swung their picks, axes, and hoes, they revealed their African heritage, synchronizing their movements to a chant led by the gang leader:

Some say Peter—UGH!
Some say Paul—UGH!

> But the God above—UGH!
> Is Lord of All—UGH![18]

The blow of the sledgehammer or hoe came on the UGH.

Black Pioneers of Coconut Grove (1880s)

The black community of Coconut Grove was established in the early 1880s. The Coconut Grove settlement, like Lemon City, was well established in 1896 when Miami was born. A white man named Charles Peacock hired two black Bahamians to work as laborers in his Bay View House, later to be called the Peacock Inn. In the days before Miami this was the only hotel between Lake Worth and Key West. The Coconut Grove community grew up around the Peacock Inn, which was built in 1882 on a gentle slope of rock overlooking the bay in the

9. The Peacock Inn, 1884. Built by Charles Peacock, a white man, the inn employed many of the early black Bahamians of Coconut Grove. It was located in what is now Peacock Park and catered to wealthy northern tourists. Courtesy Historical Museum of Southern Florida.

10. Black Bahamian women employed at the Peacock Inn, circa late 1890s. Mariah Brown, the first Bahamian whom Peacock hired, is believed to be one of these women. Courtesy Historical Museum of Southern Florida.

direction of the Cape Florida lighthouse. Today this is the site of the city's Peacock Park on South Bayshore Drive. The first Bahamian to come to work in the inn was Mariah Brown. She actually lived on the hotel premises. Later, a small Bahamian-style home was built for her up the ridge behind the hotel. This building still stands on Charles Avenue near the Coconut Grove Playhouse and is the oldest black dwelling in Dade County.

In the late 1880s more black Bahamians arrived, primarily to work at the inn and as laborers on farms in the area. They built a small settlement near the Brown home along Evangelist Street, now called Charles Avenue. This tiny, distinctly Bahamian settlement was at first called Kebo. The first black person born in Dade County, Irene Gertrude Sampson, was born in Coconut Grove on November 20, 1896. Her father, the Reverend Samuel A. Sampson, formed the first black church in the area in 1894. When she died June 19, 1996, she was the last person known by historians to have lived in south Florida in the nineteenth century.

The Odd Fellows Hall, also on Evangelist Street, was built in 1897. It was home to the black organization for which it was named and was the center of social life in the early Black Grove. It was then a two-story building. Meetings were held upstairs, and the downstairs was rented for dances and other activities. Among the social clubs to frequent the hall were the Household of Ruth and the Patriarchs. This historic building, now only one story tall, still stands at 3288 Charles Avenue next to the Mariah Brown home. The structure now houses the United Christian Church of Christ of Coconut Grove.

Bahamians played a key role in south Florida's transformation from a wilderness into rich farmland, demonstrating to skeptical whites that the agricultural practices of the islands could be successfully introduced to south Florida despite the abundance of coral rock. George Merrick, who later founded Coral Gables, noted that the Bahamian blacks changed the early white settlers' viewpoint regarding the feasibility of growing crops in the rocky country. White settlers saw the

11. The Mariah Brown home on Charles Avenue in Coconut Grove. The home, built in the mid–1880s, is Dade County's oldest black dwelling. Courtesy Sergio Campos.

12. The Odd Fellows Hall on historic Charles Avenue in Coconut Grove. The building, constructed in the late 1800s, was the center of social life in the Black Grove at the turn of the century. Courtesy Nancy Murphy.

land as forbidding and desolate from a planting standpoint, but Merrick wrote, "In the Bahamas, there is the same coral rock; and the Bahamian negroes knew how to plant on it; and how to use it; and they knew too that all kinds of tropical trees would grow and thrive on this rock. They, too, had a vital influence upon our civilization in bringing in their own commonly used trees, vegetables, and fruits."[19] Merrick also acknowledged that the way in which south Florida buildings were constructed was also influenced by Bahamian blacks, some of whom were skilled as masons. "They knew how to make a lime mortar from rock and how to use it in building rock houses and walls."[20]

The most prominent black family in Coconut Grove was the Stirrup family. This Bahamian family dynasty was established in the United States by Ebenezer Woodbury Franklin Stirrup, who was born on Governors Harbor Island in the Bahamas in 1873. Ebenezer was a mulatto and an illegitimate child. His mother had been a servant in the wealthy white Stirrup household, his father's family.

Ebenezer's mother sent him to school as regularly as she could manage; nonetheless, he grew up essentially uneducated. In 1882, when he was nine years old, his mother died. Ebenezer was taken in by relatives who felt sorry for him but apparently worked him mercilessly. According to his daughter, Louise Stirrup Davis, "He was expected to scale fish and sell them too. This being the situation, he would only go to school selectively."[21]

Determined to get out of the country, Stirrup saved his money and, in the late 1880s at the age of fifteen, left the Bahamas. He emigrated to Key West, where he worked with his uncle as a carpenter's apprentice for ten years. In 1894, at the age of twenty-one, he returned to the Bahamas to marry his childhood sweetheart, Charlotte Jane Sawyer, also twenty-one. They had ten children, six of whom reached adulthood.

While in Key West, Stirrup became disenchanted. His daughter Kate Stirrup Dean recalls that her father resented having to give part of his earnings to his elders, so he picked up and moved again, this time to Cutler in south Dade County. Cutler was a settlement fourteen miles south of the mouth of the Miami River. Here Stirrup worked as a pineapple cutter during the day. At night, he cleared land. Sometimes he was paid with land instead of money, and he invested much of the money he did earn in land.[22]

In 1899, at age twenty-five, Stirrup moved his family to Coconut Grove. Over the years, he worked as a chauffeur at the Deering estate at Vizcaya and worked on the farm which was part of the estate. He continued to speculate in real estate and gradually was able to accumulate considerable wealth. He constructed a large home for his family at the head of Charles Avenue. It became the most impressive black home in the Grove and still stands today, owned by Stirrup's descendants. Kate Stirrup Dean recalls that their house did not have running water during her early childhood. There was no fresh water system in Coconut Grove at that time; instead, most families used windmills, usually shipped from Chicago, to provide fresh water.[23]

When white pioneer Joseph Frow decided to sell some of his Coconut Grove land, Stirrup wasted no time in buying up a number of lots. Stirrup built small, Bahamian-style rental houses from the plentiful and sturdy pine trees which blanketed the south Florida area. Stirrup and his wife constructed these rental houses themselves, usually working at night, after a full day's work. In addition to helping him with the labor, Charlotte, employed as a laundress, would hold a lamp by which her husband could work. Many of the Stirrup houses still stand

13. E.W.F. Stirrup (1873–1957), Coconut Grove's most successful businessman. Born in the Bahamas in 1873, Stirrup moved to Coconut Grove in 1899. He built many of the first homes for blacks in Coconut Grove using his skills as a carpenter. Courtesy Historical Association of South Florida.

14. The Stirrup home on Charles Avenue in Coconut Grove. E.W.F. Stirrup built the home himself using Dade County pine, an unusually hard wood which grew abundantly on the high ground in Dade County. The house remains in the Stirrup family. Courtesy Sergio Campos.

in Coconut Grove. He rented these houses principally to other immigrants from the Bahamas, giving many of the new arrivals an opportunity to save enough money to buy their own homes eventually. Through these holdings, the Stirrups became one of the wealthiest families, black or white, in Coconut Grove.

The Bahamian-style cemetery in the Black Grove on Charles Avenue at Douglas Road is called the Charlotte Jane Memorial Cemetery after Mrs. Stirrup. The tombs sit above ground in the burial style often used in the Bahamas. According to Louise Stirrup Davis, the Stirrups owned the land but sold it by lots. Stirrup set aside fourteen

15. The Charlotte Jane Memorial Cemetery on Douglas Road at Charles Avenue. The Stirrups and many other Coconut Grove black pioneers are buried here. Notice the above-ground style of burial which is commonly used in the Bahamas. Courtesy Sergio Campos.

16. The entire black community of Coconut Grove, circa mid–1880s. Most of the blacks were brought to the Grove to work at Charles Peacock's Bay View Inn, which later was called the Peacock Inn. Notice the Bahamian influence on dress. Courtesy Historical Museum of Southern Florida.

lots for his wife and family members because Mrs. Stirrup did not want to be dug up after her death to make room for more bodies, a common practice in those days.[24]

At one time or another, E. W. F. "Uncle Abe" Stirrup owned much of the land that today comprises the Grove's downtown area. He also owned property along what is now Flagler Street. During the Great Depression of the 1930s, however, Stirrup lost much of the land as well as some seventy thousand dollars in cash when the Biscayne Bank failed. Despite this setback and despite having sold Henry Flagler the right-of-way when the railroad came through, Stirrup still owned 317 parcels of land in Coconut Grove when he died in 1957 at age eighty-four.

Rebecca Gibson Johnson was not yet two years old in April 1904 when she arrived in Coconut Grove from the Bahamas. Her family had come to the Grove after a brief stay in Key West. She recalled, "We lived behind the Stirrups' old home in a house on their property. The Stirrups were living in the house they had before they built the big house. My mother and Mrs. Stirrup were first cousins. They were very good friends when they were growing up. Our families were very close. The whole family used to call Mr. Stirrup Uncle Abe. He was nice with all the kids, but he was very stern. He had a horse named Snifftin. That horse could run real fast. He had a chestnut color. Uncle Abe had a one-seat buggy and he would go into Miami on it. He would take a list of everybody's orders and bring back the orders from Miami."

Johnson's memories of her childhood in Coconut Grove in the first two decades of this century provide rare insight into the beauty of the area before it was developed. She also offers a poignant picture of social life in the Black Grove community at that time:

It was a beautiful ride into Miami. The road didn't run the way it does now with Bayshore Drive running into Miami Avenue. It used to follow the water line. It went down until it met up with the road where Mercy Hospital is now. At that time Miami Avenue followed the water line. It was beautiful; it went right through the hammocks. There were lots of birds. The Florida panther was in there too—that was something that scared the boots off everyone. Mr. Stirrup used to sit on his porch with his legs crossed and just look at everybody go by. He used to say everyone was his brother or his sister. He would wave at everybody. Anything that happened overnight was told to him. He didn't have to go anywhere to hear what was going on. White and black people came. His wife was his secretary. He was a loan master. He owned houses and rented them out.[25]

Another pioneer Black Grove family, the Smiths, arrived from the Bahamas in 1916. According to Lourena Smith, daughter of family patriarch Asa Smith, the crossing from the Bahamas was slow, hot, and agonizing. Lourena, then eight years old, was traveling alone to meet her father, who had arrived earlier that year from Grand Bahama Island. Their boat was becalmed for several days within sight of the Miami coastline. In the heat of the day the motionless ocean looked like a solid thing to Lourena, as if she could walk on it. At night the face of the sea was like a black mirror staring up at her. From the deck of the sailboat she and the other passengers could see the lights of Miami twinkling on the horizon, but no wind would come to deliver them. Finally, on the afternoon of the seventh day at sea, a gentle breeze filled the sails and the sleek little sloop sliced its way into a sparkling Biscayne Bay.

Lourena's father, Asa, was born in the Bahamas on June 8, 1873. His wife, Eliza Parker Smith, also Bahamian, was born on June 6, 1874. Asa had come first to south Florida early in 1916 to clear land. Like so many other Bahamian men, he sent for his family later. By October 1916 his wife and three children had joined him.

The family then lived in a small black settlement called Ricetown, which was located at what is now Northwest Eighth Street and Twenty-second Avenue. The area was named after a white family. On the advice of George Merrick, the white founder of Coral Gables, Asa Smith purchased two lots in the area now called Golden Gate (near George Washington Carver Elementary School), and the family moved into the Grove in 1925. Grand Avenue and Douglas Road were merely sandy wagon wheel ruts at the time.[26]

Several black-owned businesses flourished along Evangelist Street in the early 1920s. At that time the black business section of Coconut Grove stretched from Hibiscus Street to Main Highway, where the ritzy Mayfair shopping complex stands today. The blacks called it Sugar Hill. Among the black businesses located there were an ice cream parlor, a bakery, a grocery store, and a dry goods store. Rebecca Gibson Johnson's description of life in the Grove is revealing:

There was a man named Vincent Alberry. He used to have a meat market down here on Charles Avenue. Mr. Vincent would go into Miami. He'd sometimes come back telling us these weird stories that would make you feel the [Florida] panther was near. He would say that he had heard the panther and that he heard women screaming for help near the Punch Bowl (a fresh water spring along the shoreline near present day Vizcaya). . . . People always believed that pirates had buried gold near the Punch Bowl.

In 1908 the Coconut Grove Playhouse had a big wall around it. There was a bicycle store on the other corner. Black boys would all rent bicycles from the shop. The boys would ride and see the girls that were working as waitresses at Camp Biscayne (a white tourist resort). That's the way they would get acquainted. There were bicycles everywhere, all the way into Miami.

There was another shop down the road from there. It belonged to Joe Major. He was one of my father's cousins. Getting around on bicycles was the livelihood of all the black boys and girls. All of them rented their bicycles for work from Joe Major's shop except on Blue Monday when nobody worked. On Blue Monday everybody went to the courthouse, where Liberty City is now, to watch who was getting thrown in jail. I remember people would not think about going to work on Monday because it was called Freedom Day. All the boys would rent bicycles and ride into Miami.

Folks went to church on Sunday. After church you were not allowed to do anything like what is done now on Sundays. You didn't play basketball and all that. This was unheard of when I was a child. They didn't have a Liberty City when I was growing up. Liberty City wasn't even heard of.[27]

In the early 1900s in order to get to Miami from Coconut Grove, one took the path along the shoreline which had been cut through the hammocks and dense woods to connect Coconut Grove and the dusty, bustling town rising at the mouth of the Miami River. According to Lourena Smith, people crossed the river into Miami in the early 1900s at a place called Tuttle Point. On the other side of the river it was called Brickell Bridge Point. On each side a large conch shell was blown to call the barge to take passengers across. The cost was ten cents to cross the river one way. Asa Smith walked the path to Miami and beyond for many years. Lourena Smith recalls that in the early 1920s, when her father worked to clear land in Broward County, his work day began at four in the morning, when he would leave the house to walk nearly to Fort Lauderdale. After crossing the Miami River before the break of dawn, he trudged north, sometimes in an early morning rain, following the swath cut through the woods for the railroad. At the end of the work day, he walked back to Coconut Grove.[28]

Early White Settlers on Biscayne Bay (1870–1894)

By the 1870s, a white family was living six miles south of Lemon City near Biscayne Bay. This was the William Wagner family, possibly the first white family living permanently in what would become Miami. Wagner had accompanied the army to Fort Dallas in 1855 to supply food for the troops and had remained after the army left. He settled on a tract of land a mile upstream from the mouth of the Miami River.

William Brickell and his family arrived from Ohio in 1871. He opened an Indian trading post on the south side of the river at the bay. Trading with the Indians primarily for pelts, egret plumes, and alligator skins in exchange for weapons, ammunition, clothing, utensils, and tools, the Brickell trading post became the area's most successful business. Brickell owned about three thousand acres of prime bayfront land stretching for three miles south of the river to where Mercy Hospital stands today, just north of Coconut Grove. His holdings included the famous bluff of white rock along South Bayshore Drive.

After the Civil War, a group of Georgians acquired the English property, formerly Fort Dallas. They founded the Biscayne Bay Company intending to produce bananas on a 640-acre farm on the north side of the river on the present site of downtown Miami. This effort failed since the soil was too poor to produce a marketable product. In 1874, one of the main shareholders in the Biscayne Bay Company, a man named Joseph H. Day of Augusta, Georgia, sent his nephew, E. W. Ewan, "a proper Charlestonian," to south Florida to see whether the enterprise could be saved.

Farming was a limited enterprise in south Florida in those early days. Without a railroad, it was difficult to get fresh fruits and vegetables out of Dade County to northern markets. Ewan reestablished the Biscayne Bay Company in the long two-story stone house that had been built by William English's slaves. He lived in the main building on the property, now much improved by the army. Indeed, the sturdy edifice would become the temporary home for many of the white pioneer families as they first arrived on the shores of the bay, and in 1874 it would become the Dade County Courthouse (the county seat was later moved to Juno). By the end of the 1870s, fewer than fifty white people lived in the area that would become Miami.

Julia Tuttle first came to south Florida in 1875, traveling with her father, Ephraim T. Sturtevant of Cleveland, Ohio. Sturtevant, an iron industrialist, had accompanied William Brickell to the Biscayne Bay area to build a winter home in a little settlement called Biscayne, eight miles north of the Miami River near present-day Miami Shores. On that first visit Julia Tuttle was struck with the splendid beauty of the place. She soon dreamed of a city in the south Florida wilderness and returned to the bay several times between 1875 and 1886 with her husband, who suffered from tuberculosis and needed a warmer climate. Unfortunately, the discovery of the south Florida warmth came too late for him; he died of the disease in 1886.

Julia Tuttle began buying up land on the Miami River as early as 1888. Fearing that her children had inherited a predisposition to tuberculosis and wanting them to grow up in a warm place, she compared the climates of California and Florida and in 1891 chose Florida

17. Julia Tuttle, "the Mother of Miami." Tuttle helped to convince Henry M. Flagler to bring his Florida East Coast Railroad to Biscayne Bay, leading to the establishment of the city of Miami in 1896. She died two years later at age forty-nine. Courtesy Historical Museum of Southern Florida.

18. Henry M. Flagler, owner of the Florida East Coast Railroad. More than anyone else, Flagler was responsible for the growth of tourism and agriculture in Florida. He owned many magnificent hotels in Florida, including Miami's Royal Palm Hotel. He died in 1913, shortly after his railroad reached Key West. Courtesy Historical Museum of Southern Florida.

as her permanent home. For two thousand dollars she bought out the Biscayne Bay Company, owners of the Fort Dallas property, and evicted Ewan. She moved into Fort Dallas on November 13, 1891.

At the close of the 1880s life moved slowly for the handful of white and black pioneers who lived in the south Florida wilderness. This was soon to change. The Great Freeze of 1894–1895 was the catalyst, Julia Tuttle was the visionary, and Henry Morrison Flagler was the means.

Flagler had been a partner of John David Rockefeller in the founding of the Standard Oil Company in Ohio. He became one of the richest men in the country. In the early 1890s he sold his oil interests and shifted his attention and considerable money to railroads. The change in Flagler's life and fortune came as a result of his wife's failing health and the imperative to move her from Ohio to a warmer and cleaner climate. Like Tuttle, he chose Florida.

Flagler first visited Florida in 1878 on a trip undertaken for his wife's health. They came only as far as Jacksonville. Having also discovered Florida too late, Flagler's wife died in 1881. Flagler remarried in June of 1883 and spent the winter in Jacksonville and St. Augustine. During this visit he decided to establish himself in Florida and to launch a new career in railroads and hotels. Flagler opened the extravagant Ponce de Leon Hotel in 1885 in St. Augustine. He improved existing rail lines to that city and by 1888 had extended rail service to Daytona. In 1893 Flagler secured a charter to build his own rail line through the untouched lower east coast of the state. With Flagler's Florida East Coast Railroad providing the life-giving impetus for the state's growth, he almost single-handedly developed the state of Florida.

New communities flourished along the railroad tracks. The railroad brought tourists from the North to languish in the warm climate and to pamper themselves in the grandiose hotels that Flagler built. The railroad also enabled the state to bloom as the nation's winter vegetable garden. Blacks served as the primary labor source in Florida for planting, tending, and harvesting the crops that rode Flagler's rails. They also provided much of the labor to build the railroad and operate the hotels.

By November 1894 the Flagler line had reached West Palm Beach, which at that time was an unincorporated community of about one thousand people. Flagler established several hotels in and near Palm Beach, including the Royal Poinciana on Lake Worth, which could accommodate twelve hundred guests and had a dining room that could seat sixteen hundred people. It was one of the largest wooden structures of its kind in the country. He also built the Breakers Hotel. Finally Flagler built as his magnificent private residence a great mansion in Palm Beach called Whitehall.

Since most of the common laborers in Flagler's land-clearing and building empire were black, Flagler was the primary factor in the expansion of the black as well as the white population in Florida at the turn of the century. However, the growth that the railroad brought to the north and central parts of the state stopped short of Biscayne Bay. In the winter of 1894 Flagler settled in at Whitehall with no immediate plans to go farther south. But three days after Christmas that year, the hand of God moved, and Julia Tuttle's dream became reality.

The Great Freeze (1894–1895)

A devastating freeze in the winter of 1894–1895 nearly wiped out the agricultural industry of the southeastern United States. For many years, the general public remembered it simply as the Year of the Ruin, but it eventually became known as the Great Freeze. Actually, it was not one but two bone-chilling and extended cold spells, hitting the South in December 1894 and again in February 1895.

Ironically, only hours before the first freeze struck, one of Jacksonville's newspapers, the *Daily Florida Citizen,* carried an article about the expected bumper citrus crop. According to the article, oranges were above-average in quality, bright, juicy, and selling at a good price. Citrus growers were hopeful and encouraged, believing that more oranges would be shipped out during that season than in any previous season in the state's embryonic orange-growing history.[29]

But on Friday, December 28, 1894, farmers in Florida and across the South waited anxiously as an unprecedented freeze engulfed their vulnerable crops. Another Jacksonville paper, the *Florida Times Union,* described what happened in north Florida:

> A northeastern blizzard, which found its center in Pennsylvania, swept the east coast, and a northwestern blizzard, which swept down from the Dakotas coursed with equal violence upon our west and gulf coast, uniting or joining forces with an increased power, enveloped the entire peninsula . . . with the chilling breath of the ice king. [Of] our bountiful and beautiful orange groves, pineapple plantations and vegetable farms . . . nothing escaped. The people, the land upon which they live, with their scorched and withered and, in many cases dead, orange trees alone remain.[30]

The next day, Floridians awakened to record-breaking low temperatures. In Jacksonville, the weather bureau's official thermometer registered fourteen degrees, one degree lower than the temperature registered during the severe freeze of 1886 and the lowest reading in the bureau's history.

Almost every interest in the state was affected by the freeze. Businesses in Florida were at a standstill. Railroad and steamship lines suffered. Trees and other vegetation looked scorched. Fruits and vegetables were covered with ice and, in many cases, frozen solid. In north Florida, fish were frozen in the bay. Poor people were particularly vulnerable. Farmers were especially hard hit, as many lost their entire income and were left destitute.

The Florida citrus industry suffered particularly. When the freeze hit, half of the season's crop—approximately two and one-half million boxes of oranges—was still on the trees and few escaped irreversible damage. Within a matter of hours, one of Florida's most promising industries was nearly ruined.[31]

By that Monday, the cold wave was practically over. Temperatures had remained below freezing for forty hours. The calamity caused by the freeze left many Florida farmers discouraged and gloomy. Others

19. Orange grove near DeLand in central Florida, December 29, 1894. Although these trees had been sprayed with water to protect them from freezing the night before, they still looked like this the following morning. Courtesy West Volusia Historical Society.

were somewhat more optimistic. Most agreed, however, that the orange trees were safe. A majority of farmers replanted, as they would have done had there not been a freeze. They anticipated the next crop to be ready for market in March and were hopeful that things would soon return to normal.

But the worst was yet to come. The greatest crop injury results when an early winter freeze is followed by a period of warm weather sufficient to initiate new growth and this in turn is followed by a second freeze the same winter. This is what occurred in the winter of 1894–1895. January's weather was mild; trees put out vigorous new shoots, and growers felt they had come through the experience in good shape. But the trees, thus rendered especially vulnerable, were killed to the ground by a second freeze in early February 1895.

This freeze was believed more severe than that of December. Cattle and sheep suffered. Some starved and others froze to death. The entire new vegetable crop froze. Again, the loss was tremendous. Florida property worth approximately $75 million was destroyed by the second freeze. The extent of the damage to the budding citrus industry can be seen from these crop figures from the Florida Fruit Exchange:

1892–93   5,055,367 boxes
1894–95   2,500,000 boxes
1895–96   150,000 boxes[32]

According to Helen Parce DeLand, whose family founded DeLand in the central part of the state, "The trees that were painstakingly restored to life were bushy, never regaining the old symmetry." The citrus industry appeared dead. Indeed, a revival of the industry was not apparent until the 1900–1901 season, and prosperity in the industry did not reappear until the 1908–1909 season.

Among the white families displaced by the freeze were the Des-Rochers, who lived near Jacksonville. Estelle DesRocher Zumwalt was seven years old when the first freeze struck in December; she recalled the event in her memoirs: "That night the thermometer dropped to nineteen degrees and the pan of milk in our screened pantry froze like ice cream. But the tragedy of it was that the bearing grove father had recently bought had frozen, too. The oranges were balls of ice and in a few days they were black and rotting on the ground under the naked trees. Father began to think about moving farther south."[33]

As countless white farmers were ruined by the freeze, so too were many blacks who owned farms and thousands more black farm workers who helped to plant, tend, and harvest southern crops. Many of the freeze victims, white and black, packed their belongings and moved south, some eventually coming as far as south Dade County. Shivering from the coldest weather most of them had ever seen, many would settle permanently in south Florida.

The Great Freeze which struck the southeastern United States in the winter of 1894–1895 propelled ruined farmers and farm workers, white and black, to settle in warmer south Florida. Ultimately, this led to the arrival of the Florida East Coast Railroad at Biscayne Bay in 1896 and the founding of the City of Miami in that year.

The black section of the new city was called Colored Town, and although other black communities developed in Coconut Grove and south Dade, it was Colored Town that became the focus of black life in Dade County. An informal color line restricted Miami blacks to living only in Colored Town, and as a result, a healthy and viable black business and professional community evolved to meet black needs. Blacks from the Bahamas continued to arrive in south Florida, and by the turn of the century a considerable percentage of the city's black population was from the islands. Their presence influenced many aspects of the cultural and religious life of the community.

The Railroad Comes to Biscayne Bay (1896)

Only the southern tip of Florida was spared by the Great Freeze. Sensing an opportunity to build the city she had envisioned, Julia Tuttle wrote to Henry Flagler. Tuttle promised to give half of her 640 acres to Flagler for the building of a city if he would bring his railroad to Biscayne Bay. William Brickell, who owned thousands of acres south of the Miami River, also agreed to donate half of his land to the new city.

A widely believed story holds that Tuttle convinced Flagler by sending him an orange blossom from her grove after the Great Freeze. However, it is contradicted somewhat by the memoirs of John Sewell, Flagler's lead man in building the city, who wrote, "Mr. Ingraham [FEC vice-president for lands and development] was in the Miami section a few days after the great freeze in 1895 that killed practically all of the citrus trees in Florida, and killed coconut trees at Palm Beach, the thermometer going down into the twenties. Mr. Ingraham found orange blooms here on citrus trees that were at that time unhurt and carried a bunch of the orange blossoms to Mr. Flagler at Palm Beach. That made Mr. Flagler decide to build his railroad to Miami as he said where one orange tree would grow, with the proper treatment, a thousand would grow."[1]

At first Flagler was reluctant, but the lessons of the hard freeze were not lost on him. Following a visit to Biscayne Bay and Julia Tuttle in February of 1895, he agreed to bring the railroad to Biscayne Bay. In February 1896, after several months of delays clearing up land title questions, Flagler dispatched one of his top foremen to Biscayne Bay to begin to clear the land for the luxurious Royal Palm Hotel which he intended to build.

The man Flagler chose to clear the land, lay out the streets, and build his hotel was John Sewell of Kissimmee. Sewell was a labor superintendent for the Flagler system and worked on Flagler's projects in Palm Beach. When asked to go to Biscayne Bay with a work crew of his choosing to start a new city, Sewell's hand-picked group consisted of twelve men, all black. These workers became Miami's first black residents. They were A. W. Brown, Phillip Bowman, Jim Hawkins, Warren Merridy (or Merraday), Richard Mangrom (or Mangrum), Romeo Fashaw, Scipio Coleman, Sim Anderson, Davie Heartly, J. B. Brown, William Collier, and Joe Thompson. According to Miami historian Howard Kleinberg, another man named Jim Clory was among the first black workers, but his name does not appear in Sewell's account.

20. John Sewell, Flagler's lead supervisor in Miami for the construction of the Royal Palm Hotel. Sewell later became mayor of Miami. He manipulated black voters to support Flagler interests in the new city. Courtesy Historical Museum of Southern Florida.

Sewell, his brother E. G. Sewell, and three white men, J. E. Lummus, C. T. McCrimmon, and T. L. Townley, departed with the twelve-man work crew from Flagler's new Royal Poinciana Hotel in Palm Beach at six in the morning on March 3, 1896. Flagler himself bid them good-bye at the train station. The men took the Flagler railroad to Fort Lauderdale, at that time the end of the line. From there they took the steamer *Della,* and at five o'clock that same afternoon arrived at the lonely dock on Avenue D, which later became Miami Avenue. There was a compelling stillness in the darkening wilderness. There was nothing around them but woods.

Sewell started by clearing the site for the Royal Palm Hotel. Miami historians have skipped lightly over what happened to the Tequesta Indian bones that were dug up to make room for the hotel. For thousands of years before the Spaniards reached Florida in 1513, the Tequesta Indians had lived on Biscayne Bay, depending on the sea for their existence. A large village stood at the mouth of the Miami River. However, the Tequestas, having no natural immunity to the many deadly diseases that the Spaniards brought with them, were virtually wiped out. When Spain finally ceded Florida to the United States in 1821, the few dozen remaining Tequestas left with the Spaniards for Cuba, where they became extinct.

Workmen encountered a Tequesta burial mound, which probably had been in use for centuries, at the site Flagler chose for the hotel. It was located at the mouth of the Miami River, now the parking lot in front of the Dupont Plaza Hotel in downtown Miami. The background of figure 21 shows the mound, which stood between twenty-five and seventy-five feet high. Sewell ordered it leveled, and the black men shown in the historic photograph of the hotel's groundbreaking obliged him. Sewell recalls in his memoirs that as he leveled the burial mound,

> I began to find Indian skeletons and altogether I took out between fifty and sixty skulls. I preserved all the bones and stored them away in barrels and gave away a great many of the skeletons to anyone that wanted them. Then stored the bones in my tool house for future reference, where they remained until the hotel was completed at the end of the year. As my tool house had to be torn down, I took about four of my most trusted negroes and hauled all of these skeletons out nearby where there was a big hole in the ground, about

twelve feet deep, and dumped the bones in it, then filled the hole up with sand and instructed the negroes to forget this burial and whereabouts of same—and I suppose they did. . . . There is a fine residence now standing over the bones—and the things that the owners don't know will never hurt them.[2]

As word spread that there was work to be had on Biscayne Bay, dozens of black men were soon camped in tents in the woods near the hotel. Clearing the streets was not, at first, a part of Sewell's job. His top priority was to clear the land for the Royal Palm Hotel. He was assigned the street-clearing task after the contractor who originally had the job failed miserably.

The problem was trying to pry the roots of the tenacious trees from the coral rock in which they were spitefully, deeply embedded. An even greater challenge to the land-clearers was a thick swath of man-

21. Some of the black men credited by John Sewell as being the black pioneers of Miami, March 25, 1896. The twelve men (not in order) are identified as A. W. Brown, Phillip Bowman, Jim Hawkins, Warren Merridy, Richard Mangrom, Romeo Fashaw, Scipio Coleman, Sim Anderson, Davie Heartly, J. B. Brown, William Collier, and Joe Thompson. Sewell is shown at left, wearing vest. In this historic photo, the men, under Sewell's orders, are destroying a Tequesta Indian burial mound to build the Royal Palm Hotel. The Tequestas inhabited south Florida for centuries before the arrival of the Spanish in the early 1500s and the Seminoles more than two centuries later. By the time the Seminoles arrived, the Tequestas were virtually extinct. Courtesy Historical Museum of Southern Florida.

22. Tents being constructed by early black arrivals, circa 1896, as word spread that there was work available at Biscayne Bay. Courtesy Historical Museum of Southern Florida.

grove hammock on the bayfront where Bayside, the Intercontinental Hotel, and Bayfront Park stand today. The impenetrable mangroves grew as thick as a man's arm and never had been disturbed.

When Sewell took over the job, the contractor who had just extended the railroad to the city urged him to use the 150 white convicts who had been working on the railroad project. Sewell preferred to use his own men but gave in and put the convicts to work clearing land for the streets. However, even they would not approach the bayfront hammock. After a few futile days, the convicts were moved out and Sewell unleashed a work gang of one hundred black men to annihilate the bayfront hammock, which they did. This is Sewell's account:

Finally the convicts were moved and I sent out word by all my negroes that I wanted one hundred negro laborers next Monday morning to start street clearing. . . . By that time the railroad was completed and the woods were full of negro laborers. When Monday morning came there were one hundred and ten negroes at my tool house waiting for me. . . . I hit the hammock first, as that had been what everybody had been afraid of and, to tell the truth, it did look like a terrible job clearing those big trees and brush and vines. . . . I had provided myself with dynamite, bush hooks, and everything else needed. I went to work with my hundred negroes without any other foreman on the work. I was determined to clear those streets and master the Miami rock. . . . When I cleared the Boulevard and Avenue B from 11th Street to First Street I had to work my men in a "V" shape, the head men with bush hooks, . . . the next row of men with axes, and the next row with grubbing hoes.[3]

Sewell and his crew made headway but were often stymied in the dense thicket by two types of trees. One was the formidable ironwood tree. True to its name, the tree was so hard that it often would break the edge of an ax. Although Sewell's men would lose as many as a dozen ax blades in a day on these stubborn trees, they ultimately prevailed.

The other problem was a poisonous tree, the name of which Sewell did not know. He was, however, very familiar with what it did to his workers. Wrote Sewell in his memoirs, "I do not know its name, but when the bark was broken and one touched the sap of this it would poison one and even the fumes of this tree would poison, and the men would suffer untold agony. With some of them, their faces would swell so that one could not see their eyes. We would handle it like we would a rattlesnake, and burn it as quickly as we would get it down and be careful not to touch where the bark was broken."[4]

Taming the wilderness around Biscayne Bay proved to be a brutal job. Practically all of the hard physical labor involved was done by blacks. Whites who were streaming into the new city were not coming to Miami to clear land or dig sewers; they were coming to go into business, to make a fast buck in the land boom, or to realize some other dream.

Whites generally disdained the menial tasks, which they described as "colored work." The view of one of Miami's earliest Jewish residents, Isadore Cohen, was probably typical. Cohen, who became one of the city's most successful businessmen, arrived in Miami in 1896 as Flagler's men were clearing the streets. Out of money and anxious to start a retail business with the stock he had brought, Cohen approached Julia Tuttle about quickly building a store. She told him that the streets were not yet laid out and suggested that he hire himself out to help clear the land for the city's streets. Cohen recorded the conversation with Tuttle in his diary:

> Had an interview with Mrs. Tuttle, who is said to be the owner of the north-side territory, in regard to renting a piece of ground for the erection of a store building. Result very disappointing. Must wait until land is cleared and streets laid out, when lots will be put on sale. On declaring that I could not wait, owing to my destitute condition, I was told to take a job clearing land, whereupon I tried to impress this naive lady that the last labor of this character my race had performed was in the land of Egypt, and that it would be a violation of my religious convictions to resume that condition of servitude.[5]

Thus, the grueling and dangerous work of breaking the stubborn land fell primarily to blacks, who now streamed into the bay area looking for work.

The Birth of Miami and Colored Town (1896–1926)

In June 1896, John Sewell's superiors in the Flagler organization told him that there were probably enough people living in the area to incorporate a city. Sewell was asked to make an estimate of exactly how many people lived on the shores of the bay at that time. He later wrote in his memoirs, "I made the survey, going to each shack or tent and boarding house making inquiry as to how many people lived at each place. When I got through and checked up we had three thousand people, men, women, and children, white and black."[6]

As the city of Miami came to life, blacks living on the bay had no political power, recognition, or influence. However, they were present at the incorporation meeting for the establishment of the city on July 28, 1896. Four days before the city of Miami was incorporated, the *Miami Metropolis* reported that there were 438 registered male voters in the precinct, of which 182 (41.5 percent) were black.[7] Essentially, the blacks were pawns of the Flagler interests in establishing and later controlling the city. State law required a minimum number of registered voters to incorporate a city, so in order to meet the minimum, Flagler's supervisors got their black workers to attend the incorporation meeting. Therefore, of the 367 voters who incorporated the city of Miami, 162 were black. All of those who voted were men, since women were disenfranchised at that time.

The first name on the charter of the city of Miami is that of Silas Austin, a black man. At one time it was believed that W. H. Artson, another black man, was the first name on the charter. A closer examination of the minutes of the incorporation meeting, however, revealed that although Artson was first on the list of eligible voters, he was not present at the meeting.[8]

Although blacks were manipulated in the process of establishing the city, they were not entirely silent at the meeting. Isadore Cohen's recollection of the event was that a "darky named Lightburn" delivered the best speech. The man Cohen referred to was Alex C. Lightburn or Lightbourn, who was born in England or the Bahamas in October 1852. In addition to establishing himself as a vocal founder of the city, Lightburn held the organizational meeting of the Greater Bethel A.M.E. Church in his home four months later.

Three years after the incorporation of the city of Miami, the black vote was needed again—this time to move the county seat from Juno to Miami. During this period, the boundary of Dade County stretched through what is now Broward and Palm Beach counties. The final countywide vote was 690 to 468 in favor of moving the county seat to

23. John Sewell's "black artillery." Sewell so designated his hand-picked laborers, referring to the fact that he could count on them to support Flagler interests at the ballot box if he needed their votes. Of the 367 men who voted to establish the city of Miami, 162 were black. Courtesy Historical Museum of Southern Florida.

24. The magnificent Royal Palm Hotel (flag over main entrance). The hotel rose with Flagler's money and black labor, and opened in 1896. Like all Flagler hotels, it was a wooden structure, painted yellow with green trim. The hotel was built on the site of what today is the Dupont Plaza Hotel's parking lot. Declared a fire hazard, it was torn down in 1930. Courtesy Historical Museum of Southern Florida.

Miami. The black vote was a strong factor in this decision. Miami's electorate cast 403 votes in this election; 398 were in support of Miami as county seat. The *Miami Metropolis* openly acknowledged the importance of the black vote in the southern half of Dade County, "Everything went off smooth from morning until night and all worked in harmony for the general good, and for once the color line was obliterated and every one of the black and tan vote counted. White men were riding through the streets with the colored fellows, and there was a full determination that the colored fellow should vote just as he wished, which fortunately was for Miami."[9]

The first Florida East Coast Railroad passenger train roared into Miami with its big bell clanging and its whistle wide open at about nine o'clock on the evening of April 12, 1896. The station was located opposite the black section. More than three hundred people turned out to mark the historic event. The city of Miami was open for business.

Julia Tuttle did not live to see the city she had dreamed of come into its own. She died suddenly on September 14, 1898, at the relatively young age of forty-eight.

Life in early Miami centered around the grandiose Royal Palm Hotel. Like all Flagler hotels from St. Augustine to Miami, the hotel was constructed of wood and painted yellow with green trim. Built at a cost of $750,000 on land donated to the Flagler organization by Julia Tuttle, the hotel was capable of serving six hundred guests.

The white business community expanded rapidly during the boom period between 1896 and 1926. The principal business street was Avenue D, now known as Miami Avenue. The other main thoroughfare was Twelfth Street, now called Flagler Street. Of course, blacks were not allowed to operate businesses along these streets. Many of these early businesses burned down in a raging fire on Christmas night 1896. After another devastating blaze on November 12, 1899, the vulnerable wooden buildings were no longer an acceptable risk and the city rebuilt itself in bricks. Buildings in Colored Town, the black settlement across the railroad tracks, remained wooden and dangerous.

25. Black workers on Flagler Street, circa 1900. Although blacks provided almost all of the physical labor used to build the city, no black person could operate a business on this street or any other in downtown Miami. Courtesy Historical Museum of Southern Florida.

Table 2.1. Birthplaces of black citizens in Miami, 1900

Place of origin	Population	%
Florida	392	40.60
Bahama Islands	212	21.90
Georgia	126	13.00
S. Carolina	97	10.00
N. Carolina	55	5.69
Alabama	41	4.24
Virginia	16	1.66
Other	15	1.55
Unknown	12	1.24
Total	966	100.00

The boom was ended suddenly by the Great Hurricane of 1926 which made a direct hit on downtown Miami. Although it survived the storm, the Royal Palm Hotel was among the ultimate casualties as the building boom ended and the city's future became a matter of great concern. Declared a fire hazard, the hotel was torn down in 1930.

According to the census of 1900, the black population of Miami prior to the turn of the century was 966, approximately 727 of whom were born in the United States and 212 born in the Bahamas. Table 2.1 shows the origin of Miami's black population in 1900. Of course, many Bahamians came to south Florida as seasonal agricultural workers and were not counted in the census.[10]

Conditions in the teeming black quarter grew worse as the population became denser. Handicapped by the lack of even basic city services, Colored Town was a squalid, congested district characterized by unpaved streets lined with rickety houses and shacks. Fire was a constant threat. The lack of adequate sanitation facilities caused chronic epidemics of influenza, yellow fever, and even smallpox. Blacks, politically impotent, could do little to improve their situation.

Some black Miami pioneers believed that the arrival of the railroad actually worsened conditions for blacks. Dr. Samuel Hensdale Johnson, a black man whose parents were early arrivals from the Bahamas, said, "In its early days Miami was a small town, where everybody knew everybody—whites and blacks. Sunday afternoons were times

26. Street scene in early Colored Town. Notice the absence of cars and the widespread use of bicycles. Courtesy Black Archives, History and Research Foundation of South Florida.

for boat trips to Ocean Beach (Miami Beach) for picnics and baseball games. As the town developed, however, the lines were drawn fast. We became hemmed in . . . Miami really became a hell-hole after the railroad arrived and Carl Fisher developed Miami Beach."[11] Johnson became Miami's first black radiologist.

As a child growing up in a city only seven years older than himself, Johnson was a witness to Miami's development during a critical stage in the city's history. He recalled that in the early days whites allowed blacks to use Miami Beach, then called Ocean Beach. There were no people living on Miami Beach at that time, and beachgoers, white and black, traveled to Ocean Beach by boat. It was not until some time later that whites stopped blacks from using the public beach.

When the rail link between Palm Beach and Miami was completed, much of the work force hired on with the grandiose overseas railroad project. Built from Homestead to Key West between 1904 and 1912, the overseas railroad was described by the hard-boiled Flagler as the toughest job he ever undertook. Good laborers were in demand across the country. The labor supply relied upon to build the Panama Canal was not available to Flagler, and the law provided that labor was not to be imported from the Caribbean. Thus black workers from the Bahamas, Cuba, and Jamaica could not be used. Flagler resorted to hiring foreign workers, particularly Germans and Italians, who were arriving in the North by the thousands, anxious to improve their lot. Most were recruited in New York and shipped to Miami for work on the extension. The intense recruiting effort did bring in some black workers, and by December 1905 the Flagler organization had set up separate camps for Italian, German, Greek, and black laborers. The *Miami Evening Record,* now defunct, reported that the Flagler organization used these workers differently. The most grueling labor was reserved for black workers. An executive committee of the organization, headed by Flagler himself, reported that blacks, being accustomed to the use of the ax, did all the rough work of clearing and that white laborers followed to do the grading.

By July 1906 the Flagler organization, having secured sufficient foreign workers, summarily fired many of its black extension workers. The *Daily Miami Metropolis* reported in a reprint from the Fort Pierce News:

The F.E.C. Railroad is about to dispense with nearly, or all of its colored section hands having made arrangements to get 800 Italians along the line in the near future. Fifty are enroute now for Eden and other points. The Sycilians they formerly tried proved too dull, but they have secured a more intelligent set of men now. The colored man seems rather too independent for that class of work which requires a man to be constantly on the job . . . but the Dago can be counted on the day after pay day as certainly as at any other time; though it is admitted he will not do as much work in a given time as a black man, but will achieve more in time, owing to his presence at all times.[12]

By May 1907, despite the destruction wrought by the severe hurricane of October 1906, the completed roadway reached Key Largo, marking the end of the first phase of the extension. Complaints from Miamians about the presence of so many foreign immigrants declined as the center of construction activity shifted from the Florida mainland toward Key West. The line reached Key West in 1912.

The project's completion was rightfully hailed as Flagler's crowning achievement, a modern-day miracle. But the price was high. By 1912 hundreds had perished in hurricanes and construction accidents. The rails themselves were soon washed away and destroyed by the great

Keys storms of the twenties and thirties. The present-day Overseas Highway was built on the nearly destroyed railroad tracks and bridges. Flagler died in 1913 at the age of eighty-three.

The first newspaper in the city of Miami was the *Miami Metropolis,* founded in 1896 before the incorporation of the city. "From its inception, the *Miami Metropolis* had an ambiguous editorial policy towards blacks. Sometimes it espoused a sympathetic, although paternalistic attitude. . . . The newspaper, however, also supported severe punishment for recalcitrant blacks."[13]

Indeed, the *Miami Metropolis* was not beyond advocating the lynching of blacks. For example, in 1897 when the city was barely a year old, the *Metropolis* carried a story about a riot in Key West. Sylvanus Johnson, a nineteen-year-old black man, allegedly raped a white woman as she was gathering flowers with three of her friends. She identified Johnson, and he was jailed. That night a mob gathered to lynch Johnson but failed because the jail keeper would not cooperate. Blacks in Key West were outraged. When a white mob tried a second time to lynch Johnson, the sheriff and an armed posse of black citizens thwarted the attempt, but a white man was killed as he approached the jail.

The *Miami Metropolis* noted that the racial trouble had been caused by C. B. Pendleton, the white editor of two Key West newspapers, who had asked indignantly on his editorial pages if there were not enough white men present to lynch Johnson. "The *Metropolis* reported [on July 2, 1897] that this statement warned blacks of a possible lynching, giving them time to organize themselves to prevent it. 'If Pendleton had remained silent,' the *Metropolis* mused, 'and a quiet meeting had been held in secret and arrangements perfected for a necktie party, it might have been accomplished with very little excitement.'"[14] The newspaper then asked for a military company or naval reserve unit to preserve order in case a similar incident occurred in Miami. "There is no telling at what moment some fiendish act similar to that perpetrated at Key West last week may occur in this city or vicinity and precipitate a race war."[15]

Blacks were often the subject of degrading humor on the pages of the *Miami Metropolis,* where they were described as shiftless and unintelligent people who loved to sing and dance. The *Metropolis,* when covering the popular black-face minstrel shows, commented on how well whites portrayed blacks. "Atkinson, in our opinion, made the most natural looking 'nigger,' and a lady in our hearing said he re-

27. Postcard of black Miami, 1906. The scene, probably posed, represents one of the earliest photographs of black Miami and, according to Miami historian Seth Bramson, is the second-most-valuable Miami postcard in existence. Courtesy Miami Memorabilia Collection of Myrna and Seth Bramson.

minded her of an old darkey who used to live on the farm where she was brought up in Georgia. His face was perfectly blank, and evidence of intelligence was conspicuous by its absence."[16] The article also mentioned that a man named "Moran made a nice chubby nigger and his well fed appearance indicated that he had been raised in a section where hog and hominy are abundant."[17]

On another occasion the *Miami Metropolis* related a story about "an unnamed black prisoner, held for petty larceny, who escaped from the county jail while emptying slop buckets. The *Metropolis* reported, 'in his flight he came across a running deer and yelled to it to get out of the way as he was coming and could not wait.'"[18]

The *Miami Metropolis* and later the *Miami Herald* regularly referred to blacks with such characterizations as darky, coon, fiend, and hamfat, often running racially degrading stories.[19] In one article discussing the need to rid the city of those blacks who were seen as loafers, the *Metropolis* noted that a certain Mr. Savage, a white man, had helped "clean out the town of the hamfat as the loafing, gambling negroes are called."[20]

Lemon City and Hardieville (1896–1926)

Many blacks lived and worked in Lemon City prior to the establishment of the city of Miami. This area continued to grow as the city of Miami to the south was taking its first faltering steps. When the Hurst starch mill began to operate in 1910 in Lemon City, it created a large and steady demand for coontie roots. Most of the diggers were black men and were paid two or three dollars a ton. Other black men in Lemon City worked in the area's tomato fields and citrus groves, while black women usually did domestic work for the well-to-do whites.[21]

28. Josephine Dillard Powell (1895–1991), one of the first black settlers in Lemon City. Her son, Richard Powell, became a long-time Liberty City resident who led Liberty City's chapter of the NAACP for many years. Courtesy Richard Powell.

29. Three of the grandchildren of Lemon City pioneers Shadrack and Lucretia Ward, who moved to Lemon City in 1894. The photograph was taken circa 1919 and shows (from left) Witlean, Wilhelmenia, and Marie Franks. Their mother was Genevive Ward, the oldest daughter of Shadrack and Lucretia. All three of these girls grew up to become Dade County public school teachers. Courtesy Wilhelmenia Franks Jennings.

By 1900 the black community of Lemon City was divided into at least three black sections, called Nazarene, Knightsville, and Boles Town. According to an old plat book, Nazarene was bounded by Northeast Seventy-first Street to the north, Northeast Third Avenue to the east, and Northeast Second Avenue to the west. The south boundary was never determined. Nazarene was part pineland and part prairie, including a muddy low-lying area called a slough (pronounced slew).

Nazarene was officially platted by a white man named Louis W. Pierce in 1900. No records explain why Pierce selected this name, and even the present-day residents don't know the origin of the name. Most believe it had something to do with the biblical city of Nazareth; others say that an old Nazarene Church used to be located in the area, and Pierce took the name from the church. Referred to as "Commodore" because he owned three boats, Pierce also owned large chunks of Lemon City and needed an area in which to house the blacks who worked his crops.

Knightsville occupied only five acres. The tiny community consisted of small lots on pineland reaching west up the ridge from Northeast Second Avenue at Sixty-eighth Street on opposite sides of a sand road scarcely two blocks long which ended near a rock pit. Knightsville was the cultural center for black Lemon City. On the north side of the sand road were two churches, St. James A.M.E. Methodist Church, near Second Avenue, and Mount Tabor Baptist Church, a block west on the same side of the road at the crest of the ridge.

Almost opposite St. James was the Odd Fellows Lodge, a two-story wood-frame building. The lower story was used for a school and the upper story for lodge meetings as well as social events. The Baptists and Methodists used the hall on alternate Sundays. The good relationship between the two churches continued after they moved west to Liberty City around 1920, where both survive today.[22]

The other black settlement in Lemon City was Boles Town, named for Elijah Boles, a black man. He and his wife Rosa came to Lemon City from Lake City, Florida. Boles Town was near or just west of present-day Miami Avenue at about Fifty-seventh Street. Before 1915 there were no access roads to Boles Town other than sand roads through the pine trees. The land had been part of the Ada Merritt homestead. Boles, who bought the property, built a number of shacks along a single street and ran a small store. From the rents he collected and the profits of his store, he became one of the most affluent blacks in Lemon City.

Early black settlers in Nazarene included members of the Barnes family. Clarence W. Barnes was born in Charleston, South Carolina, and moved to San Mateo, Florida, before the Great Freeze. There he married a woman named Lucy Long. San Mateo was an important citrus area, and Barnes worked as a farm laborer before moving to Lemon City in 1897. At first the Barneses lived in a small house on the property of B. C. Dupont at Northeast Seventieth Street near Second Avenue. When the area was subdivided, Barnes bought three lots, two of them facing Dupont Road, now called Northeast Seventy-first Street.

On one lot the family ran a tiny store selling grits, canned milk, and other staples. Barnes made a simple icebox using sawdust as insulation; he buried ice blocks in the sawdust and chipped off pieces as they were needed to cool drinks. Barnes worked as a farm laborer on nearby farms including some at Cracker Flats, as the blacks called the prairie just west of Little River.

Typical of the black lifestyle of the period, the Barnes house was split by a breezeway with two rooms on each side. They cooked on a wood stove, used kerosene lamps and lanterns, and boiled clothes in a wash pot in the yard. The family grew a few guavas and always had a

30. Lemon City pioneers Maxie Ford (left) and Horace S. Sharpe, circa 1955, in Liberty City. Both men were noted farmers and had daughters who became well-known school principals, Charlotte Ford and Isabelle Sharpe Blue. Courtesy Isabelle Sharpe Blue.

garden with plenty of okra and cabbage. They kept chickens and owned a horse, which was unusual for a black family in those days.

Another of the early black families of Lemon City was the Ford family. They lived in Knightsville near Mount Tabor Baptist Church. Maxie Ford, who died in 1956 at the age of eighty-four, was a farmer who also came from San Mateo. His wife was the former Isabel Boles, sister of the founder of Boles Town, Elijah Boles. Their daughter, Charlotte Ford, became principal of Douglass Elementary and Drew Elementary schools and a leading figure in Dade County education when black students were segregated into their own schools.

"My parents brought me here from San Mateo when I was an infant, in 1905. First we lived on the bayfront. Negroes and whites were living together—can you believe that? My father, Maxie Ford, was the greatest tomato farmer in the world. The biggest house was owned by the Reverend B. F. Goodwin. It was an ostentatious place. I remember it burned down one day, and I'll always remember how sad I was seeing that grand place burn down."[23] Charlotte Ford died in 1991.

Horace S. Sharpe married another Boles sister, Rosa. They had a home and a little store near Boles Town where another legendary figure in Dade County black education, Isabelle Sharpe Blue, was born. Blue served as principal of George Washington Carver Elementary School in Coconut Grove for many years. Interviewed long after her retirement, she remembered a grove of old lemon trees where she played as a child in Lemon City.[24]

Lemon City was swallowed up by the northern edge of Miami in the early 1900s. Houses and business supply companies replaced most of the black residential areas of Lemon City. While the old, wooden houses of Nazarene have little value, the land on which they stand is increasing in value in the growing industrial area. Lots in the area are now valued between twenty and fifty thousand dollars, depending on size. As late as 1980, however, eight old black residents remained in yellow-and gray-washed wooden houses in an area they called Naz'ree.[25]

Miami's first red-light district was known as Hardieville. As the city of Miami grew, efforts had been made to respect Julia Tuttle's wish that saloons and brothels not be allowed to operate within the city limits. The northwest area of Colored Town became the center of gambling, prostitution (a considerable amount of which involved white men hiring black prostitutes), and general rowdiness. Some of the drinking and gambling establishments were within twenty feet of the city boundary. The district was dubbed Hardieville after Dade County Sheriff Dan Hardie, who created Hardieville by herding all the prostitutes from North Miami into the area after the respectable citizens of North Miami requested that he help clean up the community. The area soon drew the uninvited attentions of the white establishment, including influential white women who may have had more to do with its demise than did their husbands.

Dr. James Jackson, after whom Jackson Memorial Hospital is named, was among several prominent citizens at a town meeting in October 1912 urging an end to all vice. Jackson said that entirely too many white men contracted venereal diseases from Hardieville prostitutes and then infected their wives. The meeting sparked the formation of the Civic League of Miami, an organization dedicated to the improvement of morals. Ultimately, the Civic League was very successful in temporarily reducing vice in Colored Town. Their success prompted local black leaders to organize their own group, the Civic League of Colored Town. Among their demands were imposing an 8:00 P.M. curfew on children, removing all immoral women from the streets, and prohibiting "good women" from going all over town unescorted after 9:00 P.M.

Black South Dade Communities (circa 1900)

In the early 1900s, the population of Dade County was expanding rapidly along the tracks of the Florida East Coast Railroad as Flagler's rails left Miami and plunged southward toward the sea. The warm climate and fertile soil of south Florida attracted many farmers, particularly from Georgia, South Carolina, and north and central Florida.

The increase in the permanent black population of south Dade County around the turn of the century was in large measure due to blacks' having followed migrating white farmers in the aftermath of the Great Freeze. By 1900 several black settlements were developing in south Dade County, including Larkins (later called South Miami), Homestead, Perrine, and Florida City.

The very first black man to buy land in Larkins was Marshall Williamson. Born in Madison, Florida, on January 31, 1890, he graduated from Georgia State College, where he learned carpentry—a trade he followed all his life. Williamson came to Larkins in 1912 and bought land. At one time he owned the land from Southwest Sixty-fourth to Southwest Sixty-sixth streets, from Sixty-second to Sixty-fifth avenues. Before he even finished building his house at 6500 Southwest Sixtieth Avenue, church services and classes for school children were being held there. In 1916, Williamson donated the land for St. James A.M.E. Church, the first church for blacks in South Miami. He also donated the land for J. R. E. Lee School on Southwest Sixty-second Avenue.[26]

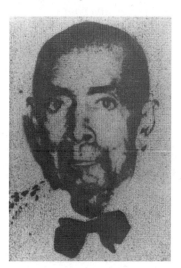

31. Marshall Williamson, the first black man to buy land in what is now South Miami. When Williamson arrived in 1912, the area was called Larkins. He donated the land for J. R. E. Lee School on Southwest Sixty-second Avenue. He also donated the land for the St. James A.M.E. Church. Courtesy Historical Museum of Southern Florida.

Above left: 32. Arthur Mays, a black south Dade pioneer. With the help of his wife, Polly, Mays helped to establish Mount Pleasant Missionary Baptist Church as well as the first medical services for blacks in south Dade. The Mayses also helped to establish the first school for black children in south Dade County. Although he could pass for white, Mays chose to live as a black man. Courtesy Historical Museum of Southern Florida.

Above center: 33. Polly Mays, pioneer and activist who worked with her husband to help south Dade blacks. For many years she drove the school bus to bring black children to school in Coconut Grove before there was a school for black children in south Dade County. Courtesy Historical Museum of Southern Florida.

Above right: 34. Johnny "Cat Man" Everett, an avid hunter of wild cats and a self-trained animal doctor. On occasion he doctored humans, in his barn, with such remedies as warm turtle blood, rattlesnake oil, and shots of potassium permanganate for gonorrhea. Courtesy Historical Museum of Southern Florida.

In 1900 black and white settlers homesteaded the high, dry land around the area now known as Goulds. A man named William Johnson—about whom nothing is known except that he was black—filed on a quarter-section later bisected diagonally by the railroad, extending from what is now Southwest 216th Street to beyond 224th Street. It included all the land that later became downtown Goulds. D. D. Cail, another black man, later purchased the northwest section of Johnson's homestead and built rental housing, a restaurant, and a large packing house along Dixie Highway south of 220th Street.

The town of Goulds, also called Black Point, was started with the arrival of the Florida East Coast Railway in 1903. A man named Gould, who was in charge of cutting ties for the railroad, operated a siding below Southwest 216th Street. The town that grew up there was originally called Gould's Siding and later just Goulds.

Goulds had an early reputation as a rough place. By some accounts, the Flagler organization recruited drifters and convicts from north Florida for the labor force there. Prisoners were released to the company to work out their sentences and then were turned loose when they finished. These accounts may or may not have been true; nonetheless, Goulds was a rough, tough place, with open saloons, killings, and fights as the usual weekend fare.

Goulds became the center of the packing house industry, bringing in hundreds of "fruit tramps" during the season. The Old Dixie Highway was lined with packing houses which have since been razed by fires, tornadoes, and hurricanes.

Among the notable early black settlers of Goulds were Gus Boles, thought to be the richest black man in the community; Jasper Harrington, who worked on the Florida East Coast Railroad from Jacksonville to Miami; Tal Roux and Arthur and Polly Mays, who opened the only black medical facility; and Johnny (Cat Man) Everett, who was an avid hunter of wildcats, an animal doctor of sorts, and all-around medicine man. The homemade remedies Everett prescribed included nine drops of warm turtle blood for whooping cough, rattlesnake oil for arthritis, and cooked rattlesnake for tuberculosis. He treated gonorrhea with shots of potassium permanganate, which he administered in his barn.[27]

Early Racial Incidents

Miami always has had racial conflict, much of it quite bloody. Blacks were usually the victims, but they never accepted their victimization quietly.

The city was barely two years old when it experienced its first serious racial incident. On June 20, 1898, during the Spanish-American War, General Theodore M. Schwan received orders to move his division of Alabama, Louisiana, and Texas volunteers to Miami. The army built a camp called Camp Miami, which housed about seventy-five hundred white soldiers, adjacent to Colored Town. Only about two thousand people lived in Miami at the time.

Choosing to disregard the staggering problems that such an influx of people was certain to create, the town's small but enterprising merchant community welcomed the infusion of much-needed capital. Henry Flagler jumped on the bandwagon, lending his wholehearted support to welcoming the troops to Miami. The *Miami Metropolis* could hardly contain its enthusiasm, cheerily reporting on June 24, 1898: "Under the efficient management of the officials of the East Coast Railroad, Camp Miami has been made the most beautiful and convenient camp for soldiers in the state."[28]

Every unbiased account suggests otherwise. The plan for the camp was well conceived but not followed. Four of the regiments found themselves beyond the city sewer lines and resorted to a crude bucket system, which was blamed for the high incidence of typhoid fever. When troops used surface wells rather than the water piped into the city, in violation of all health and sanitation rules, they paid a high price in disease. The men were unhappy from the first. The drill field was a mile away. The city offered little that was attractive to the men, who described Miami as a luxury hotel and a wilderness. Camp Miami was rowdy and poorly disciplined. It was overcrowded. The men were hot and bored. Many of them spent their time swimming naked, shooting at coconuts, and directing pranks at an indignant civilian community. Such improprieties were patiently laughed off by merchants and other community leaders who eagerly anticipated the arrival of monthly pay allotments.

Harmless fun became vicious and deadly in July 1898, when according to eyewitnesses, soldiers of Texas's Company L were outraged at the refusal of a black man to stand aside for two white women approaching him on a sidewalk. Assaulted and beaten, the man narrowly averted being lynched. He was saved by the arrival of officers who restored order.

That evening soldiers from Company L marched into the black section of Miami shooting out every kerosene lamp found burning. This resulted in the flight of many blacks to Coconut Grove, ending only after city representatives promised full protection for blacks to go to work the next morning. Miami pioneer J. K. Dorn confirmed that the quick response was prompted by economics: "Without Black labor,

White Miamians found it difficult to operate their restaurants, hotels, and stores."[29]

Racial unrest continued between the camp and blacks, culminating in an incident on July 23, 1898. Private Virgil H. Duncan of Company M, First Texas Regiment, killed a black cook named Sam Drummer when Drummer brushed against a white woman in a narrow aisle. Duncan stalked and shot Drummer in broad daylight, but he was exonerated when a Miami coroner's jury ruled that Drummer's death was caused by an unknown person or persons. The military then court-martialed Duncan, but he was acquitted without explanation and returned to active duty. At no time in the brief history of Camp Miami was any soldier arrested. Only the end of the Spanish-American War and the evacuation of the camp in August 1898 averted additional violence.

Five years later the city was again facing a serious race problem. In March 1903 a white woman named Rose Gould allegedly was raped

35. Camp Miami, 1898. This rare photo shows the camp, adjacent to Colored Town, where nearly eight thousand soldiers were housed during the Spanish-American War. There were numerous clashes between black residents and the bored soldiers. Courtesy Historical Museum of Southern Florida.

by a black man identified as Richard Dedwilley. Stunned by the assault, the *Miami Metropolis* appealed to racial passions by suggesting that lynch law might be applied to the perpetrator when he was located. In a race-baiting article, entitled "Fiendish Black Brute Brings Home to Us the Question of What Can Be Done with These Black Sons of Hell," the *Miami Metropolis* expounded on its theory of race relations:

> All kinds of remedies have been resorted to including hemp, tar and torch, and yet it seems that it is all of no avail . . . and occasionally the demon in human form breaks loose, fearing neither God nor man, bent upon the commission of a crime worse than the foulest murder. For such beings no punishment is mete. No wonder that lynchings and roastings are resorted to and such things will continue to take place North and South, East and West as long as these devilish attempts upon the virtue and lives of white women are made. If white men of Miami had gotten their hands upon him they would have made short work of putting out his worse than worthless life.[30]

Although Dedwilley was arrested on rape charges, many white Miamians were enraged by the crime and demanded immediate justice. There was even talk of an assault by whites on Colored Town.

Reflecting the rage of white Miami, the *Miami Metropolis* reported the capture of the "unholy fiend of hell" and then added, almost hopefully, that Miamians planned to treat him to a necktie party. As it turned out, the punishment meted out by the court was just as swift. After a fifteen-minute trial, Dedwilley was hanged in the yard of the county jail within the same month that the crime was committed.

Public access to the hanging of Dedwilley was denied, but in June 1906 about two hundred Miamians were allowed to witness the hanging of Ed Brown, a black man who had been convicted of murdering a white woman.

Two years after the Dedwilley incident Miami again was on the brink of racial violence. In January 1905, C. E. Davis, a white man, and his two daughters were murdered while they slept. It was determined that one of the girls had been sexually assaulted. Naturally, police investigators turned to Colored Town to find the murderer or murderers. Two black men were arrested, but they were later released when a grand jury found insufficient evidence to proceed against them.

The Color Line

By 1910 Miami's blacks numbered 2,258, nearly 42 percent of the city's population. As traditional black areas swelled, residential boundary conflicts were increasingly common. In a revealing 1911 editorial, the *Miami Herald* gave its view of the spread of the black population from Colored Town:

> A large area (in the northwest section) has been given up to Negroes. White owners of these small properties are renting them to Negroes on a weekly basis. With this kind of growth the adjacent properties depreciate in value. White people do not care to live close to colonies of Negro's houses.
>
> On the south side, around 20th Street, is the same problem above mentioned. The conditions in both directions are steadily and daily getting worse and threaten to drive out a large number of white people.
>
> The advance of the Negro population is like a plague and carries devastation with it to all surrounding property. The fact is that Miami is being badly injured and badly disfigured by the growth of these Negro sections.[31]

A major confrontation occurred as blacks from Colored Town tried to move north into a white area known as Highland Park in the early 1900s. In response, some whites called for adding more restrictions on where blacks could live, proposing at a town meeting in November 1911 to establish a residential color line. The line was to be drawn between Miami and what was then North Miami. A committee was appointed to take up the matter with property owners and others. According to Miami historian Paul George, the boundary problems moved several officials to ask the city council to pass an ordinance providing for an alley separating the races in the disputed area and to write a segregation law establishing a boundary line to keep the neighborhoods racially segregated.[32] There was intense pressure on blacks to move out. The black population increased fourfold in the ten years after 1910. By 1920 blacks constituted 32 percent of Miami's population but occupied only 10 percent of the city's available space.[33]

The color line matter officially reached the Miami City Commission in 1916. Although Ordinance 199, the Segregation or Color Line Ordinance, was tabled by the commission at its meeting on February 3,

1916, the unofficial boundary—Morse Street in the north of the city (today Northwest Twentieth Street)—remained the accepted point beyond which blacks were not to live.[34] Ultimately the color line did not restrain the northward expansion of the black population because, among other factors, white realtors continued to sell property to blacks on the forbidden side of the line. The color line did slow the process, however, and helped to keep Miami blacks crowded into a rapidly declining inner city.

Early Black Businesses in Miami (1896–1940)

As early as the 1870s, black entrepreneurs established businesses in the Lemon City area, but it was the Colored Town section of northwest Miami that was the heart of the black business community. The city's black business and professional community developed soon after the arrival of the railroad.

Blacks were denied equal business opportunities from the very birth of the city. In 1896 Lula Elizabeth James Lummus, the wife of J. N. Lummus, a pioneer on Miami Beach, wrote in the *Sanford Chronicle,* "It seems strange to me that only white men are employed as mechanics."[35]

Actually, this was not strange at all in early Miami. Exclusion from working as mechanics was not the only limitation blacks faced. They were not allowed to operate businesses that catered to white people, although white merchants could operate freely in Colored Town. Blacks resented this and protested loudly against these restrictions. The Colored Board of Trade was established at the turn of the century by the black business community as an advocate for its interests. Given the period in which it operated, it became the first relatively effective black organization other than the black church. Many of the early black business leaders in Miami belonged to the organization.

Even in this oppressive business climate, some blacks succeeded mightily. Those who became rich did so by serving the black population in some essential way. One of the first things new residents needed was housing, and the black man most successful in meeting that need was Dana A. Dorsey, probably the city's first black millionaire.

According to Kleinberg, Dorsey was born in 1868 and arrived in Miami in 1897. By other accounts, Dorsey was born in 1872, the son of former slaves, and arrived at Biscayne Bay even earlier. His early life reflected the harsh realities of blacks in the post–Civil War South.

36. D. A. Dorsey (1872–1940). A carpenter from Quitman, Georgia, Dorsey arrived in Miami at about the time the railroad was extended to Biscayne Bay. He built many of the so-called shotgun houses in Colored Town and rented them out. He was thought to be Miami's first black millionaire. Courtesy Historical Museum of Southern Florida.

The only formal education he received was from a school set up by the Freedmen's Bureau in Quitman, Georgia, where he completed the fourth grade before leaving to work. His daughter, Dana Chapman, recalled in a 1990 interview that her father's excellent penmanship was a product of the little formal education he had received. Indeed, Dorsey educated himself in most matters, including real estate where he made his fortune.

Prior to moving to Miami, Dorsey lived in Titusville, Florida, working as a carpenter for the Flagler organization. Since there were no roads to Biscayne Bay at the time, Dorsey reportedly built a raft and sailed there alone in 1892 or 1893. It was a well-timed move, as he arrived before the hundreds of blacks who came in with the railroad. Dorsey observed a critical need for housing in Colored Town, where blacks were forced to live, many in tents near their work sites.

Dorsey, the carpenter, was in the right place at the right time, and he found his niche in black real estate. On land that he purchased in Colored Town, he built small single-family homes. He never sold the houses, renting them to newly arriving blacks who were desperate to find housing. He used his rental income to purchase new property and build new houses, as far north as Fort Lauderdale. Dorsey designed and built his home at 250 Northwest Ninth Street in 1913, reportedly using scrap lumber from railroad cars for some of the interior. The home was recently restored by the Black Archives, History and Research Foundation of South Florida, Inc.

37. The Dorsey house, located at 250 Northwest Ninth Street, as it appears today. Built in 1913 of sturdy Dade County pine by D. A. Dorsey himself, the structure has been renovated by the Black Archives, History and Research Foundation of South Florida. Courtesy Sergio Campos.

In 1918 Dorsey purchased twenty-one acres of what is now Fisher Island near Miami Beach so that blacks could enjoy the oceanfront. Although one of his plans was to build a fashionable black resort, his primary aim in buying the land was to establish a place for blacks because they were forbidden to go to public beaches. Briefly the beach he owned became a popular spot for blacks to picnic. However, the land boom of 1925 skyrocketed property values and apparently forced Dorsey to sell. After he sold his island holdings to the Alton Beach Realty Company, owned by Carl Fisher, blacks living in Miami's sweltering summer heat had no access to the ocean for another twenty years.

During the land boom of the 1920s Dorsey amassed a fortune. His vast holdings throughout south Florida had increased in value to the point that he started to sell land and reinvest his money. He tried his hand at banking, building the Negro Savings Bank in 1916 so that blacks would have a place of their own to bank. At first the venture was successful, but as the Great Depression of the 1930s hit the country, the bank faced financial disaster. Although Dorsey lost thousands of dollars when the bank folded, he made sure that none of his depositors lost money. Dorsey's second wife, Rebecca, helped pull the family through this period with the substantial savings she had acquired in her own right. Despite the bank's failure, Dorsey's vast real estate holdings still provided him considerable income during the Depression.

Dorsey always collected the rents personally, walking or driving to each of his properties in Colored Town. But by the 1930s his health was poor and he could no longer drive, so he hired a chauffeur who drove him to renters as far north as Fort Lauderdale in a limousine every Sunday afternoon after church.

Dorsey also ventured into the hotel business. He built the Dorsey Hotel on Northwest Second Avenue, the first black-owned hotel in Miami. The hotel advertised in both white and black newspapers and was well known throughout the city, even though seldom used by whites. Over the years, Dorsey spent a large amount of money to modernize the hotel, including adding hot and cold running water.

Aside from his business activities, Dorsey is best known for his contributions to education. He donated a large parcel of land for black schools. In 1937, Dorsey High School opened in Liberty City. For the first time, black children in that section of Miami went to school in their own neighborhood. Through these efforts, as well as the fortune he earned, Dorsey gained the respect and admiration of the white community.

The Dorsey house was always filled with important dinner guests. Some of the white millionaires who visited were awed by Dorsey's accomplishments, achieved under difficult circumstances. Some even went to him for financial help. According to his daughter, during the Depression Dorsey lent money to William M. Burdine to keep his store open. When Dorsey died in 1940, flags were lowered to half-staff all over Miami. On his deathbed he donated the land for the Dorsey Memorial Library, which was dedicated in 1941.

Dana Dorsey was only one of many successful black business leaders in early Miami. R. A. Powers was a black furniture salesman who originally came to Miami with a white dealer who helped him start his own business. D. D. Cail rented houses, operated a restaurant, and owned a packing house on Dixie Highway. Moses Griffin ran a taxi line. Henry Wells managed the Brown and Wells dry goods and gro-

Left: 38. Florence Gaskins, the best-known black businesswoman of her day. Gaskins arrived in Miami in 1896 from Jacksonville as a widow. She operated a laundry business that catered to tourists at the Royal Palm Hotel. She also owned a real estate agency and a private school. Courtesy Historical Museum of Southern Florida.

Below: 39. Washing clothes in Colored Town. Many black women in Colored Town earned a living by washing clothes for white residents and tourists. When the first laundries were opened in Miami, some of their newspaper advertisements chided whites for allowing black washerwomen to handle their clothes, alleging that black women often allowed their husbands to wear the clothes before relaundering and returning them. Courtesy Historical Museum of Southern Florida.

cery store. Jasper Harrington, who came to Miami with the railroad and helped lay out the streets of Miami, was a successful carpenter. He built many homes east of Allapattah. J. H. Howard, a grocer and a restaurant owner, was also involved in real estate. The Reverend S. W. Brown was a South Carolinian who owned the popular Colored Town Bargain Store and other properties.

Perhaps the best-known black female business leader in early Miami was the indefatigable Florence Gaskins. She was born in 1863 in Jacksonville and came to Miami in 1896 as a widow. Ellen Johnson, an expert in local black history and the owner and manager of Lincoln Memorial Park, a black cemetery in Miami, explains that Florence Gaskins began her rise to prominence in the days of the Royal Palm Hotel. According to Johnson, "All the visitors coming down from the North used to wear white—Palm Beach white, it was called."[36]

40. The J and S Building, erected in 1925. The building, on Northwest Ninth Street between Second and Third Avenues, was named for its owners, Osborne Jenkins and William Sampson, who operated their Cola-Nip Bottling Company at this location. One of the major black-owned businesses in Colored Town, the company was known for its tasty products such as Peach Whip and Orange Smile. Courtesy Nancy Murphy.

41. W. B. Sawyer (1880–1950). Dr. Sawyer was twenty-five years old when he arrived in Miami from West Palm Beach. He started Christian Hospital, the first hospital for blacks in Dade County, and was instrumental in establishing Jackson Memorial Hospital. Dr. Sawyer owned the Mary Elizabeth Hotel in Colored Town. Courtesy William B. Sawyer Jr.

Gaskins operated a laundry business that catered to the city's tourists. She collected the laundry from the hotels and brought it to Colored Town, where she hired two or three women in the community to do the work. Eventually Gaskins prospered and began a real estate agency, a private school, and as her success increased, a Junior Red Cross chapter. In addition to being an astute businesswoman, Florence Gaskins became a dominant figure in the social circles of early black Miami.

Most black businesses were small, family-run operations. There were, however, some sizable black businesses in early Miami. The Cola-Nip Bottling Company, opened in 1920, was owned by Osborne Jenkins and William Sampson. It produced, bottled and distributed a very successful soda water. Among the sweet treats the plant produced were Orange Smile and Peach Whip. The company's old building still stands at 233 Northwest Ninth Street, near the Dorsey home.

Colored Town also had a growing black professional community. Dr. W. B. Sawyer came to Miami in 1903, and in 1918 he helped to start the Christian Hospital, the first for blacks in Miami. He practiced medicine from 1908 to 1950. In addition, he built and owned the Mary Elizabeth Hotel and Alberta Heights, the first black-owned residential development in Miami. His daughter Gwendolyn Sawyer Cherry became the first black woman to be elected to the Florida House of Representatives.

Dr. William A. Chapman Sr. was a pioneer doctor. He was the first black appointed to the Florida Department of Health and possibly the

42. The 1918 opening of Christian Hospital, the first hospital for blacks in Miami.
The hospital was erected after Jackson Memorial Hospital refused to care for a black
woman who worked as a maid for Mrs. Clarence Bush. Bush donated five thousand
dollars and five acres of land at 1218 Northwest First Place to establish the hospital.
Courtesy Historical Museum of Southern Florida.

first black doctor to travel through Florida educating the people about
communicable diseases. From Tallahassee to Key West he met with
groups in churches, schools, and homes to explain health issues. His
Overtown home at 526 Northwest Thirteenth Street was declared a
historic site in 1983; it became the site of the Chapman House Ethnic
Heritage Children's Folklife Education Center. The school board took
over the property in 1984 as part of the new campus for the rebuilt
Booker T. Washington Middle School. The Black Archives, History
and Research Foundation of South Florida, Inc., has restored the building.[37]

Dr. John R. Scott Jr. was the first African-American dentist to practice in Dade County. Scott was born in Jacksonville in 1886 and attended public school there. He later attended Florida Agricultural and
Mechanical College (later known as FAMU) in Tallahassee. Known as
Pig Iron for his athletic ability on the football field, he was also an
outstanding scholar. After graduating with honors, he entered Meharry
Dental College. Dr. Scott established his practice in the Colored Town
section of Miami in 1906. He had two locations and allowed young

43. The stylish home of Dr. William Chapman, one of Miami's pioneer black physicians. The home has been restored and is located adjacent to the campus of Booker T. Washington Middle School on Northwest Fourteenth Street near Seventh Avenue. Courtesy Black Archives, History and Research Foundation of South Florida.

black dentists to serve apprenticeships in his office. Dr. Scott was a shrewd investor in real estate and served in numerous social, civic, and church organizations. He died in 1935.

Dr. Alonzo Potter Burgess Holly was the first African-American homeopath in Miami and possibly in the state of Florida. (Homeopathy is a system of medical practice based on the theory that a drug that will produce certain disease symptoms in a healthy person will cure a sick person with the same symptoms.) Of Haitian descent, Alonzo Holly was born in about 1864 and grew up in Massachusetts, one of eight children born to the Reverend James Theodore Holly, D.D., LL.D., and his second wife. Dr. Alonzo Holly was a scholar and the author of many articles and books on blacks, medicine, and religion. He also spoke French and English fluently. Holly attended Harrison College in Barbados, British West Indies, and Atherstone College in England. In 1884 he entered the New York Homeopath Medical College and Flowers Hospital, graduating in 1888. The following year, he was appointed by the Haitian government as consul to the Bahamas, where he remained for twelve years. Before moving to Miami in 1909 to obtain better educational advantages for his daughters, Dr. Holly practiced medicine in New York and West Palm Beach. His Miami office on Northwest Eighth Street was the birthplace of many of Miami's early residents.

Other black doctors who practiced in early Miami include, "a Dr. Rivers, who practiced medicine in the city in 1896 before moving to Tampa; Dr. J. A. Butler, who also owned the Magic City Drug Store on the corner of Avenue G [Second Avenue] and Fifth Street; [and] Dr. Solomon Frazier, who arrived in 1904 and began a practice that lasted for over 60 years in the city."[38]

Kelsey Leroy Pharr came to Miami from South Carolina in 1912, working as a bellman in what later became the Dupont Plaza Hotel. He saved his money and obtained an embalmer's license from the Renouard Embalming School. For many years he was the only licensed black embalmer south of St. Augustine. In 1924 Pharr started the Lincoln Memorial Park Cemetery, the only minority-owned-and-operated cemetery in the Miami area.

Blacks were buried in the old Miami cemetery from its inception. Actually, the first cemetery especially for blacks was on Sixty-second Street in Lemon City, where a library now stands. According to Ellen Johnson, Pharr wound up owning the first black cemetery after he was asked to disinter the bodies from the Lemon City Cemetery and rebury them in the back of the city's cemetery; he later opened Lincoln Memorial Park.

Among his other projects, Pharr owned an ambulance service. He was one of the first directors of the Christian Hospital and was one of the founders of the Colored Board of Trade, the embodiment of black economic power in Miami after the turn of the century. Pharr urged blacks to own their businesses and pool their capital. Following his own advice, Pharr and the Colored Board of Trade hatched plans to buy land in the area now called Hialeah to incorporate as a black city. According to Johnson, they were thwarted when whites learned of the plan and bought the land to prevent it from being sold to blacks.[39]

Victoria Ward, a Matron of the Eastern Star Lodge, helped to establish a burial society which helped people who did not have the means to bury their family members. Similar societies existed during this period because African Americans could not readily obtain insurance. George Luther Carey began the first black-owned taxi service and was one of the community's first real estate brokers. One of Miami's first employment agencies was established by Prince Albert Miller. Willie Franks operated a charter boat service for area residents and tourists.

According to Lemon City pioneer Estelle DesRocher Zumwalt, Miami even had a black elephant trainer, whose picture with his pachyderm, Rosie, was seen all over the country, promoting Miami Beach as it was being developed in the early 1900s by Carl Fisher. According to Zumwalt, "Rosie had a colored man as trainer. She learned to be very useful. She would pull up bushes or move logs. Mr. Fisher got a cart with big wheels which Rosie could pull around, sometimes filled with children who loved the excitement of this. Rosie was more photographed than the famous Beach bathing beauties."[40]

A powerful influence in the lives of Colored Town residents was the community organizations, many of which still exist today. Among them are the Eastern Star Lodge, the Masons, the Elks, the Odd Fellows, the Love and Charity Lodge, and the Heroines of Jerico. Clubs included the Friendship Garden and Civic Club, the Algonquin Club, the Collegians Club, the King of Clubs, the Egelloc Civic and Social Club, Inc., and later the Greek sororities and fraternities.

Richard Toomey's arrival in Miami in 1912 heralded the beginning of an integral part of black Miami's emerging professional community. Born in 1861 in Baltimore, Maryland, Toomey attended Lincoln University, graduating in 1894. He proudly served his country during the Spanish-American War, becoming the first black commissioned officer during this conflict. After the war, Toomey obtained a law degree from Howard University. In 1913, at the invitation of the Miami Chamber of Commerce, Toomey opened the first African-American law practice in the city of Miami and all of southeast Florida. Segregation and discrimination prevented him from appearing in local courts, as this function was reserved for white male lawyers. Toomey nonetheless excelled as a legal writer, and his legal scholarship and analytical skills were sought by local white attorneys. Richard Toomey blazed the legal trail over which other pioneering black lawyers would travel. He died in 1948 at the age of 87.

Black businesses advertised in one of the seven black newspapers printed at different times in early Colored Town. All were operated by black owners and catered to the population they served. They were the *Miami Sun,* the *Miami Times,* the *Biscayne Messenger,* the *Miami Journal,* the *Tropical Dispatch,* the Florida edition of the *Pittsburgh*

Courier, and the *Industrial Reporter.* Most ads in these papers were small, usually stating the name of the owner and the function of the business. Others were larger, providing more information and even featuring a picture of the proprietor. S. W. Brown, who owned the Colored Town Bargain Store, was famous for his full-page ads proclaiming that his was the cheapest bargain house in the city. Eventually blacks were allowed to advertise in white newspapers. Of the early black newspapers, only the *Miami Times* survived. Founded by Henry Ethelbert Sigismund Reeves on September 1, 1923, the paper was destined to become perhaps the city's most successful black business.

Henry Reeves was born in the Bahamas, but Miami presented him with a greater opportunity to establish financial security for his wife

44. Advertisement for the hugely successful Colored Town Bargain Store, owned by S. W. Brown. Black merchants in early Miami could place ads like this one in any of the seven newspapers in circulation at various times during the first few decades of the city's history. Courtesy Historical Museum of Southern Florida.

and five children. He started his first newspaper, the *Miami Sun,* in partnership with the Reverend Samuel Sampson, Alonzo Kelly, and M. J. Brodie. After operating for only a few months, they had to suspend the venture because World War I had caused a shortage of newsprint. In 1923, when Reeves initiated the *Miami Times,* he also opened a printing shop, which did well enough to tide the newspaper over during the Depression.[41]

The Miami of 1919, when the Reeves family arrived, had many racial problems. There was no black voice. The *Miami Times* filled this void. Lynchings, the open activities of the Ku Klux Klan, and segregation were among the issues that Reeves confronted directly and courageously in the paper from its beginnings. He had taken a considerable risk in starting the newspaper anyway, since only about 50 percent of blacks in Miami during the 1920s and 1930s were literate.

At the turn of the century black business activity flourished along Second and Third Avenues in Colored Town. Before the advent of the automobile, bicycles, horse-drawn carriages, and wagons rumbled noisily along its dusty, unpaved streets. The community watering spot for the horses was a long trough on Seventh Street, between Second

45. Three generations of the Reeves family, 1965. The Reeves family owns the city's largest black newspaper, the *Miami Times.* Depicted are, from left, Garth C. Reeves Sr.; Henry E. S. Reeves, the founder of the newspaper; and Garth C. Reeves Jr. Courtesy *Miami Times.*

46. The Lyric Theater as it appears today. The building is located at Northwest Second Avenue and Eighth Street and was owned by Gedar Walker, a black man who had the building constructed in about 1917. It became the most prominent building in Colored Town and was the center of social life in the community in the 1920s and 1930s. Courtesy Sergio Campos.

and Third Avenues. "All of Miami used to water up there," said Bill Sawyer Jr., son of one of Miami's pioneer doctors, William B. Sawyer.[42]

Photographs of Colored Town during this time show elegantly dressed people busying themselves along crowded streets. According to many people who recall living in Colored Town in the early part of this century, until the 1950s or so black people always dressed up before going down on "the Avenue" (Second Avenue), even during the week.

Colored Town was constructed primarily of wooden buildings which often became firetraps. Indeed, fire was a constant enemy in all of early Miami. As mentioned earlier, much of the downtown business section, then constructed of wood, burned to the ground in the 1896 Christmas night fire, only months after the city was incorporated. As in Colored Town, the buildings were so close together that fire spread easily and quickly from one structure to the next.

Table 2.2. Businesses owned by blacks in Miami, 1900

Type of business	No.
Barber	5
Bicycle repair	1
Blacksmithing	4
Boardinghouse	2
Carpenter	5
Cigar making	1
Firewood contracting	2
Fishering	2
Fruit stand	1
Grocery/meat market	4
Ice wagon	4
Mechanic	2
Plumbing	1
Restaurant	6
Dressmaking	5
Tailoring	1

Table 2.3. Businesses owned by blacks in Miami, 1915

Type of business	No.
Auto trimming/painting	1
Baking	2
Barber shop	9
Bicycle shop	2
Blacksmith shop	1
Boardinghouse	7
Drayman	9
Dressmaking	14
Drugstore	3
Expert cutter	2
Fish market	5
Fruit stand	2
Grocery store	17
Hackman	17
Hair emporium	3
Ice dealer	1
Insurance company	3
Liveryman	2
Lunch counter	4
Meat market	4
Milliner/notions	1
Painting	7
Plumbing	1
Printing	1
Real estate	4
Refreshment parlor	6
Restaurant	11
Savings association	1
Shoemaking	2
Shoeshining	5
Tailoring/pressing	12
Theater	1
Undertaking	2
Upholsterer	2

47. The Negro Merchants Association in the 1927 Trade Week parade. The association was founded in 1927 as an outgrowth of the Colored Board of Trade and
included many of Miami's early black business leaders. Courtesy Historical Museum
of Southern Florida.

The Lyric Theater was one of the few buildings in Colored Town
that was not made of wood. This magnificent structure still stands on
Second Avenue at Eighth Street. The building opened in 1917 and was
built by a black man named Geder Walker. The Lyric Theater was the
major center of entertainment in Colored Town during the vaudeville
period of the 1920s and 1930s, showing silent movies to a full house
night after night. The structure has recently been restored by the Black
Archives, History and Research Foundation of South Florida, Inc.

Black business operations were sustained by a black working class,
which was practically fully employed and was restricted to Colored
Town in spending its money. Tables 2.2 and 2.3 reflect data from a
1915 story in the *Miami Metropolis* showing the Miami businesses
owned by blacks.

The Chauffeur's Dispute (1915–1917)

In early Miami blacks could not operate businesses that catered to whites. This led to racial confrontations, the most serious of these being the bloody dispute between black and white drivers between 1915 and 1917. Chauffeuring was a highly prized job in those days. The pay was generally better than farm work or common labor, and it was a clean job that carried a certain amount of status in both white and black Miami. In Miami, unlike other areas of Florida and the country, it was considered a white job.[43]

White chauffeurs in Miami's quickly developing tourist industry were determined to keep blacks from working as chauffeurs. The *Miami Daily Metropolis* reported on July 16, 1917, that white chauffeurs were chasing black drivers through the streets like a pack of hounds chasing a rabbit or a fox while the police looked on. A 1915 booklet distributed to attract tourists to Miami advised prospective visitors to leave their black drivers at home as most of the local garages refused service to automobiles driven by black chauffeurs. Typically, white tourists arriving with black chauffeurs were required to turn their vehicles over to white chauffeurs at the city limits of Miami. Upon leaving the city, their black chauffeurs were allowed to resume their duties.

In February 1915, a black chauffeur from Palm Beach attempted to test the matter. With three white women passengers in a car, he made a bet with a white man that he could come to Miami and drive around the city. White chauffeurs had been warned and were looking for him. The driver, unnamed in news accounts of the story, dropped off his passengers at the Royal Palm Hotel and went for a ride around the city, ending at Avenue B and Waddell Street. He was chased by several cars with Miami chauffeurs and realized that unless he gave up he would be treated roughly. He abandoned the car and walked to Colored Town. According to the *Miami Herald,* "He later appeared at police headquarters and asked for protection. He told Lieutenant McDade that 'he believed he'd take the train for Palm Beach and leave that there car here for Mistah Metcalf, its owner, to come after.' The Lieutenant took him to the railway station. He left convinced that Miami was different from West Palm and a Negro had no business acting as chauffeur in Miami."[44]

Two years later, a similar incident occurred. According to a January 1917 story in the *Miami Herald,* the black chauffeur employed by a

Mr. Camden of Virginia, who was visiting at the Royal Palm Hotel, was given police protection through the city to the hotel. "Mr. Camden immediately hired a white chauffeur, who will remain in that position while he is in the city. The colored driver was accompanied by a policeman and no attempt was made to interfere with him. The protection was promised by the city authorities before the car reached the city."[45]

In 1917 several blacks, attempting to circumvent the restrictions, started up chauffeur services catering to white customers. In response, white chauffeurs chased black drivers through the streets of Miami while the police did nothing. In July, after a black chauffeur named Fred Andrews was assaulted by several white chauffeurs, Andrews searched out one of his assailants and stabbed him. Andrews was subsequently arrested, tried, and convicted for the offense. His attackers were never caught. Racial tensions mounted in the aftermath of the Andrews conviction. A few days after the trial, rumors of an imminent black uprising surged through the white community, countered by rumors in the black community that whites were getting ready to shoot up Colored Town.

Miami came dangerously close to a major race riot when late on the night of July 15, 1917, a group of whites dynamited the Odd Fellows Hall, then the largest building in Colored Town. The explosion brought out many blacks with guns and other weapons, but violence was averted when several black clergymen pleaded for calm and police officials assured everyone that the dynamiters would be caught. Police initially offered a reward of fifty dollars and increased it to two hundred dollars after blacks complained of a half-hearted investigation. The dynamiters, however, were never apprehended.

In the end, the black chauffeurs won a victory of sorts when it was agreed that blacks would have a monopoly on the operation of buses and automobiles-for-hire in black areas. The parties to the agreement were Miami police chief William Whiteman, other white civic leaders, and the Colored Board of Trade.

Early Bahamian Immigration to Miami (1896–1926)

A significant portion of the city's black population was of Bahamian descent at the turn of the century. The large number of steamers operating between the Bahamas and Miami made travel inexpensive. Many Bahamian farm workers came to south Florida seasonally to work the crops, returning to the islands at the end of the harvest. This continued the trend that had begun decades earlier when West Indian workers sold their services abroad as seasonal laborers or until a task was completed.

By the turn of the century Miami had established an agricultural productivity that rivaled and ultimately superseded that of the Bahamas, as Bahamian soils eventually lost productive nutrients from overcultivation. Entrepreneurs in Miami attracted and exploited Bahamian labor by extensive advertising in Bahamian newspapers. For weeks at a time, the *Nassau Guardian* carried advertisements on the front page for the Ward, Eder, and Dempster steamship lines offering daily departures to and from Miami at affordable rates, about fourteen dollars in 1898.

By Miami's second decade, Bahamian labor had become essential to the local economy. James B. Nimmo, who arrived in Miami from the Bahama Islands in 1916, recalls, "Bahamians would come to Miami and Key West during the farming season. It was a pleasure to go down to the docks in Miami on a Sunday evening during the season. You'd see three or four hundred black Bahamians coming into Miami to work. Most would go back, but each season a few more would stay. That's how come you got so many Bahamian people here. In the early days, Key West and Miami had a majority of Bahamians among the blacks in those towns."[46]

In addition to contributing to south Florida's agriculture, Bahamians who came to Miami applied the skills they had mastered in the construction, maritime, and fishing industries. Their experience with oolitic limestone, which constitutes much of the islands' surface, made them more marketable in the construction trades than native-born blacks, who had come from states where this type of limestone was not found. Oolite was found abundant in Miami and, as George Merrick noted, Bahamians knew how to use this resource to construct buildings.

The United States census for 1900 reported 966 blacks living permanently in Dade County. The proportion of Bahamian-born blacks was roughly 22 percent of the blacks in the county, a much bigger territory at that time. Gender distribution of the local area blacks was not very different between Bahamian and American-born blacks, males predominating in both groups by roughly a two-to-one margin. This reflected the kind of work early Miami offered.

The predominant occupations among the two groups were different. The most often-mentioned occupation for American-born blacks
was that of common laborer (approximately 21 percent), while the
majority of the Bahamian black males reported their employment as
farm labor. Approximately 13 percent of the Bahamian males were
employed in the maritime professions: as sailors, deckhands, and other
related positions. Of the Bahamian blacks, 80 percent were able to
read and 79 percent could write, while 72 percent of the American-
born blacks could read and 69 percent could write.[47]

In pursuit of economic gain, many Bahamians silently endured the
segregation that prevailed in Miami, but some complained. According
to Florida historian Raymond A. Mohl, "While the Bahamians found
economic opportunity in Florida, they also encountered segregation
and white racism for the first time." Mohl quotes one early-twentieth-
century Bahamian immigrant—interviewed by Ira Reid for his 1939
book, *The Negro Immigrant*—who reported his disenchantment with
conditions in Miami:

> Having passed the immigration and customs examiners, I took a
> carriage for what the driver called "Nigger Town." This was the
> first time I had heard that opprobrious epithet employed. I was viv-
> idly irked no little. Arriving in Colored Town, I alighted from the
> carriage in front of an unpainted, poorly-ventilated rooming house
> where I paid $2.00 for a week's lodging.
>
> Already, I was rapidly becoming disillusioned. How unlike the
> land where I was born. There colored men were addressed as gentle-
> men; here, as "niggers." There policemen were dressed in immacu-
> late uniforms, carried no deadly weapon, save a billy; here, shirt-
> sleeved officers of the law carried pistols and smoked and chewed
> tobacco on duty. Colored Miami certainly was not the Miami of
> which I had heard. It was a filthy backyard to the Magic City.

Police brutality directed at blacks quickly emerged as a matter of
concern among Bahamians in Miami. According to Mohl, "In 1907,
islanders complained to British Ambassador James Bryce about un-
warranted police shootings of Bahamians in Key West and Miami.
Bryce urged the Foreign Office to investigate, but candidly admitted,
'There seems no doubt that the aggressors were white and the victims
black and, in such cases, little hope can be entertained of getting justice in certain Southern States. In such states as Florida,' Bryce wrote,

'Colored people are not treated with much consideration. Such cases frequently occur.'" During a subsequent investigation in 1908, a British consular official reported that in Florida it was a common occurrence for blacks to be shot by police while allegedly evading arrest.

By 1920, Mohl reported, almost five thousand black islanders, nearly all from the Bahamas, made up 52 percent of Miami's black community and more than 16 percent of the city's entire population. At that time, Miami had a larger population of black immigrants than any other city in the United States except New York.[48]

Calvin Johnson was an African-American pioneer who came to Coconut Grove from South Carolina in the early 1920s. At age ninety-five he recalled his impressions of the Bahamian blacks he saw settling in the Black Grove in the early 1920s. "They were very nice people. They had a different culture which sometimes I found difficult to understand. For instance, their eating habits were different. They ate seafood, mainly fish, crabs, conch and grits but didn't know much about vegetables. Many looked small and undernourished."[49]

In 1916 more than eight hundred workers, many of them Bahamian, were building Vizcaya for millionaire James Deering, who had purchased a large portion of the Brickell estate from Mary Brickell. At one time, Deering owned all of the land on which now stand the Museum of Science and Mercy Hospital. As the building and gardens neared completion in October of that year, the *Miami Metropolis* thus described the unfolding magnificence in detail, portraying the Bahamian work gangs in the woods near the palace: "Entering the grounds through the eastern gateway one follows a winding road through the woods. Gangs of workmen are busily engaged in setting out special trees, flowers and shrubbery along this road, and in through the woods, the weird chant of the Nassau Negro rises above the click of the shovel and hoe as the laborer sings in his high pitched voice of the wonders of his native Bahamas."[50]

Eventually, some whites became concerned about the unemployment problem created by the influx of so many island blacks and about some ship captains' unscrupulous manipulation of the immigration rule that all arriving passengers have at least five dollars before being allowed to land. Miami's powerful Board of Trade took up the debate:

That there are too many Nassau negroes in Miami was the opinion of several members of the board of trade at last night's regular meeting. One member stated that he knew for a fact over 200 Nassau negroes were in the city out of employment and the continued influx would have a tendency to make it a difficult matter to give them employment, and this would overload the city with unemployed negroes.

While it is necessary for immigrants to have at least five dollars in their possession upon landing here, it was stated by a member that it had been brought to his attention that captains on vessels bringing Nassau negroes here had been advancing the colored men the five dollars, and then, after they put foot on American soil, had taken the five dollars back and passed it on to another, in order that he might land. It was said that one five dollar bill had been the means of admitting hundreds into this country.[51]

Bahamians were a volatile element in early Miami's cultural mix. They thought themselves to be less servile than American-born blacks in Miami, who came primarily from north and central Florida, Georgia, and South Carolina. Proud of their British roots—a culture considerably more tolerant of racial diversity than America—Bahamians were often perceived by whites as radical or militant. A near-riot in Coconut Grove in 1920 convinced many whites that blacks from the Bahamas were especially problematic.

On July 30 at five in the morning a white woman was working alone in her kitchen when, according to newspaper accounts, a black man casually walked in and asked her for food. Allegedly he grabbed the woman around the neck and dragged her into the back yard. Although there was some question as to the nature of the assault, whites were convinced that the woman was raped. Several hours later, a few blocks away, detectives with tracking dogs arrested Herbert Brooks, a fifty-five-year-old black immigrant from the Bahamas in his home. The white woman positively identified Brooks as her attacker.

That night, as a mob of some five hundred white men formed near the jail, a judge decided that Brooks should be moved three hundred miles north to Jacksonville for his protection. Trailed by white vigilantes, the prisoner was taken the first one hundred miles by the police. At Fort Pierce he was placed aboard a northbound train. Brooks never made it to Jacksonville. Around noon, just north of Ormond, he reportedly jumped, head first, through the window of the moving train. His death was ruled a suicide.

Believing that the mob had killed Brooks, about four hundred of Miami's Bahamians assembled in the black Coconut Grove area on the evening of August 3. The following day, the *Miami Herald* described what happened: "Four hundred or more alien Negroes from the Bahama Islands gathered on the streets of the colored settlement yesterday morning, and becoming greatly excited, made numerous threats of what they proposed doing to avenge Brooks' death. Some people professed to believe he had been killed by the mob which pursued him from Miami to Ft. Pierce and beyond."

The gathering of angry blacks alarmed officials. For the first time in the city's brief history, they issued an order for the mobilization of the national guard. Whites were not allowed into the area, nor blacks out of it. American-born blacks declined to participate in the disturbance. In fact, the local Negro American Legion unit was involved in the pursuit of the attacker, and black men from the unit were on guard during the disturbance. Matters quieted down after Brooks's body was put on a ship to be buried in the Bahamas.

Black schools and churches developed extensively in Dade County between 1896 and 1926. Even as they did, blacks in Colored Town and elsewhere in Dade County were subjected to extensive and debilitating racial segregation, economic and political exploitation, and on occasion, beatings, maimings, and outright lynchings at the hands of racist whites. Often the police and the Ku Klux Klan were involved. Blacks did not merely accept such treatment as a matter of course, and the community was brought to the brink of race riot several times between 1896 and 1926.

Black Education in Early Miami

The education of black children was not a priority in early Dade County. The city was over thirty years old before black children were able to earn a high school diploma in Miami.

The first public school for black children in Dade County opened in 1893 in the Lake Worth area, ten years after the first white school opened. Since there were no buildings available, the school was housed in the Tabernacle Missionary Baptist Church, which charged twenty-five dollars per year to lease the church to the school. The school's first teacher was J. E. Jones, who taught throughout the 1890s. He was paid thirty dollars per month.

The first school for the children of Colored Town was a wooden building on Northwest Eighth Street between Second and Third avenues, where the Berrien Hotel later stood. Established around 1896 and commonly called Old Washington School, the school taught grades one through six. Later the Fort Dallas Land Company gave the land on Twelfth Street for a new school building where Douglass Elementary School now stands.[1]

The next school for blacks opened in Lemon City. Although the exact date of its establishment remains unknown, the *Miami Metropolis* announced on December 9, 1898, that Isaac M. Rawls had been appointed supervisor of the Lemon City Colored School. The Reverend F. A. Hamilton assumed the teaching duties for the school's fifty pupils in 1904. He was a college graduate, a rarity for black teachers of the day. The pay for white and black teachers at the turn of the century was the same, forty dollars per month. This parity would not continue. Hamilton frequently gave lectures around Lemon City and attended the Colored Literary Society meetings, which were sometimes held in Lemon City.[2]

Coconut Grove's first black school started in the early 1900s with only twelve students. Classes were held in the Methodist church on Charles Avenue under the direction of the Reverend John Davis, the minister of the church. Shortly after its establishment the school was moved from the church to the Odd Fellows Hall, also on Charles Avenue. As more children enrolled, a two-room wooden building was acquired in the thirty-six hundred block of Thomas Avenue, where the school remained for a number of years.

School board records for 1906 mention that Asa Richard had been appointed principal of Colored School Number Six, the Black Grove school that had become known as the Dade County Industrial Training School. His salary was forty dollars per month. The school offered education up to the sixth grade. In 1919 the school moved across the railroad tracks and south of the Grove to an area on Ponce de Leon Avenue, the present site of student dormitories for the University of Miami. The Coconut Grove Colored School had 105 students in 1921 and its operational cost was under two thousand dollars.

Another public school for black children in Miami was located in Colored Town across the street from the Greater Bethel A.M.E. Church, on what is now Northwest Second Avenue and Eighth Street. This school provided instruction for first through eighth grades. The Miami city directory for 1918 lists only two private black schools, Miami Normal and Saint Agnes Parochial School. However, by 1925 three additional private schools had appeared: the Harrison B. Moore Orphanage and Industrial School at 334 Northwest Eleventh Street, the Stirrup Home Training School at 333 North Twelfth Street, and Saint Alban's Industrial School on Douglas Road in Coconut Grove.

The facilities that housed these first black schools were in poor condition. Most were conducted by one or two teachers in churches or lodges, there being few county-owned schoolhouses. In the early years the school board considered any hall or building suitable to house schools for black children. Classrooms were overcrowded and many were not furnished with the necessary equipment. Drinking water, toilets, desks, blackboards, textbooks, and library books were often lacking or of poor quality in black schools.

Miami Normal was the best known of the black schools of this period. Nellie S. Powers founded the school in 1910 and served as its principal. In 1916 she led a campaign to enlarge the school to accommodate three hundred black children between the ages of three and seventeen. The Realty Securities Corporation of Miami donated a site for the new school in the Railroad Shops Colored Addition section, northwest of town. The move was supported by many leading whites, who appreciated the additional benefits that would accrue if the goal of raising six thousand dollars were realized.

The ground-breaking ceremony for the school was held on August 21, 1916. It had been expected that the building would be ready by January 1 of that year, but the opening of the school was interrupted by the First World War. As the school year began in October 1916, the *Miami Herald* carried the following story:

> The Miami Colored Normal Industrial Training and Kindergarten School will begin its seventh years' work under the direction of Nellie S. Powers this morning. . . . Mrs. Powers has inaugurated a new idea, in that she has instructed every pupil to provide his or her own individual drinking cup and the school will be kept in a thorough sanitary condition. . . . The course will include Kindergarten, Grammar School, High School, Normal, and Industrial Training. Provision has also been made for a limited number of boarding pupils during the season.[3]

By 1924, Dunbar School on Twentieth Street in Colored Town offered black children an education through eighth grade. That was as far as a black child could go in Miami's first thirty years. Before World War I, black parents had to send their children out of the county if they desired education beyond the eighth grade. African-American families often sent their older children to Jacksonville, Daytona, or out of the state, while many Bahamians sent their older children to the Bahamas for their secondary and higher education.

One of the reasons that no high school education was provided for black children in Miami prior to 1926 was that southern whites generally assumed black people to be biologically inferior to whites and therefore unable to comprehend ideas above an elementary level. Also,

48. Historic Booker T. Washington Senior High School shortly after its construction in 1927. Prior to the opening of this school, black children in Miami could not get an education beyond the eighth grade. Black parents who wanted their children to earn a high school diploma sent them away to boarding schools. The building was destroyed to make way for Booker T. Washington Middle School, which now occupies the site. Courtesy Historical Museum of Southern Florida.

whites generally believed that blacks were best suited for manual or domestic work, making it wasteful to spend public money on education beyond the eighth grade.

Finally, after considerable pressure from blacks, in 1926 ground was broken for a public high school for the black children of Colored Town, located at Sixth Avenue and Twelfth Street. Confronting opposition from whites, blacks built fires and set night watches to guard the construction site. The 1926 hurricane damaged the almost-completed structure and prevented the scheduled opening, but in February 1927 students and faculty moved into the sparkling new building. This was the

49. Eliza Granberry, the first principal of Booker T. Washington Senior High School. Courtesy Historical Museum of Southern Florida.

50. Students of Booker T. Washington Senior High School with their science teacher, circa 1931. Standing in the back row, from left, are Joseph Johnson, an unidentified man, Timothy Buggy, Eugene Duncomb, and an unidentified man. Seated, from left, are Ellen Johnson; Wilhelmena Ross; Mr. Austin, the science teacher; and Isabelle Sharpe. Courtesy Isabelle Sharpe Blue.

beginning of Booker T. Washington Senior High School, one of the most formidable high schools, white or black, in Florida. It became the intellectual seat of black Miami.

The original building was a typical south Florida masonry edifice of simple design with classical details. The structure was light and airy with very large grouped windows. It had a courtyard where many community meetings and cultural events were held. No other facility, public or private, contained an auditorium and cafeteria of equal size.

The school produced a considerable number of black physicians, nurses, scientists, attorneys, clergy, business and military leaders, and legions of black educators. Among its best-known graduates were Garth

51. The entire teaching faculty of Phillis Wheatley Elementary School in Colored Town, 1937. The school was established in 1934 and is located at 1801 Northwest First Place. Courtesy Dade County Public Schools.

Reeves, owner and publisher of the *Miami Times;* Esther Rolle, television actress; Dr. Tee S. Greer, deputy superintendent of the Dade County Public School System; and Arthur McDuffie, the insurance agent whose death at the hands of five white police officers led to the Miami riot of 1980.

Early Black Churches in Dade County (1896–1926)

Almost as soon as they pitched their tents in the woods around Biscayne Bay, blacks established their own churches. For the most part, blacks in early Dade County were prohibited from attending services at white churches. One exception was Union Chapel in Coconut Grove, now known as Plymouth Congregational Church. Black churches were established in Lemon City and in Coconut Grove prior to the arrival of the railroad. Some black churches came to occupy positions of considerable influence in black Dade County, and their ministers acquired power and prestige.

The function of the black church went well beyond religion. Not only was it the spiritual base for blacks, it was also the source of charitable efforts and mutual support in the days before public welfare. Later the black church became the foundation for social and political activism. The tradition of congregants dressing fashionably for church and addressing one another as sister or brother offered a dignity and recognition that blacks did not find in other places.

Black families looked to their churches for recognition of their individual worth and to reinforce their values for their children. Church was the place where culture was preserved and taught. Blacks expected their clergy to give political guidance and to voice black concerns, particularly complaints about the white community. For the Baha-

52. The Reverend Samuel A. Sampson, the first black minister of a church in Dade County. Sampson established the Fifty-Six Baptist Church (named for the number of its original founders) in Coconut Grove in 1894. It later became known as Saint Agnes Missionary Baptist Church and today is called Macedonia Missionary Baptist Church. Courtesy Historical Museum of Southern Florida.

53. The Macedonia Missionary Baptist Church as it appears today. Established in 1894, this is the oldest black church in Dade County. It is located on Douglas Road and Charles Avenue. Its Bahamian roots are still apparent. Courtesy Sergio Campos.

mian and other West Indian congregations, the church provided a place to preserve values and traditions brought with them from the islands.

The 1904 Miami city directory, the second published, lists nine black churches. The early directories identified black residents, churches, and businesses with an asterisk. Of the churches, four were Methodist, four were Baptist and the ninth was Episcopal. By the time the 1918 city directory was published, the number of black churches had grown to fourteen.

The oldest black church in Dade County is the Macedonia Missionary Baptist Church in Coconut Grove, established in 1894. Because there were originally fifty-six members, it was called the Fifty-Six Baptist Church. Its first location was on Williams Avenue at the home of Edith Albury, and its first minister was the Reverend Samuel A. Sampson. In 1903 the church was relocated to Charles Avenue and renamed Saint Agnes Missionary Baptist Church. The church today, located at 3515 Douglas Road, is known as the Macedonia Missionary Baptist Church. Reflecting its Coconut Grove membership, the church has strong ties to Bahamian traditions.

The first black church to rise in Miami proper was the Greater Bethel African Methodist Episcopal (A.M.E.) Church, commonly called Big Bethel. This great church was established within weeks of the city's birth in 1896 and remains a force in Dade County today. The first

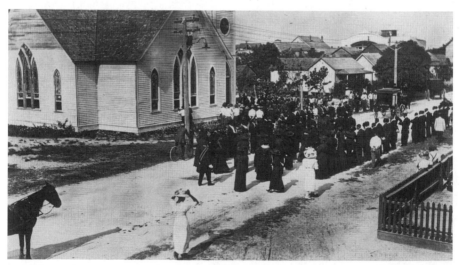

54. A funeral procession leaving Greater Bethel A.M.E. Church in Colored Town, circa 1920. Courtesy Black Archives, History and Research Foundation of South Florida.

55. The Greater Bethel African Methodist Episcopal Church (Big Bethel), the oldest black church in Overtown. It was established in 1896 at the home of A. C. Lightburn, one of the black incorporators of the city. The church was a powerful influence in the civil rights era in Miami. It is located on Northwest Eighth Street between Second and Third Avenues. Courtesy Sergio Campos.

written reference to black churches within the original city limits appeared in the *Miami Metropolis* on August 28, 1896, three months after the paper began publication. It made reference to activities at the Bethel A.M.E. Church. Three months later, the *Miami Metropolis* announced that the Bethel A.M.E. Church and Sunday school choir would give musical and literary entertainment at the Union Hall for the benefit of the organ fund. Admission was fifteen cents.

The church was formally organized on March 12, 1896, when an assembly of concerned blacks met at the home of A. C. Lightburn for the purpose of establishing an African Methodist Episcopal Church. Worship services were first held in the Lightburn home. The church later moved across the street to a tent and then into its first building, known as Little Bethel. In 1899 it was located on Eighth Street between Second and Third avenues, where it remains today.

Mount Zion Baptist Church was founded on September 17, 1896, by the Reverend T. M. Trammell. Its first permanent church building

56. Mount Zion Baptist Church was organized and built by black Baptists in 1896. The building shown here is on Northwest Third Avenue and Ninth Street. The first permanent church building was located on Second Avenue and Flagler Street. In 1898 the church moved to its present location. Courtesy Black Archives, History and Research Foundation of South Florida.

was located at the corner of Avenue G and Cherry Street (Northwest Second Avenue and Flagler Street). In 1898, the congregation moved to its present location at 301 Northwest Ninth Street. Like several other black churches, Mount Zion's wood-frame church building was completely destroyed during the 1926 hurricane.

Another old and powerful black church in Dade County is the Saint Agnes Episcopal Church, established in 1897 in Colored Town. This church was founded by the Reverend James O. S. Huntington, a white man, who was temporarily filling in as a parochial clergyman in Miami shortly after the city was founded. He was visiting John Sewell when he heard a black laundress singing as she worked. Intrigued, he asked about her church, and she told him she was a Bahamian of the Anglican Communion.

After a brief discussion, the priest realized that there was no Episcopal Church in Miami for black Bahamian immigrants, many of whom were Anglicans. As a result of his efforts, in the fall of 1897 thirty persons assembled in a private home on Northwest Second Avenue near Flagler Street, where Saint Agnes Church was established. The name was chosen because most of the founding members had been members of the Saint Agnes Church in Nassau, Bahamas.[4]

Many financial and other problems plagued the church in its early years, ultimately splitting the congregation into two groups, one of which moved out. For several years the building remained unfinished. The church was rescued from financial disorder by the dramatic leadership of the Reverend John E. Culmer, who became its pastor in 1929. Rev. Culmer would emerge as Miami's most dominant black leader of the thirties and forties, and with him rose Saint Agnes's membership and prestige.

Another of the oldest black churches in Coconut Grove is the powerful Christ Episcopal Church, established in 1901 and located on Hibiscus Street at Williams Avenue. Commonly referred to as Christ Church, during the early years this church and Saint Agnes were both

57. Saint Agnes Episcopal Church, established in 1897 by Bahamians living in Colored Town. Father John E. Culmer headed this church upon his arrival in Miami in 1929. It is located on Northwest Third Avenue and Seventeenth Street. Courtesy Sergio Campos.

ministered by the clergy of Trinity Church, a white Episcopal church in Miami. As the black community in Colored Town and Coconut Grove grew, the two churches became independent of Trinity. Christ Church was founded by Bahamians, who built a church much like the church they knew back home. They retained the name Christ Church and its Bahamian pink color.

In 1926 the Great Hurricane completely destroyed the church and the parish house. However, they were quickly rebuilt using cocina, a plentiful strong rock found in south Florida. This is the building that still stands today.

The several black Anglican churches in Dade County remained almost exclusively West Indian, making little attempt to proselytize American-born blacks. As a result, these churches are often referred to as Nassau churches rather than as Episcopal churches. The early membership of Saint Agnes consisted entirely of Bahamian blacks.

In August 1898 four families gathered at the home of John Page to establish the Ebenezer Baptist Church. The first church building was

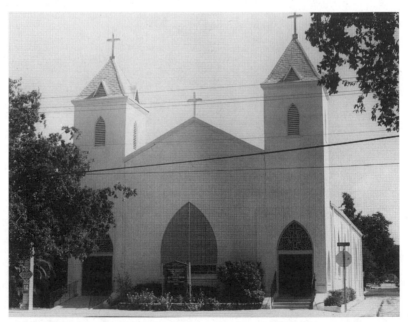

58. Christ Episcopal Church in Coconut Grove, established in 1901 by Bahamians. Named after Christ Church in the Bahamas, it gave spiritual refuge to hundreds of Bahamian families. Father Theodore R. Gibson was its most noted pastor during the civil rights era. Courtesy Sergio Campos.

on Northwest Ninth Street at Third Avenue. Friends of the founding members donated lumber for the building and church members supplied the labor. This church survives today in black Miami. Triumph the Church and Kingdom of Christ was formed in 1902 by a small group of Colored Town residents.[5]

Mount Tabor Missionary Baptist Church was formally established in 1905 in Lemon City, although many years of church activities preceded the actual founding of the church. In the late 1800s, as blacks from South Carolina, Georgia, Alabama, and Florida settled in or near Lemon City, daily social contact among them took place during lunch breaks in the vegetable fields and packing houses. Relationships among the workers grew stronger and led to weekend gatherings where the main focus was on family and religion. Since there was no church building, these meetings were conducted in private homes under the leadership of the Reverend B. F. Goodwin, the group's first pastor.

After a prayer meeting held in the home of Elijah H. Boles in February 1901, the first church organization was established. In 1905, the Reverend A. J. Thomas took the post as the second minister of the church. During his pastorate, a plot of land was purchased on Northeast Sixty-eighth Street and Miami Court, where the first church was built.

Saint John Baptist Church was established on June 17, 1906, at the corner of Northwest Second Avenue and Eleventh Terrace (Avenue G and Wood Street) in a small wood-frame building. In July 1907 the church was moved to Jackson Hall on Tenth Street between Second and Third avenues, after which the membership quickly increased. The church was led by a series of short-term pastors before being taken over on January 22, 1912, by the Reverend James Wilkerson Drake, newly arrived from Jacksonville where he had been working for the Afro-American Life Insurance Company. Drake rebuilt the church from the ground up and became one of Miami's most respected black leaders in the pre–civil rights period.

By 1912, Bahamian immigrants were settled west of Perrine. Many worked at the Ramsay-McCrimmon Saw Mill. In 1913, the Reverend S. W. White was sent to Perrine by A.M.E. Bishop John Hurst to hold a revival meeting. Because of the success of this event, an A.M.E. church was formed for the Bahamian worshipers. It became known as Pine Grover's A.M.E. Church. The church building was erected in 1914 after John and Addie Williams bought a piece of land for the building.

59. Saint John Baptist Church, established 1906. Its most noted pastor was the Reverend James Wilkerson Drake, who came to Miami in 1912 from Jacksonville. He became one of Miami's most respected black leaders prior to the civil rights era. Courtesy Sergio Campos.

This structure burned down in 1916. It was rebuilt by 1920, only to be demolished by the Great Hurricane of 1926. Bishop Hurst raised money in Jacksonville to rebuild the church, and the new structure was renamed Hurst Chapel in his honor.

Mount Pleasant Missionary Baptist Church, now located at 11591 Southwest 220th Street in Goulds, was organized in 1914. Originally, members worshiped in the home of D. D. Cail, a prominent black businessman and farmer. Later that year, a wood-frame building was erected at U.S. Highway 1 and Southwest 221st Street to house the church. The church was named by Polly Mays, one of its original members. John A. Everett, the head of south Dade's well-known Everett family, was also among the first members of the church.

Destroyed by the 1926 hurricane, the church was rebuilt on the same site. The present-day location is on land donated by Arthur Mays. In its early years this church was known as the high-yellow church, a reference to the light skin color of some of the early members, such as the Mayses and Everetts. Bodies of deceased church members were usually taken to the city of Miami for burial, but some were buried in a black south Dade cemetery associated with the Walker Funeral Home.[6]

One of the oldest black churches in south Dade County is the New Bethel A.M.E. Church, founded in 1916 by Horace Roux and J. V. Laval. The first services were held at the home of Charlie Graham, a farmer in the area then called Black Point. Its first pastor was R. W. Logan. The first building was erected in the Goulds area in 1917 and was also used as a school for first, second, and third grades. The 1926 hurricane demolished the structure, and church members worshiped at Mt. Pleasant Church until another building was erected for New Bethel in 1929. The present church building is located at 11695 Southwest 220th Street.

Saint Francis Xavier Catholic Church was established in 1927 as a mission of the downtown Gesu Catholic Church because the black

60. The Mount Pleasant Missionary Baptist Church was organized in 1914 in Goulds. Arthur and Polly Mays were among its founders. The church is located at 11591 Southwest 220th Street. It was often called the "high yellow" church because so many light-skinned blacks, like the Mays family, attended the church. Courtesy Sergio Campos.

61. New Bethel A.M.E. Church. This church in south Dade County was established in 1916 with the help of Horace Roux and J. V. Laval, two leading south Dade black citizens. The original building was constructed in 1917 but, like many other early black churches, was destroyed in the 1926 hurricane. Members worshiped at Mount Pleasant Missionary Baptist Church until a new building could be constructed. Courtesy Sergio Campos.

Catholics, most of whom were of Bahamian descent, were experiencing discrimination at Gesu. In the South of the 1920s, it was common for Catholic churches to require blacks to use the back pews and to forbid them from approaching the altar to receive holy communion with white parishioners. Instead, blacks had to wait until the end of mass to receive communion. After appealing to the bishop, Miami blacks were given permission to establish their own Catholic church. Saint Francis Xavier began in a storefront behind the Economy Drug Store, owned by pharmacist Elmer Ward, and moved to its permanent location on Northwest Fourth Avenue after Ward and other blacks raised the money in the 1930s.

Other historic black churches in Dade County include Mt. Olivette Baptist Church, established in October 1912. Its founder was also Samuel A. Sampson, by that time a Colored Town businessman, community spokesman, and civil rights leader.

A. M. Cohen Temple Church of God in Christ was organized in 1918 by A. M. Cohen. His descendants have continued his service through the years. Cohen, who came to Miami from South Carolina to work on the railroads, was among the many blacks who stood for the incorporation of Miami.

Trinity C.M.E. Church was established in the early 1920s by a small congregation from Colored Town; the old Dunbar School served as its first meeting place.

Saint Peter's Orthodox Catholic Church began in 1925 as an African Orthodox Church. Father Ernest Leopold Peterson, a priest of the African American Church, was sent to Miami from New York to head the church.

Temple Baptist Church was organized on May 19, 1930, by immigrants from the Bahamian Islands. The Reverend L. A. Thompson, its founder, came to Miami from Cat Island and served his congregation for forty-eight years.

Greater Israel Bethel Primitive Baptist Church was founded in 1912. Pastor P. D. Brantley presided over his congregation for forty-three years.

The Ku Klux Klan in Miami (1921)

Throughout the 1920s blacks in Dade County were subjected to a series of violent attacks by the Ku Klux Klan. Some of these resulted in lynchings, an increasingly common occurrence in the deep South in the twenties and thirties. Although the Klan was active in Miami in 1920, it officially announced its arrival in Miami in 1921 with a huge parade through the downtown area. Thousands of people turned out to watch the event as dozens of Klan members marched in full regalia.

White Miami did not immediately reject the Klan. In July 1927 an American Legion chapter in northeast Miami awarded the women of the Klan first prize for the most elaborate float in the Independence Day parade.

The first mob action against blacks that was probably linked to Klan activity occurred in the summer of 1920. At 9:30 P.M. June 29, two terrific explosions were heard in Colored Town. Soon after, three thousand blacks assembled at the intersection of Waddell Street and Avenue K, the dividing line between the white and black settlements. Witnesses claimed that white men threw two dynamite bombs into an unoccupied house on Avenue K. At 11:30 city officials reported that blacks were armed and gathered in groups, prompting the city to ask the American Legion for help in quelling the disturbance. An hour later, Colored Town was patrolled by over three hundred white men armed with rifles. Only residents were allowed into the area. Those responsible for the bombing were never caught.[7]

Left: 62. Poster announcing Ku Klux Klan happenings in Miami, 1926. The Klan officially arrived in Miami in 1921 with a huge parade downtown. Courtesy Miami Memorabilia Collection of Myrna and Seth Bramson.

Below: 63. Members of the Ku Klux Klan preparing to ride in a night parade in downtown Miami, 1925. Klansmen mounted on horses rode at will through Colored Town terrorizing blacks. Some members were police officers. Courtesy Romer Collection: Miami-Dade County Public Library.

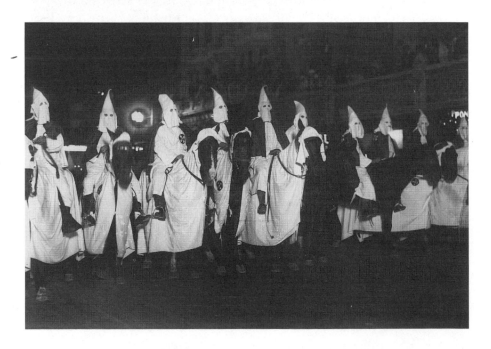

64. The Ku Klux Klan marches down Flagler Street on November 23, 1926, in celebration of Progress Week. Blacks were attacked at will, although black radicals in post-World War I Miami sometimes struck back. Courtesy Romer Collection: Miami-Dade County Public Library.

The Klan orchestrated a number of violent attacks on Miami ministers, white and black, who were perceived to be advocates of racial equality. The Higgs incident in July 1920 was one of the most noted. H. H. Higgs, a black minister from Coconut Grove, was kidnapped for allegedly espousing racial equality, intermarriage between whites and blacks, and the use of violence as a weapon against white oppression. Blacks in Coconut Grove reacted to the abduction with outrage. Believing erroneously that the minister had been lynched, hundreds of blacks poured into the streets of the Black Grove. The *Miami Herald* described what happened:

> The local police station and the Sheriff's office received a call from policeman O. L. Kennedy at Coconut Grove. He requested that every police officer in Miami be sent to Coconut Grove, as a Negro preacher had been kidnaped by four armed men in an automobile. Reverend H. H. Higgs, a Negro Baptist preacher, had been conduct-

ing revival services in Coconut Grove and due to his alleged doctrines of racial equality, resulted in a riot. Higgs was taken away by four men in an automobile and it is said that he was lynched by those men. There were over fifteen arrests that resulted from this riot.

The American Legion was called on for assistance. Guardsmen . . . and others were placed on every bridge in, and near, both Miami and Coconut Grove.[8]

Lourena Smith, who grew up in the early Black Grove, related: "Reverend Higgs was preaching to the people that they should give their children a good education so as to prevent them from having to work inside a white person's house and so that they could find a better job." Smith recalled that rioting occurred between groups of whites and blacks, and she remembered the chilling night of the Higgs abduction, when her father came home and told the family something bad had happened. "He said that when he tried to cross the Twelfth Street bridge, there were many white people there with guns. A man with a hood confronted him yelling, 'Nigger, get down off that God-damn bicycle. Where are you going? Where do you live?' Another hooded man, who apparently knew my father, intervened and prevented an incident by saying, 'Leave him alone. He's a good nigger.'" The next morning, the community donated food, clothing, and money to Reverend Higgs and his family, who left Miami to go back to Nassau.[9]

Early Grove settler Albert Gibson reported that Higgs was the president of the local chapter of the Marcus Garvey Back-to-Africa movement. Garvey was a Jamaican firebrand who rallied blacks all over the country to return to Africa. Gibson, who was also a member of the organization, said, "They beat him up good and gave him forty-eight hours to get out of town. We put him on a boat, gave him a couple hundred dollars and let him get lost. He hasn't been back since, but he dared them to come get him."[10]

Less than two weeks later, the Klan attacked another minister for allegedly preaching racial equality—this time a white minister named Phillip Irvin, who served as pastor of the Saint Agnes Episcopal Church. Eight masked men forcibly took Irvin from his home at 326 Northwest Fourth Street, beat him with a heavy strap, and tarred and feathered him. After ordering him to leave town or face worse treatment, they threw him from a speeding car onto a downtown Miami street. Blacks again were outraged.

Irvin denied having preached racial equality, and an Episcopal bishop rushed to Miami to help calm matters. The bishop dismissed the notion that a member of his clergy would advocate social equality of the races. He said the Episcopal church believed that blacks overemphasized the emotional and overlooked the moral. The bishop contended that Irvin unquestionably had taught equality as described in the New Testament and the Declaration of Independence but that he had not taught social and political equality under present conditions. Although he was promised around-the-clock police protection, Irvin left town to avoid more trouble. His abductors were never arrested.[11]

Police officials thought the same men abducted Irvin and Higgs and that they kidnapped another black man, George Brown, by mistake. Brown, a cook at the Belmont Cafe, was kidnapped while walking home. His captors handcuffed and masked him and drove him into the woods, where they tied him to a tree before realizing that he was not the man they wanted. He was released to walk back to Miami.

George Doty, a Bahamian who owned a blacksmith shop, was seized on August 25, 1921, by five white unmasked men. The abduction took place about 1:30 in the afternoon. Doty was severely lashed and given until sundown to sell his business and leave the state.[12]

In many instances blacks were merely run out of town by white mobs, a fate handed out to six blacks in January 1922 when they attempted to dance with white women on the dance floor at the Haleyon Hotel. D. A. Dorsey reportedly gave them money to enable them to leave Miami in an automobile.[13]

Two related lynchings of blacks took place in Goulds, or Black Point, in June 1923. They very probably involved Klan members. In Homestead William "Grey Eye" Simmons, a black man, allegedly killed Charles R. Bryant, the marshal of Homestead. The following account is based on work by Dr. William Wilbanks, a criminologist at Florida International University.

The story as to how the marshal was shot came largely from accounts given by a black woman, identified in the newspaper as Mary Cuzzins (or Cousins), the landlady of the rooming house in which the killing took place. She said she saw both men emerge from Simmons's room "locked in each other's arms" as they struggled for possession of Bryant's revolver. Simmons eventually gained possession of the revolver and fired several times at the marshal. Following the shooting Simmons reportedly went back to his room, changed his bloody shirt, stole a Ford truck, and drove away. In his haste to flee, he evidently ran into something and damaged a wheel, leaving his trackers a roadmap in the dirt.

The shooting caused great excitement in the southern part of the county and many search parties assembled in Homestead, despite a downpour. One group tracked the Ford truck to the Graham Negro quarters near Goulds about a half-mile west of the main highway. The search party, now a mob, came upon Simmons, who was on foot. As his name was called out, Simmons reportedly turned and, using the dead marshal's gun, began to shoot at his would-be captors. The mob returned Simmons's fire, wounded and captured him.[14]

Simmons was said to have confessed to the killing and implicated two others in a conspiracy to kill Bryant. Simmons reportedly said that he and another black man, Roy Gaines (in some accounts called Robert Gaines), had been hired by a white man to kill the marshal because of his activities against rum-runners. Simmons was lynched on the spot, within one hour of the marshal's death. The lynchers then went in search of those Simmons implicated.[15]

The mob apparently got a tip that Gaines was hiding in the woods south of Homestead. He was found and, like Simmons, summarily killed. His body was found the next morning four miles south of Homestead, punctured many times with bullets and gunshot, but he had not been hanged. Most of the black population of Goulds spent that night in the woods.

Within days of the lynchings, a coroner's jury ruled that Simmons and Gaines came to their deaths as the result of gunshot wounds from persons unknown. It appears that little effort was made to determine the identity of those responsible for the killings.

The *Miami Herald* described Marshal Bryant's funeral as the largest ever conducted in Dade County, with two thousand people in attendance. The Knights of the Ku Klux Klan assumed charge of the funeral after the church service. Two hundred klansmen and kamelias (the organization's female auxiliary) formed an automobile procession that preceded the hearse, and the procession following the hearse was fully a mile and a half long.[16]

65. Ku Klux Klan members at a rally in an unidentified place in the Miami area, circa 1925. New members had to take a pledge never to soil a sheet or disobey the Klavern Kommander. Courtesy Romer Collection: Miami-Dade County Library.

AN AFTERNOON MEAL - MIAMI, FLA.

66. Racist postcard, 1925. In addition to being abused and sometimes killed by white racists, blacks were also the subjects of twisted racist humor such as this postcard, which was used to promote Miami in the early 1900s. This card and many others depicting blacks in degrading and inhuman ways were mailed all over the United States. The alligator is stuffed. Courtesy Florida Archives.

A few days after the Bryant killing and the resultant lynchings, several whites hurled two bombs from a speeding car into an unoccupied black home in Colored Town. Nearly three thousand angry blacks were drawn to the scene. The rumor spread that blacks were arming themselves for a raid on the nearby white community. The mayor of Miami quickly dispatched his entire police force to Colored Town, along with a quasi-auxiliary army, the American Legion. By late evening, more than three hundred armed white men were patrolling the community and all streets leading into the area were closed. After several hours, most blacks returned to their homes, but the community was occupied by police for several days. The guilty parties were never apprehended.

The Back-to-Africa Movement in Miami

Many young black World War I veterans actively opposed the Klan and the racism they faced upon returning home at the end of the war in 1918. James Bertram Nimmo was one such man. He belonged to the Back-to-Africa movement founded by Marcus Garvey, the most militant of all black organizations operating in the United States after World War I.

Nimmo was born in 1898 on Acklin Island in the Bahamas. In August of 1916, his small frame emerged from the *Panama,* a steamer docked at the Miami Avenue bridge. Nimmo was typical of the genre of black nationalists in Miami after the war. He had tried to volunteer for service with the British forces when the war broke out but was rejected because of his small size. Disillusioned, he ran away from the Bahamas, landing in Miami as America slid into the Great War.

Nimmo joined the American army and was shipped off to France. "In France, you could go wherever your money could take you. I joined the army because coming to Miami was like coming into slavery. If you didn't have a job, you couldn't sit on your porch; you'd have to stay inside and keep your door closed, because police rolled up and down the streets in cars and would question you. 'Why are you here?' they would ask. 'Why aren't you working?' If you didn't have a job, they would lock you up. Farmers would come and bail you out. They would take you to their farms and work you for a period of time. The farmers would give you a minimum salary. This was common practice."[17]

67. James B. Nimmo, circa 1920. Nimmo arrived in Miami in 1916 from the Bahamas. He was an active member of the Miami chapter of the Marcus Garvey Back-to-Africa movement, known as the Universal Negro Improvement Association. The organization had a huge meeting hall in Colored Town on Fourth Court and 19th Street. Nimmo is shown here wearing the uniform of the organization. Courtesy Marjorie Wilcox.

Nimmo returned to post-war Miami in 1921 when the Marcus Garvey movement was in its infancy. The Garvey movement was a nationwide urban-based organization with large and active branches in Jamaica, Haiti, and South and Central America. There was a large and vigorous branch in Miami. The Garvey organization, also known as the Universal Negro Improvement Association (UNIA), was based in New York.

Marcus Garvey was a fiery man. He was born in Jamaica and emigrated to New York in 1916. A compelling speaker, whose oratory stopped crowds on Harlem street corners of the 1920s, Garvey attracted thousands of blacks in post-war American cities including Miami. According to Nimmo, the goals of the organization were to instill in blacks their true identity, to stimulate self-interest, and to develop self-pride.

Garvey was passionate about blackness. His vision was to establish economic ties between blacks in America and Africa, to which end the organization purchased three steamships. Shares in the White Star Line were available for one dollar each. Garvey also intended that the ships would transport black Americans who wanted to live in Africa.

Garvey had a keen sense of order and a deep appreciation of how very much black people enjoy a good parade. The organization was known for staging elaborate parades with bands, floats, and spotlessly uniformed legions of Garvey's ceremonial soldiers, some with Napoleonic hats and swords, strutting in plumes and gold sashes.

Nimmo soon became one of the most revolutionary leaders in the Miami branch of the Garvey organization. At first, the movement rented a place on Wood Street (now Eleventh Terrace) and Second Avenue. As the local movement grew, the group bought a lot and put up their own building. Some black businessmen and high church officials belonged, but most members were working-class people. Nimmo believed that prominent blacks avoided the organization for fear of being run out of town. Members of Miami's Garvey movement believed in armed resistance to white racism and were involved in a number of plots aimed at retaliation for wrongs done to blacks. Nimmo confirmed that such plans were discussed and implemented but declined to give details. He died in 1992.

Ann Marie Adker, an Overtown activist for many years, was born in Colored Town in November 1925. She was raised by her grandmother, Mariah Young, who came to Miami from the Bahamas at the turn of the century. Adker's father, Charles Young, was a member of the Garvey movement. She recalled:

My father was a member of the Marcus Garvey movement as I was growing up. It gave me a different outlook on things. The Marcus Garvey people had a great big hall just around the corner from where we lived. It was called the UNIA Hall and was located at Fourth Court and Nineteenth Street. On Sundays after church my father would take us there. Every Sunday that's where we would be. In there you had all kinds of people, from schoolteachers to just everyday people. They were all right in there learning about our history. They would tell folk tales. Now these were mostly people from the Bahamas. They told us stories that were told to them at their parents' knee. It was the most amazing thing. I remember Marcus Garvey came to Miami maybe two or three times. I was a little girl, but I remember him. He was the blackest man I had ever seen. He wasn't too tall, but he was heavy. I had heard so much about him, I had put him on a pedestal. In fact, they did have a statue of him in the entrance of the hall. This had to be like in the 1930s. The people of means—the white folks, you know—came down on the movement and they couldn't meet in that hall any more. That's when the Garvey people started this church. It was Saint Peter's African Orthodox [which exists in Overtown today as St. Peter's Orthodox Catholic Church, at 1811 Northwest Fourth Court]. They wanted to form this church so that they could have their own place that the whites could not touch. When I was twelve years old my grandmother gave me the privilege of going to any church I chose. I had been christened in Mt. Olivette Baptist Church. Since I was a Garvey follower, I leaned towards joining St. Peters, and I did.[18]

Marcus Garvey posed a serious problem for American whites, especially those living in the southern states. Rather than welcoming the idea of blacks leaving the country en masse, southern whites were particularly disturbed by the proposition because blacks were needed as laborers, domestic workers, and nursemaids to maintain the South's economic base as well as the essential comforts of many white homes.

Having attracted the hostile attentions of the American people and the ill will of the U.S. government, Garvey became persona non grata in the United States. A marked man, he was convicted of mail fraud and thrown out of the country in 1927. He died in 1940, impoverished and isolated in a poor area of London. After Garvey's death the Garvey group in Miami, as elsewhere, ceased to be a cogent force in black communities.

Black Recollections of the Great Hurricane (1926)

Before being deposed by Hurricane Andrew in August 1992, the tremendous storm that struck Miami on September 17, 1926, was known as the Great Hurricane. This powerful storm demolished much of the city but was particularly destructive in black Miami, where homes and buildings were not as well constructed as those in the white sections.

The day before the hurricane struck was a beautiful day. The sun was bright, and there was a light breeze. The *Miami Herald* carried a brief front-page story under the heading, "Hurricane Reported." The paper said that the storm was not expected to hit Florida. People in Miami went about their business unconcerned about the sketchy reports. Most had never been in a major hurricane, but on this breezy late-summer day, a cruel teacher beat at the sea, rushing towards Miami.

Unlike today, there were no sophisticated warning systems. The U.S. Weather Bureau in Miami knew that the storm was out there somewhere brewing in the southeastern Caribbean but lacked the sophisticated technology to predict accurately where the storm was headed.

On the afternoon of September 16 the lead story on the front page of the *Miami Daily News* read: "Miami Warned of Tropical Storm." The paper also reported that weather bureau chief Richard W. Gray had hoisted storm warnings about noon and warned of destructive winds in the late evening and early morning hours of the next day. Even this story caused little alarm. However, late in the day, as skies darkened and the wind picked up, people realized that a serious storm was upon them.[19]

By this time Gray was holed up in his office in the Ameri-First Building on Northeast First Street and First Avenue, watching the barometric pressure fall. It dropped so rapidly that the barograph pen had to be reset several times when it ran off the page. At 11:30 P.M. he gamely raised the red and black hurricane flags atop the building. Flailing in the furious night, the flags went virtually unnoticed. The forward gales of the hurricane were already swirling through the empty streets of the town.

By 1:50 A.M. the winds had accelerated to 57 miles an hour. Two hours later they registered 115 miles an hour.

Rebecca Gibson Johnson, born in the Black Grove in 1903, was a young woman living in Coconut Grove when the storm arrived. She recalled:

I heard the screen door slamming late at night. I thought that was strange, that no one had hooked it shut, so I got up to shut it. That's when I looked outside and saw the strangest thing. Everything was yellow. It was the middle of the night and everything had a yellow glow. I called my husband and he looked out. He said he hadn't seen anything like that in his life either. By that time, the wind was already taking our roof off. We saw the roof was starting to lift, so my husband got on the roof to try and nail it down. But he couldn't. The storm just kept getting worse. I had a baby staying with me at the time. It wasn't my baby, I was just taking care of it since its mother died. The storm was lifting everything, so we decided we needed to get out of there. We went to our neighbors, the Goodmans, who lived down the block since they had the only block house in the area. We thought this was the only thing that might save us. When we got there, Mr. Simms, a teacher at Carver who lived in the Goodman's guest house, told us there was no way the house was going to hold up in the storm. So we all went to the school. That was the hardest walk I have ever made in my life.[20]

Lourena Smith, daughter of Coconut Grove pioneer Asa Smith, re-membered the hurricane, too. The storm had come just one year after the family moved into the Grove from Ricetown. For the Smiths, the horror began about 4:00 A.M.. "My father told us that a storm was coming and everything was about to be blown away. When the bad part hit an hour or two later, we had to hide in the bathtub with a door over our heads as shelter." Smith also recalled the calm of the eye of the storm. "When the eye passed over us there was a great calm. It was right over us." At about 6:00, with the eye still hovering over them, the family evacuated their home to take shelter next door.[21]

As daylight broke, all was calm again, giving people the impression that the storm had passed. Thousands of shaken Miamians emerged from their homes to find the city still standing. Almost no one had been hurt. Hundreds of sightseers crowded onto the newly constructed Venetian Causeway leading to Miami Beach, virtually basking under a blue sky and bright sun. Ignorant of the danger ahead, people liter-ally danced in the eye of the storm as it passed directly over down-town Miami.

Half an hour later, the northern eye wall of the storm slammed ashore. As the other side of the storm struck with awesome force, its winds attacked the city at 138 miles an hour. The water level at the mouth of the Miami River rose nearly twelve feet, virtually in minutes. Hun-dreds of people were trapped, and many drowned on the unfinished causeway as the sea rushed in ahead of the storm's force.

Louise Stirrup Davis, one of E. W. F. Stirrup's younger daughters, recalled that her older sister Kate left the sanctuary of the well-built Stirrup house during the time that the sky suddenly cleared. "She got caught just a few doors down the street. It took her over an hour to get home. . . . When morning came, we all thought it was over. This was when the eye of the storm was passing right over us. People went out into the streets and collected all kinds of things. Some came back to the school where we had taken shelter with hundreds of shoes. I thought that was so crazy, collecting shoes at a time like that."[22]

Black Grove pioneer Calvin Johnson recalled the fierce storm, too: "That was a bad one. During that time we were living in a shotgun house [small wood-frame house built in the Bahamian style] down on Charles Avenue. The wind was blowing so hard that it picked up the house we were in and moved it to another location. This all happened while we were still inside the house."[23]

In the end, much of Miami lay in ruins. Biscayne Boulevard looked like a yacht basin, so many boats had been swept ashore. Downtown, the streets were full of mud and fish. The stench was horrible. Many houses and cars had been swept into the bay. Hungry and homeless people wandered the streets. So many were destitute that department stores were converted into shelters. Typhus broke out. Scores of people died, most from drowning, as the hurricane washed completely across Miami Beach and inundated Miami, Hollywood, Fort Lauderdale, and even Moore Haven on Lake Okeechobee, where the greatest damage was caused by a tidal wave.

In Miami, the smell of death was everywhere. Unfounded rumors appeared in northern newspapers that race war had broken out in the city. Total casualties in the disaster were 392 dead, 6,281 injured, and 17,784 families affected by losses. Miami was in near total darkness during the nights immediately after the storm. Electrical power had been knocked out except for the McAllister Hotel and the offices of the *Miami Herald,* to which the Florida Power and Light Company managed to lay one wire.

The majority of the damage to Miami homes and businesses was to rooftops and windows. It was estimated that ten thousand homes were unroofed or otherwise damaged. Glass was scattered everywhere, and most home furnishings and decorations were damaged by the water. The damage just to homes, not businesses, was estimated at $5 million, a huge amount at that time.

Most of the relief stations were located in Colored Town, reflecting the damage to that area. Colored Town, with its flimsy shacks and shotgun houses, unpaved streets and nonexistent sewer system, was the most devastated area of the city. The Miami Chamber of Commerce visited the area and found the worst destruction in a block bounded by Northwest Seventh and Eighth avenues and by Northwest Twenty-second and Twenty-third streets. Of the thirty-nine houses in that block, ten were destroyed and ten others were unroofed. Several of Miami's struggling black churches were completely demolished.

Hundreds of blacks did their part to help rebuild the community. The Florida East Coast Railroad brought in 300 blacks from Jacksonville and 250 from south Georgia, primarily to clear debris. A branch of the Citizens' Relief Committee opened in black Miami on Northwest Tenth Street and Second Avenue to supply the demand for hundreds of black laborers to clear the streets of refuse, to bury the dead, and to provide common labor for rebuilding the city.

Blacks were pressed into cleanup work whether they wanted to be involved or not. According to one newspaper report, "There were some Negroes that were not working. Raids were made by the Sheriff's office on occupants of pool rooms. Those that were arrested were given the choice to either work or stay in jail."[24]

The process of rebuilding proved to be expensive. The city of Miami sent out an international appeal for help. President Coolidge designated the American Red Cross to raise relief funds for the people of Miami. Nearly $3,000,000 was raised in addition to $161,697 raised from local donations. The Cuban people were particularly generous. Immediately after the storm, the Cuban government sent a battleship loaded to the gunwales with 250 tons of provisions and supplies, along with fifty thousand complete doses of typhoid vaccine.[25]

In terms of its historical importance, the 1926 hurricane was a property storm. Although hundreds of people were killed, this was not its legacy. Rather, it was that the storm flattened the city just as it was starting to stand on its own. The incredible Miami land boom was at its zenith. Land speculators, investors, and residents reconsidered Miami as a safe place for investing their future or their money. In the aftermath of the Great Hurricane, Miami's economic boom of the 1920s ended.

Blacks and the Police in Miami (1896–1928)

Relations between Miami's blacks and the police have never been good. Miami's early police officers were mostly from small towns in the South, and their attitude towards blacks was suspicious and hostile. Black old-timers tell of the days when police officers would ride through Colored Town looking for black men who were not working. Such men routinely would be locked up under vagrancy laws which were applied more readily to idle blacks than whites, because southern whites were suspicious of blacks who did not appear to have jobs.

The city of Miami did not hire black patrol officers until 1944, and at first they could not arrest white people. Most of early Miami's police officers were poorly trained and few had significant experience as law enforcement officers. They were hired under a good-old-boy system. A great many of them came from Georgia and other southern states that had been hurt by the Great Freeze. Miami's police officers treated Miami blacks as blacks were generally treated in the South at that time: Black people had no rights that white people were obliged to respect.

The Colored Board of Trade was the most vocal and visible black advocacy group in Miami in the early years of the city's history. The board accused the Miami police establishment of outright terrorism in Colored Town. From the beginning, the Miami city jail had an inordinately high proportion of black inmates, leading some blacks to believe they were being unduly scrutinized by the police. According to Miami historian Paul George, of the thirty-five inmates in the county jail in September 1904, thirty-four were black.[26]

In the 1920s the *Miami Metropolis* railed against the Miami police and the local judicial system, asserting that it was almost impossible to convict a white man of the murder of a black person in Dade County.

68. Miami police station. This building was constructed in 1909 as Miami City Hall, with the police station in the small building at right. After becoming the police station in 1928, it was the scene of many acts of brutality by Miami police officers against blacks and others. The building was demolished in 1958 and was replaced on this site at 51 Southwest First Avenue by the Miami federal building. Courtesy Historical Museum of Southern Florida.

The newspaper condemned Miami justice as an outrage and the product of infamous discrimination.

Black Miami had to contend with a succession of Dade County sheriffs, all of whom kept a wary eye on Colored Town. R. J. Chillingworth vigorously tried to prevent blacks from voting in municipal elections. His successor, Dan Hardie, campaigned on a platform that advocated arresting suspicious characters first and letting them explain afterwards. Hardie referred to his pack of bloodhounds as "nigger" hounds.[27]

By the 1920s outright torture was secretly practiced by the Miami police, primarily against black prisoners. A 1926 Dade County grand jury witness testified that a black man accused of stealing an automobile had been beaten on the soles of his bare feet with a heavy copper-bound ruler for about ninety minutes by a police officer at the city jail.[28]

According to a 1928 Dade grand jury report, Miami police were using a crude electric chair to get confessions. The helpless victim was placed in the chair and suddenly the current was turned on. If the victim tried to leave the chair, he was immediately knocked back by blows from the attending police officers.[29] Witnesses stated that it was commonly known around the station that the chair was sometimes used on black women, who were often indecently exposed during the process.

A number of witnesses testified that live electric wires were applied to the exposed bodies of persons held on a table by officers. Sometimes the shocks were administered to the prisoner's genital area.

According to the grand jury report on the operation of the Miami Police Department in the 1920s under Chief H. Leslie Quigg (one of the longest-serving police chiefs in the city's history), the department was dominated from within by "a well-constructed organization of unknown strength, slowly but surely destroying the freedom of our citizens, meaningless and cruel practicing habits destitute of moral or civic motive and serving only to gratify a malignant passion."[30] The grand jury pronounced Quigg wholly unfit for the office of chief of police.

Then in 1928 the city was shocked by the Kier case. This was a sensational murder case involving the killing of a young black man by several white Miami police officers who were holding the man in custody. After the killing, the officers attempted to cover up what had happened. The actual killing took place in July 1925, but the truth did not begin to emerge until three years later. The silence was broken when one of the policemen involved in the killing testified to the grand jury that police had murdered the man.

This story began on the evening of July 16, 1925, when police sergeant M. A. Tibbits of the Miami Police Department was reportedly shot by an unknown assailant near a baseball park in Colored Town. Tibbits and three other officers, William Beechey, John O. Caudell, and Thomas R. Nazworth, were said to have been responding to an anonymous call about a disturbance at the park. Tibbits claimed he had been shot in the abdomen while searching the park.

In the same edition of the newspaper with the Tibbits story, the *Miami Herald* reported that a black man, identified only as H. Kier, had been shot and killed. Kier's body was found near Northwest Seventh Avenue in Colored Town. His head was riddled with bullets.[31]

The search for Kier's killer and Tibbits's assailant faded to back-page news with few leads available in either case. In 1928 William H. Beechey, one of the officers involved in the incident, testified that he and detectives Nazworth and Caudell were in the car that had allegedly responded to the disturbance complaint on July 15, 1925. Beechey said there was no disturbance and that Kier, the black man who was found shot to death that same night, had been in the car with them.

Kier was a bellman at the El Comodoro Hotel in downtown Miami and was arrested after a hotel guest complained that Kier had told her daughter that a male guest, presumably a white man, wanted to meet her. The mother was offended by Kier's action and had him arrested.

A police officer named E. W. Pierce apprehended Kier in the hotel lobby. It would later be reported that the hotel manager told the arresting officer, "Don't kill him here." Kier was taken to police headquarters. At this point, Miami Police Chief H. Leslie Quigg reportedly ordered Pierce and another officer to take Kier to a lonely spot and beat him, but Pierce begged off the assignment.

Beechey also testified that he and the three other officers (Tibbits, Caudell, and Nazworth) took Kier for that drive. He said he expected to take Kier to the northwest quarter of Miami, slap him around, and send him north, a common police practice at the time. But what Beechey claimed to have witnessed went beyond the usual treatment afforded to troublesome blacks.

Beechey testified that on a deserted road detective Nazworth got out of the car, hauled Kier from the car, threw him to the ground, and drew his revolver. Kier struggled to his feet. Nazworth's first shot went wild, apparently striking Tibbits. Nazworth continued to fire at Kier. When Kier was dead, the four men left him on the highway and rushed Tibbits to Jackson Memorial Hospital, where he was treated for his gunshot wound.

Chief Quigg arrived at the hospital shortly thereafter to see Tibbits. Beechey claimed that he told the chief what had happened. Nazworth, who had done the shooting, gave the chief a different account. He

Left: 69. Miami Police Chief H. Leslie Quigg who recruited untrained white men from Georgia and sent them into Colored Town to enforce the law. A 1928 Dade County grand jury described Quigg as wholly unfit to be chief of police because of widespread brutality in the department under his leadership. Courtesy Romer Collection: Miami-Dade County Library.

Right: 70. Miami police officer Melville Tibbits, 1925. At about this time, Tibbits and Police Chief Quigg were charged with the murder of H. Kier, a young black man accused of insulting a white woman. Both were acquitted in 1928 by an all-white jury. Courtesy Romer Collection: Miami-Dade County Public Library.

claimed there had been a struggle, that Kier took the gun and shot Tibbits, that Nazworth was able to wrestle the gun away from Kier, and that Nazworth then shot Kier. According to Beechey, Quigg advised the men to agree on a story and stick to it.

With these revelations, the city of Miami was under great pressure from some whites and many blacks to investigate the incident. But Miami Mayor E. G. Sewell, brother of John Sewell, announced that the city had no intention of investigating the officers' alleged misconduct. The grand jury saw it differently. In March 1928 Miami police officers Tibbits, Caudell, and Nazworth and chief of police H. Leslie Quigg were charged in the Kier killing. For the chief of police, the charge was first-degree murder.[32]

The Quigg trial was an absurd parody of justice. One prospective juror, a white man named Peeples, admitted to having known Quigg for about twenty years and admitted believing that the white race is superior. He was accepted on the jury. During the trial, applause swept the courtroom when one of Quigg's attorneys said that if Kier had insulted a member of his family, he would have treated him more roughly than officer Pierce did.

On April 29, 1928, after less than three hours of deliberation, the jury returned not-guilty verdicts for all of the police officers. Although temporarily out of office, Quigg later returned as Miami's police chief.

Quigg's replacement was Guy Reeve, formerly the chief of detectives for the department, who proved less tolerant of abusive behavior by his officers. The department dismissed an officer who beat a black man during a raid staged in November 1928. The following January, a coroner's jury for the first time found a policeman guilty of unjustifiable homicide in the killing of a black citizen. His punishment was dismissal from the department.

In the winter of 1928 a particularly gruesome police killing took place in Miami. The victim this time was a fourteen-year-old black boy named Spelman Kemp. He and two other boys were caught by a white Miami police officer pilfering eggs from a railroad car. When hailed by the officer, the boys dropped their booty and ran. The officer fired a shot which hit the child in the back.

The boy was taken to a hospital, where he died. A Dade grand jury later reported, "The little boy, conscious of his approaching death, stated that the officer who had shot him kicked him while he was lying wounded on the ground. Another witness testified that he heard the officer say to the boy, 'What did you run for? Did you think I wouldn't get you? . . . I have a d——- good mind to finish you now.'" This particular officer had killed four people since he joined the Miami Police Department. No action was taken against him in the Kemp shooting.

The 1928 grand jury's report berating the Miami police department is so revealing that portions of it are presented here:

> We have been greatly disturbed because of the necessity of reporting to the court and revealing to the public such discoveries and disclosures involving our police department as will shock the public conscience, tend to make mockery of law and order and breed contempt for law enforcement officers generally, and no opportunity has been overlooked by this grand jury to obviate the necessity of such a report. It is a terrible truth to reveal that the crimes for which indictments have been returned against police officers are equaled by a number of other such crimes that have been disclosed to this grand jury, but for the commission of which no indictments have been returned because of our inability to fix individual responsibility. We find that on one occasion a prisoner was reported by police to have committed suicide in his cell by hanging. Yet the undertaker and the physician who examined the body as well as other witnesses, scorned the idea of suicide, testifying that there was no broken neck, and no indications whatever or even slight evidence of death by strangulation. Evidence has been given that this prisoner was unmercifully beaten and tortured the night preceding the report of his alleged suicide, but we cannot definitely and conscientiously fix the responsibility of his death on any individual at this time. We find that on another occasion a prisoner's pleadings for mercy and groans of agony attracted the attention of outsiders who, from a vantage point in the darkness, were able to see only a part of the torture and cruelties administered by unidentified police officers, and which were continued until the prisoner's pleadings and groans ceased—then the room was darkened and apparently vacated. A careful investigation has not yet disclosed the further disposition of this prisoner.
>
> We will not attempt to relate here the innumerable indignities, insults and brutalities to which many citizens are said to have been

subjected by police officers inside and outside the city prison, many of whom charged with offenses of minor natures and many charged with no offense at all. Much of this testimony, and especially the testimony of those claiming to have been personally subjected to such treatments, we have discounted and have made allowance for their prejudices, giving the accused the benefit of every possible doubt, but many such stories of torture, indignities and inhumanity have been corroborated by physicians who were called upon to administer treatment for the injuries complained of. Within the present week an aged citizen, a white man, died and in the opinion of the attending physician injuries received by him in Miami police station some time ago contributed largely to his death at this time. The identity of the offenders may never be known, death having removed the evidence.

When the testimony began to unfold this state of affairs we were hopeful of later finding that such practices were unusual and rare, and were neither sponsored nor condoned by those in charge, but to our amazement it developed beyond all doubt that the persons in charge of this department of our city government not only condoned and ratified such violence on the part of their subordinates but in a number of instances have themselves led the assault and become the chief executioner.[33]

The impact of the grand jury report on the operation of the Miami Police Department was negligible. Antiblack violence by Miami police continued openly until at least the creation of Metro-Dade County in the late 1950s.

In the decade leading up to World War II, Klan activity declined in Dade County. However, by the 1940s the Klan was back, continuing its public intimidation of blacks well into the 1950s. Often police officers were among its members. Miami's John B. Gordon Klavern No. 5, named after a Confederate general from Georgia, welcomed travelers to the city in the forties with a huge billboard at the city limits. In 1951, the Klan was believed to have been involved in the bombing of Carver Village, a Miami apartment complex for whites which had begun renting to blacks.

There were other white racist groups operating in Dade County in the thirties and forties, one of which exceeded even the Klan in its racial and religious hatreds. According to historian Stetson Kennedy, Miami was headquarters for the White Front, a storm-trooper-type outfit active in Miami from 1939 to 1941. Members of the organization went about town in Nazi-like brown shirts and threatened Jews with blackjacks and brass knuckles. Its relatively small membership consisted of local Klan dissidents, some German Americans, and a few White Russians.[34]

But the mainstay of antiblack activity in Dade County in the 1940s and 1950s was the reactivated Klan. In the summer of 1946 the Klan emerged as the culprit in an attempt to intimidate a black union official. Roosevelt Winfield, a shop steward at the Miami International Airport, was accosted by three men in hoods and gowns. He said he was told to stop his union activity or he would be drinking water from the bay. Union officials warned that this, the third instance of intimidation against Winfield, was the work of the Ku Klux Klan.

As a result of increased Klan activity, the Dade County Civil Rights Council was organized, and the Klan's reemergence prompted the Greater Miami Ministerial Association, an influential white group, to issue a statement denying any connection to the Klan. While the Klan was desperately trying to recruit new members in Miami, many white pastors reminded their congregations that the Ku Klux Klan was not part of organized religious faith.

Even some white Florida politicians openly opposed the Klan in the mid–1940s. After hearing reports that the Klan was trying to reorganize, both candidates in the 1946 U.S. Senate race in Florida, George Smathers and Congressman Pat Cannon, condemned the Klan. "America has outgrown mob rule," said Cannon. "However provoked or righteous a minority group may believe itself to be, I can see no justification for any attempt to settle social matters by men without authority taking the law into their own hands." Smathers said, "If the Ku Klux Klan is sowing hate, deceit, division or intolerance, then the Klan is against democracy and I am against the Klan."[35]

PART 2

THE BARRIERS FALL

Colored Town entered its heyday in the early 1930s, and the golden age lasted for nearly four decades. Many of the great entertainers of the period, white and black, played to packed houses along Colored Town's Little Broadway, as Northwest Second Avenue was called in those days. Business boomed for black business owners and professionals as the black middle class carved a niche for itself in postwar Dade County. Many black communities developed in other parts of the county during this time. Influenced by the presence of so many northerners and military operations in south Florida, these years also marked the beginning of the civil rights period in Miami.

The Heyday of Colored Town (1930–1960)

Colored Town comes alive as a mango-colored sunset fades to black. The smell of hot fish and conch defines this place. So does music. One door up from the Lyric Theater on Second Avenue, Hartley Tootes's house band at the Rockland Palace is warming up. Led by a mournful saxophone, the band nurses a slow, undulating blues song, filling the Miami night with its soul. A line has already formed for the first show at the Harlem Square Club two blocks up; Count Basie is playing there tonight. The Cotton Club, on the Avenue near Seventh Street, is featuring Billie Holiday.

The bustling streets are lined with stylish, shiny cars, many of them convertibles, encased in chrome. Willowy men in zoot suits and wide hats glide down Second Avenue brandishing long gold chains from their pockets. Perfumed women in silks and sashes swish from one shop to another. Old black men still in their work clothes gamble, curse, and laugh in a back alley.

There is an hour's wait for a table at the popular restaurants along the Avenue, but you can buy still-warm sweet potato pies and "sho'nuf" Georgia-style barbecued ribs from the sidewalk table set up by the members of the Mount Zion Church choir on an empty lot next to the church. They have hot fish sandwiches and pickled pigs' feet, too. For a nickel, you can buy a freezing-cold bottle of Cola-Nip peach soda, sold from washtubs filled with chipped ice.

The Ritz Theater has a full house tonight. *Key Largo,* the runaway
Bogart film, is heading the bill. Also showing are highlights of Joe Louis's
latest heavyweight title fight. Colored Town has two other movie theaters. At the Lyric, now showing an all-black musical, scores of people
stand in line for the next show. At the Modern, in the twelve hundred
block of Third Avenue, a new western is playing to a full house.

This was Colored Town on a sizzling Saturday night in its heyday.
Many such Saturday nights came and went during Colored Town's
zenith. Dirt and disease still plagued the community. The crowded
little shotgun houses were there, and the suffering inside them was no
less than in earlier or later periods. But Colored Town's time had come,
and it would not last forever. On nights like this, not even the choir
ladies from Mount Zion thought about tomorrow. Trumpets, drums,
strings, and basses owned the night.

Despite the overcrowded conditions and other problems in Colored
Town in the thirties, forties, and fifties, the vibrant culture of black
Miami flowed along northwest Second Avenue. Blacks were not allowed in white hotels, nightclubs, or restaurants except as employees.
However, many whites crossed the railroad tracks regularly to frequent the pulsating night spots of Colored Town. During this period
there were many prosperous black-owned businesses thriving as a result of the complete and pervasive social and economic isolation of
blacks at that time. As Colored Town hit its peak, this forced concentration of purchasing power made at least a few Miami blacks very
wealthy.

Second Avenue was originally known as Avenue G during the Flagler
era, and most of the city's black business establishments were located
there. Because of the high quality of entertainment to be found in Colored Town during its heyday, Second Avenue between Sixth and Tenth
Streets gained a national and international reputation as Miami's Little
Broadway. It was also known as "the Strip" and "the Great Black
Way."

For over three decades the Avenue became *the* place to be seen in
black Miami. Among the famous entertainers frequently performing
in Colored Town were Ella Fitzgerald (who introduced her nationally
popular tune "A Tisket a Tasket" in Miami), Cab Calloway, Benny
Goodman, Louis "Satchmo" Armstrong, Bessie Smith, Billie Holiday,
Nat King Cole, Count Basie, Josephine Baker, B. B. King, Sammy Davis

Jr., the Inkspots, James Brown, Sam and Dave, Dionne Warwick, Aretha Franklin, and many, many others.

William (Bill) Sawyer Jr., son of one of the city's pioneer doctors, and his wife, Bernice, ran the Mary Elizabeth Hotel. This historic hotel and its famous Flamingo Lounge were the epicenters of Colored Town in its glory days. As Little Broadway rose to its zenith, the hotel saw many of the great talents in entertainment and sports pass through its doors. "Basically, the Mary Elizabeth Hotel never closed!" said Bill Sawyer. "Blacks weren't allowed to stay on Miami Beach back then. All the big white entertainers would come over and jam all day and all night long at the Mary Elizabeth, and this entertainment was free! People like Tommy Dorsey and Jimmy Dorsey and that fella who beat them drums so well—Gene Krupa! They'd stay all night for free. They just wanted a chance to get up on stage and play."[1]

71. Cab Calloway, a very popular singer during the heyday of Colored Town, performs in the Clover Club. Calloway was a nationally known star and often was booked to perform in white and black clubs in Miami. Courtesy Historical Museum of Southern Florida.

"You had more whites than colored most times," said Bernice Sawyer. "Many musicians stayed at our hotel. As a matter of fact, Cab Calloway started me drinking Moscow mules, a drink that had gin in it, and I don't know what else!" The Sawyers, unlike other nightclub operators in Colored Town, had a license to remain open until five in the morning. They usually stretched it to keep the club open around the clock.

The Rockland Palace was the only other black-owned hotel. According to Bill Sawyer, "The Palace was popular in the late 1920s and 1930s. In the twenties, the club was named the Della Robia. It was a nightclub where they always held dances and all. It was located between Eighth and Ninth streets on Second Avenue. The Rockland Palace had Hartley Tootes's big band as the house act. They were based

72. The famous Zebra Lounge in the Mary Elizabeth Hotel. During the heyday of Colored Town, this was the epicenter of the area's entertainment. Courtesy William B. Sawyer Jr.

73. The incomparable jazz singer Billie Holiday (standing far left) at Georgette's Tea Room, a favorite gathering place for the black social elite of Miami. Courtesy Historical Museum of Southern Florida.

74. Four young women just inducted into Alpha Kappa Alpha Sorority, late 1930s. By the 1940s and 1950s, black fraternities and sororities were replacing the elitist black social clubs of the earlier era. Courtesy Isabelle Sharpe Blue.

75. Members of the Idle Hour Art and Social Club, a group of domestic workers who had Thursdays off, 1930s. Courtesy Black Archives, History and Research Foundation of South Florida.

at the Rockland Palace, but they traveled around the country playing gigs."

Another popular hotel was the Sir John Hotel, first named the Lord Calvert in the 1940s and 1950s. The Lord Calvert Whiskey Company bought the property and built the hotel, but the company was in financial trouble. The Sir John Whiskey Company took it over in the mid-fifties and made it even more popular than the Lord Calvert had been. Prior to the Sir John, the only established black hotels in Miami were the Mary Elizabeth Hotel and the Rockland Palace.

Garth Reeves, retired publisher of the *Miami Times* newspaper, covered many of the events in Colored Town during its heyday. He thus recalled the entertainment of that era at the popular Harlem Square Club and the Rockland Palace:

During the winter, the Beach would be loaded with entertainers and stars. In the fifties they'd bring in the best like Bill Robinson, Bojangles, Harry Belafonte, Nat King Cole, and Count Basie's and Duke Ellington's orchestras. I came back from college in the 1940s, and I loved the big bands.

We had one or two bands every single weekend because there were two large clubs that competed with each other for the best acts: the Rockland Palace and the Harlem Square Club. Oh, they had the top entertainers, and it cost a dollar and a quarter in advance, or a dollar and a half at the door. That's all it cost to see those entertainers! Boy! For pennies, you could see the greatest bands of all time.

The Rockland Palace always had a good house band. Some good musicians came out of there. I remember the first house band the Rockland Palace had was Hartley Tootes. He had a great band. After him came Snookum Russell. There was also Chick Webb and Ella Fitzgerald. The Pool, another club, had acts like Louis Jordan.

It was incredible, all right. Everyone had a great time. Everyone looked forward to the weekend because we knew there would be some grand entertainment. Sam Cooke was a great favorite down here—Oh boy! They turned out for Sam Cooke! The bands would play mostly on Sunday nights. The nightclubs were set up to hold fifteen hundred people, but there were usually many more folks than that. I sure don't know how we did it though!

I remember one white band who was playing in Colored Town, Tommy Dorsey. They played a dance at the Harlem Square Club. I remember distinctly because I was standing by the bandstand and—what was the name of that drummer? Buddy Rich. He was having a good time. He'd gotten too much to drink during intermission and Tommy wouldn't let him come back on the stage. Tommy was a strict disciplinarian—professional, you know—and you couldn't be drunk on his bandstand.

The Harlem Square Club was owned by a guy who lived out on the Beach, Al Goldman. He used to invite his friends over. I remember when we had a great band he would put the whites upstairs and the blacks downstairs. We were segregated in our own community, but that's the way it was.

Actually, it was against the law. It was on the local books that we couldn't have mixed audiences like that, but nobody paid much attention to it when there was a big-name entertainer in town. In fact, by about the middle of the set, blacks and whites were sitting all over! They weren't caring about color and racial differences.

They were great days. Everyone seemed to be having a real good time. I don't remember any real disturbances, racial or otherwise.

The music brought everybody together and seemingly united people. It cut across racial differences.[2]

During the heyday of Colored Town, one of its most prestigious restaurants was the Polite Cafe, located in the one thousand block on Second Avenue across the street from Kelsey Pharr's funeral home. "All the big shots ate there," recalled James C. Dunn, who arrived in Miami from central Florida in the 1930s, before he was twenty:

Cab Calloway and the rest of the big entertainers got their hair done at Chinks Barber Shop, which was in the one thousand block on Second Avenue. They had five or six chairs and they were busy all week, but filled up all day on Fridays and Saturdays.

You could buy the finest clothes you could find in New York right here in Miami on Second Avenue. Block after block was filled with stores. You couldn't hardly walk between the buildings all along Second Avenue there were so many stores, and people were making money hand over fist.

A lot of men bought their zoot suits at the Broadway Men's Shop in the nine hundred block on Second Avenue. The man who worked in there wore all these sharp fancy clothes, sort of like a model, and the guys would see him and try to dress like he did. In the thirties men wore these expensive leather pointed shoes with thin soles and everybody wore hats. Keeping your shoes shined was no problem. They had three or four shoe shine stands on every block in those days.

Railroad Front was the name they gave to the three or four blocks facing the railroad tracks between Fifth and Eighth streets in Colored Town. Many of the houses along there were used for prostitution. At Eighth Street and the railroad track was a house they called the White House. All of the women there were black, but they all looked like white women.[3]

Ann Marie Adker, who became a leader in Overtown, was a young woman in the heyday of Colored Town. She recalled clearly the nightlife and furious business activities there when she was in her twenties:

Every nightclub carried its own caliber of people. The clubs like the Mary Elizabeth and the Sir John Hotel were hotels where the big entertainers from out of town slept. Those were the more high-class clubs. Now, the Calypso Club which was out near Twentieth Street and Third Avenue, that was a larger place than some others and it catered to a different type of people. It had local entertainers. Some went on to other places. Princess Carlotta was the main headliner of the Calypso Club. This was a female impersonator. To go in there and see him in his fabulous gowns for the first time was really something.

Every year they had these semiannual balls. People would attend those balls religiously. No expense was too great to look better than someone else. We had what you call dressmakers in those days. Don't mind that we couldn't go to a Burdines. Some of those dresses were originals Burdines couldn't buy. Brown had his Cadillac taxi service. Of course you called Brown's so that when you arrived at the ball you got to get out in front of the Rockland Palace and be escorted in. It was each evening gown prettier than the one before. People would line up on the opposite side of the street to see who was going in.

Several areas within Colored Town developed into small neighborhoods. These included Good Bread Alley, so named because of the warm, rich smell of fresh-baked breads which permeated the air from a nearby bakery, Hatchet Bay Town, Chinatown, Martin's Lane, Railroad Front, and Gambler's Lane.

Officially the area commonly called Colored Town was first referred to as the Central Negro District. In 1937 the name was changed to Washington Heights. But by the late stage of the heyday, black people most often referred to the area as Overtown. According to Ann Marie Adker, who lived in the area all of her life, it may have been because one had to go "over" downtown to get to Colored Town from Coconut Grove. "Years ago when you would see people catching the jitney, like from Coconut Grove up here, they would say, 'I'm going *over* town.'"[4]

In addition to its stunning nightlife, Colored Town in its heyday was the scene of many parades and sporting events. One such event, the Orange Blossom Classic, endures today. According to Miami historian Arva Parks, "Because they were all but excluded from Orange Bowl activities, the black community organized their own Coconut Festival. As the Orange Bowl Queen led the parade down Biscayne Boulevard, the Coconut Queen led the parade down Northwest Second Avenue. An all-black Coconut Festival football game was held at Dorsey Park. In 1949, the Coconut Festival became the Orange Blossom Classic. The parade continued down Second Avenue, but the football game between the Florida A & M University Rattlers and a visiting team was played in the Orange Bowl Stadium. For that one event, blacks were allowed to sit in seats out of the end zone."[5]

Many famous black athletes came often to the hotels and clubs in Colored Town, particularly to the Mary Elizabeth. These included such greats as Joe Louis, Sugar Ray Robinson, Roy Campanella, and many others. "Another person who frequented the Mary Elizabeth was Walter Winchell," said Bill Sawyer. "When Joe Louis was retiring, he made the announcement in my office at the Mary Elizabeth. Walter Winchell covered the story about Louis's retirement. Louis and Roy Campanella

76. Platform at the Miami depot of the Florida East Coast Railroad, circa early 1950s. Notice the group of four black people at center: The women's stylish dress was typical of well-dressed ladies of the period. Many blacks who visited Colored Town during its heyday came by train in segregated passenger coaches. Courtesy Miami Memorabilia Collection of Myrna and Seth Bramson.

77. Redcaps (baggage handlers) at the Miami depot of the Florida East Coast Railroad, circa 1938. Station master William McDonald is in railroad uniform, front center, with two unidentified police officers. Florida's three major railroads, which included the FEC, employed thousands of black men like these during Florida's rail era from the late 1890s to the 1950s. Many of these men lived and spent money in Colored Town during its heyday. Courtesy Miami Memorabilia Collection of Myrna and Seth Bramson.

were always hanging around the hotel all day and all night." Sawyer described his long relationship with the prize-fighter:

> I first met Joe Louis when he began coming to Miami at the start of his popularity. You would think he was Jesus by the way people acted! They would line up, not for one block but for block after block after block, just to see him walk down the street. But he was as nice as anybody would want to be. I remember the little children from the neighborhood would come and ask me to introduce them to the different celebrities staying at the hotel, like Jackie Robinson and Sugar Ray Robinson. They would ask the celebrities to make an appearance out to the school to raise money, but most of the time these fellows would turn the children down. But Joe Louis—he never turned anybody down! He would go all the way to Opa-Locka to make appearances for the kids.

78. Malcolm X, with camera, taking a photograph of Muhammad Ali in an Overtown nightclub, 1964. Courtesy Howard Bingam.

In this poignant description of his relationship with baseball great Jackie Robinson, Sawyer sheds light on the absoluteness of racial separation in early Miami, as even the first black man to play major league baseball was relegated to a hotel in Colored Town when the Brooklyn Dodgers were in Miami:

> Jackie Robinson was a good person. I used to have to lend Jackie Robinson money when he was going over to Latin America before he got in the big leagues. I remember the owner of the Brooklyn Dodgers would come to the hotel to check on Jackie when Jackie Robinson was first accepted. They paid me well, too, to help take care of Jackie, because he wasn't allowed to stay with them downtown.[6]

Baseball was a popular sport in black Miami. The famous Negro Baseball League played games in Miami often. Apparently, so did Fidel Castro. "I used to play baseball on the streets here in Miami with Fidel Castro," said Bill Sawyer. "In the 1930s and 1940s a man named Mr. Valdez, who was Latin and a friend of Castro's, operated the barber shop in the Mary Elizabeth. That's where all the Spanish people would hang out. His shop was like the headquarters for them. Castro was one of those people who used to be there. Valdez was really like a community leader. Castro went to the University of Florida, I think. He was a very good ball player . . . in fact, at one time he was going to try out for the big leagues."

Mary McLeod Bethune, the nationally known black educator and founder of Bethune-Cookman College in Daytona, owned a drug store in the Mary Elizabeth Hotel. "We used to know her well," said Bernice Sawyer. "Her son operated the drug store and we would let her use space in the hotel to raise money for the college, . . . I'll tell you one thing about her; when she used to walk into a room where men were sitting, she would stop and say, 'Gentlemen! Stand up! Don't you see a black lady in your presence?' And they'd all stand up, rather sheepishly. Incidentally, Mary Bethune was very good friends with Eleanor Roosevelt." Bill Sawyer noted that although Carl Fisher (the developer of Miami Beach) helped Mary Bethune raise money out on the Beach, she still had to stay in Colored Town hotels.

79. William B. Sawyer Jr., the son of Miami pioneer doctor William B. Sawyer, at home in Overtown. Sawyer managed his father's Mary Elizabeth Hotel at the epicenter of Colored Town in its heyday. The Sawyer family still owns considerable properties in Overtown. Courtesy *Miami Herald.*.

In spite of Colored Town's many problems, by the 1950s it was home to several monied black families like the Sawyers. Some of them were getting worried. Their status was the result of white-imposed racial segregation which forced blacks to spend their money in black-owned businesses. Now, with social change in the air, the black elite was facing an uncertain future. After the social restrictions on blacks began to ease, some blacks were taking their money elsewhere. Black visitors from other cities, who used to flock to Colored Town, now in increasing numbers went to the Eden Roc Hotel or the Fountainbleau Hotel on Miami Beach.

The end was in sight for Colored Town. "Integration really did a job on us," said Bernice Sawyer. "Although it was for the best, black people were then able to stay in the bigger hotels on the Beach, like the Fountainbleau. The Mary Elizabeth lost its magic. It went to nothing."

The death knell was struck with the decision in the early 1960s to run Interstate 95 right through the community. This decision alone displaced thousands of people from Colored Town, which was now more frequently called Overtown. According to Miami observer Ray Mohl:

The building of Interstate 95 in the Miami metropolitan area provides a devastating example of the human and social consequences of urban expressway construction. A 1955 plan for the Miami expressway, prepared by the Miami City Planning Department, routed a North-South Expressway along the Florida East Coast Railway corridor into downtown Miami—a route that had little impact on housing in nearby Overtown. However, a new plan prepared in 1956 for the Florida State Road Department shifted the route to the west and directly through Overtown. Despite community objections, the new route was accepted by the road department and supported by various downtown Miami officials and groups like the Chamber of Commerce. Specifically, the Florida East Coast Railway right-of-way was rejected, as the plan stated, in order to provide "ample room for the future expansion of the central business district in a westerly direction."

Consequently, the new expressway ripped through the center of Overtown, wiping out massive amounts of housing as well as Overtown's main business district—the business and cultural heart of black Miami. Some 40,000 blacks made Overtown home before the interstate came, but less than 10,000 now remain in an urban wasteland dominated by the expressway. One massive expressway interchange alone (I–95 and I–395) took up about twenty square blocks of densely settled land and destroyed the housing of about 10,000 people.[7]

The decision to run the interstate through the black community was deliberate, intended to displace a large segment of the black population so that the valuable land on which Colored Town sat could be used to expand the downtown business district. The use of urban renewal monies to displace inner-city minority populations was the national trend at the time, and the division of Colored Town was avoidable. As noted earlier, a second corridor along the Florida East Coast Railroad right-of-way was available and was considered but rejected. That choice would not have decimated black Miami, but downtown business interests vehemently opposed the FEC Railroad corridor. The so-called Seventh Avenue corridor was selected, and the geographical transformation of Colored Town began.[8] Today, parking lots for the Miami Arena stretch along Second Avenue where the Rockland Palace and the Cotton Club once stood. A litter-filled empty lot at the

80. Interstate Highway 95 through Overtown. The construction of this highway represented a deliberate decision to destroy a significant portion of the community and to displace thousands of blacks. Primarily as a result of the expressway, Overtown declined in population from about forty thousand to fewer than fifteen thousand people within a few years. Courtesy Sergio Campos.

corner of Second Avenue and Tenth Street marks the spot where the Harlem Square Club reigned over Little Broadway.

In Ann Marie Adker's view, "Urban renewal came in and took the land my grandmother left me—you might as well say they took it. They gave me what they wanted me to have, which meant that I couldn't afford to buy back anything. We lived at 1925 Northwest Fifth Avenue. In 1947 they started something black people had never heard about: home inspections. They would come in and tell you that all of the electrical plugs had to be in the walls. Then they wanted to put in sidewalks. For that they wanted six or seven feet of your property. Some of the people had to cut off their front porch to give them those six or seven feet. When you opened your front door, you were in the street."[9] Adker said that many Overtown residents began moving out as urban renewal took hold. In the end, thousands of blacks were pushed out of the city's most historic neighborhood in order to make way for urban renewal.

A sprawling public housing project at Third Avenue and Twentieth Street has replaced the Cafe Society. A twisted network of soaring highways covers the spot on Fourteenth Street between Third and Fourth Avenues where the Ritz Theater once stood. Today on the Great Black Way, only the indomitable Lyric Theater remains as a lonely reminder of the golden age of Colored Town.

The Second World War and Postwar Years (1940–1954)

Dade County was a great staging and training area during the Second World War. With hundreds of thousands of military and civilian support personnel stationed in Dade County, American military bases and offices proliferated. When the war started, Miami's blacks were solidly behind the war effort. In May 1943 a huge parade and rally in Colored Town kicked off a major war-bonds drive. In early 1945 American Legion officials revealed that almost half of the 56,781 Florida blacks in the armed forces were from Dade County. Still, blacks complained that white recruits were being inducted faster than blacks.

As anxious as they were to join the war effort, blacks were inducted into segregated units and were essentially assigned to menial jobs. The United States Navy openly recruited blacks into positions of servitude such as mess cooks and stewards, and many were glad to be accepted. A Miami recruiting ad aimed at blacks read: "Training received is

Above: 81. Eleanor Roosevelt
visiting the Servicemen's Club in
Colored Town during World War II.
Mrs. Roosevelt was the first wife of
a president to invite a black woman,
Mary McLeod Bethune, to dine at
the White House. Courtesy Historical Museum of Southern Florida.

Left: 82. Annie M. Coleman, one of
the first women to become involved
in social issues as the civil rights era
began in Dade County. Coleman was
a strong advocate for the rights of
blacks. The Coleman Gardens
Housing Project is named after her.
Courtesy Historical Museum of
Southern Florida.

such that many will be able to qualify as caterers, stewards or waiters in restaurant or hotel work when they return to civilian life."[10]

Given the large number of black servicemen and women from Dade County, local blacks urged the American Legion to form a Negro veteran's organization in Miami, raising funds for the purchase of the property from the relatives of slain local veterans. In September 1945 a center for returning black veterans was announced in Miami. It was named the John Griffin Post and was opened on June 27, 1946, on Northeast Third Avenue in Colored Town.

Effective social change for blacks began in Miami almost as soon as the first black soldiers from the North hit the streets of segregated Dade County. Local whites had feared that black military personnel in Miami might have to be allowed to use the whites-only public beaches, which were being used to teach white sailors to swim. In order to avoid this, the Dade County Commission on March 14, 1944, gave the navy permission to establish a temporary beach for Negro trainees on Virginia Key.

Having been denied access to the ocean since D. A. Dorsey's short-lived Fisher Island black resort project in the 1930s, local blacks took notice. In early May 1945 Miami blacks began agitating for a permanent bathing beach in Dade County. The goal of the agitation was not to integrate the county's white beaches, but to pressure the county to open a beach exclusively for blacks. To press home the point, a group of blacks, led by Father Theodore R. Gibson of Coconut Grove's Christ Church, tested their right to use county-owned beaches by swimming at whites-only Baker's Haulover Beach on May 9, 1945. With this event, the civil rights movement in Dade County began, more than a decade before it did in other cities in the South.[11]

The wade-in at Baker's Haulover galvanized the Dade County Commission to act to prevent further efforts at integrating public beaches. On June 6, 1945, the county park superintendent announced that the Virginia Key Beach for Negroes, formerly the training beach for black sailors, was expected to be available within thirty days, and on August 8, less than three months after blacks waded in at Baker's Haulover, Virginia Key Beach was opened to blacks. On that day, more than one hundred blacks participated in the formal opening. Boat service to and from the beach began at nine that morning from Seventh Avenue and the Miami River. Within two weeks, nearly four thousand blacks had used the new swimming facilities. County officials said that atten-

83. An unidentified woman with a sign for Virginia Beach. The sign had been blown down by a storm in 1946. The county opened the beach on August 8, 1945, in order to prevent blacks from using public beaches, which were reserved for whites. Courtesy Florida Archives.

dance had exceeded expectations, with the result that two boats were operating daily to and from the beach, with three boats on Sundays and Wednesdays. The park director reported that there had been no disorder of any kind and that as soon as materials were available, further development of the beach would be made.

As more and more blacks came to the city during the war, service centers were established to meet their social needs. Vocational training centers built in Miami and across the nation were operational for both white and black veterans at the end of the war. For the first time, millions of blacks were the beneficiaries of government support in obtaining education, training, housing, medical, and other benefits. This substantially contributed to the stabilization and growth of the black working and middle classes in the 1940s and 1950s—not only in the South, where so much had been denied blacks for so long, but also throughout the United States.

At the end of the Second World War, blacks in great numbers began to migrate from the rural South into the cities of the Northeast and into growing southern cities such as Atlanta, Richmond, and Miami. As the civil rights era dawned, there was throughout the urban South a well-entrenched and growing black working class upon which the movement could be built. It was this group, for example, rather than the black middle class, that became the very backbone of the civil rights movement in Miami. Its presence on the historical stage at this time was due in no small measure to the postwar benefits granted to black veterans in the 1940s.

84. A "Jim Crow" segregated passenger coach, circa 1948. The car depicted in this rare photo belongs to the Atlantic Coast Line Railroad and is leaving the Miami station on October 6, 1948. Passenger cars used by whites were much more comfortable than this. Blacks were required to ride in separate passenger cars on railroads in the South until the 1960s. Courtesy Miami Memorabilia Collection of Myrna and Seth Bramson.

By the early 1950s, thousands of servicemen and women, and many of the civilians who came with them, settled permanently in Dade County. This began a change in the political and social fabric of the community. Miami's southern white population was being inundated by northern whites with somewhat different racial attitudes and experiences. Dade County's population was changing from small-town southern conservative to transplanted northern liberal. For this reason, relatively more moderate political and social views were heard in Miami during the civil rights period than in other parts of the state.

Many black veterans from the South, including many in Miami, felt that they and their progeny were entitled to equal treatment under the law since blacks had done their part to preserve the country. In spite of the changes following World War Two, white racism had not abandoned Miami. The Ku Klux Klan still had a visible presence in the county. As agitation by local blacks increased and as many black veterans settled in Dade County, some with a more enlightened world view as a result of their participation in the war, Miami became ripe for social conflict.

Postwar Black Communities in Dade County

Between 1920 and 1945, the white population of Dade County expanded more rapidly than did the black population. In 1920 blacks made up 29.7 percent of the total population of the county. As Table 4.1 shows, blacks made up only 17.7 percent of the total county population by 1945.

As Dade County grew dramatically in population following the Second World War, competition for space became more keen between blacks and whites. One incident left wounds that even today remain unhealed.

Since 1917, Railroad Shops Colored Addition had been a black community with an industrial school, park, and playground. The area was bounded by Northwest Forty-sixth and Fiftieth streets and Twelfth and Fourteenth avenues in an area now known as Allapattah. The district had been established to house the blacks who serviced Flagler's trains after they rolled into Miami. Railroad Shops was so named because the Florida East Coast Railroad had its service and repair facility there. An advertisement in the 1917 City of Miami Directory encouraged prospective settlers to relocate to "Railroad Shops Col-

Table 4.1. Black population of Dade County, 1920–1945

Year	Total	Black
1920	42,753	12,680
1925	111,332	28,869
1930	142,955	29,894
1935	180,998	35,924
1940	267,739	49,518
1945	315,060	55,877

Source: Carney, "Population Growth," 53.

ored Addition, an attractive suburb." The agent, T. J. Hannan, was located in Colored Town, at 102 Avenue G. By the mid–1940s, several black families were settled in Railroad Shops. When the county decided in 1947 that a school was needed for white children on the Railroad Shops site, many blacks refused to move. Using its right of eminent domain, Dade County evicted about thirty-five black residents from their Railroad Shops homes on August 1, 1947.

The evictions started around eleven in the morning. By early afternoon, the personal belongings of the resisting homeowners had been removed by police officers and were scattered in their front yards. Amid their belongings, some residents spent that night under a sky heavy with rain. They were drenched.

The evictions were difficult to accept, particularly for the older residents. Ruby Strickland recalled that her seventy-four-year-old mother, who lived in Railroad Shops, was among those resisting the order to move. Strickland went by her mother's house that morning, trying to persuade her to move in with her. "She told me not to touch anything in her house. She wasn't going." Later that day a friend on a bicycle informed Strickland that her mother had been evicted. When she arrived at her mother's house, she found the family's possessions on the ground. "They had put a padlock and a no trespassing sign on the door. My mother said to me, 'Ruby, if I had a hammer.' That's all she said. She didn't shed a tear." The Strickland family got forty-five hundred dollars for ten lots and their five-room house.[12]

The 1940s saw the birth of Liberty City, a predominantly black community that sprang up near the Liberty Square Housing Project, which opened in the late 1930s. As the Overtown population grew, row upon row of crowded, ramshackle houses sprang up along the district's dusty unpaved streets. There was little or no running water and no indoor plumbing. Electricity, fast becoming commonplace in white residential areas, was practically unknown in Colored Town. Children and young adults died of tuberculosis and other contagious diseases at a high rate. Crime—primarily bootlegging, prostitution, and gambling— thrived. Many of the customers were white men from the other side of the railroad tracks. The worsening conditions, combined with white resistance to expansion of the city's black population into white residential areas to the east and south, led to the creation of a new black district to the north and west, which later became known as Liberty City.

The Liberty City area was developed by Floyd Davis, a white man who purchased most of the land for the development from several black families. Davis hired a black man, Alfonso Kelly, to sell lots to blacks. Many blacks in Lemon City and Overtown were reluctant to move to the new black area, considering it too far out in the sticks. But Kelly, a man of considerable charm and persuasive abilities, sold many parcels in Liberty City. According to Richard Powell, now in his eighties, his family was among the first dozen black families to settle in Liberty City.[13]

The origin of the name "Liberty City" is not known, although it was probably linked to Davis, the white developer of the area. The now-defunct black newspaper, the *Miami Tropical Dispatch,* advertised land for blacks in other areas under the same name. The developer of those properties was also Floyd Davis.

Father John E. Culmer was a moving force in the establishment of the Liberty Square Housing Project. In 1929 Father Culmer of Saint

85. Alonzo "Pop" Kelly, who sold lots in Liberty City to blacks in the early 1930s. Many blacks believed the new community to be "too far out in the sticks" from Colored Town. With the opening of the Liberty Square Housing Project in 1937, Liberty City expanded rapidly. Courtesy Black Archives, History and Research Foundation of South Florida.

86. Horace Sharpe Jr., son of Lemon City pioneers, in front of one of the first homes built in what became known as Liberty City, circa 1923. Courtesy Isabelle Sharpe Blue.

Agnes Episcopal Church (one of Miami's leading black churches then and now), became disturbed over the tuberculosis deaths of several of his young parishioners and started a crusade to improve conditions in his community. He brought his concerns to the attention of the Greater Miami Negro Civic League and volunteered to serve as chairman of the league's fact-finding committee. In the early 1930s his citywide campaign for better housing and sanitation for blacks won the support of the editor of the *Miami Herald,* who agreed to publish a series of columns on the unhealthy conditions in Colored Town.

The *Herald*'s exposé brought national attention to conditions in Miami, and eventually President Franklin D. Roosevelt himself sent officials from the Works Progress Administration to visit Colored Town. As a result, plans were made for constructing one of the first federally funded public housing projects in the nation. Consisting initially of thirty-four units, the project was erected between Northwest Sixty-second and Sixty-seventh streets and became known as Liberty Square. This was the second federally supported public housing project in the nation and the first one to be built in the South.[14]

Liberty Square was planned and built in a parklike setting. The buildings were simple and inviting. The community center contained a recreation hall, a nursery, a doctor's office, a consumer cooperative store, a federal credit union, and classrooms for tenant education programs. Every family had a garden. Most grew flowers as well as vegetables. Liberty Square had modern kitchens and bathroom facilities, hot and cold water, gas and electricity. In Overtown, residents were still using tin washtubs, oil lamps, wood stoves, and iceboxes. It was not unusual for relatives and friends of those living in Liberty Square to visit the project and ask to take a bath in a real bathtub or to drink a glass of water containing ice cubes.

James E. Scott was the first administrator of the Liberty Square project. Scott personified the social and moral standards of the Liberty Square community. He insisted that residents take care of their homes and the common areas of the project. As a result, the housing project was virtually spotless at all times during his administration. It was so well kept that some black families built large expensive homes across the street.

87. The Liberty Square Housing Project as it appeared shortly after opening in the late 1930s. This was the first public housing project for blacks in the South. Constructed between Northwest Sixty-second and Sixty-seventh Streets, it initially consisted of thirty-four units. Several millions of dollars were spent in recent years to completely overhaul the buildings and grounds. Courtesy Historical Museum of Southern Florida.

Scott was born on June 17, 1890, in Savannah, Georgia. He graduated from Hampton Institute with an advanced degree in business administration. After volunteering for the armed services, he was selected for officers' training school. Upon his discharge, Captain Scott organized and served as the director of the Community Health and Thrift Center in Norfolk, Virginia.

In 1925 he relocated to Miami and helped launch the Colored Association for Family Welfare, which was to be a community center and day nursery. In 1927 Scott became the executive director of the organization, which had changed its name to the Negro Welfare Federation. Scott held the view that the group should help people to help themselves. Because of his untiring efforts on behalf of the organization, its name was later changed to the James E. Scott Community Association. Today it is the oldest social service agency serving the black communities of Dade County. Also named after Captain Scott is Dade's largest public housing project, James E. Scott Homes, located in the northwest section of Miami.

A new black elite class began to develop in Liberty City as the new housing project attracted more and more middle-income blacks. One of the places that attracted black celebrities, entertainers, and social climbers in the heady days of Liberty City's birth was Georgette's Tea Room at 2550 Northwest Fifty-first Street. Miami's black social elite held Sunday teas there as a matter of course. During the 1940s Georgette's was the place of choice to strut the latest fashions from New York or Paris on a Sunday afternoon. Today it is a private residence on Dade County's list of historic places.

Brownsville was another black community that developed quickly in the postwar period. Originally a white settlement, this farming development was started in the 1920s by a white man named W. L. Brown. The area is near the White Belt Dairy, bounded by Northwest Twenty-seventh Avenue on the east, Northwest Thirty-second Avenue on the west, Northwest Fifty-fourth Street on the north, and Northwest Forty-first Street on the south.

What was originally the black section of Brownsville was called Brown's Subdivision or Brown's Sub. In the late 1940s, despite white opposition, blacks started to move into the all-white section of Brownsville, and the resultant white flight caused the area to be virtually all black by the mid–1960s. The Brownsville Improvement Association helped promote many needed projects and activities, including preserving the concept of home ownership as a cornerstone of the community. Neal Adams, one of the founders of the organization and the third black to serve on the Dade County Commission, was a grocery store operator in Brownsville.

Opa-Locka also developed during this period. Its name was probably derived from the Indian word "Opatishawaukalocka," which means "hammock in the big swamp." In the 1940s railroad construction probably was a factor in the location of a black settlement along the tracks near Northwest 135th Street, east of Northwest Twenty-seventh Avenue. Opa-Locka was settled by many black laborers laying tracks for the Seaboard rail line.

An adjacent area, Bunche Park, was settled by black veterans of World War II who worked in Opa-Locka or other nearby communities. Named to honor Dr. Ralph Bunche, a black statesman, this community was Dade's first government housing development for black veterans. The author's parents, James and Corine Dunn, originally from DeLand, Florida, purchased a home there in 1951. They had five sons. Corrine Dunn became a north Dade activist and was instrumental in the establishment of a family health center adjacent to Bunche Park.

The black community of Richmond Heights was established in 1949. It was the first and largest private housing development built exclusively for black veterans of World War II and was one of the first preplanned residential areas for blacks in the country. A white couple, Frank and Mary Martin, founded and platted the entire subdivision to encourage black veterans to seek home ownership. It became a haven for black professionals, including many who were new to the county. In the 1950s living in the Heights was a status symbol. Although the structures were typically concrete block structures with two bedrooms and one bath, a local newspaper referred to this area as "the Negro's Shangri-la."

Nonetheless, most blacks remained crowded into Colored Town, now increasingly referred to as Overtown. They could not afford to move to Richmond Heights or elsewhere, so the expansion of public housing in the 1950s and 1960s gave many the option to escape the slums.

According to Dr. John O. Brown, who became one of Miami's most active civil rights leaders, there could have been a lot more public housing in Dade County if not for a few whites who wanted to get rich.

A white man named Luther Brooks and a handful of other whites opposed just about every proposal to build public housing the city or the county tried to build. They wanted to provide housing for the thousands of blacks who were being displaced from Overtown by urban renewal and the construction of the I–95 expressway. The group hired the Bonded Collection Agency to collect their rents on the hot, cramped, and poorly designed two-and three-story apartment buildings that began to rise like weeds throughout northwest Dade County. Blacks came to call these buildings "concrete monsters."

They put people in these apartments without any training on how to live in homes like this. You would see people throwing dishwater out the back door and trying to flush uncooked scraps of chitterlings and collard greens down the toilet.[15]

The Bonded Collection Agency still controls dozens of concrete monsters, particularly in Overtown and in northwest Dade County.

88. "Concrete monster" in Overtown. Apartment buildings like this were so dubbed by many of the blacks who lived in them because they were overcrowded, not air-conditioned, and had no play areas for children. Primarily white developers constructed these buildings in order to cash in on the displacement of thousands of blacks by urban renewal and expressway construction. Courtesy Sergio Campos.

The civil rights period in Dade County predated the civil rights period in other parts of the South by at least a decade. It was led by the activists of the time, notably Father John E. Culmer of Saint Agnes Episcopal Church in Colored Town and later, Father Theodore R. Gibson of Christ Church in Coconut Grove. Legal matters for the movement were handled by a tenacious black lawyer named G. E. Graves Jr. Black demands for voting rights came first, and by the late 1940s the whites-only Democratic primary was struck down by the U.S. Supreme Court. Blacks in Dade County and elsewhere in the South found their political voice. In time, racial restrictions in public accommodations and housing were removed. Although some whites resisted the expansion of blacks into previously all-white neighborhoods, the desegregation of housing was a fact of life by the early 1970s.

The Movement Begins

Prior to the civil rights movement in Dade County, black people were truly second-class citizens. Relations between black and white people in Dade County were cordial, as long as black people understood that they were not the social equals of whites. The "whites only" signs, as prevalent in Miami as they were in other southern cities, stood everywhere as reminders in case someone forgot. Blacks could not use public parks or other facilities. They could not vote in the Democratic primary. Public schools were segregated. Black students could not attend the University of Miami or any of Florida's other state-supported colleges except Florida A & M University in Tallahassee. Blacks were excluded from living in certain neighborhoods. Certain jobs were not available to black people, and blacks were excluded from most labor unions.

Corine Dunn worked as a maid on Miami Beach in the 1930s and 1940s. "Black workers on Miami Beach had to have an ID card that was issued by the Miami Beach Police Department. It had your picture on it and your fingerprints. If you wanted to work on the Beach, you had to carry that card."[1]

Social mores of the time dehumanized blacks, requiring them to defer to white people. If a black person met a white on the sidewalk, the black person was expected to step aside. Blacks were required to ride in the back of buses in the South, including Miami. Since many whites did not care to try on clothes that might have been worn by a black person, blacks were not allowed to try on clothes at Miami department stores, including Burdines and Sears. Whites were permitted to do so. The only blacks allowed to use the elevator at the Burdines store were members of the Dorsey family, in recognition of D. A. Dorsey's financial help to the Burdines during the Depression.

Black educator Eunice Liberty arrived in Miami in 1930. She believed that discrimination against women, white and black, in pre-World War II Miami was worse than discrimination against black men. According to Liberty, "Women were not allowed to eat in Burdines for a long time. They even let black men in to eat there before white or black women. Roxy Bolton, a white feminist activist from Coral Gables, was the one who fixed it so women could go there and eat. Black nor white women didn't eat in Burdines for a long, long time."[2]

Such was the status of black people in Dade County at the dawn of the civil rights movement. As the decade of the 1940s unfolded, a few changes for the better began to take place. In the late summer of 1944, a precursor of white and black cooperation appeared in the *Miami Daily News* announcing the city's first multiracial group specifically organized to address problems between whites and blacks relating to housing, health and recreation. The committee was composed of six white and six black members.

Members of the Dade County Interracial Committee toured sections of Miami's black communities in order to observe living conditions firsthand. Some officials expressed surprise and concern that rents were as high in slum areas as they were in regular rental areas. Following its tour, the committee announced that eliminating slums in the black sections of Miami was its major aim. The committee also said that it would press for better housing and support for a hospital to give private treatment to Negro patients.

Things also began to change in the Miami Police Department. Since the city's birth, Miami whites had been strongly opposed to hiring blacks as police officers, as was generally true throughout the southern states. In fact, Miami may have been the first city in the South to hire blacks as members of its permanent police force.

When blacks complained about the lack of black police officers in Colored Town, the usual response was to put meaner and tougher white officers on the streets. The following 1920 *Miami Herald* story revealed prevailing attitudes among whites in Miami:

> J. Kingsley Fink, Miami Police commissioner, answered the request of the city's colored board of trade to employ colored officers on the city's police force by declaring that there will be no colored officers on the force if he has anything to do with it.
>
> As a direct result of the board's request, the police began a strict enforcement of the law aimed at the negroes by raiding a 2 block area in the colored settlement. Police chief Raymond Dillon also opposed the hiring of colored officers and joined the police commissioner in effectively turning down the request.[3]

Because of continued advocacy by blacks, in September 1944 a hand-picked group was sworn in to become the first black patrolmen hired as a permanent part of the Miami Police Department. The recruitment of John Milledge, Ralph White, Clyde Lee, Ed Kimball, and Moody Hall had taken place under extreme secrecy, since many whites were opposed to blacks on the police force. There was even concern for the safety of the new patrolmen. In the beginning, they were limited to patrolling the black section of the city. Technically they were not police officers, but patrolmen. They had the authority to arrest blacks but not whites. According to a black police officer hired in 1947, not until 1963 could black Miami police officers arrest whites.

Ralph White, one of the original black patrolmen, felt that black Miamians were very receptive to them. "Sure there was resentment by whites, but overall the attitude was good and the arrangement worked."[4] In March 1945 the assignment of black police officers was expanded to include the black section of Coconut Grove, which the city of Miami had annexed by that time.

In September 1945, Miami's Negro patrol unit celebrated its first birthday. What had begun with five black patrolmen had grown to a force of fifteen police officers, and three more blacks were expected to be hired soon. The city's safety director said that the Negro unit had proved itself far beyond expectations, winning a permanent place in Miami's law enforcement. Besides foot patrols, black officers manned a bicycle patrol squad which operated from midnight to eight in the morning. White officers were excluded from black areas unless on

89. Judge L. E. Thomas, the first black judge in the South since Reconstruction. Judge Thomas presided over cases brought to court by the city's first black patrolmen in the late 1940s. He is shown here in the 1950s. Courtesy Black Archives, History and Research Foundation of South Florida.

special assignment. In 1946 black Miami police officers were admitted to civil service rank, meaning they were eligible for pension and retirement benefits.

Judge Lawson E. Thomas was Miami's first black judge. In 1951 he began presiding over the municipal court at the new Negro police precinct at Northwest Eleventh Street and Fifth Avenue. There he handled the cases of blacks arrested by the city's Negro police force, consisting of over forty officers by the late 1940s. Thomas is believed to have been the first black judge in the South since Reconstruction.

The new black officers were barely on the job when, in 1946, tragedy struck. John Milledge was patrolling outside Dorsey Park on November 1, 1946, during a football game between Dorsey High School and a black high school from Gainesville. From the darkness between two houses across the street, in the seventeen hundred block of Northwest Fourth Avenue, a .22-caliber rifle was aimed at Milledge and a shot was fired, sending a bullet through the officer's throat. Twenty minutes later, John Milledge died at Jackson Memorial Hospital.

Another black officer, James Washington, was watching the football game when he heard the shot and saw Milledge fall. Later Washington said, "That man sure tried to live."[5] Two men were seen running from the scene of the crime. All of the other black officers were called to duty, and an intensive search was conducted. Although a reward of one thousand dollars was offered, the assailant was not found and the case remained unsolved for over forty years.

In July 1989 a witness came forward. Mary White, a black woman, notified Miami police that she had a story to tell. White said that she was sitting on her porch near the crime scene on the day Milledge was shot when a man with a rifle came running by. She noticed that the man had an impaired left eye. Willie Smith, a friend of the man who was running with the gun, was with White at the time. Smith knew the man with the rifle to be Leroy Strachan, but Smith told White he would hurt her if she spoke to anyone about what she had seen. Until Smith died, more than forty years later, White told no one what she saw that day.

Immediately after the shooting, Strachan left Miami for New York where he lived with his father, buried in anonymity. With White's statement in 1989, the case was reopened. New York police tracked down the suspect in Harlem. He told police he had killed Milledge after an argument. According to Strachan, he was only trying to scare Milledge. Strachan was held in a New York jail while he fought extradition to Florida for trial. He had maintained a spotless record since his arrival in New York, holding a steady job and becoming a senior leader in his church. People in New York who knew Strachan were shocked to learn of his arrest; many supported his futile fight to avoid returning to Dade County.[6]

The case was finally closed in September 1991 with a plea bargain, under which Strachan pleaded guilty to manslaughter. He was freed almost immediately, because the nineteen months he had spent in a Manhattan jail fighting extradition counted toward his 364-day jail sentence. He returned to New York a relatively free man, notwithstanding the fact that he had killed a patrol officer.[7]

Profiles of Miami Civil Rights Leaders

The most active black organizations in the beginning of the civil rights movement were the National Association for the Advancement of Colored People (NAACP), led by the Reverend Edward T. Stephenson and later by Father Theodore R. Gibson and Dr. George Simpson; the Congress on Racial Equality (CORE), led by Albert D. Moore and Dr. John O. Brown; the Crusade for Voters, chaired by Otis James; and the Negro Ministerial Alliance, which was organized by several black ministers.

The groups operated in different arenas toward the same goal—equality for blacks. The NAACP primarily used the courts. The activist organization CORE led demonstrations, including most of Miami's downtown lunch-counter sit-ins. The Ministerial Alliance participated in much of the desegregation dialogue between black and white groups. The Crusade for Voters moved to increase the empowerment of blacks at the ballot box. Other activist organizations also operated in the county, including the Urban League, which was seen as comparatively conservative at that time, and the Black Muslims, which was viewed by whites as hostile, if not dangerous. The Reverend Martin Luther King's Southern Christian Leadership Conference, which was active in many other southern cities, did not have an active chapter in Miami. However, the Reverend Edward Graham and a number of other black leaders cooperated with King in his work elsewhere and brought Dr. King to Miami twice.

90. Thurgood Marshall (second from left) meets with Miami civil rights activists, circa 1952. Marshall would later become the first black justice of the United States Supreme Court. At the time of this photograph, he was general counsel for the national NAACP office. Miami attorney G. E. Graves is seated at far right. Courtesy Historical Museum of South Florida.

91. Martin Luther King Jr. at Miami's Variety Children's Hospital (now Miami Children's Hospital) April 4, 1966. Dr. King visited Miami several times during the civil rights movement. Courtesy Miami Memorabilia Collection of Myrna and Seth Bramson.

Father John E. Culmer (1891–1963)

Father John E. Culmer was Miami's first major black leader. He came to Miami from Tampa in 1929 to lead Colored Town's Saint Agnes Episcopal Church, which was in financial ruin and still suffering from a scandal in 1916 involving a former priest. Culmer emerged above his predecessors and contemporaries as the preeminent black leader of his day. Exalted by his followers, he was able to command the attention of the white media and power structure. Through the national black media, he enjoyed a reputation around the country as Miami's most articulate black spokesman.

John Edwin Culmer was born on May 22, 1891, the second child of Edwin James and Ellen Spiro Culmer of Savannah Sound, Eleuthera, Bahamas. His father was a farmer, and his mother a schoolteacher and seamstress. The Culmer family was also relatively well educated and musically inclined.

Despite his father's request that he take over the family farm, in 1911 he left the Bahamas to become a minister. He first went to New York and then to Philadelphia, but he was not able to gain admission to a seminary because of his race.

Disappointed, he returned briefly to Savannah Sound before traveling to Miami, again seeking acceptance to a seminary. While exploring different avenues to achieve his goal, Culmer settled in the black Coconut Grove area and sustained himself with a variety of jobs. Despite his superior education, he worked as a common laborer, helping to clear land in Coconut Grove and Miami Beach. The pay was low, and the surge of black labor made for poor living conditions. His shelter consisted of a space on a barren floor in a room that he shared with other laborers, sleeping and working in shifts.

While working in the fields one day, he severely cut his foot. The truck transporting field hands was not due to return from town until the end of the day. Culmer limped back in the direction of Coconut Grove in search of medical attention. While making his way back, he hailed a number of passing buggies being driven by whites but was ignored or greeted with racial epithets. Eventually, Mrs. Arthur Curtis James, the wife of a prominent white man, stopped and took him to her home, where she cleaned and bandaged his wound. She was impressed with his training and desire to become a minister and offered to finance his education if he could enroll in a seminary.[8]

In 1914, Culmer managed a dry goods store which served as an outlet for the Burdines Department Store and was a member of the Christ Episcopal Church, where he served as organist and Sunday school teacher. Having found more stable sources of income, he purchased two lots, built a home at 3357 Douglas Road, and married Nancy Elizabeth Taylor.

Culmer's desire to become a minister was eventually realized by chance when a white Episcopal priest named Father Sopher, from Coconut Grove's Saint Stephen's Episcopal Church, visited Christ Episcopal Church and noticed how capably Culmer played the organ. As they talked, Sopher learned that the organist wished to become a minister and that he had no children; therefore, the priest offered to recommend Culmer for acceptance as a candidate for the ministry.

With this recommendation and Mrs. James's financial help, Culmer obtained a bachelor's degree in music from Oskaloosa College in Oskaloosa, Iowa, in 1916. He then studied at the Bishop Payne Divinity

School in Petersburg, Virginia. In 1919 he earned a Bachelor of Divinity degree and finally entered the ministry. After his training, Father Culmer went to Tampa, where he served as priest in charge of the Saint James Episcopal Church.

During his work in Tampa, he exhibited extraordinary leadership skills. Under his ministry, Saint James Church completed a brick church building, built a new rectory, installed pews, retired its mortgage debt, and nearly doubled its membership. He gained a reputation in Tampa's black community as an articulate advocate for minority rights, while whites saw him as a pragmatic and trustworthy promoter of good relations between the races. By 1929 Saint James was recognized as one of the foremost black churches in Tampa. Its membership was shocked and angered upon learning of Culmer's pending transfer to Miami in September 1929.

Saint Agnes was one of Miami's oldest churches, initially assembled in October 1897. The church had been struggling under the cumulative effects of a scandal involving its priest, the destruction caused by the 1926 hurricane, and general financial burdens. An ideological split was also developing among the membership.

With aroused race consciousness among blacks in Miami after World War I, some members of the church sought an affiliation with the African Orthodox Church, an outgrowth of the Marcus Garvey Back-to-Africa movement. This new church retained all the trappings of the Episcopal Church and offered emancipation from white bishops in favor of a black church with black bishops, priests, and deacons. Some members did join the African Orthodox Church in 1922 and later formed the Saint Francis Xavier Church in the early 1940s. This church still exists in Overtown.

Faced with a fragmented and disillusioned membership, Culmer quickly reorganized the congregation. His enthusiasm infected the church. With financial contributions from the membership and a loan from the American Church Building Fund Commission, he supervised the completion of the new church building within fourteen months of his arrival. The first service in the new Saint Agnes Church was held on November 30, 1930. Culmer eventually added a marble altar and the first Moeller pipe organ ever acquired by a black church in Miami.

As in Tampa, Father Culmer proved highly adept at promoting social change. His effectiveness in improving the social conditions of Miami's black community stemmed from a shrewd sense of what gains were realistically feasible at any given time and an ability to rise above the intimidations that daunted others. He was able to maneuver in both the white and black communities. Although Culmer had his critics, blacks generally perceived him as a courageous leader who fearlessly strove to obtain equal rights for Miami's black residents, yet Miami's white community did not perceive him as a threat to its interests or security.

In 1934 Culmer initiated a citywide campaign to improve housing for Miami's blacks. Through columns in the *Miami Herald,* he exposed the horrifying living conditions in Colored Town. This exposé led the mayor to appoint Father Culmer to a committee studying slum conditions in the city. An allocation of federal money ultimately led to the building of the Liberty Square Housing Project, the first such project for blacks in the southeastern United States.

In spite of his successes, or possibly because of them, some blacks were critical of Culmer and suggested that he was not aggressive enough in dealing with whites. Culmer expressed his views about Miami's black leadership in a 1938 letter to the editor of New York's widely read black newspaper, the *Amsterdam News,* and again in a 1940 article in the NAACP's *Crisis* magazine. In his letter to the *Amsterdam News,* Culmer discussed an issue that has been alive among Miami blacks throughout their first century on Biscayne Bay—perennial in-fighting. He suggested that blacks could receive more consideration if they displayed more unanimity of opinion and action, citing petty jealousies and leadership rivalries as doing more to impede the progress of blacks than anything else.

In the 1930s, some whites, including the Klan, became concerned about the increasing resolve of Miami blacks to vote in the primaries. As a result, the Klan embarked upon a campaign to intimidate blacks. Klansmen often marched through Colored Town on election eve and warned of dire consequences should blacks attempt to vote.

Father Culmer's activism in voting rights was a key factor in attaining safe voting conditions for blacks in the primary election of 1939. As publicity director of the Interdenominational Minister's Alliance, Culmer wrote to H. Leslie Quigg, chief of police, requesting protection for black voters. His request was granted, and for the first time blacks participated in a city election in record numbers.

At about this time a Klansman asked a white member of Saint Agnes Church to recommend someone from the black community to address

92. Father John E. Culmer (1891–1963). Father Culmer arrived in Miami from Tampa in 1929 to lead St. Agnes Episcopal Church. He became Miami's most influential black leader of the 1930s and 1940s, regularly writing articles on Miami for national black publications such as New York City's *Amsterdam News*. Courtesy Historical Museum of Southern Florida.

white concerns at a Klan meeting. The parishioner recommended Father Culmer, who accepted the invitation. The precise nature of the discussion is not known. However, Culmer said he warned the Klan that if it continued to intimidate black people, he and other blacks would don Klan hoods and gowns and march alongside Klansmen in Colored Town to show that they would not be oppressed in their own community.

Father John Culmer died in 1963.

Elmer A. Ward (1891–1991)

Elmer A. Ward was a notable figure in the Dade County civil rights movement. Ward was born on July 27, 1891, in Charlottesville, Virginia. He was the grandson of a slave and one of eleven children born to David and Florence Ward. After graduating from the Charlottesville public schools, he attended Howard University, spent two years in the army, and obtained his pharmacist license from the University of Toledo in 1924.

Ward came to Miami in 1926 and opened the Economy Drug Store at 1101 Northwest Third Avenue. He retired from running the drug store in 1955 and devoted himself fully to political causes. As a leader of the city's chapter of CORE, Ward became an activist in fighting the racial barriers facing blacks in Dade County. In 1942 he became the first black person to serve on a Dade County Circuit Court jury. Ward participated in the demonstrations that led to the desegregation of the area's theaters, restaurants, golf courses, and beaches.

Known as Dr. Ward, he also made his mark in banking in the 1960s, serving on the advisory board and as vice-president of First Federal Savings and Loan, the first black to achieve such a post. In 1975 Ward said, "I don't believe in violence, but I have been a militant since I was fifteen. I'm a nonviolent political activist." In recognition of his contributions to the community, Ward Tower, at 2200 Northwest Fifty-fourth Street, a $3.6 million federally subsidized housing project for senior citizens and the handicapped, was named for him. Elmer Ward died in Miami on October 3, 1991. He was one hundred years old.

Grattan Ellesmere ("G. E.") Graves Jr. (1919–1992)

Grattan Ellesmere Graves Jr. was born in Lawrenceville, Virginia, on February 11, 1919. When young Graves was in elementary school, the family moved to Washington, D.C., where he received the balance of his formal education, including a law degree in 1943 from Howard University. On January 13, 1946, Graves arrived in Miami to practice law. He thought that most blacks in Miami were complacent and uninvolved in changing the city's racist system. According to Graves, very few middle-class blacks or members of the black monied class joined the Miami NAACP. He believed they were afraid to be associated with the organization. He also believed that the black monied class generally resisted social change, citing as an example the blacks who owned hotels and other businesses in Colored Town and who thus stood to lose if the social order were changed.

In 1948 the white leadership of the city decided to remove a large number of blacks from property near downtown which was needed for expanding white-owned businesses. A series of meetings was called to discuss the matter. After attending these meetings, Graves realized that it was a foregone conclusion that blacks were to be moved, the only question being discussed was where to move them. Graves was the first to effectively confront Miami's power structure about the planned unilateral removal of blacks from their homes, and he became an instant hero among Miami blacks as a result.

In the early and mid–1950s, Graves became increasingly involved in civil rights cases in Miami. A number of significant statewide civil rights cases originated in Dade County, and Graves was involved as NAACP attorney in almost all of them. He was also a close associate

93. Attorney G. E. Graves (center) and Father Theodore R. Gibson riding a Miami public bus in a protest effort to desegregate public transportation during the Miami civil rights era. Courtesy Historical Museum of Southern Florida.

of the Reverend Theodore R. Gibson, the city's preeminent civil rights leader. The two of them hatched many of their civil rights strategies in the kitchen of Graves's home.

Graves lived in Liberty City until his death on January 17, 1992, at age seventy-two. According to Dr. John O. Brown—himself a noted figure in the Dade County civil rights movement—G. E. Graves was one of the unsung heroes of the community.

Edward T. Graham (1905–1987)

The Reverend Edward T. Graham was the pastor of the historic and powerful Mount Zion Baptist Church in Overtown during Miami's civil rights period. He became a major figure during that time by leading a number of demonstrations.

Graham was reared on a South Carolina farm in the days when a black child's education was considered to be complete after the fourth grade. With the help of a grandparent, Graham worked his way through private schools and eventually won a master's degree from Columbia University. The more education he received, the more he questioned segregation.

Graham came to Miami as a worker with the United Serviceman's Organization at the outbreak of World War II. He became active in the Miami chapter of the NAACP, which was spearheading integration efforts in the county. Graham ultimately became president of the chapter. Thereafter, he was in the foreground of the Dade County civil rights struggle, going on to become the first black to serve on the Dade County Commission. He died in 1987.

John O. Brown, M.D. (1922–)

Dr. John O. Brown was another of Miami's civil rights giants, fearless in his attack on the race discrimination he found in the city when he arrived in 1955. Brown had moved to Miami after completing his training in ophthalmology at Alabama's Tuskegee Institute and soon opened his practice. It was not long before he was in the thick of the area's burgeoning civil rights struggle.

John O. Brown was born in Colbert, Oklahoma, on October 23, 1922. He grew up in Wewoka, Oklahoma. His parents, Edward D. Brown and Gayler Hill, were Texans who had moved to Oklahoma during the land boom that opened up that state. During World War II Brown married Marie Faulkner of Atlanta, Georgia, whose father was a well-known Congregational minister and dean of the chapel at Fisk University. The couple raised four children, three boys and a girl. Having experienced many instances of racial discrimination as a youth, and having served in the war as an officer in the U.S. Army's famed all-black Ninety-second Division (also known as the Buffalo Soldiers), Brown was particularly incensed at being subjected to second-class citizenship.

By the late 1950s, Dr. Brown was head of the Miami chapter of the Congress on Racial Equality (CORE). From that position he spearheaded most of the activism that was associated with the civil rights movement in Dade County. He was an active force in civil rights cases. One of his sons was among the black children who sued the Dade County Public School System to force desegregation of public schools. He led the marches to integrate lunch counters and public beaches. He was a potent member of the tight circle that led and inspired the move-

94. Dr. John O. Brown, one of the giants of Dade County's civil rights movement. An ophthalmologist from Oklahoma, Brown arrived in Miami after World War II and immediately became a leader in the movement in Miami. His son was one of the twelve black children who sued the Dade County School Board to force desegregation. Courtesy Dr. John O. Brown.

ment in Miami. Although not as well known as Theodore Gibson and Edward Graham, John O. Brown was no less a hero in the struggle for black equality in Dade County.

According to Dr. Brown, the black middle and upper classes in Dade County assiduously avoided the civil rights movement. "They couldn't get forty black schoolteachers to join the NAACP, and it only cost two dollars a year to join. Schoolteachers were the upper class, but they were afraid of losing their jobs. It was the little man who came to the rallies and chipped in his fifty cents or a dollar that carried the movement in the black community." At that time, there were several branches of the NAACP organized in Dade County. Brown said, "The Miami branch of the NAACP was the weakest one. Richard Powell, the head of the Liberty City branch, and Bessie Brunt, who was president of the Opa-Locka chapter, gave us more support. We went to them when we needed money."9

M. Athalie Range (1915–)

Mary Athalie Wilkinson was born in Key West on November 7, 1915. Her grandparents were originally from Nassau, Bahamas, but her parents, Edward L. Wilkinson and Grace Shultz, were also born in Key West. The family left the Keys when she was five or six years old, and she grew up primarily in Miami. Mary Athalie Wilkinson Range is a

1939 graduate of Booker T. Washington Senior High School. Although she did not receive a formal college education, she later attended the New England Institute of Anatomy and Embalming and is a licensed funeral director. She heads the Range Funeral Home, the city's most successful black funeral home.

Mary Athalie Wilkinson married Oscar Lee Range, who was from Valdosta, Georgia. They had four children—Myrna, Patrick, Oscar, and Gary—and lived in the Liberty Square Housing Project in the early years. Oscar Range became a licensed funeral director, and the Ranges opened their funeral home in 1953. After her husband's death seven years later, Mary Athalie Range continued the business.

Range's political involvement began in 1948 with the PTA of her children's school, Liberty City Elementary School, then located on the present site of Charles R. Drew Elementary School. According to Range, conditions at the school were deplorable. With an enrollment of some twelve hundred children, the school consisted entirely of portable class-rooms, having no permanent building. It had twelve toilet facilities for girls and about the same number for boys. There was no lunchroom, even though school cafeterias had long been common in white schools. Booker T. Washington High School had had a cafeteria when Range attended; so had her elementary school.

There were no grassy areas or trees on the grounds of Liberty City Elementary. The children had only outside drinking fountains, fed by uncovered water pipes merely laid over the ground. The water was so undrinkable that parents who could afford it gave their children ther-mos bottles of ice to take to school; others gave their children mayon-naise jars filled with chipped ice. The school was one of the few Dade County schools still operating on double session.

In the late 1940s, Range was elected president of the school's PTA. She was adamant about getting a hot-lunch program at the school, which led to a rare confrontation between black parents and the Dade County School Board. In a 1991 interview, Range recalled:

Some of the parents began to suggest that we write the school board and tell them that we were not satisfied with the conditions under which our children were being educated. I felt that writing letters never helped, so I said rather than writing letters let's all get together and go down to the school board as a group. The parents were all very cooperative with this idea.

That PTA meeting was on a Tuesday, and the school board met on Wednesday. We decided we would go that Wednesday, and we went to the school board unannounced. About 125 people went to the meeting. It was a very great surprise to the school board members. We got there very early because we did not know when the meeting started. We filled up every seat in the auditorium; consequently, the other parents who were accustomed to going and talking were left without a seat. They delayed the meeting for an hour hoping that maybe we would go away.

Finally, the superintendent called the meeting together, and I shall always remember what he said: "We have an unusual situation here today. In order to get our meeting moving, we have a large group of Negroes here so we are going to hear what they have to say. If there is a spokesman among you, you may come up." I went up and spoke for fifteen minutes without a note. One of the school board administrators walked out of the meeting afterwards and asked our school principal, "Who was the silver-tongue derringer they sent down here to hang us?"

As a result of the confrontation, arrangements were made with Miami-Jackson Senior High School (an all-white school at the time) to transport food from its cafeteria to the elementary school, and Range and the other parents were promised a new school building complete with a cafeteria of its own. A large portable building was brought onto the school grounds to serve as a temporary cafeteria, and hot lunches were available to the black children of Liberty City Elementary from then on. The school board also kept the promise to construct a new school. It was the first black school to be built in Dade County in twenty-one years. Mary Athalie Range was established as a black leader. City hall was next.

Range described her entry into Miami politics in the mid–1960s, when Miami blacks were emerging as a force in city politics:

It was during the time that Mrs. Alice Wainwright, who was the first female commissioner for the city of Miami, became a little disenchanted and said she did not want to serve anymore. This was going into what we refer to as the Roaring Sixties. Rosa Parks had refused to sit on the back of the bus. Black people were beginning to flex some muscle. When Alice Wainwright decided she did not wish to run again, immediately we began to look for some black who could probably fill that vacancy. After much deliberation I was chosen.

In the 1964 primary race for the commission seat, Range outdistanced her closest opponent by five hundred votes but was faced with a run-off election against white candidate Irving Christie. She lost the run-off by one thousand votes, a very small margin. She had about seventeen thousand votes and Christie about eighteen thousand. Range was critical of how Christie managed to win. By her account, "The evening before the election, there was a big sound truck going around the white sections of town saying, 'Unless you get out and vote in tomorrow's election, you may have a Negro deciding your fate on the commission.'"

There were also problems in the black areas. Range explained, "Because people in the black community are not well-versed in politics, they could be told almost anything. Many who were allowed to get off their jobs to go to the polls during the first primary vote were told by their employers, 'Oh no! You voted for Mrs. Range the first Tuesday. They will count it this time.' There was a lot of bitterness in the community."

Robert King High was Mayor of Miami at the time. He had aspirations to become the state's next governor. Consequently, said Range, High thought he should do something to increase his popularity in the black community. Following Range's failed election attempt, the mayor encouraged one city commissioner to relinquish his seat so that Range could be appointed to the position. Thus, in 1965 Mary Athalie Range became the first black person to serve on the Miami City Commission. She subsequently won the seat outright in the following election. She was elected to a third term and in that election got more votes than the mayor.

After she became a city commissioner, a horrible fire in a black area of Miami took the lives of eleven people. An investigation revealed that a space heater was to blame. Range responded to this tragedy by leading the commission to pass an ordinance outlawing space heaters in the city.

In the mid–1960s Range virtually forced City Manager Mel Reese to hire the city's first black motorcycle patrolman. According to Range, Reese was opposed to the idea when she first approached him on the subject. He reportedly commented that this was one section of the police department "that was not going to be a checkerboard."[10] During this time, the city was attempting to acquire the land needed to establish the Alice Wainwright Park near Vizcaya, and Range's vote was desperately needed. High called Range the day of the voting to sound her out on the matter. She agreed to support the proposition to establish the park on the condition that the city train black motor-cycle patrol officers. The bargaining worked. The meeting and voting were postponed until the first black trainee mounted his cycle. That officer was Robert (Bob) Ingram, who later became chief of police and mayor of the city of Opa-Locka. Alice Wainwright Park was es-tablished immediately after Ingram was selected.

Range's style of popular activism and in-your-face confrontation followed her from the school board to city hall. In the late 1960s trash pick-up around black sections of the city was erratic; Range said that garbage in the black areas of the city was picked up when sanitation workers had nothing else to do. In a 1967 commission meeting, Range reported that there were some apartment buildings in Liberty City where garbage sometimes piled up for two weeks. She introduced an ordinance mandating twice-weekly garbage collection all over the city of Miami. The vote on the proposition was postponed twice. Range invited supporters to her home, where she told them to bring some garbage to the next commission meeting and deposit it on the com-missioners' desks. Blacks with bags of garbage packed the meeting, and the ordinance was expeditiously passed.

Range left the commission in 1972 and was succeeded by Father Theodore R. Gibson. Governor Reubin Askew later appointed her to the state cabinet as secretary of community affairs, where she served from 1970 to 1973.

While Range was in her cabinet post, the state suffered a tremen-dous drought, placing farmers in dire straits. The Everglades burned uncontrollably. A group of farmers approached Range and asked her to visit hard-hit agricultural areas. The devastation made an impres-sion on her, and she met several times with the governor. He was co-operative and sent a team of specialists with Range to survey the dam-

95. M. Athalie ("Mama") Range in 1971 with Governor Reubin O. Askew. She was appointed by the governor as the first black person to sit on the Miami City Commission in 1965. She was later appointed Florida Secretary of Community Affairs. Political leaders, including U.S. presidents, still highly prize the advice and support of Athalie Range. Courtesy Florida Archives.

age by helicopter. As a result of her leadership, more than $8 million of state and federal money was allocated to deal with the crisis.

After Range left her cabinet post, President Carter appointed her to the national AMTRAK board for a two-year term. Range was one of the first blacks in Florida to support Jimmy Carter's campaign for the presidency in the late 1970s. She introduced Carter to black groups even before he announced that he was running for president.

By the 1990s M. Athalie Range had retired from active public life. She remains a dominant figure behind the political scene in Miami and continues to run her business with her son Patrick. She is affectionately and respectfully called "Mama" Range, and her political support for candidates at the local, state, and national levels is still assiduously courted.

Father Theodore R. Gibson (1915–1981)

As the civil rights era matured in Miami, the most important figure to emerge from among the black leadership of that time was the Reverend Canon Theodore R. Gibson. In the early 1960s he was the rector of the powerful Christ Episcopal Church, planted deep in the heart of the Black Grove. When Gibson began his ascent to power in Miami politics, this church had about eight hundred members. He was Miami's most important black leader since Father John E. Culmer who, like Gibson, had Bahamian roots and was the leader of a black Miami Episcopal church.

Gibson was born on April 24, 1915, to Bahamian immigrant parents. He was born in a three-room frame house in Miami's northwest section. His mother worked as a maid and laundress to send him to college. He never accepted the doctrine of segregation, even in his youth. His mother said that he never knew the second-rate feeling that segregation produces in blacks born in the American South.

From a young age, Gibson viewed the social and geographic barriers placed on his race as a moral wrong. He saw his best friend horsewhipped by the Ku Klux Klan on the streets of Miami. Gibson considered anything anyone did against blacks to be a personal affront.

Gibson attended St. Augustine College in Raleigh, North Carolina, and Bishop Payne Divinity School, now part of the Virginia Theological Seminary. Christ Church was his third placement after graduation. Loquacious and eloquent, by the late 1950s Gibson was into the thick of things in post-war Miami. He was pugnacious, cunning, and forceful in his verbal assaults on injustice and those who were responsible for it.

In the early 1960s, Gibson and a white Coconut Grove woman named Elizabeth Verrick teamed up to attack the slum problems in the Black Grove. Their efforts led to visible improvements. For example, the black section of the Grove was connected to the sewage disposal system; previously human excrement had been collected by a truck called the honey wagon, the approach of which required no announcement.

Gibson's later contributions, though more subtle, were also very important. He was a key figure in mending relations between blacks and whites in Coconut Grove. He fought for school desegregation and pressed for more jobs for Hispanics and blacks. After stepping down as president of the Miami NAACP in 1965, Gibson was elected president of the Florida Council of Churches in 1970.

By early 1972 Gibson was involved in Miami politics. Miami City Commissioners J. L. Plummer and Sidney Aronovitz persuaded him to run for a seat on the commission. Gibson was elected and served on the Miami City Commission until 1981, never losing an election.

During his service on the commission Gibson played a large role in reforming Miami's civil service laws. For years he put pressure on city managers to appoint more blacks to top administrative posts, often meeting with resistance. It was Gibson who cast the pivotal vote that reformed the Miami civil service laws and made more city jobs available to blacks and Hispanics. He continued to strive to prevent layoffs of sanitation workers, public-safety employees, and others.

Miller J. Dawkins, a Miami-Dade Community College administrator endorsed by Gibson to take his seat, ultimately succeeded Gibson on the commission. Father Gibson died in September of 1982. He was

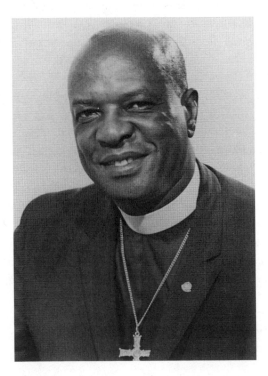

96. Father Theodore R. Gibson (1915–1982), the most preeminent civil rights leader of the 1960s and 1970s. Gibson was pastor of the venerable Christ Episcopal Church when he was elected to the Miami City Commission in 1972. He also headed the Miami chapter of the NAACP during the civil rights movement in Dade County. Courtesy Historical Museum of Southern Florida.

buried in the old Miami City Cemetery, where his mother and father are also buried.

Voting Rights

The incorporation of the city of Miami in 1896 and the vote to move the county seat from Juno to Miami shortly afterwards marked the beginning and end of meaningful black involvement in city affairs for more than six decades. By 1920 registered white voters in Dade County outnumbered black voters fourteen to one, although nearly one-fourth of the population was black. This was typical of southern communities during this time. In fact, since the early 1900s the black vote in the South had been essentially meaningless. The Democratic party controlled southern politics: Winning a Democratic primary in southern states was tantamount to winning the general election. State statutes going back to 1897 and 1901 enabled the then-conservative and racist Democratic party of Florida to exclude blacks from membership. Thus, blacks were effectively disenfranchised and neutralized as a political force in the state. Since they could not vote in the whites-only Democratic primary, their other choice was to squander their votes on unappreciative Republican candidates in general elections. For the privilege of doing so, they were required biannually to pay a one-dollar poll tax. Not many bothered.

Although Republicans in the South profited somewhat from heavy black support in national elections, they could not afford to alienate white voters by appearing to appeal to blacks. Therefore, Republicans tended to minimize the importance of their black support.

The question of black participation in the political process generated many overt threats and acts of violence against blacks. Dade County Sheriff R. J. Chillingworth flagrantly attempted to prevent blacks from voting, even angering many whites. In 1899, several whites protested to city and county authorities about Chillingworth's intimidation tactics, going so far as to hang the sheriff in effigy.

At a large 1939 rally in Miami, white extremists launched a campaign to discourage blacks from participating in the approaching nonpartisan city commission election. A vivid description of the terrorism appeared in the May 3 *Miami Herald:*

> The park rally, last of the primary campaign, was attended by more than 2,000 persons. It was followed by a Klan parade and lighting

of more than 25 fiery crosses. . . . Hundreds of red-lettered warning cards were spread through Miami's negro section Monday night as the Ku Klux Klan staged an automobile protest against negro voters in today's primary election.

The crosses carried on a huge truck at the head of a parade of about 75 cars bearing uniformed and hooded men were dropped at one block intervals. A dummy dressed to represent a negro was suspended in a noose from a power pole. On the front of the figure a large red-lettered sign read: "This nigger voted." . . . The hooded occupants of one automobile . . . dangled a hangman's noose from the window of the car. . . . Warning cards thrown from the window read: "Respectable negro citizens are not voting tomorrow. Niggers keep away from the polls." The warnings were signed in inch-high letters, KKK.[11]

The Klan campaign backfired. Several black leaders, including Sam Solomon, who headed his own black-oriented newspaper, and the Reverend John E. Culmer reacted to the threat by telling city officials that black voters intended to challenge the Klan by going to the polls in

97. Dummy burned during the 1939 Miami election campaign. The Ku Klux Klan reportedly burned this effigy in Colored Town in order to discourage blacks from voting. However, the intimidation backfired. Led by Sam Solomon and Father John Culmer, blacks voted in record numbers in the election. Courtesy UPI/Corbis-Bettmann.

record numbers. On election day in 1939, under heavy police protection led by Chief H. Leslie Quigg, nearly a thousand black voters went to the polls, marking the first time in Miami's history that blacks had made a concerted effort to register and vote. Although there was some internal squabbling among black leaders concerning who should take credit for the successful effort, it had been supported by a number of black and white leaders as well as by the *Miami Herald*.

In the 1940s the whites-only Democratic primary came under severe scrutiny by the federal courts. The United States Supreme Court ruled as unconstitutional the exclusion of blacks from the Texas primary, spelling doom for the continuing exclusion of blacks from primary elections in Florida as well as other southern states. In 1944 the black political dam in Florida first broke, although haltingly, in Tallahassee. In that year, six blacks were allowed to vote on the Democratic ticket at one Tallahassee precinct, while at another precinct three blacks were refused the right to vote.

The next year a group of Miami blacks protested to the governor that any legislation preventing them from voting in Democratic primaries would be a violation of their constitutional rights. This particular protest was prompted by a study being conducted by a committee under the direction of Florida attorney general, J. Tom Watson. The study pondered what to do about the Texas rulings, which apparently granted blacks the right to vote in Florida's Democratic primaries.

Blacks had good reason to be wary of Watson. His search for ways to include blacks in the primary did not result from enlightenment on his part. As Florida's top lawyer, he had fought a losing battle against black voter participation. Assuming that the committee was seeking ways to get around the court ruling, the protest group's letter declared that any legislative proposal the committee might make for that purpose would be an error. Actually, Watson made three proposals, one of which allowed blacks to vote in the Democratic party's primaries but at segregated polling places. In July 1945 Watson arranged a joint meeting between the Florida Democratic party's executive committee and a black organization, the Progressive Voters League of Florida, in an effort to avert any friction from blacks voting in the party primary.

By 1945, the national Democratic party leadership had seen the handwriting on the wall and, being desperately afraid of Republican domination of the black vote in the South, was making friendly gestures to blacks for the first time. Candidates for the Miami City Commission appeared before black voters for the first time in April 1945, acknowledging blacks as voters and making campaign promises such as improving sidewalks, trash collection, and building conditions.[12]

On January 22, 1946, the Democratic party of Florida made history when members of the party's state executive committee, without discussion and with only a few dissenters, voted to eliminate the barrier to Negro voting in the party's primaries. For the first time since 1904, the resolution fixing membership qualifications did not specify that the primaries were limited to white people. The committee did, however, resolve to provide separate voting boxes for blacks and whites.

The next day the *Miami Herald* tried to put a positive light on the idea of blacks voting:

> When the Supreme Court ruled that Negroes had the right to vote in Texas, it set a precedent for other states to soon follow. Among them is Florida. While this may have angered many Florida Democrats who were trying to block the resolution, the decision should also be viewed positively. It may allow various leaders in the negro community the opportunity to advance the lot of the colored people. And so, instead of having a disastrous impact, the bill awarding Negroes their voting rights must be seen as a step towards reaching the ideals of a true democracy.[13]

The registration of black voters in Dade County soon got underway in earnest. Election officials prepared themselves for a record-breaking turnout by blacks, anticipating that a large proportion of the fifty-seven hundred blacks registered as Republicans would switch their party affiliation. The names of black voters were kept separate, however, in case the Dade party leadership decided to follow the state committee's recommendation for separate balloting.

According to M. Athalie Range, in the years before the civil rights movement there were two men who were true political activists. One was funeral director Sam Solomon, who was active during the Culmer years. Another was T. R. Harrison, an uneducated preacher who did not have a congregation and simply went around preaching wherever he was allowed. Range remembers him as being very conscious of the politics of the day. "He had a little group that he tried to educate concerning voting. About 1948 they drove him away from the polls.

98. Political activist Sam Solomon, who helped to get blacks to participate in the 1939 Miami elections in the face of strong opposition from the Ku Klux Klan. M. Athalie Range described Solomon, who was also a writer and commentator on issues affecting blacks during the 1930s and 1940s, as one of the city's most unappreciated early black leaders. Courtesy Historical Museum of Southern Florida.

He was beaten several times and received quite a few scars on his face." Harrison at that time was working for the Afro-American Insurance Company. "His early efforts at building black political awareness have never been recognized," said Range.[14]

In the 1950s black voters became more important to political candidates as black voter registration and participation in Dade County politics increased. By the early 1960s the Crusade for Voters' goal was registering sixty-five thousand black voters in Dade County. They succeeded in boosting the rolls from about twenty thousand to thirty thousand. While the committee was nonpartisan, it got some of the credit for the heavy black support given to Claude Pepper in his successful race for the 1962 Democratic congressional nomination.

By the mid–1960s, a black political machine had emerged in Miami. Its inventor and driving force was a rotund and well-liked black man called Uncle Charlie Hadley, who became a political legend. He was immediately recognizable at any political gathering: standing five foot seven with a 250-pound frame and his trademark, striped suspenders. Charles Rudolph Hadley of Miami was a powerful political leader in Florida for more than three decades. During those years, to court the black vote was to court Uncle Charlie. He delivered the black vote in city and county contests as well as in state and national elections.

Above: 99. Blacks lining up to register to vote as Democrats. Blacks were not allowed to register as Democratic party members in Florida until 1946. Prior to that time, the vast majority of black voters in Florida and in Dade County were registered as Republicans. Courtesy Historical Museum of Southern Florida.

Left: 100. Joe Lang Kershaw, a Dade County public school teacher and the first black person to be elected to the Florida House of Representatives since Reconstruction. Courtesy Historical Museum of Southern Florida.

Operation Big Vote, which Hadley started in the late 1950s in Miami, was the first and most formidable black voter registration and vote-gathering apparatus in Dade County. For more than twenty-five years, Hadley led voter registration drives, door-to-door campaigns and get-out-the-vote efforts in Dade County's black communities. Hadley was an early supporter of Miami Congressman Claude Pepper in Pepper's initial campaigns. His nephew, Howard Gary, became Miami's first black city manager in the late 1970s. Hadley raised Gary from his boyhood and was his mentor during Gary's tenure in political life.

Born January 8, 1918, in rural Cairo, Georgia, Hadley was one of eleven children. In order to obtain a better education, he left home to live with his uncle in Tallahassee but had to drop out of school for long periods in order to support himself. He nevertheless finished high school in 1936 at the age of twenty-three. In 1940 Hadley graduated from Florida A & M University and three years later moved to Miami with his wife, Ella. He began working with the Dade County Health Department, from which he retired in 1962.

Hadley was elected the unofficial mayor of black Miami in 1959 through a postcard poll, and he took that responsibility seriously.

101. Representative Gwendolyn Sawyer Cherry, daughter of Miami pioneer physician Dr. W. B. Sawyer, became the first black woman to serve in the Florida state legislature. She was killed in an automobile accident on the Florida State University campus on February 7, 1979. She was succeeded by Carrie P. Meek. Courtesy William B. Sawyer Jr.

102. Congresswoman Carrie P. Meek. Meek was elected to the U.S. House of Representatives in 1986, becoming the first black person from Dade County to be elected to Congress. In 1982 she was the first black woman to be elected to the Florida senate. She formerly worked as an administrator at Miami-Dade Community College. Courtesy Carrie P. Meek.

103. United States District Court Judge Wilkie D. Ferguson Jr., the first black person from Dade County to serve as a federal judge. Judge Ferguson grew up in Opa-Locka. He is married to Dade County Commissioner Betty Ferguson. Courtesy Wilkie D. Ferguson Jr.

Housing and health-care issues remained close to his heart until his death in 1985 at the age of seventy-two. A public library in Liberty City, a park, the Hadley Gardens apartment complex, and Charles Hadley Elementary School were named in his honor.

The first beneficiary of black political activism was Dade County public schoolteacher Joe Lang Kershaw, who was elected to the Florida House of Representatives in 1968. Another early beneficiary was Gwendolyn Sawyer Cherry, daughter of Dr. William B. Sawyer, an early Miami physician. Gwendolyn Cherry was one of Dade County's most successful black women. She is noted as having been the first black woman elected to the Florida House of Representatives. She was also an attorney, an educator, and an author.

Cherry was born in Miami in 1923 and continued to call Miami home throughout her life. She served in the state legislature from 1970 until she died in a one-vehicle accident on the Florida State University campus in Tallahassee on February 7, 1979. She was fifty-seven years old.

Between 1965 and the present an ever-increasing number of black public officials have been elected or appointed in Dade County. One Dade County black, attorney Jesse J. McCrary Jr., was appointed Florida secretary of state. He served from 1978 to 1979. Another black man, Howard Gary, became Miami's first black city manager in 1981. He served until 1984, when he was fired by the city commission. The move to oust Gary was led by Mayor Maurice Ferre, who paid the price for it. Although blacks had supported Ferre heavily in previous elections, they abandoned him in the election following the Gary firing, ending his tenure as Miami mayor. Although Ferre had joined M. Athalie Range, the first black on the commission, in pushing through many advances for blacks, Ferre was unfairly accused of having racial motivations during his confrontation with Gary. In fact, blacks in Miami were greatly empowered under his leadership as mayor.

The black vote in Dade County became increasingly important in the decades following black enrollment in the Democratic party in the late 1940s. In 1957 whites were about evenly divided on the controversial proposal to establish a supergovernment that would take over many of the functions of the cities in Dade County. However, with the promise of jobs and empowerment, blacks signed on and voted heavily for the new metro government system. The issue barely passed in a hotly contested election. In the early 1970s blacks also saved the proposal to build a rapid-rail mass transit system in Dade County. Again, blacks voted heavily for the system, while whites and Hispanics were about evenly divided. This time, too, it was the promise of jobs and empowerment that carried the day with black voters.

In the 1990s Dade's black vote was enhanced when a local court ordered the Dade County Commission to organize itself into single-member districts. This meant that each county commissioner would represent a specific area of the county and would no longer be required to run for office countywide. The matter had been pressed by a group of black and Hispanic candidates who sued the county on this issue. Since minority candidates tended to raise far less money in their campaigns than white candidates, the single-member district decision was seen as a boost to the electability of minority candidates. As a result of single-member districts, black representation on the county commission was significantly increased in the early 1990s. Today four blacks serve on the commission. The seats on the Dade County School Board were similarly reorganized in 1996, leading to the election of an additional black school board member in September of that year.

In 1996 there were 760,353 registered voters in Dade County: 318,912 were white non-Hispanics, Hispanics accounted for 275,034 of the total, blacks numbered 155,851, and 10,556 were listed as "other." Following the national trend, the overwhelming majority of black voters in Dade County are registered as Democrats. In 1996 there were 137,796 black Democrats, as compared to 7,169 black Republicans and 10,605 blacks with no party affiliation.

Tables 5.1 through 5.6 illustrate the blacks elected or appointed to public office since 1965.

In September 1996 the Federal Bureau of Investigation and the United States Attorney announced that three well-known blacks were involved in a grandiose kickback and bribery scheme. Two were sitting elected

Table 5.1. Blacks elected to Florida State House of Representatives

Name	First elected
Joe Lang Kershaw	1968
Gwendolyn Sawyer Cherry	1970
Carrie P. Meek	1979
John "Gus" Plummer	1980
James C. Burke	1982
Willie Logan, Jr.	1982
Jefferson Reaves, Sr.	1983
Darryl L. Jones	1990
Larcenia J. Bullard	1992
James Bush III	1992
Kendrick B. Meek	1994

Table 5.2. Blacks elected to Florida State Senate

Name	First elected
Carrie P. Meek	1982
William "Bill" Turner	1992
Darryl L. Jones	1992

Table 5.3. Blacks elected to Dade County Commmission

Name	First elected
Earl J. Carroll	1968
Edward T. Graham	1972
Neal Adams	1976
Barbara M. Carey	1979
Arthur Earle Teele Jr.	1988
James C. Burke	1993
Betty Ferguson	1993
Dennis Moss	1993

Table 5.4. Blacks elected to selected city commissions

Name	City	First elected
Athalie Range	Miami	1965
Rev. Edward T. Graham	Miami	1979
Father Theodore Gibson	Miami	1972
Leroy "Spike" Gibson	South Miami	1968
Albert W. Tresvant, Sr.	Opa-Locka	1970
Juanita Smith	Florida City	1980
Otis Tommy Wallace	Florida City	1980
Miller James Dawkins	Miami	1981
Roscoe Warren	Homestead	1981
Willie Logan, Jr.	Opa-Locka	1980
Danny Brown	South Miami	1986
Laura Saunders	Florida City	1986
Ollie Bell Kelley	Opa-Locka	1986
George Lipkins	Opa-Locka	1986
Helen L. Miller	Opa-Locka	1986
Mary E. Allen	Opa-Locka	1986
Israel Andrews	Florida City	1988
Steven A. Barrett	Opa-Locka	1988
Betty Banks	South Miami	1989
Eugene Berry	Florida City	1990
Daisy M. Black	El Portal	1993
Tommy Dorsett	Florida City	1992

Table 5.5. Blacks elected mayor, selected cities

Name	City	First elected
Albert W. Tresvant, Sr.	Opa-Locka	1975
Willie F. Logan, Jr.	Opa-Locka	1980
Juanita Smith	Florida City	1984
Helen L. Miller	Opa-Locka	1982
John Riley	Opa-Locka	1984
Otis Tommy Wallace	Florida City	1984
Robert E. Ingram	Opa-Locka	1986
Daisy M. Black	El Portal	1994
Steven A. Barrett	Opa-Locka	1990

Table 5.6. Blacks elected to Dade County school board

Name	First elected
William "Bill" Turner	1971
Joyce H. Knox	1978
Frederica Wilson	1992
Solomon Stinson	1996

officials, Miami City Commissioner Miller Dawkins and Metro-Dade County Commissioner James Burke. Also implicated was Miami's former city manager, Howard Gary. Dawkins was accused of accepting a twenty-five-thousand-dollar bribe from Unisys, a large computer company that had been awarded a $20 million contract to provide computers to the Miami Police Department. James Burke and Howard Gary were allegedly involved in a kickback scheme involving the sale of millions of dollars' worth of county bonds. Burke and Gary have denied wrongdoing, and neither had been charged at the time of this printing. But Miller Dawkins pled guilty to accepting a bribe and was sentenced to more than eighteen months in prison and fined heavily.

Dawkins's seat on the city commission was filled by the appointment of Richard Dunn, a black minister who ran unsuccessfully for the city commission just weeks before the scandal broke. Reverend Dunn tried desperately to hold on to the traditional "black seat" on the Miami City Commission but lost it to a Cuban-American. The November 1996 race for the seat put Dunn in an ethnically tinged political struggle between the black and Cuban American communities. Some prominent Cuban Americans supported Dunn and pleaded with their fellow Cubans to help keep black representation on the commission. They failed: Dunn got only 13 percent of the Hispanic vote in the race; blacks gave Dunn over 90 percent of their vote. White Miamians also preferred Dunn. But the political tide had turned forever in Miami. Blacks and whites will eventually lose representation on the commission altogether unless some form of single-member district representation can be instituted.

The Desegregation of Housing in Dade County

The federal courts in the 1940s began to rule clearly that racial segregation in American life was wrong. This included racial segregation in housing, especially in public housing. In postwar Dade County the

104. Caught in a public-corruption scandal called Operation Greenpalm, Miami City Commissioner Miller Dawkins, left, in September 1996 enters the Miami federal building with his long-time friend T. Willard Fair, head of Miami's Urban League, to answer charges of accepting a bribe. He later pleaded guilty to the charges. Courtesy *Miami Herald*.

demand for housing increased significantly, in that a considerable number of people, black and white, in the armed services and in war-related jobs, moved to south Florida during and after the Second World War. As blacks began to exert pressure to move into what had been historically white neighborhoods, white resistance was immediate, vocal, and sometimes violent.

In June 1941 a large group of irate white Coconut Grove residents protested to the city's planning board about the encroachment of the Grove's black population into the white section of the town. Their complaints came after the Dinner Key Realty Company asked for a zoning change which would have allowed the company to build two homes for blacks in the traditionally white section of the Grove. In a theme that would be heard loud and often in Dade County and elsewhere, whites claimed their property values would drop if blacks were allowed to move in. The Miami Building Department confirmed that permits had been issued for two black residences, but both permits awaited a final decision by the city planning board.[15]

The chairman of the planning board promised that a definite line would be established dividing the white and black sections. Dinner Key Realty reported that it had approached every white person affected by the project and offered to buy him or her out at reasonable prices. Victor Griley, attorney for Dinner Key Realty, promised that if the property was rezoned for blacks, the company proposed to build a dividing wall similar to the one constructed by the federal government to separate blacks in the Liberty Square Housing Project from their white neighbors. Parts of that wall still stand.

The Miami City Commission ultimately revoked the request by the two black families for building permits in the white Grove, in effect killing the Dinner Key Realty proposal.[16] The two lots involved in the dispute were located at the southeast corner of Hibiscus Street and Florida Avenue. This area today is virtually all black.

The Ku Klux Klan was an active element in white resistance. In August 1941 over five hundred white residents of northwest Dade, some carrying banners, arrived at the Dade County courthouse in private cars and chartered buses to oppose a proposed 250-acre black settlement on Northwest Seventh Avenue. The courthouse was overflowing with protesters carrying petitions with over twelve hundred signatures. Among the protesters were members of the John B. Gordon Klan Number 24, which had reportedly participated in a demonstration a few nights earlier in which crosses were burned. The zoning board, after hearing all the protests, refused to rezone the disputed property.

Despite white resistance, there was tremendous pressure on the city and county to rid themselves of black slum housing. In the early 1940s the housing authority was ready to spend $5 million on black housing projects, but continued white resistance made it difficult to find acceptable locations for the construction of public housing for blacks. Black housing areas in Goulds and Perrine on the west side of the Florida East Coast Railroad were unopposed, so these two areas were approved. Three other areas were approved for low-cost housing projects in Homestead, Goulds, and west of Red Road between Northwest Fourteenth and Twenty-fifth Streets.

In June 1944 white residents of Coconut Grove again protested a proposed rezoning. This time the proposal was made by the Federal

Housing Authority for construction of fifty duplex dwellings for black war workers. Although many protesters denied racial motives, they clearly opposed blacks moving into the white neighborhood. The request for reclassification of the property was ultimately withdrawn.[17]

There were problems in far northwest Dade County, too. On May 9, 1945, Opa-Locka voters were just six votes shy of unanimously approving an ordinance restricting black businesses and residences to an area east of Twenty-second Avenue. In Miami Springs it was much the same. In November 1945, after Circuit Judge Stanley Milledge outlawed housing segregation, the Miami Springs city council came to the support of property owners opposing the ruling. Two black couples, Milton and Willie Mae Coleman, and Jack and Claudia Wilson, were arrested and charged with violating the county's zoning regulations when they attempted to move into a Brownsville area zoned for whites.

In May 1946 the municipal planning board recommended that a twenty-four-acre tract in Coconut Grove be used by the Miami Housing Authority to provide low-rent housing for blacks. The planning board, attempting to offer "suitable protection" to white Grove residents, recommended that a wall and a seventy-four-foot buffer strip be constructed between the white and black sections.[18] Parts of this wall remain standing today.

In this vein, a plan to build low-income housing in the northwest section, which had been approved in early 1946, ran into fire from whites. More than three hundred property owners organized to fight the proposed development of 744 acres for black housing. Whites even considered establishing their own township to ensure that the area remained closed to blacks.

In April 1946, the Florida Supreme Court issued a historic ruling. Dade County's power to segregate black residential districts, which had been granted by a special act of the 1937 legislature, was ruled illegal. In a unanimous opinion, the court declared that it found nothing to authorize zoning out any group solely on the basis of color or race. It should be noted that the Florida Supreme Court was not trailblazing; it was merely following the lead of the federal courts, which had begun to rule that racially segregated housing was unconstitutional. As a result of this decision, charges were dismissed against the two black couples who had been arrested in the Brownsville dispute.[19]

In May 1946, the *Miami Herald* weighed in on the black housing question:

Now that elections have passed, it is once again vital that Miami finds a suitable solution to one of its most urgent problems, the negro housing situation. . . . [Legislators] must seek new ways of improving the living conditions of the Negroes, as well as ease the objections of white residents. Our negro problem is the white man's responsibility. It has, and continues, to grow more acute each year. There is no issue of White Supremacy, nor social equality involved. It is a matter of self-preservation, decency and humane conduct.[20]

In another editorial in July 1946, the *Miami Herald* revisited the issue. Even more than in its May piece, the paper laid the responsibility for Miami's slum problems squarely in the hands of whites:

Miami's downtown negro section is a standing disgrace to this community. This statement defies challenge or contradiction. This responsibility rests wholly and solely on the white population of metropolitan Miami. This, too, is beyond questioning or dispute. The negro is not permitted to establish himself at will under the social system that is maintained here.

The problem is for our white citizens to solve entirely. The solution of this pressing problem, however, devolves upon our officials. Solving [the problem] must be done in an orderly fashion, conformable to the realities of the situation. The responsibility is ultimately in the hands of those charged with the final determination and decision.[21]

By the late 1940s whites in Brownsville and other traditionally white neighborhoods were moving out as the inevitable expansion of the black population enveloped entire northwest neighborhoods. Because of continued white opposition and in spite of the state supreme court ruling only months earlier, in 1947 the Miami City Commission again rejected a plan to expand the black section of Coconut Grove.

One of the pivotal events in the advancement toward equal access to housing took place in the late 1950s when Frank Legree, a black man, bought a house on Northwest Fifty-fifth Terrace in an all-white section of town. Legree was purchasing the home for his mother, who was moving to Miami from Knoxville, Tennessee. Legree had been able to purchase the home because of block-busting tactics by white realtors. These realtors knew that there were growing pressures for black housing. They also knew that panicked whites would accept

105. Alley view, looking north between Fourth and Fifth Avenues at about Thirteenth
or Fourteenth Street in Colored Town, circa 1930. By the 1930s and 1940s living
conditions in Colored Town were at their worst. Pressure mounted to find new
housing areas for blacks. Courtesy Romer Collection: Miami-Dade Public Library.

unrealistically low prices for their houses as they moved out en-masse
when a neighborhood was desegregated. And finally, the realtors knew
they could quickly sell the abandoned homes to blacks at inflated prices.
Thus, a real estate bonanza evolved, stimulated by greed and propelled by racial fears. Blacks broke out of their traditional residential
boundaries, not because of egalitarian concerns on the part of whites,
but because some white realtors decided to stimulate business for themselves by forcing racial change in some neighborhoods.

The Legree move provoked such outrage among whites in the vicinity that some even took to picketing the house with signs reading, "We
want this nigger moved" and "whites only." As the Legree contro-
versy simmered, the local branch of the Ku Klux Klan became aroused
and its statewide leaders became involved.

The Klan involvement became known to G. E. Graves, who paid a white man, H. Shaffer, to join the local Klan group as a spy. Graves, who as noted earlier had often represented civil rights causes in the courts, met secretly with Shaffer. One night, in hushed tones, Shaffer told Graves that the Klan planned to ride against the Legree house the next night, that a cross would be burned, and that the house was to be set to the torch. Shaffer said that Klavern members had drawn straws to see which ten men would do the deed and that he had been one of the ten. Graves took Shaffer to the home of State Attorney Richard (Dick) Gerstein, who was skeptical until Graves produced Shaffer. With an admitted conspirator in his pocket, Gerstein, with Graves and Shaffer in tow, went to see the chief of police, Walter Headley. Chief Headley launched into a verbal attack on Graves for stirring up trouble; but faced with Shaffer's self-incrimination and the active involvement of the state attorney, the chief was moved to set a trap for the Klan at the Legree house the following night.

Graves next went secretly to the media. Notified of the planned Klan attack on the Legree home and the trap being laid by police, a number of news reporters and at least one television crew were sworn to secrecy and joined the covert operation. Thus, a large contingent of police, media, and others privy to the operation, including Graves, hid themselves in the bushes near the Legree house.

Late that night a truck carrying several white men and a huge wooden cross turned onto Fifty-fifth Terrace. The truck stopped at the Legree house. In the quiet of the night, white men planted the Klan's cross on the lawn of the home. Suddenly, the police popped out of hiding, yelling "Halt! Police!" With a television camera whirring and microphones open, the police arrested the Klan members, including Shaffer, who was released later. With this, the demonstrations against the Legrees ended.[22]

In the early 1950s, relocation of blacks anywhere other than into black areas was still fiercely resisted. According to Dr. John O. Brown, a white man named Fred Hockett was a leading opponent of racial integration in Dade County. He was hardly alone. When Overtown blacks tried to move into an all-white area called Carver Village in 1951, they were greeted by explosions of dynamite. On the evening of September 23, 1951, a hundred pounds of dynamite exploded behind an unoccupied sixteen-unit apartment house in the northwest sixty-eight hundred block of Tenth Avenue in Carver Village. The bombing caused great agitation in the community, even among some whites. The culprits were never found.

According to Florida historian Stetson Kennedy, the FBI refused to investigate the Carver bombings on the grounds that such incidents were not a violation of federal civil rights laws when citizens were not in their homes or places of worship at the time of the attack. The Department of Justice agreed to investigate only the damage done to mailboxes by the blasts.

Since the 1960s racial segregation in Dade County housing has become far less apparent than in previous decades. Today there is a notable trend toward desegregation of housing in Dade County. According to the 1990 census, the process of housing desegregation is moving more quickly in Dade County than it is in other parts of the state and nation. The apparent desegregation may, however, reflect a tendency of Caribbean-born blacks and Hispanics, many of whom are black, to

106. Carver Village apartment building after bombing. On the evening of September 23, 1951, a one-hundred-pound dynamite bomb exploded behind this unoccupied apartment house in an all-white area called Carver Village. The bombing was meant to discourage blacks from moving in. Courtesy Historical Museum of Southern Florida.

integrate traditionally white neighborhoods rather than native-born black Americans moving into formerly all-white neighborhoods. Nonetheless, despite some relative improvement in housing desegregation, in 1990 the vast majority of Dade County's black population continued to reside in the northwest section of the county, with heavy concentrations in the Overtown, Allapattah, Liberty City, Brownsville, West Little River, and Opa-Locka areas.[23]

Housing discrimination continued to be a problem in Dade County into the late 1990s. In November 1996 a housing discrimination suit in Kendall in southwest Dade County was settled in favor of the black plaintiffs who complained that a Kendall property owner had refused to rent to them because they were black. The plaintiffs received over $1 million.

Other Desegregation in Dade County

As was evident in the move to obtain their own public beach, blacks in Dade County began their struggle for civil rights very tentatively, first demanding separate but equal facilities and then, following favorable opinions from the federal courts on the rights of African Americans, threatening to use public facilities reserved for whites only. Such was the case with the publicly owned golf course near Miami Springs, which was reserved for whites.

In 1949 fourteen blacks calling themselves the Cosmopolitan Golf Club, including Elmer A. Ward, *Miami Times* publisher Garth Reeves, Joseph Rice, and a black lawyer named John D. Johnson, showed up at the links. They were permitted to play, but the city attempted to curtail full use by offering restricted access in the future. With G. E. Graves as their attorney, the black group threatened court action. City officials suggested that at least one day a week be set aside for blacks to use the new golf course. They offered blacks access to the golf course on the day that the links were usually closed anyway for maintenance and watering purposes. Blacks rejected the offer and sued the city. The Florida Supreme Court upheld the city's right to keep the course segregated, but Graves appealed in federal court. In October 1950 the United States Supreme Court handed Miami officials a summary slap in the face. The Court held unanimously that Miami's rule denying blacks unrestricted playing privileges on the municipal golf course was unconstitutional. Without even hearing the city's defense, the Court vacated the Florida Supreme Court decision and sent the case back to

Tallahassee for reconsideration. Subsequently, blacks were able to use the public golf course in Miami without incident.

Access to jobs was also a target of early civil rights activity in Dade County. According to G. E. Graves, in the 1950s whites and blacks involved in the building trades agreed that whites would work on jobs in white areas and that blacks would work on jobs in the black areas. This was considered to be a good arrangement at the time, except that there was little or no work to be done in the black areas, while the downtown section and white residential communities were expanding. By their own agreement, blacks sat on the sidelines.

As the black population grew in the postwar period and as blacks were being pushed out of Colored Town, the cheap two- and three-story apartment buildings, now called concrete monsters, began to appear in black sections of Dade County. Under the agreement between black and white building contractors, this should have meant plenty of construction jobs for blacks; it did not turn out that way. White contractors hired white plumbers, painters, and bricklayers to build these structures in black areas. The contractors argued that they were hiring whites because they had to employ union workers. Since blacks were not allowed to join most labor unions, this pretext effectively froze them out of jobs. Eventually, a group of black plumbers asked Graves to help them organize their own labor unions to avoid this dilemma. Unionization would also help them investigate the claim that white contractors paid city inspectors to deny licenses to blacks. Graves's involvement was a major step toward the breakdown of racial barriers in Dade County trade unions and thus to the economic improvement of blacks in the construction trades.

Even though Graves ultimately lost the federal suit against Miami's building department, the city soon started giving licenses to black plumbers. Graves was also instrumental in the formation of unions for black painters and workers in other construction trades. By the 1960s, blacks were being admitted to most local trade unions.

Prior to the removal of racial restrictions on the use of public transportation in the South, it was customary and legally required for blacks to sit in the rear while whites sat in the front. On June 7, 1956, the local chapter of the NAACP demanded an end to racial segregation on buses in Dade County. The organization announced the possibility of a boycott of the Miami Transit Company, a potentially disastrous move in light of the large number of blacks riding the buses to work.

The move came as a shock to whites since there had been few incidents on Miami buses such as those that had triggered boycotts in Tallahassee and in Montgomery, Alabama.

According to the *Miami Times,* the policy of seating whites from the front and blacks from the rear had been loosely enforced in Miami. In fact, seating was on a first-come, first-served basis; a black person was not required to give up his or her seat for a white person. Yet, in separate incidents in Miami, three blacks were arrested when they refused to move to the rear of the bus. Two of them, Bessie Kurbo and Rudolph Reid, were charged under the city's disorderly-conduct laws but not under the state's segregation laws.

The Reid case attracted considerable attention. Reid, a nineteen-year-old black man, refused to move to the rear of a Miami Transit bus in June 1956 and was found guilty of disorderly conduct by breach of the peace. Reid was represented by G. E. Graves. He was fined fifty dollars by Judge Francis Sobieski of the municipal court. In passing sentence, the judge said a simple incident like this could lead to further trouble between blacks and whites. Judge Sobieski also stated that if charges had been brought under the state's segregation laws, he might have thrown them out as unconstitutional. Graves said he would not appeal the ruling, but indicated that a suit testing the validity of Florida's bus-segregation laws would be filed in federal court.

In his closing arguments, Thomas O'Connell, assistant city attorney, said the incident involving Reid was quite obviously provoked and invoked by the NAACP. He added that Reid deliberately sat in a section of the bus where he was not supposed to sit, and therefore he was guilty of conduct that could lead to a race riot. Reid denied that the incident was planned.

In 1957 another incident occurred. Charles Nesbitt, a twenty-year-old Opa-Locka black man, suffered a lacerated face when he was struck with a money changer by a white bus driver after refusing to move from the front section of a Miami bus. In the end, it was Nesbitt who received a jail sentence for breach of the peace and profanity. The bus driver was not charged in the incident.

Bus segregation in Miami came to an end in 1957, when a federal judge ruled that bus segregation laws and ordinances in Florida were unconstitutional and therefore unenforceable. The ruling was handed down by Judge Emmett Choate, the judge who had ruled that segregation of the City of Miami's golf course was unconstitutional.

Soon after winning their way to the front of the buses, Dade County blacks took the drivers' seats. It is readily apparent to today's Dade County bus passengers that an inordinate number of the drivers are black. This is no accident. It is the product of a strike in the late 1950s by white bus drivers against the privately owned bus company then serving the county. To break the strike, management invited blacks to drive. A key figure in the events was, again, attorney G. E. Graves.

Because Graves had been active in the formation of black labor unions, an official of the bus company asked him to send over some black drivers to replace the striking whites. Graves was not comfortable with the thought of strikebreaking, but in the interest of obtaining a foothold for blacks as bus drivers, he got several black men to accept immediately the vacated drivers' slots. The protracted strike was never effectively ended, since Dade County later purchased the bus company and started to operate the public buses. Many white drivers never returned to work. In 1990 Graves reflected upon the strike: "Those white drivers are still out on strike, and it's been more than thirty-five years."

The desegregation assault on Crandon Park, the largest whites-only beach, began in 1958 when CORE decided to challenge Dade County on the exclusion of blacks from the park. The group had determined that there was no law against blacks using the park. Father Theodore R. Gibson volunteered to go before the Dade County Commission to get the county's official position on the matter.

On the day Gibson went to the commission meeting, twenty to thirty CORE members assembled in the office of the NAACP on Third Avenue in Overtown. They were prepared to go to Crandon Park but agreed to wait to learn the outcome of Gibson's appearance before the commission. The CORE group was in constant contact with Gibson by telephone and knew that his appearance had been put off all morning. Shortly after noon the members lost their patience, and led by Dr. John O. Brown, they piled into their cars and headed for Crandon Park.

When they arrived, they caught the county attendants at the beach by surprise and demanded to use the bathhouse. When the attendants hesitated, they used the facilities anyway. Several Metro-Dade police cruisers arrived. Apparently under orders to do nothing, the police made no arrests. "From that day on," said Brown, "black people have been using Crandon Park."[24]

The Miami branch of the NAACP launched a drive against racial segregation in public swimming pools. Father Theodore R. Gibson announced the initiative just days after several black women were refused admission to the city-operated Manor Park Pool.

After members of the NAACP met with city officials seeking unlimited use of all tax-supported recreational facilities, City Manager Ira Willard ordered all city facilities opened to blacks. His decision was not based on goodwill toward blacks, but on City Attorney William Pallot's assurance that no valid law could bar blacks from the publicly owned facilities. Nevertheless, the city commission reversed this decision just twenty-four hours later. During Miami's one day of integration, six blacks used two city-operated pools.

G. E. Graves and Father Gibson, representing the Miami branch of the NAACP, met with city officials. Graves handed them citations of eleven federal court decisions stemming from the Equal Protection Amendment to the Constitution in an effort to avert a lawsuit, but it was to no avail.

In September 1960, a federal judge ruled that Miami could not deny entrance to blacks at Manor Park Pool. The suit—the first one affecting the city's swimming facilities—had been filed by the NAACP as Graves had promised. Although only Manor Park had been mentioned in the suit, the ruling applied to all city-owned facilities. A federal appeals court later upheld this lower court's ruling.

In April of the following year, about one hundred blacks protested strongly when they were denied admittance to a dance at Bayfront Park Auditorium. The benefit dance was sponsored by the local chapter of the Heart Association, and it included guest appearances by two black singers, Johnny Mathis and Damita Jo. Heart Association officials and Miami's mayor, Robert King High, stated that they had no objections to blacks attending the dance. However, the committee of disc jockeys responsible for the event decided to keep the affair segregated.[25]

Ultimately, city officials agreed that blacks could not be denied access to any public recreational facility, including Bay Front Park. By the early 1960s all such facilities had been desegregated.

The Miami civil rights movement was marked by several significant events leading to the gradual breakdown of the city's long history of racially segregated public eating places. Even though department stores in Miami did a large amount of business with blacks, none indicated any intent to change their policies. According to Dr. John O. Brown, blacks were simply refused service and no store wanted to be first to break with the tradition. The first demonstration against segregated lunch counters in Dade County was led by CORE in 1959 during its national convention, which was being held at the Sir John Hotel in Miami. The group demonstrated at Jackson's-Byron's lunch counter in downtown Miami. Several members, most from out of town, were arrested. After the CORE demonstration, blacks thought they had worked out an amicable solution with store owners. "They [the store owners] said they would be willing to try it if we all would work together," said Brown. "Then the media asked us what had been accomplished. We told them that it had been agreed that blacks would be served at the lunch counters. The media then went to the store owners and asked them if it was true that blacks were going to be served at their lunch counters. Fearful of losing white customers, they denied that an agreement had been reached. That's when the Miami CORE chapter instituted the lunch counter sit-ins."[26]

To gather support for their drive against local discrimination, CORE invited an Alabama boycott leader, the Reverend Fred L. Shuttlesworth, a nationally known civil rights leader and close associate of Dr. Martin Luther King Jr., to speak in Miami. In early September 1959, the Birmingham minister spoke in front of more than six hundred people, including about one hundred whites, at the Greater Bethel A.M.E. Church. Along with other speakers, he urged local citizens to support the committee in its use of nonviolence as a means of combating racial segregation.[27]

On March 11, 1960, when seven black clergymen led by the Reverend Edward T. Graham attempted a sit-in demonstration at the lunchroom of Burdines downtown store, the police denied them entrance. The police department had been alerted to the planned demonstration and had ordered the arrest of anyone involved. After talking with store security and police officers for about thirty minutes, the ministers decided to leave the store.[28] A boycott of downtown stores was subsequently agreed upon at a mass meeting at Mt. Zion Baptist Church. This decision infuriated Mayor Robert King High, who that same day had met with his biracial committee to resolve the sit-in threat. The boycott was postponed, however, to allow officials from the Ministerial Alliance, a black activist group, and CORE, the NAACP, and the City of Miami to meet.

At this point a white man named John Turner entered the picture. According to Brown, he was the most effective white leader during the civil rights period in Miami. "He was a businessman. He got Bob High [Miami's mayor, Robert King High], Hood Bassett of Southeast Bank, and others to start meeting seriously with local black leaders to work something out. From this came the Dade County Community Relations Board." According to Dr. Brown, the blacks who attended these meetings were Father Theodore R. Gibson and Dr. George Simpson, who represented the NAACP; A. D. Moore and Brown himself, who represented CORE; and the Reverend Edward T. Graham, who represented the Ministerial Alliance.

In April 1960 the biracial committee proposed a plan that would allow all stores to open their lunch counters to blacks at the same time. This plan became a reality on August 1, 1960. On that day, three teams of two CORE members each were served lunch at the counters of W. T. Grant, F. W. Woolworth, and S. H. Kress department stores. Other downtown stores, such as Burdines and McCrory's, were to follow. The agreement led Miami to become the first city in Florida to take down racial barriers at lunch counters.

"None of this would have happened had it not been for John Turner," said Brown. "He was a Scotch-Irish man and he knew how to get things done. When he snapped his fingers, Bob High jumped. He got people with clout on that board." According to Brown, Turner exerted tremendous influence in the white business community. "It was John Turner who introduced Maurice Ferre, who would later become Miami's first Hispanic mayor, to the black community. Maurice was just a little boy, still wet behind the ears, but he had political ambition."[29] John Turner died at the height of the civil rights movement.

Brown had special praise for several other white CORE stalwarts who stood up for blacks. These included Ruth Perry, a librarian from Miami Beach who served for many years as CORE secretary; Shirley and Milton Zoloth; Thalia Peters; and Phillip Stern.

According to Brown, two-thirds of the people from CORE who joined the sit-ins were white. "Had it not been for white people, there never would have been a CORE chapter in Miami. Jack Gordon of Miami Beach, who later became a powerful state senator, and his wife, Barbara, were among our most visible supporters." Gordon represented CORE in its negotiations with downtown department store owners during the lunch counter sit-ins. According to Brown, another white man named Leonard Turkel and his wife, Annsheila, were also active in helping the organization deal with the store owners. "He was a businessman who later became chairman of the board of the Overtown Family Health Center," said Brown.

Howard Dixon, a white attorney, represented blacks during the civil rights period in Miami. He also worked with Dr. Brown. Dixon gave the following account of his relations with his white neighbors during his period of activism in Dade County's civil rights movement:

> When we came here I think, for me, there was just no question in my mind that the injustice that was going on around us was unbearable. And I have to say that we were fearless. Nothing frightened us. We were not frightened about our ability to make a living. Maybe it was just stupidity. The danger of it was never anything we thought about. We would fight with friends of ours who would say, "Well, I can't do that. I'm an insurance man. I'll lose all my clients if somebody finds out." And we would have those big arguments all the time.[30]

As downtown lunch counters were being desegregated in early August 1960, a group of eighteen people was arrested for attempting to integrate the lunch counter of Shell City Store, a large department store in Liberty City. The August 18 arrests were unprecedented in the Dade County civil rights movement. Immediately after the demonstration, CORE Chairman A. D. Moore called for a boycott of the huge store. Pickets surrounded the store and handed customers leaflets pointing out CORE's concerns. The objective of the boycott was to persuade customers not to shop at the store until it changed its policies regarding serving blacks at its lunch counter.

CORE also pressed the store management to drop all charges against CORE members who had been arrested in the attempt to desegregate the store. Some of those arrested preferred to remain in jail even though CORE offered to post their bail of one hundred dollars each. On the Monday following the arrests, the defendants pleaded not guilty and asked for a trial without a jury.

Howard Dixon, the head of the Florida Civil Liberties Union, defended the Shell City demonstrators in August 1960. Shell City executives testified at the trial that they asked the racially mixed group to leave because "it would mean loss of business to us to serve mixed groups based on what we believe to be the desire of the majority of the white people of this country." Another white attorney representing the demonstrators, Tobias Simon, argued that there was no constitutional barrier to discrimination by private citizens, but for store executives to use the authority of the state to enforce their private acts of discrimination was unconstitutional.

The eighteen defendants were convicted and placed on probation for one year by Judge George E. Shulz. The matter was settled in September 1962 when the Florida Supreme Court ruled that it was a misdemeanor rather than a felony for a person to refuse to leave a restaurant after being requested to do so by the management. Ultimately, all department store eating facilities in Dade County, including Shell City, were desegregated.

In May 1960 public and staff eating facilities at Jackson Memorial Hospital were peacefully integrated when forty blacks had lunch in the hospital's cafeteria. Henry Wells, spokesman for the hospital's seven hundred black employees, was fired just a few hours after leading the peaceful integration of the cafeteria. Kermit Gates, director of the hospital, denied having fired Wells, a laboratory assistant, for his role in the integration. Gates later explained that Wells, who had been on the job for three weeks, was ineligible for employment in the hospital because he was an army deserter.

The Gibson Case (1963)

In the late 1950s, Miami's NAACP leadership met in a glass-fronted room on Northwest Third Avenue on the third Thursday of every month. At that time, it was one of the most controversial groups in south Florida. The local NAACP's goal was to eliminate all forms of racial segregation by 1963. In asserting this aim, the group claimed to represent the 110,000 blacks in the metropolitan area.

The Reverend Theodore R. Gibson, the organization's leader throughout the turbulent 1960s, estimated the local group to have a membership of one thousand in 1963. His was a new voice. In 1959 he enunciated the group's plan in the *Miami News:* "The NAACP in Miami . . . is perfectly willing to listen to sweet reason in its demands for equality and to work with responsible organizations toward a sensible approach to racial problems—up to a point. . . . We'll appeal to your reason, but when that fails, we'll appeal to your hide."[31]

Early in his tenure as Miami NAACP chapter president, Gibson came to the most crucial confrontation of his public life, one which would ultimately be resolved by the U.S. Supreme Court. It was a conflict rooted in the nation's preoccupation with communists in the 1950s and the concern among politically conservative Americans about communist influence within the civil rights movement.

At the national level, this phenomenon was played out before the brutalizing McCarthy committee (the House Committee on Un-American Activities) under the leadership of Senator Joseph R. McCarthy. Many unwilling and innocent citizens were dragged into hearings before the committee in its search for communists in the American government. Florida's version of the McCarthy committee was the Johns committee of the Florida Senate, named after conservative State Senator Charley Johns. It operated in much the same way as the McCarthy committee did in Washington: by innuendo, public ridicule, and harassment of those targeted in the search for subversives.

In the 1950s, whites who openly supported the NAACP and its goals were at risk of being subjected to the wrath of the Johns committee and their fellow white sympathizers. This made it difficult for the NAACP to publicly help white candidates who were known to be sympathetic to black causes. Gibson understood this. "We realize the danger of waving banners and making speeches in favor of a particular candidate," he explained in a 1959 interview. "The word is put out from the top and it filters down. Our people know how we feel about a candidate. We reward our friends and punish our enemies."

About one-fourth of the members of Miami's NAACP chapter were white, although, according to Gibson, many wished to remain anonymous: "I'd get a note from someone saying, 'Here is a contribution.' I take that to mean the person is with us, but doesn't want a membership. I understand. People have their own problems. . . . Then there is the political aspect. Aspirants to public office have found that the Negro community is a force to be reckoned with. But the office seeker must also consider that he could alienate a large conservative bloc by openly espousing the NAACP."

Many considered the NAACP to be a suspect organization. They believed that the movement for racial desegregation must have been led, or at least influenced, by communists. Both the McCarthy and Johns committees assumed that the NAACP, as the lead organization in the civil rights movement, was a hotbed of subversives. In 1959, the Johns committee demanded that the Miami chapter of the NAACP hand over its membership list to allow the committee to decide if, indeed, communists operated inside the organization. Gibson staunchly refused. He agreed to testify from memory but insisted that he would not give up his organization's records. He and the Reverend Edward T. Graham, the organization's former president, were arrested and charged with contempt of the legislature.

The news coverage of the Johns committee's investigation led to a drop in the membership of the Miami NAACP. By Gibson's account, "A lot of people evidently thought we might be forced to give them up. This drove from the rank-and-file many who feared, with good reason, that exposure of their names would mean economic reprisals. . . . Once these people became convinced that the leadership would go to jail to protect the membership lists, they returned and brought others with them."

Gibson felt this kind of investigation was not only unnecessary but that it ultimately worked to the advantage of genuinely subversive groups. He asserted that the NAACP's organizational machinery made it virtually impossible for a subversive element to gain control, because each candidate for a leadership position had to be nominated by a committee, then screened, and then elected by the membership body. "If the [Johns] committee is sincere about wanting to check on subversive affiliations of our members, it needs only to give us the names of its suspects. We'll throw them out fast," he said.

In his refusal to turn over the membership list, Gibson cited the First and Fourteenth Amendments to the Constitution, which pertain to the right of assembly, the right of association, and the equal protection of the rights of all citizens. Nonetheless, Dade Circuit Court Judge W. May Walker pronounced the two ministers guilty, sentenced them to six months in jail, and fined them twelve hundred dollars each. The convictions enraged black Miami. Gibson and Graham appealed the decision to federal court.

Overnight Gibson and Graham were catapulted to the head of the local civil rights movement. By virtue of their intransigence, they were seen by their supporters as courageous. In New York, the national NAACP office said that the survival of the NAACP in Florida hung in the balance. In Dade County, blacks closed ranks behind the two ministers, raising money to pay their fines. On September 15, 1963, a major rally was held at Overtown's Mount Zion Baptist Church. The *Miami Times* exhorted blacks to fill the church to overflowing:

These men at all times have shown a fearlessness and devotion to the cause of freedom that should be an inspiration to all of us in the Miami area. Their stand for freedom is not only a personal one with them, it is a thing which includes all of us in this area. Their present sentence to six months in jail, plus a fine of $1,200 each (or another six months in jail if the fines are not paid) is only another manifestation of their devotion to the cause of freedom. Lesser men would not have stood as firm and as courageously as these two men have done. Their sentences are evidence of this.[32]

The Gibson case was a classic clash between the individual and the state. A bitterly divided U.S. Supreme Court issued one of its most important decisions during the American civil rights era in February 1963 when the Court, in a five-four decision in favor of the two ministers, concluded that the Johns committee had only a limited right to fish for communists in the membership rolls of nonsubversive organizations. The majority opinion, two concurring opinions, and two dissenting opinions filled forty-eight pages with the clashing views of the nine justices. Justice Arthur Goldberg said there was "an utter failure" to show a connection between the Miami NAACP and subversive activities which was sufficient to justify violating the organization's freedom of association. "The Florida Committee is not seeking to identify subversives," Goldberg wrote; "It is the NAACP itself which is the subject of the investigation. Compelling such an organization to disclose its membership presents . . . a question wholly different from compelling the Communist Party to disclose its own membership." Goldberg called protection of the right of freedom of association "all the more essential when an organization is unpopular with its neighbors. To impose a lesser standard would be inconsistent with the maintenance of those essential conditions basic to our democracy," he wrote.[33]

"I thank my God," Gibson replied. "The NAACP, as I have said many times, is not communistic; has never been on the attorney general's list, nor any other subversive list, and I feel and believe that it never will be. The NAACP is simply a good American organization."[34]

The desegregation of public education did not come easily to Florida or to Dade County. The response in Tallahassee and at the Dade County School Board was to resist the 1954 *Brown v. Board of Education* U.S. Supreme Court decision, which ordered a halt to racial segregation of public schools. Many gradualist approaches were introduced and discarded as blacks and their white allies in the movement brought more and more pressure on the school system to integrate. Finally, with no remaining legal options available, in late 1959 the Dade County School Board relented and announced that black students would be admitted to Orchard Villa Elementary School the following school year. The desegregation of higher education proceeded with somewhat less resistance.

Throughout the desegregation process, blacks have had some allies. This should not be forgotten or dismissed. Some whites fought for black rights in housing, public facilities, trade unions, and so forth. In some instances white programs and facilities desegregated voluntarily as a matter of principle, quietly admitting blacks in the late 1950s and early 1960s. Further, Miami avoided the violence that was seen in some parts of Florida during the civil rights period.

The Desegregation of Public Schools in Florida

Prior to the historic *Brown* decision, blacks were segregated into inferior public schools in the American South. In some southern states, blacks were not allowed to attend school at all; in others, such as Florida, black schools were constructed only if blacks paid double taxes. By 1870, only about 10 percent of southern blacks were enrolled in some kind of school, a percentage significantly lower than white enrollment.

Following the Civil War some whites attempted to intimidate blacks with violent acts, including the burning of black schools. However, with the passage of the Fourteenth Amendment to the Constitution, blacks began to have access to segregated public education. The operation of dual public education systems in the South had been legally justified since 1896, when the U.S. Supreme Court held that the separation of the races was not a violation of civil rights, as long as equal facilities were provided for blacks. This separate-but-equal doctrine had guided public education in the South until 1954.

After the *Brown* decision made separate-but-equal schools unconstitutional, things began to change, albeit slowly. On May 17, 1954, the Court declared unanimously that the segregation of public-school students solely on the basis of race violated the equal protection principle of the Fourteenth Amendment to the Constitution. It also ruled that school segregation violated the Constitution regardless of whether schools for blacks appeared to be as good as those for whites. For the majority, Chief Justice Earl Warren wrote that separating black children from others of similar age and qualifications solely because of their race generates a feeling of inferiority which may affect their hearts and minds in a way unlikely ever to be undone.

Florida was among the seventeen states that were most directly affected by the decision. Preceding the decision, Florida State School Superintendent Thomas D. Bailey had expressed his view that desegregation orders by the Court would not immediately affect Florida, since the cases at issue originated in South Carolina, Virginia, Delaware, and Kansas.

After the decision Bailey set the gradualist tone for the state's approach to school desegregation. "The law has been determined," he said. "We feel that so far as this state is concerned, the adjustment to it, when the time comes, will be sanely, judiciously, and humanely carried out to the satisfaction of our Colored and White citizens alike."[1]

The Florida legislature opposed the court ruling and tried to find ways to avoid implementing it, including passing a law that authorized the assignment of pupils to schools based on health, safety, order, and educational welfare, but not race. The result did not change the segregated schools. Although he would later be remembered as a political moderate who helped move the state through the desegregation process, Florida's Governor LeRoy Collins accepted segregation as a part of Florida custom and law and promised to use the lawful processes of his office to maintain it.[2]

On March 12, 1956, Florida's two U.S. senators, Holland and Smathers, and six of the state's eight congressmen, Bennett, Sikes, Herlong, Rogers, Haley and Mathews, were among the nineteen senators and seventy-seven members of Congress from the South who issued the so-called Southern Manifesto, pledging themselves to use all lawful means to reverse the U.S. Supreme Court's desegregation decision. Only Democrat Fascell and Republican Cramer did not sign.

On March 12, 1956, at a top-level conference, the governor, cabinet members, and other high-ranking state officials established a committee of jurists and lawyers to study legal means to retain segregation. Headed by L. L. Fabisinski, the committee recommended to the 1957 legislature that the law grant county school boards the power to assign pupils to schools. The committee also recommended authorizing the governor to regulate the use of public places to preserve domestic order and granting him the authority to use all the state's law enforcement officers, including the state militia, to suppress disorder. According to Florida historian Carlton W. Tebeau, Governor Collins asked the 1957 legislature to approve the committee's work in order to preserve domestic order, keep down inflammatory propaganda, and help improve the living standards of blacks. The lawmakers went further and passed, over the governor's opposition, an interposition resolution alleging that the Supreme Court had enacted new legislation in *Brown v. Topeka Board of Education*.[3]

The interposition resolution stated that the governor should interpose the authority of the state between the citizens and the national government's effort to enforce the *Brown* decision. Although the Florida legislature approved these measures, it was Collins's moderation rather than the intransigence of the legislators which prevailed. As a result of his leadership and moderate approach, desegregation in Florida, for the most part, proceeded slowly but not violently (protracted violence in Saint Augustine was a notable exception).

One of the whites willing to stand in support of blacks, even as the state dug in its heels against desegregation, was State Representative John B. (Jack) Orr Jr. According to historian Howard Kleinberg, the Miami-born Orr stood alone on the floor of the Florida House to vote against the legislature's attempt to preserve racial segregation after the *Brown* decision. On July 25, 1956, the legislature, gathered in special session to preserve segregation, voted eighty-nine to one in the House. In a twenty-minute speech which left the chamber tense and silent, Orr, the lone dissenter, told his colleagues: "I believe segregation is morally wrong. The existence of second-class citizenship is repugnant to our great democratic principles. . . . For us to set an example of hypocrisy and deceit, of disregard for our laws will surely do more harm to our children than will result from their being seated in a class-room next to one whose skin color is of a different hue."[4]

Although his speech was not subjected to derision in the House, the response in Miami was another matter. One politician warned Orr that he wouldn't get enough votes at the next election to serve as pall-bearer at his political funeral. Letters poured in calling him an anti-Christ, a traitor, and Public Enemy Number 1. His family was threat-ened. Having already won the Democratic primary for reelection, Orr faced only token Republican opposition and was returned to Talla-hassee. However, his words came back to haunt him and he paid the price in 1958, when he was defeated in a nasty campaign by a pro-segregation Democratic challenger. Orr was redeemed in 1972, when the citizens elected him to be Dade County mayor. Kleinberg notes, "Orr was not without human frailty; he had a history of marital and drinking problems. He was elected mayor of Dade County but the wars—both public and personal—took their toll."[5] Orr's life came to a painful end at a relatively young age. He died of cancer in 1974 at age fifty-four.

The Desegregation of Dade County Public Schools

The first real challenge to Dade County's dual educational system be-gan in 1943. A courageous black teacher named Hubert C. Reynolds filed a lawsuit challenging the Dade County Public School System's practice of routinely paying black teachers less than white teachers—a practice which the school board justified by saying that white teach-ers were simply better than black teachers. Reynolds, who taught at Booker T. Washington Senior High School, became a voice for most of Dade County's black population because education was not the only field in which blacks were paid less than whites for performing the same work.

Reynolds claimed that the school board enforced racially discrimi-natory salary schedules. His attorneys asserted that although black teachers were paid at the minimum salary level without regard to their seniority, white teachers received a progressively higher salary for each year of service. The Dade school system agreed that lower salary levels prevailed for black teachers. However, it pointed out that the differ-ence in pay was justified because of the lower effectiveness of the black teachers, as measured by a score on a rating system which the school board had adopted in 1941. The board claimed that the rating system regulated salary regardless of race or color. Superintendent James Wilson testified for the defense, claiming that although the instrument used to rate teachers may not have been scientifically accurate, it was as good as any instrument being used at the time. Wilson also stated that the white teachers, as a group, had a much greater degree of effectiveness than black teachers and that they were superior in completion of reports and protection of school property.

In addition to the differences in pay, white, but not black, teachers were given contracts. The school system's rating committee argued that contracts were offered to white teachers to keep up their morale, while black teachers did not appear to be disturbed by the omission.

Two years after the suit was filed, the case was decided. Federal judge John Holland dismissed the charges against the Dade school system, ruling that the rating system used in setting teachers' salaries was not discriminatory. Dr. Gilbert Porter, who organized Florida's black teachers in the 1940s to fight race discrimination in public education, recalled that Reynolds was fired and railroaded out of Miami soon after the court ruling.[6]

With respect to school desegregation itself, Dade County's school board, like most others in the South, failed to move with "all deliberate speed" as ordered by the Supreme Court in the *Brown* decision. This foot-dragging prompted a series of lawsuits by black leaders in Dade County. One of these was filed by Dr. John O. Brown and several other blacks. Dr. Brown was the president of the Miami chapter of CORE at the time.

The suit, seeking an end to segregation in Florida schools, was filed in federal court on June 12, 1956. The plaintiffs included the Reverend Theodore R. Gibson, father of Theodore R. Gibson Jr., a student at Dunbar Elementary; Prince Hepburn, father of Scheren Hepburn, who was ten at the time and attended Liberty City Elementary; Albert Reddick, father of Cleo Reddick; J. O. Brown, father of J. O. Brown Jr.; James Lenton Parker, father of Theresa Parker; and Richard Powell, father of Richard Powell Jr., who was eight years old and a student at Poinciana Elementary.[7]

The suit asked the court to order the Dade County School Board to devise a plan which would expeditiously desegregate the schools, because the parents' 1955 petition to the school board to abolish segregation as soon as practicable had been ignored. The named defendants included the school board, its individual members, and school superintendent W. R. Thomas, whom the plaintiffs wanted enjoined from enforcing Florida's segregation laws. Brought under the equal rights provision of the Fourteenth Amendment to the Constitution, the suit described the plaintiffs as representatives of a class that included all parents of black school children.

The school system resisted vigorously. Dr. Joe Hall, the school superintendent who succeeded Thomas, admitted that his recommendation to bar the children from the white schools was due to their race. He said that the children would face a hostile environment, creating an unfavorable learning situation.

In 1958 while this case was being decided, State Representative John B. Orr Jr. proposed the establishment of a citizens' committee to aid in the desegregation process. Members of the committee would be appointed by the school board and would aid in setting up a legislature of eighty high school juniors and seniors who, with adult help, would work out a desegregation program to be presented to the school board. Other students would be selected by the first group of students, based mainly on their scholastic standing and their character. Their plan would be introduced on a trial basis. Orr believed that whites on both sides of the issue would find the plan acceptable because it gave them time to work out other plans if necessary. He believed the approach would be acceptable to blacks because it attempted to comply with, rather than to defy, the law.[8]

The Dade County Public School System had several other plans to carry out the desegregation order, all gradualistic and in accord with the state's unhurried approach to school desegregation. One of these plans—then in effect in the Washington, D.C., schools—called for the desegregation process to begin in the first grade. The theory behind the plan was that six-year-old children start their school lives without prejudices and, therefore, more easily accept one another.

Yet another plan was to establish a junior college, which would be a thirteenth-and fourteenth-grade public school that any qualified student, regardless of race, could attend on a voluntary basis. The community college, or junior college, had been proposed for white students only prior to the desegregation order. Under this plan the community college would become a center for any student who wanted higher education beyond the twelfth grade. Another plan, used in Louisville, Kentucky, was to select certain schools to be desegregated, which students could attend voluntarily.[9]

In late 1959 the Dade County School Board lost the desegregation lawsuit filed by the black parents and students. The school board announced that black students would be admitted to Orchard Villa Elementary School beginning in the next school year, but this did not lead to integration. Many whites chose not to send their children to the desegregated school and transferred them to other schools instead. When Orchard Villa opened that fall, it had fewer than a dozen white students. By that Christmas it was an all-black school.

White resistance to school desegregation continued as various plans were introduced, each of which had the ultimate effect of maintaining a segregated school system. On March 17, 1960, U.S. District Court Judge Joseph Lieb approved the school system's freedom-of-choice plan, allowing parents to apply to admit their children into any school regardless of the school's attendance area or their child's race. This voluntary desegregation approach continued with little movement toward real integration.

In 1964 the U.S. Congress passed legislation which gave the federal government a way to punish states for not desegregating their schools. It also provided monetary and technical aid to school districts that were complying with desegregation plans. This bill gave the U.S. attorney general the power to bring suits on behalf of individuals who had been denied access to public schools because of their race. Furthermore, it withheld federal funds from programs that discriminated. As a result of the legislation, the rate of integration increased significantly in the southern states. Another positive outcome of the legislation was that education took equal standing with health and welfare as reflected in the newly organized Department of Health, Education and Welfare (HEW).

The Desegregation Center at the University of Miami, working with HEW, developed several approaches and suggestions to desegregate public schools in Dade County. The U.S. Fifth Circuit Court of Appeals was also involved. According to Dr. Gordon Foster, Director of the University of Miami Desegregation Center, sections of Dade County were excluded from the desegregation process mainly because of their political influence. For example, hundreds of black children from Over-

107. Students arriving for the start of the school year at newly desegregated Orchard Villa Elementary School in 1960. This was the first public school in Dade County to desegregate. Within weeks the school was virtually all black. Courtesy Historical Museum of Southern Florida.

town were bused to schools on Miami Beach, but few, if any, white students were bused to inner-city schools from Miami Beach.[10]

By the late 1960s, sixteen schools remained all black, including one high school, Miami-Northwestern; three junior highs, Allapattah, Drew, and Brownsville; and twelve elementary schools. Federal District Judge C. Clyde Atkins, who now handled Dade's school desegregation suit, explained that those schools were not being integrated due to several exceptional situations, including traffic hazards, special programs at the schools, possible damage to educational programs as a consequence of changes, school capacity, walking distances, and natural barriers. However, in June 1963 the Dade County School Board officially declared the system desegregated.

In July 1969 HEW reported that the Dade school system was still a dual system and not in compliance with the Civil Rights Act of 1964. Forty-two of the 217 schools in the system were all black, in part as a result of the system's failure to move white students to black schools. The following month, Judge Atkins assumed jurisdiction over a suit filed by a group of white parents from South Miami Heights which sought to block the plan to send their children to Mays Junior High, a virtually all-black school. They argued that the school board adopted the plan to transfer their children in violation of the state's sunshine law. The white parents had prevailed in the state court; but when Atkins took over the case, he approved the school board's integration plan. He also noted that the board's continuation of thirty-eight all-black schools did not meet constitutional standards. Atkins then ordered a feasibility study to learn the possibility of desegregating all of the schools by February 1970. When Dade School Superintendent Dr. E. L. Whigham responded that this could not be done, the court gave the board until February 1, 1970, to come up with a new plan.

Judge Atkins held a hearing on January 22, 1970, to discuss the new plan, which consisted of desegregating eleven all-black schools and leaving alone twenty-eight predominantly black schools. The judge delayed the transfer of students until September 1970, but ordered the transfer of 1,976 teachers by February 1, 1970. Teachers would first be given the opportunity to transfer voluntarily, and those who did not volunteer would be assigned to a different school by lottery, leading to a teacher population mirroring the racial makeup of the student population in each school. Judge Atkins also ordered the administration to set up nondiscriminatory standards for demoting or firing faculty and staff whose jobs were eliminated in the transfer. The school board's latest plan was declared unconstitutional, and the court demanded that every school be integrated by September 1970. The law did not give Judge Atkins the authority to order massive busing, and according to school officials busing would be necessary to desegregate the schools. Therefore, Atkins asked for a new plan by April 1. In the meantime, the schools closed for one week in order to transfer teachers. The system reported in February 1970 that 1,221 teachers had volunteered for transfer and that only 60 teachers had resigned, a number only slightly higher than during a regular school year.

The effort to integrate faculties was not successful in the long term, however. Seventeen years later, in June of 1987, it was determined that the system's faculty and staff were still segregated, as 67 of the 249 public schools in Dade County still had segregated staffs.[11]

According to School Superintendent Whigham, the cost involved in transferring teachers and students was $454,000, and the system could budget only $226,000 for that purpose, leaving the rest of the money to come from the state or the federal government. To solve this problem, the school board approved two resolutions calling on Florida's congressional delegation to request funds for desegregation. As a result, Dade as well as many other southern school districts received millions of dollars in federal desegregation assistance.

On August 12, 1970—after years of court interventions, lawsuits, and plans with various school pairings, clusters, and other assorted approaches to the desegregation problem—the U. S. Fifth Circuit Court of Appeals ordered even more school desegregation in Dade County through the pairing of fifty-three schools, leaving eight schools black. On June 4, 1971, Judge Atkins declared the system unitary. However, on June 22, 1971, black parents, in conjunction with the Classroom Teachers Association and the American Civil Liberties Union, requested that the court reenter the desegregation picture because too many black children still attended all-black schools. Atkins denied a new hearing.

Still the issue of school desegregation refused to go away. In the fall of 1977, a new elementary school opened in a white area only five blocks from South Dade's Richmond Elementary School. Richmond had an 80 percent black and 20 percent white student body; Pine Lake Elementary, the new school, had a 90 percent white and 10 percent black population. It was a formula for conflict. Although the two schools were a perfect match for pairing to attain racial balance, the Dade County School Board decided on March 22, 1978, not to change the schools' attendance boundaries in order to do so. Judge Atkins later ordered the pairing to be done. Kindergarten through third grade were taught at Pine Lake, and fourth through sixth at Richmond. An alliance of black and white parents from both schools challenged the pairing decision. The U.S. Fifth Circuit Court of Appeals denied their request, holding that the group with a right to a hearing would be those parents who supported more integration, not those opposing it.

Busing was not a primary tool in the desegregation process in Dade County, at least not massive busing, because it was forbidden by school board guidelines. Busing was, however, significantly expanded as a result of the desegregation effort. Because the federal courts ordered a great deal of pairing, grouping, and boundary changing in the 1960s and 1970s, buses were used to transport black students to white schools and white students to black schools. In August 1970 school officials anticipated that an additional four to five thousand students would be bused, and that twenty to thirty more buses would be needed.

Nine years later the busing issue took center stage in Dade County. According to Dade School Superintendent Dr. Johnny L. Jones, a black man, the problem was that more blacks were being bused out of their communities than whites. Black parents began to suggest that racial integration was taking place at the expense of their children. Many wondered if it was worth it.[12]

In January 1983, for the first time, a group of black and white parents came together to plead with the school board to put a stop to busing. Ruth Page, a black mother, wanted the school boundaries of south Dade's R. R. Moton Elementary changed even if it meant resegregation. Moton had been desegregated since 1971 when the school had been grouped with two all-white elementary schools, Perrine and Bel-Aire, which required elaborate busing.

Parents of both races from all three schools supported Page at a public hearing before the school board attendance boundary committee. The committee members rejected the plea after two hours of debate, deciding that the changes sought by the parents were not beneficial to the students. According to Lucille Montequin, the school board's administrator responsible for equal educational opportunity, the parents' proposal would resegregate the school and racially isolate the black students.[13]

Two months after this committee hearing, in March 1983, there was a hearing before the school board. The attendance boundary committee made recommendations to balance attendance at under- and overpopulated schools using busing. A black great-grandmother, Viola Pearson, commented, "I'm sick of this busing. I don't want my children getting up at five in the morning and waiting in the rain and cold for a bus that sometimes never comes." At this hearing parents also asked for an equal busing system, meaning that the same number of whites would be bused to black schools as blacks to white schools. Approximately 70 percent of the students then riding buses were black. Despite the angry parents, the board decided not to make any changes. The decision was influenced by school board attorney Frank Howard, who said that any attempt to resegregate schools would almost certainly face a court challenge.[14]

In February 1985 the number of students bused for desegregation purposes increased to about 23,000. Of these, about 19,000 were black. In April of the same year, the Dade County School Board voted to delay busing 39 white children from Miami Lakes Junior High to Lake Stevens Junior High, in a predominantly black residential area, and 186 white sixth-graders from Miami Shores Elementary to Horace Mann Junior High, also in a predominantly black neighborhood. The board concluded that the condition of the black schools was not good enough to accept new students.[15]

This enraged many black parents, who wondered aloud how it could be that the schools were not good enough for white students but were all right for blacks. The board decided to improve the academic programs at both black schools and transfer the white students the following year.

Some of the students being bused included those who took advantage of the majority-to-minority transfer program which had been established by Judge Atkins back in 1970. This type of school transfer allowed a student to leave a school in which his or her racial group was in the majority and go to one in which his or her group was in the minority. Since then and up to 1984, 96 percent of the transfer students were black. The problem by December of 1984 was the overcrowding of some white schools by black students.[16]

To solve this problem, the school board decided on February 20, 1985, that blacks could not be transferred to white schools that were 15 percent or more overcrowded. The new policy also stated that blacks could not transfer to white schools once the number of blacks reached 37 percent. That meant that there were twenty-eight white elementaries to which blacks could not transfer, even though less than 37 percent of their students were black, because the schools were overenrolled. There were also thirty-one white schools to which blacks could not transfer because their black population was over 37 percent.[17]

Another approach to desegregation tried in the 1980s and 1990s is the use of magnet schools, wherein specialized courses are only offered at one school which attracts students of all races from all over the county. Of the state's seventy-five magnet programs in 1989, thirty-six were in Dade County, and the number of black students benefiting slightly outnumbered whites and Hispanics.[18]

As public schools desegregated, the number of private schools in Dade County dramatically increased. During the desegregation process in public schools, private-school enrollment consisted of approximately 94 percent white students. According to Dr. Gordon Foster of the University of Miami Desegregation Center, school desegregation reached private schools much later, when the Internal Revenue Service announced on July 10, 1970, that the government would no longer allow tax-exempt status to private schools with racially discriminatory policies. The IRS also said that gifts to schools that lost their tax-exempt status would not be considered charitable contributions, and would therefore not be tax-deductible. Although not required to have black students enrolled, the schools had to have racially nondiscriminatory admission policies. In 1970, five private schools in Dade County were granted tax-exempt status, although none of them had blacks enrolled. Officials at those schools stated that no black students had applied.[19]

By the early 1990s the full integration of the Dade County Public School System had not yet occurred. Dr. Foster blamed the failure on housing patterns. He said that Dade County did not have a lot of desegregated housing, making it difficult to accomplish its school desegregation goals. The best solution would be to scatter publicly supported low-income housing sites around the county, but attempts to build such housing met resistance in white and black middle- and upper-income neighborhoods. For this approach to succeed, an unlikely alliance of private developers, banks, and the government would be required.[20]

One result of school desegregation was the demise of traditionally black high schools. The last graduating class marched at Booker T. Washington Senior High School in 1967, bringing to a close the institution's long and illustrious tenure as one of Florida's great high schools. The next year, the school was changed to seventh through ninth grades and all its students were black. Later the school became a ninth-grade center paired with Ada Merritt and Citrus Grove junior highs. In 1979 Ada Merritt closed, and its students were transferred to Booker T. Washington. By this time the building was in decline and the school became one of the county's inner-city schools, with all of the problems the phrase connotes.

In 1986 a new Booker T. Washington Middle School was approved, and it opened in 1989 on the property next to the old building. By 1990 enrollment consisted of 1,650 students: 71 percent Hispanic, 28 percent black, and less than 1 percent white non-Hispanic.

All-black Mays Junior-Senior High School in south Dade was at its peak in the early sixties, attended by black students from various economic levels. Staff morale was high. In 1968 Earl Wells, a black man and one of the system's most respected educational leaders, became principal. Then the desegregation process began.

Boundary changes and other desegregation-related decisions led to busing many of the black Mays students to white schools some distance away, where they were not universally welcomed. Racial disputes between blacks and whites at predominantly white South Dade Senior High School caused some of the Mays students to flee the school and return to Mays.

As a result of the school board's desegregation plans, Mays, too, was ultimately reduced from a high school to a junior high. As in other black areas of the county, the academic sinews of the black south Dade community were severed. In 1969, Mays held its last commencement exercise. The student population of the new Mays Junior High was virtually all black.[21]

Mays became a magnet school in 1989 and today offers special programs for the study of the arts and literature. It attracts voluntary students from various areas of the community. In the early 1990s approximately 165 students were in the magnet program, most from the predominantly white Kendall area. Overall student enrollment was 40 percent Hispanic, 30 percent black, and 30 percent white non-Hispanic.[22]

Also as a result of desegregation efforts by the school system, in 1965 George Washington Carver Senior High School had its last graduating class. Black Coconut Grove students in the tenth, eleventh, and twelfth grades were assigned to Coral Gables Senior High School, and in 1967 Carver also became a junior high. In 1971, as with Booker T. Washington, Carver became a seventh-grade center. By the 1994–1995 school year it had a student population of approximately 39.4 percent Hispanic, 21.6 percent black, and 37.2 percent white non-Hispanic. It also had one of the school system's most popular magnet programs, specializing in foreign languages.

The Desegregation of Higher Education in Dade County and Florida

Even before the famous 1954 *Brown* decision, Florida and several other southern states were under pressure to provide higher-education opportunities for blacks; however, the separate-but-equal doctrine was

Table 6.1. Racial and ethnic distribution of all students, University of Miami, 1990–1995

Race/ethnicity	1990	1991	1992	1993	1994	1995
White	8,118	8,430	8,082	7,815	7,308	7,204
Hispanic	2,634	2,852	3,039	3,111	3,180	3,329
Asian	815	904	965	996	990	1,052
Black	983	1,069	1,124	1,160	1,301	1,305
Am. Indian	29	34	47	39	33	39
Unknown	1,325	956	898	721	922	612
Total	13,904	14,245	14,155	13,842	13,734	13,541

Source: *University of Miami Fact Book,* Fall 1995.

still in effect. Accordingly, the state cabinet voted in October 1946 to provide scholarships for qualified black students so that they might attend out-of-state colleges that provided courses not offered at Florida A & M University, the state's publicly supported university for blacks. The ten-thousand-dollar scholarships were offered in compliance with the United States Supreme Court ruling that the state must provide the same college educational opportunities for blacks as for white students.

In March 1950, eleven southern states defended their position before the United States Supreme Court. The states insisted that the Court would destroy the whole public school system in the South if it outlawed the separation of blacks and whites. The states viewed segregation as a police power needed to prevent riots and eventual chaos in public education and recreation. Among the states involved were Arkansas, Florida, Georgia, Kentucky, Louisiana, Mississippi, North Carolina, and Oklahoma. The Court ultimately rejected this argument.

The University of Miami was racially segregated from its birth in the 1920s. The university's athletic teams even resisted playing northern teams with black players. In 1946, University of Miami officials barred the university's football team from playing a Pennsylvania team with two black players, but by 1950 the university was playing integrated teams. The university admitted its first black students in 1961 and hired its first black instructor in 1962. In 1967 Ray Bellamy became the university's first black varsity athlete. By the mid–1980s, two to three thousand blacks had graduated from the university. By the fall of 1995, there were 1,305 black students at the university, about 9.6 percent of the student population. Table 6.1 reflects the racial and ethnic composition of students at the University of Miami from 1990 through 1995.

Rather than admit black students to its junior colleges, Florida school officials authorized the establishment of twelve black junior colleges following the *Brown* decision. When the Dade County School Board began attempts to establish its black junior college, the local NAACP chapter objected, arguing that establishing such a junior college would be a continuation of segregation. The school board decided to open a separate branch of Miami-Dade Community College called the Northwestern Center rather than establish a separate black junior college. This center was established at Miami Northwestern Senior High School. The faculty at that center was black, but it was allowed to participate on the college advisory committee and in the administration of the main campus, located near the Opa-Locka Airport in northwest Dade.

According to McCarthy in his recent book on black Florida, "This may have been the first time in the nation that such an arrangement was attempted. When several black students requested admission to the all-white main campus of the junior college, the school board allowed seven of them to register in the fall of 1960, thus establishing at Miami-Dade Community College one of the first desegregated public schools in Florida and in the whole southeastern United States. By the early 1960s, officials closed down the black center and transferred its black students and 11 black teachers to the main center."[23] In 1966 a black student was elected as student-body president.

Of about 279,000 community-college students in Florida in 1992, 10 percent were black and 10 percent Hispanic. Community-college faculties were 9.3 percent black and 4.8 percent Hispanic, and professional employees were 14.9 percent black and 4.2 percent Hispanic. Most of the minority enrollment in Florida community colleges was at Miami-Dade Community College. That institution has graduated 16,388 black non-Hispanic students since then. In 1995 its enrollment was 21.4 percent black. Table 6.2 shows the 1995 enrollment of ethnic groups at Miami-Dade Community College.

Florida Memorial College, which was founded in 1879 in St. Augustine, was moved to north Dade County in 1968. The college is

Table 6.2. Racial and ethnic distribution of students, Miami-Dade Community College, 1995

Race/ethnicity	No.	%
Black	10,815	21.4
Hispanic	30,117	59.6
White	8,585	17.0
Other	1,013	2.0

approximately 96 percent black and carries an enrollment of sixteen hundred students.

Table 6.3 shows the enrollment at Florida International University (FIU) from 1991 through 1996, reflecting an increase in black enrollment from 9.56 percent of students in 1991 to 13.77 percent in the fall semester of 1995. FIU had the largest enrollment of black students of any of the nine state universities except Florida A & M University, the historic all-black state university.

The desegregation of higher education in Florida moved slowly. Indeed, after a brief rise in black enrollment at predominantly white institutions in southern states, black enrollment stagnated, then declined precipitously by the mid–1980s. In 1975–1976 there were 5,455 blacks in five southern states who had graduated from a state college, and by 1984–1985 there were only 5,514.[24]

Under a 1983 federal court order, states such as Arkansas, Florida, Georgia, Oklahoma, and Virginia adopted plans to further desegregate their public colleges and universities no later than the 1985–1986 school year. In 1987 the NAACP, through its Legal Defense and Educational Fund, accused these five states of failing to obey the court order. The desegregation plans consisted of increasing black enrollment in white colleges and universities in both undergraduate and graduate programs, increasing the number of black professors, and improving programs and resources at black universities. The NAACP noted that the five states failed to attract a significant number of black high school students and that there had been no improvement in the number of blacks graduating from the colleges.

The NAACP also specified that the programs and facilities in black universities were deficient when compared to those in white schools. The organization wanted the U.S. Department of Education's Office

Table 6.3. Black student enrollment, Florida International University, 1991–1995

Period	Total students	Black students	% black
1991–92	23,332	2,231	9.56
1992–93	22,387	2,260	10.09
1993–94	23,842	2,641	11.07
1994–95	26,501	3,324	12.54
1995–96	28,096	3,870	13.77

of Civil Rights to force the states to comply or be punished by losing federal funds. In Florida the number of black students enrolled in colleges had decreased gradually from 1977 to 1987. Black high school students going to college declined from 8,792 in 1977 to 6,831 in 1984. The percentage of blacks in graduate schools also dropped, from 5.4 percent in 1981 to 4.8 percent in 1986. Educators blamed poor academic preparation as a major factor in explaining these figures.[25]

In 1988 the federal government threatened to drop some funding from state colleges and universities in Florida and the other states unless they met desegregation standards. Of the Florida colleges or universities included, none were in Dade County.[26]

PART 3

RACE RIOTS AND CIVIL DISTURBANCES
(1968–1995)

The decade of the 1980s was Miami's time of fire. The horrendous riot of 1980 was the darkest moment in the life of the city. As a cataclysmic event, it eclipsed even the Great Hurricane of 1926, which wiped out the city only physically. By contrast, the riot of 1980 assaulted the very psyche of Miami. The city was engulfed in flames for four frightening days in May that year, as mobs, arsonists, looters, and murderers fought police for control of the streets. Eighteen people died, and property damage totaled more than $100 million. Liberty City was left in ruins, and Miami itself seemed mortally wounded.

The riot followed the acquittal of five white Dade County police officers in the beating death of a young black man named Arthur McDuffie. It began just as the magnificent blooms of thousands of royal poinciana trees opened, painting the city in fiery red. In that resplendent state, Miami slid inexorably into the abyss.

Race riots on such a scale had not been seen in America since the 1960s, when many cities, including Miami, dissolved into riot. Miami's sudden explosion reminded the nation and the world of the fragility of race relations in the United States. The riot destroyed Miami's newly acquired international reputation as the rising star of the Western Hemisphere. The city was declared in the national press to be the most racially torn city in the country. In the aftermath of the riot and with the arrival of thousands of immigrants from Cuba and Haiti, the city emptied itself of its white population.

Its innocence lost, Miami began to look inside herself. All was not well. The riot was not caused by poverty: If blacks rioted because of poverty, they would be in a continuous state of riot in America. The riot was not the result of boredom or the lack of recreational facilities for inner-city youth: There have never been adequate recreational facilities for inner-city youth in any major city in the country. The riot was not caused by the arrival of hundreds of thousands of immigrants in less than two decades: If immigration had been the reason, blacks would have rioted in the early 1960s, when the influx of immigrants was at its height. Certainly, these were underlying causes, but the riot itself was sparked by injustice. When an all-white jury failed to convict the white police officers who killed a black man for what amounted to a traffic violation, black Miami was consumed with rage.

The road back has been slow and uncertain. Two other major race riots shook the city in 1982 and 1989. Both involved Hispanic police officers killing young blacks. For those who lived through the decade of fire, the psychological scars have been deep. For many the next race riot is only one newscast away.

There is good reason for this sort of pessimism. Despite efforts by business and community leaders to address the perceived causes of the riots, on the steamy streets of black Miami today, the social and economic conditions that undermined public order in 1980 remain unresolved. Moreover, the police are no more welcome in Liberty City and Overtown today than they were when McDuffie was killed nearly twenty years ago. Even so, to prevent future conflagrations, we must better understand those of the past. In the last two decades Miami has provided copious such occasions upon which to reflect.

From 1968 to the deadly riot of 1980, there were many racial clashes in Dade County—almost all of them involving disputes with the police. In addition, several black political leaders who had come to power in the aftermath of the civil rights era were swept from office in disgrace in the 1970s. Some blacks believed that this was unfair and that their leaders were subjected to more scrutiny than were white leaders. By August 1968 Miami was in full riot, as the Republican national convention met on Miami Beach to nominate Richard Nixon for his first term as president. This disturbance was followed by another, in the Brownsville area in 1970, called the Rotten Meat Riot since it was instigated by a dispute over the sale of tainted meat. Between 1970 and 1979 over a dozen mini-disturbances took place in black communities from Opa-Locka to south Dade.

The 1968 Riot

Racial disturbances are usually preceded not only by an immediate, precipitating incident but also by events that may have happened months or even years earlier. Such an incident occurred on the evening of February 4, 1968, when two white officers of the Miami Police Department arrested a black seventeen-year-old named Robert Owens and charged him with carrying a concealed knife. On the way to the police station, the officers took Owens to a half-finished span of bridge on the new Dolphin Expressway, where it rose to cross the Miami River at Fourth Avenue. They forced him to strip, and then dangled the naked youth by his heels more than a hundred feet above the dark waters of the river.

The incident was later reported in the press. Black Miami was furious. It was also reported that several weeks before the Owens incident, a delegation of blacks had asked the chief of police, Walter Headley, to remove from his Liberty City beat one of the officers who later became involved in the bridge incident. They believed that the officer exhibited antiblack conduct. Headley responded by telling the delegation that he thought their complaint was silly.

In addition to problems with the police, there were complaints about the failure of the Dade County business community to help blacks, despite widely publicized promises to do so. As the tension increased, the black leaders who had been counseling their followers against violence began to lose their influence to more militant black activists.

During this time the Republican national convention came to Miami Beach to nominate Richard M. Nixon for the presidency. Although there was no direct link between the Republican national convention and the riot, the presence of the Republicans and the huge entourage of national and international press accompanying the convention inspired Miami branches of some black political groups, such as the Congress on Racial Equality (CORE) and the Black Panthers, to organize political rallies in the black community. The largest of these rallies was set for one o'clock on August 7 at a community center in Liberty City. It was rumored that professional basketball star Wilt Chamberlain, a Republican in town for the convention, would attend.

Between one and two o'clock, about thirty people, most of them teenagers, gathered at the site of the rally to see Chamberlain. Although the athlete never arrived, several reporters, including two from television networks, were present. A few uniformed Miami police officers looked on from a parking lot south of the rally site, and two black intelligence officers from the Dade County Public Safety Department mingled in the crowd.

By half past two some 150 people had gathered for the rally and the crowd overflowed into the street. As the crowd grew, it became more and more restive. A few rocks were thrown at passing cars, prompting the police to call for five more squad cars and a canine unit. As they arrived, they became the target of the crowd's hostility.

By four o'clock the crowd had grown considerably and had virtually taken over Sixty-second Street at Seventeenth Avenue. Teenagers were now throwing bottles, rocks, and other objects at passing cars. At five o'clock two roadblocks were set up, reducing traffic through the area, and the police withdrew to reorganize. The crowd in the streets continued to swell. By seven that evening nearly three hundred people had gathered at the intersection of Sixty-second Street and Seventeenth Avenue.

Then came an ideal target: It was a white man driving east on Sixty-second Street in a pickup truck decorated with a bumper sticker that read "George Wallace for President." (George Wallace was the racist governor of Alabama who literally stood in the schoolhouse door to block the federally forced integration of the University of Alabama in the late 1950s.) The truck was too tantalizing a target to be denied, and it provoked a virtual shower of rocks and bottles. The driver understandably panicked and lost control of the truck, striking another vehicle before coming to a halt. With shouts of "Get Whitey!" the crowd, now a mob, swarmed over the truck, trying to get at the driver. A group of black men who had been standing in a doorway pulled the man to safety inside a nearby bar while his truck was overturned and set afire by an angry group of black youths. The 1968 riot was on.[1]

Almost immediately, other groups of black youths moved east along Sixty-second Street, breaking into and looting white-owned businesses. Word of the disorder was spread by radio reports, which brought hundreds of blacks from nearby apartment buildings. Although the vandalism and looting were started by groups of young black males most of whom were between fifteen and twenty, they were soon joined by adults, both men and women.

The police had no plan for coordinated action. Regrouping at a nearby command post between 7:10 and 8:00 P.M., police units with sirens blaring rushed from scene to scene trying to arrest looters. Rioters merely waited for them to leave an area before moving in to resume looting. With more than two hundred officers massed in the area, the police appeared to have restored order by 8:00. Many people drifted away. Vandalism and looting became sporadic.

Then, incredibly, the riot was given a new lease on life about a half-hour later. It was inadvertently reignited by the arrival of Miami Mayor Steve Clark and Florida Governor Claude Kirk with an assemblage of assistants, security personnel, and news reporters, including television crews from national networks. Their presence brought people back into the streets. At various street corners Mayor Clark and Governor Kirk addressed groups of astonished blacks, asking them to go home. But the masses had already been at home, and some wondered aloud why they had been called out of their homes only to be told to go back. Someone threw a rock at a police vehicle. A nervous police officer fired a warning shot into the air. The 1968 riot was on again.

At 9:30 P.M. various officials, including Governor Kirk, the Reverend Ralph David Abernathy of the Southern Christian Leadership Conference, Dade County Mayor Charles Hall, and Miami City Manager Melvin Reese, met with area residents at the headquarters of the Liberty City Community Council, at Sixty-second Street and Thirteenth Avenue, to discuss problems and grievances. The officials promised to send representatives to a meeting set for eleven the next morning. Black leaders then helped the police to disperse the crowd.

The following day, three hours before the meeting was to begin, groups of teenagers gathered on Thirteenth Avenue and threw rocks at passing vehicles. Again the Miami police rerouted traffic. By eleven o'clock, the crowd in the area numbered nearly three hundred, but the officials had not arrived. Macon Williams, a black member of the governor's staff who handled matters relating to blacks and economic opportunity, was present. However, council leaders considered him merely a messenger with no authority to act, and they refused to confer with him. At noon no other representatives or officials had appeared. The crowd, noting their absence, was growing angry, and the situation was deteriorating rapidly.

The police and fifty highway patrolmen in full riot gear used a riot truck and tear gas to disperse crowds along Sixty-second Street. Receiving what they took as sniper fire, they fired warning shots in the air from shotguns and semiautomatic rifles. Some of the rioters responded by throwing rocks and bottles at the police. People ran wildly for cover. When the several minutes of shooting were over, a young black child had been wounded and two black men had been shot dead.

At approximately five o'clock, in the wake of the injuries and deaths, the governor called in 950 national guardsmen and gave the Dade County Sheriff's Office overall command of anti-riot operations. A curfew extending from six in the evening until six in the morning was

108. National guard troops posted at barricades on Northwest Sixty-second Street, August 9, 1968. Courtesy *Miami Herald*.

set for the area, and all bars and liquor stores in Liberty City were closed. Police killed two more black men over the next two days before order was finally restored.[2]

The Rotten Meat Riot (1970)

In June 1970 the city again faced a racial crisis, this one in Brownsville, adjacent to Liberty City. This mid-June spasm of violence became known among Miami's blacks as the Rotten Meat Riot. The incident was sparked by black anger over a white-owned grocery store called Pic-and-Pay. Blacks had long complained about the store and had given its owner, Fred Weller, a white former public-school social-studies teacher, a list of complaints which included customer dissatisfaction with the quality of the store's meat, its high prices, and its extra charges for cashing welfare and Social Security checks.

Picketing of the store began June 12 following an altercation between Weller and Gladys Taylor, a hefty black woman who was head of the Dade County Welfare Rights Organization. Taylor claimed that

Weller caller her a nigger when she complained about being charged $1.25 to cash a $157.00 welfare check. In an interview after the riot, Weller denied that he used the term nigger. "She said, 'I'm going to put your white ass out of business,' and I told her, 'You take your black ass and go somewhere else and shop.'"[3]

By either account, this was no way to talk to Gladys Taylor, a woman of substantial physical presence with a booming voice and the temperament of a rattlesnake. The irascible Taylor often appeared at school board and county commission meetings where she was renowned for cursing people out; indeed, Taylor elevated ordinary street-cursing to a virtual art form. When Weller crassly invited her to leave the store, the exchange between them must have reached new depths, even for Taylor.

After three days of peaceful picketing and an unsuccessful meeting between blacks and Weller, sheriff's deputies appeared at the store and, according to black witnesses, fired tear gas at the pickets. Some blacks responded with a volley of rocks and bottles. Two white motorists were pulled from their cars and beaten, their vehicles set afire. Molotov cocktails were thrown into other cars and through store windows. The rumor spread that snipers had taken up positions on roofs and in apartment windows. The police responded by sealing off the area and arresting several rioters.

On June 16 Weller's attorneys persuaded Dade Circuit Judge Henry Balaban to issue a temporary injunction forbidding picketing at the market. But the violence continued, first spilling over into Liberty City, then the following day into the black section of Coconut Grove. Although the Pic-and-Pay store was guarded by police during the rioting, some damage was done when a fire was set in the rear of the building.

Neither of the two persons shot by the police during the disorder turned out to be rioters. Lison C. Morris, the white owner of a construction company located a few blocks north of the Brownsville riot area, was shot as he and four other men watched the disturbance from the rooftop of their building. Police officers thought they were burglars and reported that the men had fired on the police as officers approached the building. Morris said the officers stormed in, firing at him and his friends.

George Curtis, an eighteen-year-old African American, was shot by police in the neck and shoulder. Although no gun was ever found, the police accused him of being a sniper. At Curtis's trial, seven white policemen so testified. There were no other witnesses. An all-white jury found him guilty of assaulting police, and he was sentenced to five years in prison. In preparation for the trial, the youth had passed two lie-detector tests. During his appeals, Dade Circuit Court Judge Alphonso Sepe freed him on a one-dollar bond. In 1975, after five years of legal proceedings, the state dropped the charges when a relentless *Miami Herald* reporter found witnesses who testified that Curtis had not been armed and had not been in the apartment from which the police claimed he had fired at them.

Mini-disturbances (1971–1979)

In their 1984 book, *The Miami Riot of 1980: Crossing the Bounds*,[4] authors Porter and Dunn noted that between July 1970 and January 1979, Dade County experienced thirteen outbursts of racial violence. Some of those incidents are summarized below.

February 22, 1971

Black youths from Coconut Grove pelted cars on West Dixie Highway in the aftermath of the police shooting of Joseph Veargis, a black seventeen-year-old who was riding in a stolen car. Veargis was shot after he supposedly pointed a pistol at police. It turned out to be a chrome-plated tear-gas gun. After firebombs were tossed at white motorists, seriously injuring one man, police sealed off the black area of Coconut Grove and placed sharpshooters with rifles atop key buildings. The violence spilled over to Coral Gables High School, a predominantly white and Hispanic school which served students from Coconut Grove. Police reported that twenty-five to thirty black students assaulted several white boys and three white girls.

March 23, 1971

In Opa-Locka, ten miles north of Miami, police sergeant James W. Teppenpay shot a black bystander, Joseph Lee Scott, during a shootout with robbers. The next evening an angry crowd of about six hundred blacks gathered in front of a local bar. According to news reports, acting Opa-Locka City Manager William S. Griffiths, yielding to the crowd's demand that Teppenpay be suspended, told them, "You can watch me type out the suspension notice on the policeman who shot the man last night."[5] The blacks also called for the ouster of Opa-Locka's police chief, Herbert Chastain, and shouted grievances, primarily claims of mistreatment by the Opa-Locka police. Griffiths said he would take their complaints under consideration, but the promise was not enough.

Sniper fire, car stonings, and store looting were reported that night. Stahl's General Store, a white-owned business, was gutted by fire. The next day Opa-Locka officials declared a 7:00 A.M. to 7:00 P.M. curfew. Police continued to receive reports of sniper fire. The following night, two white-owned nightclubs in the black area, a liquor store (the Park Bar), and a deserted former nightclub (the Harlem Gardens) were burned. At the Park Bar, looters used hand trucks to carry away cases of liquor.

By March 25 an uneasy truce had been established, and the Opa-Locka City Commission agreed to appoint two lawyers acceptable to blacks to investigate their complaints. Frank A. Howard Jr., a white man, and Jesse J. McCrary Jr., a black man who would later become Florida's first black secretary of state, prepared a twenty-four-page report and submitted it on May 10. The report criticized the Opa-Locka police for insensitivity but did not substantiate specific complaints of police abuse of blacks. It was also critical of the Opa-Locka city government, which Howard and McCrary accused of burying their heads in the sand. Black leaders were described in the report as less than candid when they reported to their followers that the police chief had ignored their grievances. Blacks who participated in the disturbance were also criticized for having resorted to violence.

January 24, 1979

Two county police officers saw a thirty-five-year-old black man involved in what the officers said was a drug sale on Sixty-second Street in Liberty City. After a two-block chase, the officers caught, subdued, and handcuffed him, but the chase had drawn a crowd. The police report of the incident indicates that another black man interfered with the arrest and, after a brief chase, was also arrested. The sight of police chasing people back and forth angered the growing crowd. Groups of young blacks started throwing rocks at the police and white passersby, and some twenty units were called in. The disturbance lasted two and one-half hours.

William McLeod, a black witness, told the *Miami Herald* the next day: "The police had [the first man] down on the ground, and [the other man] said, 'Hey, man, you ain't got no business kicking the man like that.' And the cop said, 'When I finish here, your ass is going to jail.' And they chased him down the street and arrested him."[6] Several Liberty City residents insisted that one of the men was clubbed and kicked repeatedly after he was handcuffed. One of the officers accused in this incident, Alex Marrero, would be named in 1980 by three other police officers as the one who struck the blows that killed Arthur McDuffie, igniting Miami's 1980 riot.

Fallen Black Leaders

Before the great riot occurred in 1980, several events combined to lead many African Americans in Miami to believe they were victims of discrimination. Among these were the separate falls from grace of several of Dade County's most powerful black leaders. Some blacks felt it was open season on prominent black leaders. The first to fall was civil rights hero Rev. Edward T. Graham, in 1975.

Graham had been a giant in the Dade County civil rights movement in the 1950s. He was directly responsible for many of the peaceful demonstrations that led to the breakdown of racial barriers in the county. As pastor of the venerable Mt. Zion Baptist Church in Overtown, Graham was in a pivotal position of influence and leadership in the movement, which was essentially led by the black clergy (with support from some prominent members of the white clergy). Well-known and respected in Miami, Graham was first appointed to the Miami City Commission in 1970. Two years later, he was elected to the Metro Commission in his own right. An investigation led by Assistant State Attorney Martin Francis Dardis implicated Graham and several other metro commissioners in an alleged bribery scheme in October 1974.

The investigation involved Surfside builder Leonard Roeder, who complained that George MacLean, former manager of Miami's Dinner Key Auditorium, was criminally harassing him to pay approximately twenty thousand dollars in order to gain approval of a condominium project in Miami Beach. Alan Rothstein, a former Miami city attorney, was also implicated in the investigation. MacLean pointed the finger at Rothstein, who happened to be the attorney for the project. Dardis pressured MacLean to testify against Rothstein in exchange for immunity. MacLean accepted the deal because the authorities had well-documented footage of him accepting a payoff in a Miami Beach parking lot. Rothstein, under the threat of a grand-larceny charge, was also granted immunity if he agreed to name public officials who had been involved in the scam. The two men named five county commissioners, including Graham, all of whom were reported to be accepting zoning bribes. Both MacLean and Rothstein submitted to and passed polygraph tests. The Metro Commission was plunged into a major scandal.

Graham had frequent social contacts with Rothstein, who testified that he handled the payoffs for Graham. He admitted that he frequently met Graham for lunch at a downtown Chinese restaurant called Suzanne's. He alleged that he paid Graham one thousand dollars per favorable vote. On May 9, 1975, Graham and two of the other commissioners were found guilty of accepting zoning bribes and were forced to resign from the commission. In 1978, however, the State Supreme Court overturned the convictions. Consequently, the charges were dropped, but the damage to Graham's reputation was irreparable. He died in relative obscurity in March 1987.

Metro Commissioner Neal Adams also fell from prominence in the mid–1970s after having been appointed in 1975 following Graham's conviction. He ran a grocery store in Brownsville, where he became an active force in grassroots organizing for political power and community betterment in the civil rights era. Adams organized and ran the Brownsville Improvement Association and the Brownsville NAACP Youth Council. He encouraged blacks in the community to register to vote. Especially concerned with the welfare of the community's underprivileged youth, he initiated a number of special programs to keep them off the streets and to involve them in constructive activities. His demeanor was unassuming and mild-mannered (almost to the point of self-deprecation), but his civic activism won the respect of many of the area's blacks and whites.[7]

Adams was suspended from the Metro Commission in 1979 pending the outcome of two felony indictments: operating illegal bingo games and maintaining a gambling house. According to Florida law, only registered charities could operate bingo games. The state claimed that Adams sublet the Northside Bingo Hall two or three nights a week under the names of his organizations and that he personally received over four hundred dollars a month from the games.

James Bailey, manager of Adams's operation, later testified that almost identical amounts of cash were paid to the two organizations that leased the bingo hall, yet checks were written to the organizations. This implied that Adams was intentionally diverting proceeds from the games to personal use and was attempting to conceal his doing so.

Adams was not without influential support. Several state, federal, and local officials took the stand on his behalf, but to no avail. Adams was found guilty on both counts. He could have received up to five years in prison, but the presiding judge chose to take into account Adams's past service to the community. Ousted from his seat on the commission, Adams lost the right to hold future public office and received two years' probation and a five-thousand-dollar fine. The trial judge said Adams may have tried to do too much for his community.

Only a month after his sentencing, the conviction was overturned and Adams's rights were restored. Despite his having vowed never to seek any kind of public office again, Adams's passion for public service prevailed and he attempted an ill-advised political comeback in 1979. He ran for the same seat that he held five years earlier but failed badly in the attempt. He lost to educator Barbara Carey, the black woman who had replaced him on the commission. He dropped out of political sight thereafter.

Then came the greatest fall of all. In the months leading up to the riot of 1980, Dade County was stunned by the fall of Dr. Johnny L. Jones, Dade's first black school superintendent.

Jones was born on July 26, 1933, in Greenville, North Carolina. His father, William Henry Jones, a carpenter and handyman, and his mother, Lucy, were strict disciplinarians. Because of his parents' financial problems, Johnny learned to work hard and hit the books, knowing it was the only way to succeed. After school he earned extra money shining shoes and picking peanuts on nearby farms. Throughout his academic career Jones was seen as a high achiever.

When it came time for college, Jones chose Florida Normal College in St. Augustine, which he attended for only a short time. He transferred to Bethune-Cookman College in Daytona Beach, majoring in English. He achieved a good academic record, and graduated from college in June 1955. Having difficulty landing a job, he enlisted in the Air Force. Shortly thereafter, he married his college sweetheart, Mildred. The couple lived in Montana, where Johnny Jones was serving as an

Air Force personnel specialist. After he finished his military obligation, Jones and his wife moved to Bradenton, Florida, and both found teaching jobs at Lincoln Memorial High School, an all-black school.

Johnny Jones was an immediate hit. He became involved in helping students in new projects through fund raising and advertisements. Although teaching was his first love, his ambition was to be an administrator. For that he needed a doctorate degree, and he earned it from the University of Idaho in 1963. Upon receiving his degree, Dr. Jones moved to Miami, where he became an assistant principal at predominantly black George Washington Carver Junior High School in Coconut Grove. From there his ascent to power was quick and steady. He was made coordinator of the school system's evaluation unit in 1966; principal of Liberty City's Drew Junior High in 1967; director of secondary schools for the north central area office in 1969; area superintendent of the northwest area office in 1971; and deputy superintendent for school operations in 1973.

Just when his career in the school system was beginning to peak, his personal life was shaken. In 1976 he filed for divorce from his wife, who received custody of their daughter, Joni, then seventeen. On January 22, 1977, Jones married Maytye Hammond, a teacher and opera singer. With his new wife and a bright future ahead, Jones charged on toward the superintendency.

Superintendent of Schools Dr. Ed Whigham resigned in 1976 and recommended Jones as his successor. However, the school board gave the position to a white man, Dr. Leonard Britton, the other deputy superintendent at the time. This decision sparked anger among many blacks, some of whom saw the school board as having been racist in its decision. In May of 1977 the tables were turned. Jones achieved his long-awaited goal when he won a third-ballot victory over Britton, granting him the superintendency.

Jones moved quickly to consolidate the power of the superintendent. Although he brought new and talented blood into the administrative ranks of the school system, Jones also elevated some of his friends into a tight circle of unofficial power, which some believed ruled the system with an obvious hand.

Jones had a take-charge style. He was a stylish dresser, always impeccable in appearance. He showed up unannounced at schools for surprise inspections and was known to have relieved principals of their duties on the spot. He was a student-oriented superintendent. He vir-

109. Dr. Johnny Jones, the first black superintendent of the Dade County Public School System. Dr. Jones was a strong advocate for students. He was swept from office in the infamous "gold plumbing caper" in 1979. Courtesy Dade County Public School System.

tually stopped the school system's practice of expelling the so-called bad kids to the streets. He felt that all school children should be in a school building, no matter how bad they were. He made providing quality education to black and disadvantaged students a high priority.

Jones became a major player in the county's power structure. He was an Orange Bowl committee member, a University of Miami trustee, and a board member of the Miami Dade Chamber of Commerce, among other positions of influence. His presence was nearly ubiquitous in the media. According to William "Bill" Perry, a close advisor and friend, Jones could walk with the kings and with the grassroots people. To many blacks, Jones's stature had reached almost messianic proportions. There were whispers that he might be looking ahead to becoming the nation's first black secretary of education. Then, it all fell apart.

In 1979, in what was coined the "gold plumbing caper," Dr. Johnny L. Jones, the county's top black role model, was indicted for using school system funds to purchase bathroom fixtures for a vacation home he was building in Naples, Florida. Prosecutor Ira Lowery professed that the evidence was cut and dried. The order for plumbing fixtures consisted of a six-foot tub, a three-bowl sink, a bidet, low-boy toilets, a jacuzzi, and gold-plated fixtures. At the time this order was placed, Jones ordered changes on the building plans for his Naples home. The changes called for similar fixtures. The fixtures, which Jones claimed were for a new class at MacArthur South Senior High School, almost perfectly matched the color scheme in his Naples home.

After one of the most sensational trials in Dade County history, Jones was found guilty, and on December 4, 1980, he was sentenced to three years in prison and five years' probation for his involvement in the gold plumbing caper. He was also fined five thousand dollars and required to perform four hundred hours of community service during his probation. Solomon Barnes, a descendent of one of Lemon City's pioneer black families and the principal of MacArthur South High School, was accused of assisting Jones in the plumbing scheme. He, too, was convicted and was sentenced to serve five years in prison.

Jones was convicted by an all-white jury. The state had used its peremptory challenges to excuse five blacks from serving on the panel. Blacks in Miami were incensed, but defense attorneys Fletcher Baldwin, William Frates, and Terry Bienstock wasted no time in filing the appeal. Prosecutor Ira Lowery denied that the state overstepped its bounds by excusing the five black potential jurors. The prosecution proclaimed that the potential jurors were biased, as the black community had convinced itself of Jones's innocence even before the trial began.

Several months later, Jones was back in court defending himself against charges related to his involvement with a textbook supplier who claimed that Jones was accepting bribes. During the course of that trial, Jones was charged with witness tampering and solicitation of perjury. He was convicted on the bribery charge.

On February 26, 1985, the gold plumbing caper conviction was reversed by the state's Third District Court of Appeals. The appellate court agreed that the state had acted improperly in excusing the black potential jurors. This decision was a clear descendent of the Florida Supreme Court's 1984 landmark ruling in *Neil vs. Florida,* which held that either side in a criminal trial may be called upon to explain its exercise of peremptory challenges when it is suspected that the challenges were used in a racially discriminating manner.

During the appeal, Jones remained free on bond and worked a few odd jobs. He worked as a salesman for a fruit-drink company and then as director of a private social-service agency. With partners, he later opened a restaurant on Biscayne Boulevard called The Place, where he practiced his special abilities as a cook.

On September 23, 1984, Jones was again in the news when the car he was driving accidentally crashed into a house in northwest Miami, crushing six-year-old Allan Duroscar to death. Jones claimed that two cars were racing down the street and swerved in front of him. He said he lost control of the car, which traveled 145 feet, jumping the sidewalk and knocking down a traffic sign just before it crashed into the Duroscar home. The police said that the boy was crushed between the grille of the car and an inside wall of the house. A witness gave an account which supported Jones's version. Jones passed a roadside sobriety test and suffered only minor injuries in the accident. He was charged with careless driving.

In May 1985, Jones finally faced his first experience of prison after the Florida Supreme Court said it had no jurisdiction to review the issues raised by Jones's appeal on the bribery conviction. Jones was ordered to jail on a two-year sentence, where he continued to operate his restaurant on a work-release program. He was allowed to leave the North Dade Detention Center each morning at eight and return at midnight, except on Mondays, when he was required to stay behind bars. He was not allowed to return home at any time and was forced to pay the county seven dollars a day for room and board. After serving less than a month on the work-release program, Jones was released from jail. Dade Circuit Judge Ellen Morphonious decided that Jones should be allowed to be free until his appeals were exhausted.

On August 10, 1985, the former school superintendent was acquitted of the careless-driving charges. County Judge Alfonso Sepe said that eyewitness accounts that another car forced Jones off the road were more credible than the prosecutor's diagrams and the opinion of an accident-reconstruction expert with limited experience. "Justice prevailed this time," said Jones after his acquittal. Jones said that the knowledge that he had caused the death of young Allan Duroscar "tears me up inside, and I have to live with that for the rest of my life."

After his temporary release from prison, Dr. Jones was plagued with many personal problems. Financial difficulties seemed to follow him wherever he went. In October 1985 Circuit Judge Daniel L. Levy ordered that his restaurant, The Place, be sold at public auction. In his ruling, Levy granted an $84,211 foreclosure judgment against Jones and his partners, who included his daughter, Joni Fortune. Later that month Jones faced tax-fraud charges related to failing to report income in 1978 and 1979, his last two years as superintendent. And in October 1985, Dr. Jones was ordered to jail to resume serving the two-year sentence for the bribery conviction. Throughout that sentence, Jones was allowed to participate in the work-release program again.

Dr. Jones was released from jail for the second time in December 1985 after he asked the court to reduce his sentence. "I've learned much. I've suffered much. I feel that I failed the children. For that, I'm sorry," he said. Judge Morphonious listened to his plea and changed the sentence to two years' probation. As part of the probation, the judge said that Jones must organize a new community service program. This obligation required Jones to work four hours a day, five days a week for the remaining two-year sentence, a total of 2,080 hours.

On July 3, 1986, the state attorney's office announced that Jones would not be retried on the grand-theft charges in connection with the gold plumbing case. In making the announcement, Janet Reno, the state attorney, reported that two key prosecution witnesses refused to cooperate. One had been convicted of theft and sentenced to six months in jail and the other proclaimed that if subpoenaed, he would invoke his right against self-incrimination. Dr. Jones died on December 3, 1993. He was the epitome of the black fallen star.[8]

Other Incidents (1979)

In the fifteen months preceding the 1980 riot, a series of five highly sensitive incidents reinforced the belief widely held among blacks that they could never expect fair treatment from the criminal justice system of Dade County. The first involved a black school child and a white Florida highway patrolman.

At three o'clock on January 9, 1979, an eleven-year-old black girl was walking home from school in rural Homestead in south Dade County. Willie T. Jones, a white member of the Florida Highway Patrol, stopped her at South Dixie Highway and 312th Street. Jones told her that a girl fitting her description had stolen candy from a nearby store and ordered the child to get in the back of his car. The frightened girl complied, whereupon Jones drove her to a field, parked his cruiser, and moved into the back seat with her. Under the pretense of searching her, he fondled the girl's breasts while she quietly wept. She later told her uncle, with whom she was living at the time, that the trooper then told her to remove her panties. She said she refused and started to cry aloud. The officer withdrew his demand but proceeded to touch the child's vaginal area through her underclothing. Jones then drove the girl to a spot near her home and dropped her off.

The child was so distraught that, at first, she told her uncle and aunt only that a policeman had picked her up and accused her of stealing. That evening, however, she told them the whole story, including the words she remembered the policeman saying before he drove off: "We're still friends, aren't we?" Her uncle called the highway patrol office to report the incident, and an investigator was sent to his home a few hours later. The girl remembered the trooper's name tag. His last name, she thought, was Jones. The investigator showed her photographs of several troopers, including one of Patrolman Willie T. Jones, whom the girl readily identified as the patrolman who had picked her up.

After more than three weeks of investigations, during which he failed a lie-detector test regarding the incident, Jones was arrested and charged with lewd and lascivious assault on a child. He was allowed to resign from the patrol before the precise time of his arrest; thus, the record would show that he had resigned because of personal problems and that he was unemployed when arrested. At his arraignment he was not required to post bond and was released in his own custody.

The girl's relatives said they were advised by their attorney, Otis Wallace, a black man, to keep quiet about the case to protect the child and because he might eventually file a civil suit against the state on the family's behalf. The Dade State Attorney's Office, the Florida Highway Patrol and, of course, Jones's attorney also kept quiet about the incident. Their silence, however, helped create the later perception among blacks that there had been a conspiracy to suppress publicity.

The state requested that as punishment the trooper be required to undergo psychological treatment and that he pay for the child's counseling. No jail time was requested. The girl's uncle agreed to the arrangement. But Dade Circuit Judge Jon Gordon, to whom the case was assigned, was uncomfortable with the case. He viewed it as an arrangement between the state attorney's office and the defense attorney to go easy on Jones, and he wondered in open court whether the matter would have been handled differently if the victim had been white and the offending officer black. He said the case smacked of racism and removed himself from it, whereupon it was turned over to Judge David Levy.

On August 9, 1979, seven months after the incident, Jones pleaded *nolo contendere* to the charges and was given three years' probation. He was told by the court that he could never work again as a police officer, and he was ordered to undergo psychotherapy and to pay for any psychiatric care the girl might require. Less than four months after the trial, Jones, who was married and the father of two children, was pronounced to be no longer in need of psychological treatment. This pronouncement was made despite Jones having been diagnosed as a borderline psychotic and despite suspicions that he had committed previous similar offenses.

Jones made only two monthly payments for the girl's psychiatric treatment. Then living with her mother in South Carolina, she was described by her mother as withdrawn and suffering from frequent nightmares. Only after the trooper had become delinquent in payments for the child's counseling did the family decide to make the story public.

Under severe criticism from blacks, now that the whole arrangement had been publicized, Judge Levy and the state attorney explained that they had agreed to the sentence because the girl's family had agreed to it, pointing out that the girl's uncle wanted Jones to receive treatment rather than punishment. In July 1980 Jones was indicted by a federal grand jury on charges of illegally arresting and sexually abusing the girl, both violations of her civil rights. Before Jones could be arrested, however, he left the county and has not been heard from since.[9]

One month after Trooper Jones assaulted his victim, several white Dade County police officers were accused of assaulting a black junior high school teacher in an incident that enraged blacks. Shortly after seven o'clock on the evening of February 12, 1979, officers conducting a drug raid knocked on the door of Nathaniel Lafleur's home at

9245 Northwest Twenty-fifth Avenue. According to Lafleur, who was watching television at the time, this is what happened.[10]

At the knock on the door, he called out, "Who's there?" An unfamiliar name was given in response, so Lafleur asked again, "Who's there?" and again was given an unfamiliar name. He opened the door and saw several men, one dressed as a police officer, pointing a gun at him.

Lafleur slammed the door, locked it, and awoke his friend, Loretha McCrary, who was sleeping on the living room couch. He ran to the bedroom, closed the door, called 911, and reported that the police were breaking into his house. The police then broke in. They pushed the woman onto the couch and said they were looking for narcotics. When McCrary told them, "You've got the wrong house," a rifle was put to her face.

As Lafleur cowered near a closet, the officers knocked out a panel in the bedroom door. He said the officers threw him on a bed, kicked him in the kidney, and pistol-whipped him while one officer held a pistol to his head, demanding to know where the drugs were. He said he was told they would blow his head off if he didn't tell them.

At this point, according to Lafleur's account, his twenty-year-old son, Hollis, arrived home. Hollis said he asked a plainclothesman on the porch what was going on. He was told that the police had a warrant, but when he asked to see it, an officer, later identified as John Mullally, pulled his wallet from his back pocket (with his badge in it), hit Hollis in the face with it, and struck him in the eye with his fist. Hollis said he was grabbed from behind by another officer, who was not identified, and was hit twice over the head with a flashlight.

The search of the Lafleur home lasted two and one-half hours. Lafleur was charged with resisting arrest. His son was charged with obstructing an officer in the performance of his duties. Both were also charged with battery on a police officer. A loaded pistol was confiscated, but no drugs were found. After being treated at a hospital, Nathaniel Lafleur was released the next day on a bond of about two thousand dollars. Doctors found blood cells in his urine, indicating kidney damage. His eye was red and swollen, and he had a badly bruised knee.

As it turned out, Loretha McCrary was right. The police had raided the wrong house. Two days later county officers raided a house nearby at 9121 Northwest Twenty-fifth Street, the one they had intended to search the first time, and confiscated half an ounce of marijuana. No arrests were made.

The police account of what happened at the Lafleur house differed from Lafleur's story. According to the police, Officer James Leggett knocked on the door and told Lafleur they had a search warrant, whereupon Lafleur slammed the door on Leggett's hand, causing lacerations and swelling. The police burst into the house and chased Lafleur into his bedroom. Officer Vincent P. Farina said he saw Lafleur run over and reach under the mattress of his bed, then run into a closet. The officer pulled Lafleur from the closet and handcuffed him. The officers reported they found a loaded pistol under the mattress. The police account of Hollis Lafleur's involvement was that he refused to wait outside when asked to do so. He allegedly swore, said he was going inside, and then pushed Officer Mullally aside, whereupon a struggle ensued.

On February 16, four officers were suspended without pay for their part in the raid. Officer Leggett, the only officer in uniform, was not suspended. At the request of E. Wilson Purdy, the director of public safety for Dade County, State Attorney Janet Reno, who would later become United States attorney general in the Clinton administration, dropped the charges against Lafleur and his son. Purdy wrote a letter of apology to the school teacher. The department also changed its policy to one requiring that at least a sergeant or a lieutenant be present whenever search warrants were served. The Dade County grand jury, however, refused to indict the officers for criminal wrongdoing. Because of the extensive press coverage of the raid and its aftermath, including numerous editorials in local newspapers, Lafleur's name became a household word in black and white homes throughout Dade County.

Later in 1979 another racially charged incident occurred. On the evening of September 2 Randy Heath, a twenty-two-year-old black man, was driving with his sister Theresa through a warehouse district in Hialeah, the county's third-largest city, when, according to Theresa, he stopped the car and went to urinate. As he stood next to a warehouse wall, he was approached by Larry Shockley, a white off-duty Hialeah police officer. With his gun drawn, Shockley ordered Heath to put his hands against the wall. Shockley later testified that he thought Heath was a burglar.

In his first account of the incident, Shockley stated that Heath resisted and was shot during a struggle. During an investigation more than five months later, Shockley stated that Heath did not resist and that after placing his cocked pistol behind Heath's head, the gun accidentally went off, fatally wounding Heath. The day after the shooting, the Hialeah Police Department announced that Shockley had been suspended with pay pending an investigation by the state attorney's office. A later investigation by a local newspaper showed that Shockley had not been suspended.

Instead, one month after the killing, he was given a week's leave with pay to attend the National Police Revolver Championship in Jackson, Mississippi. Two months after the shooting, Shockley received a merit-pay increase on the basis of a departmental report noting that Shockley patrolled aggressively and exhibited a high degree of initiative. Where he needed to improve, the report said, was in the area of tactfulness.

For reasons never clarified, the state attorney required nearly five months to take the Shockley case to a Dade County grand jury, which cited Shockley for negligence in mishandling his weapon but found no evidence of criminal wrongdoing. Some blacks accused the state attorney of racism and of failing to expeditiously prosecute those cases in which blacks were victimized by whites, especially by white police officers. Janet Reno denied the charges.

At the close of the 1970s a mistrustful and angry black Miami slipped from pessimism to cynicism. As blacks fumed, the stage was now set for the greatest of all Miami riots.

It was Miami's darkest hour. On May 17, 1980, the world watched as Miami erupted in its most violent racial spasm in the history of the city. Sparked by the acquittals of several white Dade County police officers in the beating and killing of an unarmed black motorcyclist named Arthur McDuffie, the riot cost over $100 million in property damages. It raged for four days, and eighteen people, most of whom were black, lost their lives. In the confused aftermath of the riot, blacks were promised economic and political change. The end result has been disappointing, since none of the post-riot measures has significantly impacted the lives of inner-city blacks in Miami or other Dade County communities.

Two other very significant racial disturbances occurred in Miami after the 1980 riot. Both involved questionable police shootings. In 1982 in an Overtown video arcade, a young black man named Nevel Johnson was shot and killed by Miami police officer Luis Alvarez as Johnson played video games. Within minutes Overtown was in full-scale riot. Alvarez was ultimately charged with acting recklessly and with culpable negligence. He was found not guilty. No major outburst followed the verdict.

Then, in 1989 in Overtown another Miami police officer, William Lozano, killed two young black men, Clement Anthony Lloyd and Alan Blanchard as they raced northward on a motorcycle in an attempt to evade another police officer. Claiming he was in fear for his life as the motorcycle bore down on him, Lozano fired, killing the driver. His passenger died after the motorcycle slammed into an oncoming car. Again, Overtown was in riot, and other sections of Miami followed.

The McDuffie Incident (1979)

On December 17, 1979, in the dead of night on a deserted Miami side street, a group of at least six, and possibly as many as a dozen, white Dade County police officers beat a black motorcyclist named Arthur McDuffie to death. He was handcuffed during the assault. Even though the events of that tragic night unfolded in gruesome detail in the press, blacks did not riot in response to the killing itself. It was the failure of the criminal justice system to convict those who committed it; and more than that, it was the intentional exclusion of blacks from the trial jury that inflamed many black people. As in the trial of Dr. Johnny L. Jones, blacks had been intentionally excluded from the jury box by a bevy of defense attorneys using peremptory challenges. The rage would not be constrained.

The killing took place in late 1979. At 5:00 P.M. on Sunday, December 16, McDuffie, a divorced thirty-three-year-old black insurance agent and the father of two small children, left the house in northwest Dade County where he lived with his sister, Dorothy. He was riding a 1973 black and orange Kawasaki 900 motorcycle, which he had borrowed from his cousin, George Randolph. He was on his way to visit Lynwood Blackman, a friend for the past ten years, who lived at Fifty-ninth Street and North Miami Avenue. McDuffie had promised to tune the engine of a car belonging to Blackman's neighbor. When McDuffie arrived shortly before 5:30, he found he did not have the right tools, so he sat on his cycle and talked to Blackman's two daughters. When Blackman came outside at 5:30, he saw McDuffie heading west on Northwest Fifty-ninth Street.

McDuffie visited a female friend for several hours, possibly until as late as 1:00 A.M. Then he got on his motorcycle and headed north in the general direction of his sister's home. He never made it.

At 1:15 A.M. on December 17, McDuffie was seen by a white police officer, Sergeant Ira Diggs, heading north along North Miami Avenue. He slowed down at a red light, according to a police report, and "popped a wheelie," a stunt in which the cyclist pulls up his front wheel and takes off. McDuffie was said to have made a provocative gesture toward Diggs, who sat in his police car parked near the intersection. McDuffie then raced away.

Sergeant Diggs gave chase. Exactly why McDuffie tried to flee was debated later. One theory was that his driver's license had been revoked. Whatever his motivation, McDuffie was soon pursued by more than a dozen police cars in a terrorizing chase, which lasted eight minutes and at some points exceeded one hundred miles an hour. He finally stopped at the corner of North Miami Avenue and Thirty-eighth Street as police units swarmed in.

The first units to arrive were those of Officers Mark Mier and Charles Veverka, followed closely by William Hanlon and Sergeant Diggs. Mier

110. Arthur McDuffie who, while handcuffed, was beaten to death by several white Dade County police officers in December 1979. An all-white Tampa jury's acquittal of all the officers involved on May 17, 1980, resulted in the great riot of that year. From Bruce Porter and Marvin Dunn, *The Miami Riot of 1980: Crossing the Bounds*. Courtesy of Porter and Dunn.

drew his service revolver, aimed it at McDuffie, and ordered him to freeze while Veverka approached McDuffie and grabbed him by the shoulder, pulling him off the motorcycle. Veverka later claimed that at this point McDuffie turned around and, with his right fist, swung at and grazed him. Additional units continued to swarm in, including some from the Miami Police Department. The City of Miami officers present were Sergeant Wayne English and Officers John G. Gerant, Alexander Prince, and Richard Gotowala. All of the officers on the scene were white.

McDuffie was severely beaten by no fewer than six, and possibly as many as twelve, Dade County officers. George Yoss, an assistant state attorney who prosecuted the case, reported that McDuffie managed to fight back in the beginning even though Veverka held him in a bear hug, but then he was pulled away from Veverka by other officers engaged in the melee. In three minutes, it was all over. McDuffie lay immobile, his head split open and his brain swelling uncontrollably. He died four days later.

Immediately after the incident, a rescue unit was called and police headquarters was advised that the man involved in the arrest had suffered head injuries. McDuffie, already slipping into a coma, was taken to Jackson Memorial Hospital. Officer William Hanlon, who later became a key witness for the state, called the Liberty City headquarters of the Public Safety Department (PSD) with the first version of the incident. Over the radio, he told a lieutenant that McDuffie had been injured falling off his motorcycle.

In their attempt to conceal the facts, Hanlon and several other PSD officers tried to make it appear that McDuffie had lost control of his motorcycle when trying to turn a corner, that he was thrown from the motorcycle, lost his helmet, and struck his head on the curb. Hanlon admitted later that he kicked McDuffie's motorcycle, stepped on McDuffie's glasses, and placed McDuffie's watch on the road and shot at it with a spare revolver which he kept strapped to his ankle. At the trial of the officers who were later indicted, Hanlon explained that he committed the last act for no reason other than pure vandalism.

A marked patrol car also ran over the motorcycle to make it look as if it had been damaged in an accident. Officers used their night sticks to break all the glass gauges on the motorcycle. This act, although designed to hide their crime, ended up being incriminating. The medical examiner and other investigators who inspected the motorcycle wondered how an accident in which a cycle fell on one side or the other would result in broken glass on both sides.

At 4:58 A.M. headquarters ordered Officer Robert Hinman to conduct a routine investigation of the accident scene. When Hinman arrived he found that the scene had been cleaned up or, in police jargon, destroyed. Hinman reported over his radio to headquarters that there was "no way I can investigate it if the scene has been destroyed. I can respond to the emergency room and sit and hold the guy's hand but there's nothing else I can do with it." Headquarters asked, "Why did they tow all the stuff so quick?" Hinman replied, "I have no idea."[1] At 5:30 A.M. with growing concern among the involved officers that the accident version might not hold up, the sergeant at the scene radioed headquarters:

Sergeant Evans: That guy last night?

Headquarters: Yeah?

Evans: He was hit with kelites [police flashlights].

Headquarters: He was hit with kelites?

Evans: Uh-huh.

Headquarters: Oh, shit.[2]

Sergeant Evans's report on the McDuffie beating reached Commander Dale Bowlin, senior officer in the Liberty City PSD headquarters, at midmorning on the seventeenth. The inconsistencies made him suspicious. "We discussed the reports that same day, in the afternoon and throughout the day. We questioned the officers about the accuracy of the reports. We were not satisfied."[3]

He was not the only one to raise questions. The county medical examiner, Dr. Ronald Wright, brought in on the case after McDuffie's death, also had his doubts. He did not believe that the extensive injuries to McDuffie's head were caused by a fall from a motorcycle. McDuffie appeared to have been beaten to death with a blunt object like a galvanized pipe, police nightstick, or heavy-duty kelite flashlight. Wright began to work closely with Commander Bowlin, with Bowlin's boss, Major Willie Morrison, a black man, and with the department's internal review section. Their suspicions increased on December 18 after internal review talked to the City of Miami officers who were on the scene but not involved in the incident. Interviews with these officers convinced Bowlin and the others that McDuffie had been severely beaten. At this point, internal review notified the state attorney of the case.

On December 24, the first article about the inconsistencies in the reports of McDuffie's death appeared in the *Miami Herald*. Two days later Officer Charles Veverka became the first broken link in the chain of conspiracy. As he later told a newspaper reporter, he was at home on Christmas Eve with his children, thinking about McDuffie's children, who would face their first Christmas without their father. He decided to turn himself in. Veverka went to police headquarters with his father, a PSD lieutenant, and told his superiors what he knew of the beating. A total of nine police officers were suspended in connection with the death of Arthur McDuffie: Ira Diggs, Michael Watts, William Hanlon, Alex Marrero, Herbert Evans Jr., Mark Mier, Charles Veverka, Joseph Del Toro, and Eric Seyman. Four of the suspended officers (Marrero, Diggs, Watts, and Hanlon) were charged with manslaughter and tampering with evidence. A fifth, Sergeant Evans, was charged with tampering with evidence and leading the coverup. Eula McDuffie, the victim's mother, responded to the arrests with a theme that would be adopted by Miami blacks: "They beat my son like a dog. They beat him just because he was riding a motorcycle and because he was black."[4]

McDuffie was buried on December 29, wearing his full-dress corporal's uniform of the U.S. Marine Corps. The highly emotional funeral, including riveting television images of McDuffie's flag-draped casket, his grief-stricken mother, and his former wife and eight-year-old daughter, was widely broadcast that evening.[5] The next day, a gripping close-up picture of McDuffie's tortured mother was carried on the front page of a local newspaper. Although blacks were most vocal in their rage, most whites were also appalled by the killing.

When it was announced that the police officers were being charged only with manslaughter instead of murder, the black newspapers and radio stations ran angry commentaries accusing Janet Reno of being a racist and calling for her resignation. In response, Reno argued that the facts of the case did not warrant filing murder charges and invited anyone with more evidence to come forward. No one did.

On January 1, 1980, however, the state attorney announced that suspended officers Charles Veverka and Mark Mier had been granted immunity and would testify as witnesses for the state. The following day, with Veverka and Mier now apparently willing to say that Alex Marrero struck the blows that caused McDuffie's death, and with Hanlon saying that McDuffie was handcuffed when Marrero struck him, Reno announced that the charge against Marrero would be raised to second-degree murder. "We increased the charges," said Assistant State Attorney Yoss, "not because of pressure from the black community, which was commonly held to be the reason, but because we now had evidence that Marrero acted in a way that was eminently dangerous to another, evincing a depraved mind regardless of human life, which is second-degree murder."[6]

On January 3 two dozen blacks joined by a handful of whites marched in protest of the McDuffie killing in front of the county's criminal justice building. They carried signs reading "Justice for McDuffie" and "Right the Unrightable Wrong." A story about the killing and the demonstration was carried in a national magazine as the case attracted attention outside of Miami.

Reno assigned the case to Hank Adorno, her most experienced prosecutor, to head a team of what she considered her best assistant state attorneys. The state also decided to try all the officers at once instead of independently, a move that drew considerable criticism after the trial. Local coverage was so pervasive that defense attorneys asked for the trial to be moved out of Dade County because it was impossible for the officers to receive a fair trial in Miami. Blacks in Miami, however, feared that if the trial were moved, there would be a greater chance for the officers to be found not guilty. The Tampa branch of the NAACP pointed out that only a few months earlier there had been a strikingly similar case in which a white Tampa police officer had been acquitted by an all-white jury of fatally beating a young black motorcyclist stopped for a routine traffic violation.

On March 3 Judge Lenore Nesbitt agreed that the trial should be moved and ordered the case to be tried in Tampa. "The case is a time bomb," she said. "I don't want to see it go off in my courtroom or in this community."[7]

On March 28 Judge Nesbitt dismissed the two felony charges against William Hanlon on the grounds that the state lacked the evidence to proceed against him. The state attorney's office then dropped its lesser charges against Hanlon, provided him immunity from further prosecution, and announced that he would testify as a witness for the state along with officers Veverka and Mier.

The trial began March 31, and immediately the team of defense lawyers used their thirty-four peremptory challenges to remove blacks from the pool of potential jurors. (Peremptory challenges of prospective jurors may be used by either side to remove potential jurors without having to give a reason. Since the officers were being tried together, they had a total of thirty-four such challenges.) "We wanted a black on that jury as badly as they didn't want one," said Yoss. "We knew how many blacks were in the group of potential jurors waiting to be called in. We would send someone down to the room to look to see how many were left. By about the third week of jury selection we realized that they had enough challenges left to bump all the blacks waiting to be called. Realizing we were going to have an all-white jury, we tried to get the best six we could."[8]

From the medical examiner's testimony in the early stage of the trial, it became clear that when McDuffie's skull was fractured, he was lying face down with his head against the pavement or, more likely, the curb. That position gave no possibility of his head recoiling from the blows, accounting for the fact that his skull was split open. He was handcuffed at the time. The medical examiner graphically described the force used to inflict McDuffie's fatal injuries:

Prosecutor: Would you describe to the members of the jury, as best as you can, what amount of force would be necessary to cause that particular fracture, the one between the eyes?

Wright: It's the equivalent of falling from a four-story building and landing head first.

Prosecutor: On what?

Wright: On concrete.

The state then brought forth its key witnesses, the immunized police officers. The first was Charles Veverka, who admitted to pulling McDuffie from his motorcycle and exchanging punches with him. He said, however, that within seconds of his physical contact with McDuffie, other officers, including Sergeants Diggs and Marrero, literally snatched McDuffie from him and proceeded to beat him violently with nightsticks and kelites. Veverka described for the jury how Marrero battered McDuffie while he lay helpless on the pavement:

Prosecutor: What did Officer Marrero say?

Veverka: The words I heard were, "Easy. One at a time."

Prosecutor: What did Marrero do?

Veverka: I observed him, with either a kelite or a nightstick, holding it with both hands and bringing it over his head and come down twice across the top back area of Mr. McDuffie's head.

(The prosecutor asked Veverka to demonstrate to the jury the way he saw Marrero strike McDuffie.)

Veverka (demonstrating): I observed him straddle Mr. McDuffie in this manner, kelite or nightstick, whichever it was, holding it with both hands, bring it back over his head and come down on the side or the back of the top area of his head.

Prosecutor: How hard did he hit him?

Veverka: Oh, extremely hard.

Veverka testified that although he was standing several feet away from McDuffie, blood splattered on his pants leg. The questioning then turned to the coverup. Veverka said that Sergeant Evans was the leader. Veverka testified that he heard Evans say something like, "The bike needs more damage," and that Evans told Hanlon to get in the car and ride up on the bike. When Veverka heard a crashing sound, he looked up and saw a police unit sitting on top of the motorcycle.

Veverka next testified that Sergeant Evans advised him to write up the incident, making it appear that McDuffie had injured himself in a fall from the motorcycle before he was touched by the officers at the scene; Veverka complied. Under cross-examination by defense attorneys, Veverka admitted that he submitted several false reports of the incident and that he had lied to the police investigators in the coverup attempt.

The defense's major focus was to raise questions about the credibility of the immunized officers and to have it appear that the officers were lying to conceal their own involvement. Indeed, the defense accused Veverka and Hanlon of striking the blows that actually killed McDuffie. As the trial proceeded, it became increasingly difficult for the jury to discern who did what during the two or three minutes of the beating.

Another immunized officer, Mark Mier, next took the stand. Mier's testimony jolted the state's case by contradicting Veverka on two key points. First, Mier testified that on his arrival at the scene, apparently within moments of the arrival of Diggs and Veverka, he pointed his service revolver at McDuffie and ordered him to freeze. Looking down the barrel of his gun at McDuffie, thus having a clear view of McDuffie's actions, Mier testified that he saw McDuffie throw no punches. The jury was left to decide for themselves whether Veverka was lying about the punch in order to make it appear acceptable that he, too, struck McDuffie.

Mier testified that he also saw Marrero straddle McDuffie and strike him with his kelite or nightstick. But Mier contradicted Veverka in his description of the way in which Marrero struck the blows. Mier said that they came not in a chopping, overhead fashion, as Veverka had testified, but in a side-to-side fashion, from right to left. The jury now had to decide which, if either, of the two versions they would believe.

The defense attorneys attacked Mier's credibility on the grounds that he, too, had participated in the coverup: "Would you tell me," said one defense attorney during Mier's cross-examination, "is there some way that the members of this jury, or anyone in this courtroom, can tell when you mean it and when you don't mean it, when you swear to tell the truth, so help you God? I mean, is there a little smile on your lip, or are your ears turning red, or is there some way we can tell when you're telling the truth and when you're not?" He replied, "No, sir."

Next, the state called John Gerant, an officer with the Miami Police Department, who had been present the night McDuffie was attacked, but who was not accused of any wrongdoing. Gerant's testimony was crucial because he was not an immunized witness. Unlike Veverka, who admitted hitting McDuffie, and Mier, who helped in the coverup, Gerant had nothing to hide regarding his own actions that night. In his initial testimony, Gerant supported Veverka's account of the way the fatal blows were dealt. He said the man who struck McDuffie hit him in a chopping overhead fashion, as Veverka had testified. Gerant, however, seriously damaged the state's case and shocked the courtroom by pointing not to Marrero as the man who dealt the killing blow, but to another defendant, Michael Watts.

As chief prosecutor Hank Adorno explained to CBS News after the trial, the state's case suffered severely from the Rashomon syndrome — the tendency of eyewitnesses to see things from different perspectives and angles, and at different times. "The Watts beating occurred at the beginning, before Marrero ever got there. The Marrero beating occurred later on. I think, any time that you're trying a case . . . based solely on eyewitness recollection of an event, you're going to have three people looking at the same things and seeing different things. And that's what I had to get across to the jury. That doesn't mean . . . it didn't happen; it means that they're looking at it from different [viewpoints]."

In addition to the conflicting testimony from immunized witnesses, another issue the jury had to consider was the character and possible culpability of the state's key witnesses. Were they any better or worse than the officers against whom they were testifying? In no instance was this issue more straightforwardly presented than in the testimony of William Hanlon. Judge Nesbitt had granted Hanlon a directed verdict of acquittal of the felony charges against him three days before his testimony against the other officers began. The state immunized him and forced him to take the stand; Hanlon became the third officer to accuse Marrero of striking the fatal blows. Under pressure from a defense attorney, however, Hanlon indicated that he was not beyond thoughts of brutality that night.

Hanlon described the casual nature in which he suggested to several officers how McDuffie's legs could be broken. Edward Carhart, a defense attorney, told CBS News after the trial that this was about the most chilling thing he had ever heard a witness say in a courtroom: "You have a man lying there handcuffed, semi-conscious, and Mr. Hanlon says it popped into his mind, 'You could break a man's legs if you wanted to.' And he walked over to demonstrate how it could be done. I find that an incredible thought process."

In the defense portion of the trial, Diggs and Marrero were called to testify. Diggs denied hitting McDuffie, but it was Marrero's testimony that added a new element to the trial. Marrero admitted to struggling with McDuffie, including striking him several times. Marrero said, however, that he did it because McDuffie was trying to take his gun away from him.

News reports of Marrero's testimony claiming that McDuffie went for his gun were met with serious skepticism in black Miami. Marrero, the only officer charged with second-degree murder, was also the only one who claimed that McDuffie tried to reach for a police officer's gun. McDuffie's mother and brother insisted that McDuffie was not the sort to fight police officers.

At 11:52 A.M. on Saturday, May 17, after almost four weeks of testimony, the case went to the jury. In Miami it was a clear spring morning, with temperatures in the mid-seventies. The media had reported that the case had gone to the jury, but after such a long and complicated trial it seemed doubtful that verdicts would be returned quickly. Yet after just two hours and forty-five minutes of deliberation, the jury returned to the tense courtroom. From a crowded pressroom, dozens of reporters waited to relay the news to Miami. Into the unblinking eye of the single camera allowed into the courtroom, the clerk read the verdicts to a hushed audience:

We, the jury . . . this seventeenth day of May 1980, find the defendant, Michael Watts, as to count three of the information, manslaughter by unnecessary killing, not guilty. We, the jury . . . find the defendant, Herbert Evans, Jr., as to tampering with or fabricating physical evidence as charged in count five of the information, not guilty. We, the jury . . . find the defendant, Ira Diggs, as to count three of the information, tampering with or fabricating physical evidence, not guilty. We, the jury . . . find the defendant, Alex Marrero, as to count one of the information, second degree murder, not guilty.[9]

Thus began Miami's decade of fire.

The Riot

It took thirteen minutes for the clerk to read all the verdicts, and although the judge had warned against outbursts in the courtroom, the reading was followed by screams and weeping. The chief defendant, Alex Marrero, who had faced the second-degree murder charge, broke into tears and had to support himself by leaning on a wall. Frederica McDuffie, Arthur McDuffie's ex-wife, who had planned to remarry him before he was beaten to death, led McDuffie's sobbing mother through the crush of reporters. "My son! My son!" she cried, supported on both sides by members of her family. "They're guilty. They're guilty in God's sight and they have to live with this."[10] A dozen or more television cameras recorded it all for the evening news.

At 2:24 P.M. the news went out over the Associated Press wire, and most Miami radio stations interrupted their regular programming to report the verdicts. Several minutes later, WEDR, a radio station popular among young blacks, received so many angry and hysterical phone calls that Clyde McDonald, the afternoon deejay known as Iceman, became alarmed and called station manager Jerry Rushin at his home to ask what he should do. Rushin told McDonald to put him on the air from his house. "I knew all hell was going to break loose because

111. Miami police officer Alex Marrero weeping at his acquittal, 1980. Marrero was accused of being the one who struck the blow that cracked Arthur McDuffie's skull. Courtesy *Miami Herald*.

of this," Rushin said later. "I thought if I could get them thinking about something else, it might ease things." In his broadcast, Rushin proposed that the city's black leaders meet on Monday morning with State Attorney Janet Reno "to get some answers."[11]

Many Miamians, white and black, were shocked by the acquittals. For blacks, the trial had a significance that went beyond the McDuffie case. It represented the truest, most damning test of the entire legal system; the system they had been counseled was their best hope for achieving equal treatment in American society. For blacks, the gray areas of the case—the contradictory testimony, the credibility (or lack thereof) of the police witnesses, the way the prosecution had conducted its case, the expertise of the defense attorneys—all had little meaning. The fact remained that a number of white police officers had beaten an unarmed black man to death for a traffic violation and had not gotten so much as a slap on the wrist from the courts.

"For outsiders, I think, it would be impossible to appreciate the shock that went through the black community," said Major Clarence Dickson, the highest-ranking black in the Miami Police Department at the time. "I think it is safe to say that you'd almost have to be black to understand. All their grievances, all their distrust of the system, all the beliefs people had in the evils of the system—suddenly, it all turned out to be true."

Back at WEDR, the Iceman's phone lines were solidly clogged with angry callers. "People were saying they didn't want to wait until Monday morning to do something," Rushin later reported. By 3:45 P.M. three to four hundred people were milling around outside the station, talking animatedly about the verdict and shouting out their rage. "They were saying that the white jury had let off those white cops; that they wouldn't take it anymore and they wanted to do something."

"Whenever something like this happens, they look to the radio station. They think we can do something that other people can't." In an effort to calm people, Rushin brought several crowd members inside to let them express their frustration and anger on the air. Rushin says he forgot to make a tape of the day's broadcast, but at least one listener, Major Dickson of the Miami Police Department, wrote down what was said. "Rushin was saying things like, 'It's a cryin' shame, that all-white jury turning those white officers loose. How long can we continue to take this nonsense? When are we going to rise up and be heard?'" Often, Dickson said, Rushin's voice cracked, and he appeared to be on the verge of tears. Then came the community people, most of them women, with much sobbing and crying out, "Where can we go? What can we do?"

Another WEDR listener was a twenty-one-year-old black counselor in an ex-offender program run by the city, who usually kept the radio on while she worked. "You could feel the tension from the radio," she remembered. "You could hear it building up, and you could feel the hurt in his voice. You knew he felt really mad." Crowds of young blacks, many with large transistor radios balanced on their shoulders, were congregating near African Square Park on Sixty-second Street and also along Twenty-second Avenue near the site of the largest housing project in the county, the James E. Scott. The anger that poured over the airwaves echoed their own. "We had watched the trial every night," said one nineteen-year-old youth who was there. "All those pictures and descriptions explaining how they beat the man to death, and they found those guys guilty of nothing? Not nothing? That's like saying the man didn't die."

On every streetcorner, the litany of perceived wrongs was repeated: the Johnny Jones case, the Nathaniel Lafleur case, the Randy Heath incident, the Trooper Jones case, which in the minds of some blacks was tantamount to the rape of a black child by a white policeman, the constant mistreatment and harassment of black men by police, the failure of the city to do anything to fix up Martin Luther King Boulevard, the Cuban takeover of the city, the competition with Haitian immigrants—all came to the forefront.

Flanked by cinderblock bars, pool halls, mom-and-pop grocery stores, and one- and two-story public housing projects, Sixty-second Street looked like any other ghetto main drag in the city. Although the area was completely black, the street served whites, too, as the principal east-west access to I–95, Miami's major north-south highway. Whites also drove into the area on weekend nights looking for cocaine and marijuana, which were sold openly on street corners near African Square Park.

At about five, the first rocks and bottles were lofted at cars driven by whites along Sixty-second Street. One person who remembered just when it started was Betty Wiggs, an administrator in the Haitian Refugee Center on Twelfth Avenue at Sixty-second Street. She reported:

I was in my office on Saturday doing some paperwork. It was a very hot day and quite a few people were on the street. Around four-thirty or five o'clock, things began to get noisier than usual, so I took a peek outside. There were definitely more people than usual on the street, and I could hear some of them talking about the verdict in the McDuffie trial. Just as I was turning to go back inside, a small car passed down Sixty-second Street with what seemed like two white people in it. Just as it approached the light at Fourteenth Avenue people started throwing things at it. Someone yelled, "Get the crackers." There seemed to be a lot of tension and anger on the faces and lips of the people standing there. I went back inside and gathered my things. As I came out I could see some young men standing by the walk-light. They seemed to be pushing the light to make the cars stop there. I could feel that something was about to happen, so I left.

In Liberty City, as the police knew from previous disturbances, it was not unusual for young blacks to throw objects at cars to express their anger or to create excitement. "Rocks and bottles on Saturday night are more or less a common thing here," said Lieutenant Randall McGee, who was a platoon commander at the Liberty City Precinct of the PSD that afternoon. "It was nothing you'd ordinarily get too excited about." At the Liberty Square Housing Project, near African Square Park, some older people had even set up aluminum lawn chairs in front of their whitewashed bungalows to watch the fun.

At about 6:00 P.M., a rumor spread that a white man speeding along Sixty-second Street had shot a black child. It was only a rumor, but on that afternoon it was taken as factual. The Miami Police Department's rescue squad responded to a call about the incident, but was told that the child had already been taken to the hospital. Local hospitals had no record of such an admission. Nevertheless, the rumor added to the existing tension and drew hundreds more to Sixty-second Street.

By 6:15 the crowd was so large, and the flying rocks and bottles so thick, that the Miami Police Department, which patrols that section of Liberty City, pulled its few squad cars out of the area and set up roadblocks to divert white drivers. Their efforts were fruitless, however, because of a shortage of personnel and barricades.

At about 6:20 the mob got its first victim: a white derelict who was beaten and bloodied by young blacks at Sixty-second Street and Thirteenth Avenue. The police received several calls about a man down at that location, and at 6:30 an unmarked Miami Police Department car driven by Sergeant José Burgos tore down the street, picked up the man, and sped off. Before entering the area, Burgos had asked for a backup car, but he decided to try to save the man on his own. Accounts are sketchy at this point, but apparently Burgos's backup car left its post on Seventeenth Avenue, where it had been guarding the western entrance to Sixty-second Street, to aid in the rescue effort. As a result, several cars operated by unsuspecting whites entered the riot area. The way was opened for disaster.

One of these cars was a cream-colored 1969 Dodge Dart driven by eighteen-year-old Michael Kulp. With him were his twenty-two-year-old brother, Jeffrey, and a friend, Debra Getman, twenty-three, asleep in the back seat. The Kulp brothers, who had come to Miami from Spring City, Pennsylvania, a year earlier, had spent the day at the beach with Debra. Jeffrey sat alongside his brother in the front seat. The car had no radio, and Debra later told homicide detectives that none of the three had heard anything about the McDuffie verdicts.

As reconstructed by the police and eyewitnesses, the car was suddenly struck by a shower of rocks and bottles as it was going east along Sixty-second Street at Thirteenth Avenue. A chunk of concrete came through the windshield, striking Michael in the head and causing him to swerve onto the sidewalk. There, the car struck a seventy-five-year-old man named Albert Perry, fracturing his ankle, and a ten-year-old girl, Shanreka Perry. Moments before, Shanreka had been playing in her yard nearby when she spotted her sister and aunt walking toward a grocery store across Sixty-second Street. She started out to join them. Her aunt feared for the girl's safety in the growing chaos and remembered shouting back to her: "Girl, you better go home." That was the last thing Shanreka remembered.[12]

The Kulp car struck her and drove her up against the stucco wall of one of the buildings in the housing project, crushing her pelvis, severing her right leg, and smearing the wall with a wide swath of blood. Amid cries of horror and anger, the bleeding girl's leg was wrapped in a blanket from someone's clothesline. A black taxi driver coming down Sixty-second Street was hailed by the enraged crowd. The driver took the child to Jackson Memorial Hospital.

According to eyewitnesses, the accident further inflamed the mob, which dragged the Kulp brothers from their car and beat them savagely. Debra, who had been jolted awake by the barrage of rocks, managed to get away from the car and ran through the project to a street on the other side. Blacks helped her into a taxi, and she escaped with only a few cuts on her face.

From all accounts, the Kulp brothers were beaten continuously by a variety of people for about fifteen to twenty minutes. They were punched, karate-kicked, and struck with rocks, bricks, bottles, and pieces of concrete, one of which weighed twenty-three pounds. At one point, someone picked up a yellow *Miami Herald* newspaper dispenser and brought it down on Jeffrey Kulp's head. They were shot several times with a revolver and run over by a green Cadillac, whose driver then came over and stabbed them with a screwdriver.

An hour after the Kulp beatings, three other whites, Benny Higdon, twenty-one, his brother-in-law Robert Owens, fourteen, and Robert's friend, Charles Barreca, fifteen, were stoned and beaten at almost the same spot, and nearly as brutally as the Kulps. Of the three, only Barreca made it to the hospital alive, but he died there shortly afterward. "In my thirty years on the force, it was the most violent crime I've ever seen," said Sergeant Mike Gonzalez of the Miami Police Department's homicide squad, who directed the murder investigation. "We get a lot of cases where you have extreme violence—people beating up people and stabbing them and what not—but nothing like this." Gonzalez tried three times that night to get to the scene of the Kulp and Higdon murders, only to be driven back each time by angry crowds. "We weren't able to do any real investigation until it was all over," he later reported. "All we did that night was try to keep score."[13]

The fifth victim, Bertha Rogers, fifty-five, was driving north that night on Twenty-second Avenue in her 1966 Chevrolet Malibu, when, at about 9:30 she was struck by a shower of rocks in front of the Scott project at Sixty-ninth Street. Someone reached in and grabbed her purse. Gasoline was poured over her, and she and the car were set afire. A bystander got her out of the car and drove her to Jackson Hospital. She died of severe burns on May 22.

Forty-five minutes later, three blocks away on Twenty-second Avenue, a car driven by Emilio Muñoz, a sixty-three-year-old Cuban-born butcher, was stoned and overturned outside the Scott project at Seventy-second Street. As Muñoz lay pinned in the wreckage, the crowd beat and jabbed him with sticks. Then someone threw gasoline over the car and set it aflame. According to the medical examiner, however, Muñoz was already dead. Blood from the beating had trickled into his lungs, choking him to death. He would not be extricated from the charred car until the next day, at about the same time as a fishing boat waited in the harbor at Mariel, Cuba, to bring his wife and son to the United States.

The body of Chabillall Janarnauth, twenty-two, a light-skinned immigrant from Guyana known as "Shab" by his fellow workers in a Miami drafting shop, was found on Twenty-seventh Avenue near Fiftieth Street just before eleven o'clock. He was so severely mutilated that a friend identified him only by his brown boots and his distinctive hair and eyebrows. The police theorized that he had been beaten and then run over several times with his own car, which was never found.

The last victim that night was Mildred Penton, sixty-five, who was returning from the Flagler Dog Track with her husband and daughter when the crowd threw rocks at her car on Twenty-seventh Avenue near Forty-eighth Street. "We were just driving along and suddenly it felt like a brick building was falling on the car," her husband John said later. Mildred Penton was struck in the head by a brick and lost consciousness. After four days in a coma, she awoke briefly but then went back into a coma and died five weeks later.

The white people injured but not killed during the riot ranged from those with superficial glass cuts to those who were shot or beaten so severely that they were left permanently disabled. In all, 417 people were treated at the area's nine hospitals during the three principal days of rioting. No uniform statistics were kept according to race and time of admission, so it is difficult to be precise about victims and injuries at various times during the riot.

Shortly after the McDuffie verdicts were announced, officials of the local branch of the NAACP and other prominent blacks thought of holding a rally that night at the Metro Justice complex near downtown, not just to express their anger at the verdicts but also to dissipate energy that might lead to violence. "It was designed," said George Knox, former attorney for the City of Miami, "to be an orderly expression of hostility."[14] Director Jones of the PSD gave permission for the rally. It was announced at about five o'clock over WEDR and WMBM, the city's black-oriented stations, and also over many white stations.

By 7:45, about one thousand people stood in the parking lots and sidewalks in front of the Metro Justice Building, mostly young blacks but also some older blacks and even some whites. "In the beginning it seemed fine," said Michael O. Fowler, a UPI reporter who by now had heard reports of bottle throwing at cars but as yet knew nothing of the deaths in Liberty City. "People were talking freely, even joking." As many as three thousand had assembled when, because there was no public-address system, the crowd became increasingly restless over the lack of action. There were rhythmic chants of "justice, justice, justice," and "Reno must go." Someone got them singing "We Shall Overcome" and the gospel song "Amen." The crowd swayed in time to the music, but the atmosphere became tense. Many of the young people had their transistor radios with them, and news of what was happening in Liberty City was beginning to spill over the air.

The PSD had allotted fifteen officers to monitor the rally, but they were hopelessly outnumbered and considered it prudent to stay out of sight. Part of a smaller group headed for the front of the PSD headquarters. Three or four shirtless young men gestured taunts at the police inside the building. Egged on by each other, one finally kicked a hole in the glass front door.

The situation was quickly out of control. While the rally organizers pleaded for order, the crowd shouted its rage over the injustice of the McDuffie verdicts and of white society in general. Two PSD officers who had been watching events from a distance drove their cruiser into the crowd, apparently trying to scatter people, then sped off. The act added another provocation. Even blacks who under normal circumstances never would have done so found themselves drawn into acts of violence.

One such man was a thirty-two-year-old lawyer who worked for the state and attended the rally with his wife and ten-year-old son. "I remember being consumed with rage," he said, "and feeling that somehow I had to dramatize it." He had felt that way twice before, he said: once after the death of Dr. Martin Luther King Jr. when he and other black students at an Alabama college occupied an administration building in defiance of the police, and the other after the death of Robert F. Kennedy.

"Now I felt that I had to do something. I didn't want to let the moment pass." The first thing he did was to stand fast when a police car tried to move slowly through the crowd to break it up. "I refused to back down. I refused to move for him. Even though I was a public official, in a sense, I didn't identify with any official at that time. I identified with my black brothers, and all I could think about was how the criminal justice system I had respected put its foot on my neck and face." His anger was so intense that he ripped antennas off police cars parked nearby, an act of criminal vandalism that continued to shock him weeks later. "I remember thinking what kind of impression I was making on my son; what it meant seeing his father like that. But I also wanted him to know what it was about and why I was angry."[15]

At one point Knox went into a police car and used its loudspeaker to steer the crowd away from the PSD building and to the Justice Building. But then another police car from the tiny suburb of Sweetwater, answering a call from the PSD for outside assistance, careened to the edge of the crowd, its siren blaring and lights flashing.

Amid the confusion, a rumor spread that the car had run over the foot of a black girl. In response, a dozen men overturned an empty PSD car nearby and two other cars belonging to county officials. Rags were inserted in their opened gas tanks, and while some blacks tried to stop them by standing in their way, others tossed lighted matches past them and toward the gasoline-soaked rags. One car burst into flames, then another. The crowd erupted into a full-scale riot. They smashed the glass doors of the Metro Justice Building and set fires inside its marble lobby, terrorizing the desk clerks on weekend duty. They overturned several more cars and set them afire.

In back of the building, the attack on PSD headquarters resumed. The few police officers trapped inside the building frantically called for help.

By about ten o'clock the police had at last mustered enough forces, seventy armed officers in all, to move in with a credible show of force. As soon as the rioters saw police officers wearing face shields and carrying riot batons marching toward them in columns ten deep, they quickly melted away toward Liberty City and other points north. The rioters then destroyed the mostly white-owned businesses in their own neighborhoods.

The police strategy to quell the riot was first to seal off the major riot areas and then to restore order with a massed force of police and national guard officers. The first of these goals was officially achieved at 10:36 P.M. Saturday, more than five hours after the riot started, when an effective perimeter was established along 105th Street to the north, the Miami River to the south, Thirty-seventh Avenue to the west, and Sixth Avenue to the east. Whites, however, were still filtering into the ghetto along the side streets, as evidenced by a white couple's encounter with the mob on Twentieth Street at about 10:45 P.M. A more accurate estimate of when an effective perimeter was established would be midnight or 12:30 A.M., when the first guard units arrived in the city.

The second part of the strategy, the show of force, was not put into effect until Sunday night, nearly twenty-four hours later, because the problem involved trying to control people who did not wish to be controlled. Furthermore, Governor Bob Graham had instructed authorities that the National Guard was not to use live ammunition and that guardsmen were to be deployed only alongside police officers. Even with the help of one thousand National Guard troops brought in by early Sunday morning, the authorities were still spread painfully thin.

"First you need enough men to go in and move people out of an area," said Captain Douglas Hughes. "Then you need more men to

112. Miami in flames during the 1980 riot. This view is of the Norton Tire Company, which was located in Liberty City. The company later moved to the suburbs, taking many jobs with it. Courtesy *Miami Herald* .

113. Looters arguing over their spoils. These men are arguing about who will get what following their looting of a television repair shop on Northwest Fifty-fourth Street during the riots of 1980. Courtesy *Miami Herald*.

stay and hold areas that have been taken back. We could do one or the other, but not both at the same time."[16]

Between eleven o'clock and midnight on Saturday, scattered incidents of looting and burning were breaking out in black communities all across Dade County, but none of these areas suffered rioting on the scale of the impoverished center of northwest Dade County, Liberty City. By eleven, thousands of people were in the streets, and many were furiously tearing apart the commercial fabric of the community.

By Sunday, the city and county fire departments had recorded 213 fires in the Liberty City area alone, with 21 additional fires in Opa-Locka and 13 in Perrine. In the dark hours of early morning, the city glowed as if it had come under a large-scale incendiary attack.

Of all the commercial streets in the ghetto, Seventh Avenue, the eastern boundary of the riot, was the most thoroughly looted and burned. Along an approximately three-mile stretch, virtually every business with lootable goods was hit; many were also torched and, several weeks after the riot, bulldozed flat. The pattern of what happened to Seventh Avenue was similar to that of other commercial streets throughout the ghetto.

The riot came to Seventh Avenue about six o'clock, when a black man was seen running toward Seventh from Seventieth Street repeatedly firing shots into the air like a cowboy fresh into town from a cattle drive. Generally, however, rioters were distracted by the anti-white violence that was going on several blocks to the west. Serious looting started two hours later. Susan's Meat Market, a Cuban-owned business at Sixty-fourth Street, was the first store to be looted. Witnesses said it went at eight o'clock.

Then the Edison Furniture Store at Sixty-ninth Street was looted and burned to the ground. By midnight on Saturday, looting victims included Eagle Street, whose safe was carted away; the Pantry Pride supermarket at Sixty-second Street, which moved out after the riot;

114. Black business owners surveying damage after the looting of their store in Liberty City during the 1980 riot. The popular view that black businesses were spared by rioters was incorrect. Courtesy *Miami Herald*.

and Shelter Electric, a lighting-fixture store at Sixty-seventh, which was also burned to the ground. At 2:30 A.M. looters cleaned out the display bikes at the Harley-Davidson franchise at Seventy-seventh Street.

By three o'clock Sunday morning the riot entered a lull, common in such disorders, during which rioters took a break from their frenzied activity and went home.

The eight white victims of the riot all died — or, as in the Kulp case, were fatally injured, some time on Saturday night. The nine black deaths occurred on Sunday and Monday, as the police and guardsmen moved in and took back sections of the city.

Four blacks had been killed by early Sunday morning. Elijah Aaron, forty-three, father of five, an irrigation-system worker who had to quit his job after two heart attacks and kidney problems, was shot to death on Twenty-seventh Avenue and Forty-fourth Street by a PSD patrol officer who claimed that Aaron was looting a tire store and that he had pointed a pistol at the officer. Abram Phillips, twenty-one, father of one, was shot by a Miami police sergeant at Twenty-second Avenue and Seventy-second Street after Phillips, according to the sergeant, had fired four shots at him with a pistol. Michael Scott, a seventeen-year-old student at MacArthur High North, a school for problem students, was killed by a security guard at the Jet Food Market on Twenty-seventh Avenue and Fifty-fourth Street. Kenneth China, twenty-two, was found dead on Twenty-sixth Avenue and Fifty-third Street from what a police report said was a stray bullet.

Late Sunday afternoon three more blacks were shot by whites driving through black areas. Andre Dawson, fourteen, had run after his sister, who had gone to a store on Third Avenue and Eighty-third Street despite her mother's warning to stay near home. Suddenly, a blue pickup truck or van raced down Eighty-third Street and three shots rang out, two of which stuck Dawson in the head.

At about the same time, forty-four-year-old Eugene Brown, a cement finisher and father of three, who liked to talk of the day he would open his own construction business, was driving two of his children and his wife to a U-Totem store on Eighty-third Street at North Miami Avenue to get some orange juice. The store had been partially looted the previous night but was still open for business. While Brown waited in the car, his family went toward the store. Shots were fired from what witnesses said might have been a blue truck, and Eugene Brown died while his wife crouched behind the car.

The third victim was claimed about six o'clock that Sunday afternoon when a thirty-five-year-old truck driver named Thomas Reese was drinking beer among a crowd of thirty while they watched the fire at a grocery store on 103rd Street at Thirteenth Avenue. Up the street, two teenaged boys threw rocks at passing vehicles. Witnesses remember that Reese had just finished telling them to stop when the boys scored a hit on a truck. The vehicle skidded abruptly to a stop, and the driver fired shots at the crowd. Everybody scattered, but before Reese could get behind cover, he received a fatal bullet wound in his back.

The most controversial police shooting occurred Sunday night on the corner of Second Avenue and Forty-second Street in the Haitian district of the city. There, at about eight o'clock, a Miami police officer shot a thirty-nine-year-old Haitian minister named LaFontant Bien-Aime as the minister was driving in his van with his thirteen-year-old son, Kensy. The police officer, Karl Robbins, said he was chasing looters from a furniture warehouse on the corner when suddenly a van bore down on him as if trying to run over him. Robbins's report states that he fired his shotgun at the driver while jumping out of the way.

Bien-Aime's family maintained that he had not been looting but was on his way to his church a block north of the shooting scene for his regular Sunday night services. A subsequent grand jury investigation issued no indictment of the officer after the state attorney's office said it found evidence that the minister had indeed been inside the furniture warehouse.

The last black to die in the riot was Allen Mills, thirty-three, a janitor at a luxury apartment house on the Rickenbacker Causeway. He was shot to death by two Miami police officers at 4:30 P.M. Monday on the corner of Seventh Avenue and Fifty-fourth Street. According to the police, Mills, who had done time for armed robbery and was then on probation for shoplifting, had been riding his bicycle around the area and acting erratically. At one point, they said, he threatened police officers with a four-inch folding knife, then rode off. In another confrontation, the police said Mills attacked two officers at a barricade and was shot seven times. He ran twenty feet before he fell.

By midnight on Sunday the riot was running out of steam. Some three thousand National Guard troops were in the area, and although only half this many were actually available for street duty, they still provided the police sufficient numbers to shrink the perimeter and discourage systematic looting. Many of the arson calls were instances of fires blazing up again. What looting remained was carried on by scavengers sifting through the ravaged and burned-out buildings in search of goods left behind by the earlier waves. It was also approaching Monday morning, when many people had to get up and go to work.

As dawn broke on Monday, the city was still shaken and fearful. Stores and offices in downtown Miami closed shortly after lunch following a false rumor that blacks had burst out of Liberty City and were on the rampage. The command post log at the PSD's Central District noted: "Situation becoming stabilized." On Tuesday, burglary calls to the 911 number dropped to their pre-riot level. The police made only ten arrests all day for riot-related activity.

By Wednesday it was over. Most of the National Guard was sent home. Barricades at perimeter checkpoints were opened. The public schools, which had been closed on Monday and Tuesday, opened their doors and took thousands of children off the streets. Although the curfew remained in effect until Friday, Director Jones of the PSD extended the evening hours until ten. For the first time in five days, the PSD log for Wednesday night recorded: "There were no unusual problems throughout the day." In the end, Miami's age of innocence was consumed in flames and blood.[17]

The Aftermath

Only 135 riot defendants, or 13.5 percent of the 997 cases that went through the system, were sentenced at all, including those given probation. According to William Moriarty, director of the Criminal Justice Coordination Division of the Criminal Justice Council, the percentage of defendants who normally end up receiving at least some kind of sentence is about 32 percent, or two and one-half times as high as was the case with the rioters. Prosecutors dropped about 85 percent of riot defendants' cases or referred them to a pretrial intervention program, where the charges were dismissed if the defendants stayed out of trouble for several months. Many simply failed to show up for their trials. Although warrants were issued for their arrest, it seems unlikely that the warrants were ever served.

In the months following the riots, a series of emotionally charged, riot-related trials was held in Miami. Defendants were identified with the assistance of people who saw what had happened in the Kulp, Owens, Barreca, Higdon, and Muñoz murders. Most of these had occurred in areas near the Liberty Square Housing Project on Sixty-second Street.

In October 1980, two black male defendants, James McCullough, eighteen, and Frankie Lee James, twenty, were tried by a racially mixed jury on second-degree murder charges in the death of Jeffrey Kulp and the attempted murder of Michael Kulp. Mary Kinsey, a thirty-five-year-old black woman, testified for the state; and a statement given by McCullough himself, in which he admitted that he had kicked Kulp once in the chest, was used against him. On October 28 McCullough was found guilty of manslaughter, and on December 11 he was sentenced to fifteen years in prison. Because of his age, the sentence was later reduced to four years in prison and two years of community control, a probationary period in his community. Frankie Lee James was acquitted of all charges.

In February 1981, four young black men—Leonard Capers, his brother Lawrence Capers, Samuel Lightsey, and Patrick Moore—were tried by another racially mixed jury for the murders of Benny Higdon, Robert Owens, and Charles Barreca, who were dragged from their cars and beaten to death. Lightsey made a taped admission to the police that he had pulled Owens from the auto after it had been forced into a parking lot. He said he had punched Owens a few times as he lay on the ground. Moore also admitted to standing over Higdon with a .25 semiautomatic pistol and firing point-blank three or four times. The Capers brothers did not deny that they were at the scene, but along with Lightsey, they accused two other black youths, Nathaniel Lane and Lonnie Bradley, of being the main attackers in the fatal beatings.

After more than five days of deliberation, the longest in Dade County history, a jury which included three blacks found Lightsey guilty of second-degree murder, and he was sentenced to life in prison. The Capers brothers were found guilty of three counts of third-degree murder, and each received three consecutive sentences of fifteen years in prison. Moore was acquitted.

In early March 1981, the trial of Lonnie Bradley, eighteen, and Samuel Williams, thirty-two, both black, was slated on charges of second-degree murder in the slaying of Owens, Barreca, and Higdon. The charges were dropped after the state's two key witnesses could not identify Williams in a police lineup and when another witness recanted her earlier statement implicating them.

Nathaniel Lane, eighteen, described by other defendants as the chief culprit in the beating deaths of Higdon, Owens, and Barreca, was tried in April 1981 on charges of first-degree murder. The key witness was Doris Jones, a black woman who lived in an apartment overlooking the parking lot in which the murders occurred. She knew Lane and testified that she recognized him as a key figure in the mob that beat the three white motorists.

The trial resulted in a hung jury, split on racial lines. The whites voted to convict and the blacks to acquit. Lane's second trial in July 1981 also ended with a hung jury, split along racial lines. The state made the unusual decision to try him a third time in December. This trial, too, was heard by a biracial jury, and although not split along racial lines, it again was unable to reach a verdict. The state finally gave up, and Lane was released.

On July 16, 1982, Lane was back in jail, this time charged with shooting an unarmed black youth in the neck in an attempted robbery at a rock concert in Overtown. The victim was paralyzed as a result. Lane was identified by several witnesses, all of them black, but he denied the charges, claiming that he, too, had been the victim of an attack. Lane was convicted of attempted first-degree murder and armed robbery and sentenced on March 29, 1983, to two consecutive life sentences.

On March 7, 1982, after three and one-half hours of deliberation, a biracial Dade County jury found Ira Lee Pickett, a black man, guilty of first-degree arson and burglary with assault in the mob attack that left Emilio Muñoz burned beyond recognition after his car was torched at the height of the riot. Pickett, a former garbage collector, signed a confession in which he admitted setting the car afire. Pickett was sentenced to fifteen years in prison.

The whites who cruised the riot neighborhood in the blue pickup truck or van randomly shooting at blacks were never arrested. The killings suggested an old southern refrain: death by persons unknown.

Although there was concern at the federal level that the Miami violence might spread to other cities, the Carter administration took the position that the riot was caused by circumstances unique to Miami: for example, the turmoil resulting from the large influx of Cuban and Haitian refugees. A month after the riot, however, a *Miami Herald* survey of Dade County blacks found only 4 percent of those interviewed thought the immigration influx had contributed to the riots. Officials in the Carter administration claimed that the rapid succession of racially explosive cases in the Dade County criminal justice system was unusual and specific to the Miami area.[18]

As the week of the riot wound down, the president dispatched Attorney General Benjamin Civiletti to Miami. His assignment was to assess the truth of charges by Miami blacks that the criminal justice system was racist, and to consider the propriety of intervention by the Department of Justice. On May 21, Civiletti announced that a team of civil rights lawyers from the Department of Justice had moved into Dade County to look into thirteen police-brutality complaints, including the deaths of six blacks shot by the police during the riots.

The White House also established a special task force to develop an economic recovery plan for Miami, headed by Frank Jones, domestic expert and general counsel to the Community Services Administration. Jones was to coordinate the federal effort with state and local initiatives, devise an overall plan, and submit the plan to the president. Jones told a delegation of Florida business and political leaders several weeks after the riot that the president wanted the Miami recovery plan to be a model for other cities. Some local blacks and elected officials associated with Carter's reelection effort were summoned to the White House, the task force visited Florida several times, and it was decided that the president himself would visit Liberty City on June 9 while he was in town to deliver a speech to a national convocation of the Opportunities Industrialization Corporation in Miami Beach.

The federal task force and the president's local supporters selected a small group of business and political figures to meet privately with the president at the James E. Scott Community Association (JESCA) Center in Liberty City. The group included Frank Borman, president of

Miami-based Eastern Airlines; Alvah Chapman, president of the Miami Herald Publishing Company and one of the most influential men in Dade County; Mayor Ferre of Miami; Athalie Range, Miami's most highly respected black leader; and about a dozen other prominent blacks and whites.

The president's arrival was well known, and a large crowd of blacks gathered early outside JESCA's headquarters. There was considerable confusion, however, as to the meeting's purpose. Some of the local leaders who met with President Carter assumed that he had come to Miami to announce when and how much federal money Miami would receive to aid in the rebuilding. It was also widely assumed that Carter had come to tell them how far he was prepared to go in order to help the community recover.

The president's idea for the meeting was quite different, however. He had not come to talk, but to listen. He wanted to hear about initiatives taken by local leaders in both public and private sectors. Before committing federal funds, the president wanted to know specifically what the community was doing to help itself. Carter's expectations were not met, because at this point, barely three weeks after the riot, there were no local initiatives.

In the meeting, President Carter made it clear that the local leadership should not expect the federal government to carry the entire financial burden. In response, the Miami leaders complained that no one had asked them to prepare plans to discuss with the president. "Our people weren't asked to prepare anything," said Lester Freeman of the Chamber of Commerce. "They were just called and asked to show up."[19]

The meeting broke up after ninety minutes. The president left the building and entered his limousine with Athalie Range, an early Carter supporter during his election campaign. As the motorcade pulled away, several bottles and rocks were tossed by young blacks in the rear of the crowd. A few struck the president's limousine, and Athalie Range grabbed Carter's arm impulsively. "He just patted my arm and just said, 'It'll be all right,'" she reported in an interview in 1991. The incident provided local leaders with an embarrassing end to an already depressing day.

Ultimately the federal response consisted largely of loans made available through the Small Business Administration (SBA). Of about $40 million targeted for first-year use in the riot area, only a little more than half was ever loaned. Moreover, nearly 90 percent of the $22 million actually loaned in response to the Miami riot went to whites or Hispanics, and fewer than half of these people ended up reopening their establishments in the riot areas. The SBA loans during the year following the riot facilitated the reestablishment of numerous businesses which had been affected by the riot, but not in riot-impacted areas. Indeed, the real impact of the loans seems to have been to help draw riot-damaged businesses away from the inner city rather than to keep them there.

According to the Greater Miami Chamber of Commerce, some new businesses had opened in the Liberty City area by July 1982, but most were small, service-oriented businesses rather than the larger manufacturing and retail businesses existing there before the riot. The federal government also increased support for its Comprehensive Employment and Training Act (CETA) program in Miami, which made available substantial sums of money to train the unemployed and, in some cases, to support them in their jobs for a predetermined period during which prospective employers were encouraged to hire them as regular employees. In one form or another, more than $6 million in federal riot relief was spent in this manner, with mixed results.

Although drafted by the Carter administration, the federal aid package was left to be implemented by President Reagan. That caused additional problems, one of the most serious being the Reagan administration's effort to cut back or terminate the CETA program and the Economic Development Administration (EDA), an agency that was supposed to figure prominently in redeveloping the riot area. The EDA did dispense nearly $10 million for riot relief in Dade County, but while some of its programs were operated in conjunction with other federal agencies, its demise seriously set back an already sluggish recovery effort. Measured against the standard of Carter's promise to construct a model for governmental riot response, the federal plan does not seem to have been a resounding success.

In 1981, the City of Miami agreed to pay $100,000 to the family of Arthur McDuffie. Metro commissioners agreed to pay the family $1 million.

Perhaps the most significant change to occur in the aftermath of the riot was the 1984 Florida Supreme Court decision prohibiting the elimination of prospective jurors based upon their race alone. This decision resulted from the case of Jack Neil, a black man charged in the fatal shooting of a Haitian immigrant in the early 1980s. Prosecutors had used their peremptory challenges to excuse prospective black jurors, presumably on the theory that they would be more sympathetic to the defendant. Only one black was selected to the panel, but as an alternate. Neil was convicted, and he appealed. The Florida Supreme Court ordered a new trial, ruling that it was time in Florida for jurors to be selected on the basis of their individual characteristics and that they should not be subject to rejection solely because of their skin color.

Until the Neil decision, blacks were infrequently seated on certain juries due to a variety of factors: attorneys had nearly unlimited discretion to use peremptory challenges; blacks were underrepresented in the jury pool because they were underrepresented on the voter registration lists, from which all prospective jurors were drawn; and for some blacks, jury duty presented an economic hardship which caused them to seek to be excused.

Ten years after the riot, the *Miami Herald* published a status report on the recovery efforts. Two of the primary organizations dedicated to restoring neighborhoods were making fewer and fewer loans to the areas they had set out to help. Miami Capital Development, Inc., won a $4.8 million federal grant in 1980 to spur growth in riot-torn areas, but by 1990 most of its loans had flowed to communities outside the central fury of the riots: West Little River, Edison-Little River, and Opa-Locka. Increasingly, Miami Capital's loans, presumably intended primarily to assist small black businesses, were being directed toward businesses owned by Hispanics.[20]

The Business Assistance Center (BAC), the other organization formed to help the area recover from the riot's impact, was created in 1982 and infused with $6.9 million to loan to Liberty City businesses. But the BAC changed its strategy and by May 1990 was lending money to black-owned businesses from Brickell Avenue to deep south Dade County. Executives for both groups defended their records. According to them, the two organizations had created hundreds of jobs and dozens of businesses. The BAC argued that the most effective benefit to the black community would come from fostering a black middle class on a countywide basis. Still, their critics believed that the groups had forsaken the neighborhoods that needed help the most.

The Nevel Johnson Incident (1982)

On the evening of December 28, 1982, Nevel Johnson Jr., a twenty-year-old black male, was playing a video game at a popular local recreation establishment in Overtown. At 6:07 P.M. two uniformed officers, Luis Alvarez and Luis Cruz, both Hispanic, entered the game room. Shortly afterward, a shot was fired and Johnson lay motionless on the floor. This fatal incident sparked a three-day civil disturbance in Overtown.

According to Miami Police Chief Kenneth Harms, the officers entered the pool room on a self-initiated check because the pool room, located at 1495 Northwest Third Avenue, had a history of narcotics dealings. Harms said that Officer Alvarez noticed what appeared to be a gun under Johnson's clothing and asked Johnson, "What's that?" Johnson replied, "That's a gun."

Alvarez placed his left hand on the bulge and with his right hand drew his own revolver. According to the police account, Johnson made a quick movement and the officer's gun discharged. Police believe that the gun was placed toward the back of Johnson's head, probably resting against his neck. The fatal bullet hit Johnson as he turned toward the officer, entering over his left eye and exiting through the top of his skull. Johnson carried an unregistered .22-caliber revolver, according to the police, although the officers on the scene did not know where the gun was when homicide investigators arrived.

Several witnesses at the scene had different versions of what happened. Jeffrey Hoskins, a nineteen-year-old high school friend of the victim, insisted that Johnson was not armed. He said the officers walked in and Johnson was unaware of their presence. In Hoskins's account, Alvarez "swung him around and pulled out a gun and drew the gun to Nevel's head. . . . He never had a chance to say a word before the shot went into his head."

Three others who claim to have witnessed the shooting offered different versions. One said Johnson had a gun in his pocket, and another said he was not carrying a gun "but somehow ended up with one in his hand as he lay wounded on the ground moments after the shooting." The third witness said he never saw a gun, neither before nor after the shooting. All three witnesses did agree on one thing: Johnson was shot without provocation and without making a threatening movement. Willie Watkins, owner of the arcade, said, "Even if he did have a gun, he knows I don't allow any horseplay in here. But he was the kind of kid I could walk over to and say, 'Let me have it,' and he'd give the gun to me."[21]

The police insisted that Johnson's gun bulged out of his trousers and that this was the reason Alvarez drew his weapon. Nevel Johnson's brother-in-law was standing right behind Johnson playing another video game at the time of the incident. He said he saw the gun Johnson was carrying but said that Johnson probably wore it for his own protection.

Immediately after the shooting, Overtown erupted into a full-scale riot. Several hundred blacks set police cruisers ablaze, sprayed one cruiser with bullets, looted several stores, and trapped the two detectives inside the video arcade.

The riot did have its moments of heroism. The video arcade employees kept back an angry crowd trying to force its way into the arcade where Alvarez and his partner were trapped. In another incident of bravery, a white Florida Industrial Commission judge, Rosemary Usher Jones, made a wrong turn at Northwest Twentieth Street, a turn that took her directly into the heart of the growing riot. Suddenly, the first concrete block came flying through the window of her

115. The Overtown video arcade on Northwest Third Avenue where Nevel Johnson was killed by Miami police officer Luis Alvarez in December 1982. Courtesy Sergio Campos.

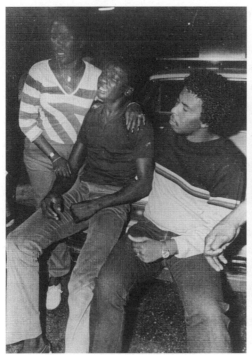

116. The brother of Nevel Johnson, waiting for news of his brother's condition at Jackson Memorial Hospital. Courtesy *Miami Herald*.

117. Overtown in 1982 riot. A woman and child warily cross Northwest Twentieth Street at Second Avenue two days after the Johnson shooting. Courtesy *Miami Herald*.

Volvo. She tried to keep driving, although she already had glass on her eyelids and in her hands. When rioters started rocking her car, two black girls came to her aid, telling her, "Don't go that way. They'll kill you. Let us help you."[22] One of them slipped into the driver's seat, and the judge ducked down out of sight. The girls couldn't move the car through the crowd but did manage to get to the same arcade where Johnson had been shot. Her pursuers had already torn open the Volvo's doors and snatched the judge's purse, rings, and a bracelet when the arcade owner, Willie Watkins, and three others wrested the judge away from the crowd and hurried her into the arcade. Watkins and his friends even managed to recover some of the judge's personal items. They stayed with her until a SWAT team arrived.

Johnson's immediate family, including his mother and father, never believed the police account of what happened. They said he had no previous arrest record and never carried a gun. "They shot my boy in cold blood," said Johnson's mother. "He doesn't own no gun. We never had a gun in the family. He's never been in trouble. They shot my boy in cold blood and everybody's going to know it soon as I talk to my lawyer. Everybody's going to know the truth soon enough. We got nothing to hide."[23]

Meanwhile, members of the Ku Klux Klan gathered on Brickell Avenue and Southeast Twenty-fifth Road to pass out literature supporting the police of Miami and advocating the rights of white people. Community activist William Perry, director of the local chapter of PUSH (People United to Save Humanity), said that what happened to Johnson and the rioting that resulted were predictable, given economic and social conditions in the city. He also forecast a worsening climate, considering the employment situation and the way black people were treated in Miami.[24]

Five agencies, including the FBI, made inquiries into the disturbance. City Manager Howard Gary, a black man, promised an investigation into the shooting with no whitewash and announced that the two officers involved had been relieved of street duty, even though a preliminary police report concluded that the shooting appeared to be accidental. The Miami branch of the NAACP announced that it would investigate whether the official probes were conducted fairly, and it appealed for calm.

Homicide investigators interviewed eight witnesses to the shooting. Three said that Johnson had a gun. None said the .22 pistol found at the scene was left by police to make it appear as though the shooting was justified.

It was later revealed that when Alvarez led his partner into the game room he was outside his assigned section of the city. The arcade was located in Sector 40 of the Police Central District, a predominantly black area east of I–95. Alvarez was assigned to Sector 30, a primarily white area composed mostly of Latinos. Miami City Manager Howard Gary said that Alvarez committed a violation of police procedure when he and his partner left their assigned areas, adding that the only time an officer is to leave his zone is for emergencies or in response to direct instructions. He also said that Alvarez would be punished if found guilty of the violation but did not say how.

A police panel met and recommended that Alvarez be found guilty of minor procedural violations for leaving his assigned duty area and modifying his police revolver without permission, an act which some experts believe left the gun with a hair trigger. The panel suggested a two-week suspension as punishment.

Alvarez selected Roy Black, one of the defense attorneys in the McDuffie case, to represent him. The prosecutor, Benton Becker, was not as well known. He had negotiated the pardon of former president Richard Nixon in 1974 and represented Gerald Ford during his vice-presidential confirmation hearing. He had also served as White House counsel.

On February 17, 1983, a Dade County grand jury charged that Alvarez acted recklessly and with culpable negligence when he shot Johnson. Alvarez faced a maximum penalty of fifteen years in prison and a ten-thousand-dollar fine if convicted. Several blacks in Overtown criticized the indictment and insisted that Alvarez be charged with murder.

Roy Black asked Dade Circuit Court Judge David Gersten to transfer the Alvarez trial to another county. Black contended in his motion

118. Miami police officer Luis Alvarez in court, January 1984. He was accused of shooting Nevel Johnson to death in an Overtown video arcade in December 1982. Courtesy *Miami Herald*/Tim Chapman.

119. Attorney Roy Black, who defended Luis Alvarez. The highly regarded Miami attorney argued, in part, that Overtown is a dangerous community and that Alvarez was correct to react as he did in shooting Nevel Johnson. Black also represented one of the black defendants accused of killing a white person during the Miami riot of 1980. Courtesy Carlos Cuba.

that the riot would be fresh in the minds of potential Dade County jurors and that an impartial jury could not be seated in Dade County. The judge denied his request, and the trial began on January 18, 1984.

Of the thirty prospective jurors who were selected, three blacks on the panel were dismissed because of prior arrest records, one due to a prejudicial remark he made about Alvarez and one who had known Johnson's father for forty years. Ultimately, an all-white panel was chosen, including five non-Hispanic whites and one Hispanic. Both alternate jurors were Hispanic.

During the trial, Black called Johnson an armed criminal, claiming that Johnson had robbed a woman of her purse two months before the shooting. "We don't know if (Johnson) intended to shoot the officers or shoot his way out of the arcade." Prosecutor Laeser pressed that Alvarez made many mistakes that fateful night, one of which included leaving his assigned patrol zone without telling his supervisors and failing to tell Cruz what he was going to do inside the arcade. Laeser argued that Alvarez stood too close to Johnson when he put his service revolver within a foot of Johnson's head.

The prosecutor told jurors that Johnson's hands were raised in surrender when Alvarez's gun discharged; defense attorney Black countered that his client shot in self-defense as Johnson reached for a revolver hidden in his waistband. Alvarez told the jury, "I shot because I had to shoot. If I wouldn't have fired, I would have been the one shot." Yet Parks Fitzbugh, a Miami-Dade police psychologist who had interviewed Alvarez right after the shooting, testified that Alvarez indicated the shooting was an accident, not an act of self-defense.

Key witness Jeffrey Hoskins made conflicting statements about what happened. In an interview he said that the officer came in and grabbed Johnson by the head and then swung him around and shot him. Later he recanted that statement. He also said that Alvarez and Johnson exchanged no words; however, another key witness, Antonio Bell, said that he heard them talking. Hoskins was shown photos of six Hispanic Miami police officers, including Alvarez; but when asked to identify Alvarez, he picked the wrong officer.

The trial lasted nearly two months; it took the jury only two hours to reach a verdict: not guilty. Immediately after the verdict, outbursts of violence and looting reoccurred in Liberty City and Overtown, but they were not as serious as the initial riot and were quickly quelled by police. In 1984, Miami city commissioners approved a $460,000 settlement with Johnson's parents. The settlement, part in cash and part annuity, brought the family about $1.1 million.

The Lozano Incident (1989)

Miami police officer William Lozano was twenty-nine years old when his actions on a busy Overtown street plunged Miami into its third major racial disturbance of the decade. He joined the Miami police department on February 4, 1985, one of many police officers in his family. Lozano had never been disciplined, and his evaluations ranged from average to good. He was a perfect marksman.

Clement Anthony Lloyd, one of the two blacks killed in the Lozano incident, was twenty-three years old. He was a native of the Virgin Islands. He had held odd jobs until he found a job running a car wash. In 1984 Broward deputies arrested him with ninety pounds of marijuana in a suitcase at the Fort Lauderdale International Airport. He pled guilty and received three years probation. In 1987 he was arrested for violating his probation, and he had several driving violations. Allan Blanchard, the other black man who was killed in the incident, was twenty-four. He had been living in Miami for two months. Originally from Saint Croix, Blanchard had no police record and was unemployed.

The Lozano incident started on January 16, 1989, when Lozano and his partner, Dawn Campbell, a white female officer, were called to an apartment building near Northwest Third Avenue and Sixteenth

120. Allan Blanchard, victim of a 1989 police shooting. Blanchard, a passenger on a motorcycle being driven by Clement Lloyd, was killed when the cycle crashed after Miami police officer William Lozano shot Lloyd as he sped toward him on an Overtown street. Courtesy *Miami Herald.*

Street for a domestic dispute. Once it was settled, they went outside and were approached by Eddie Johnson, a black man, who wanted to report a stolen license plate decal. At this time, Lozano went to the trunk of his police car to search for a form to make out the report.

When he found none, he picked up his radio to call a nearby police unit. Moments before, Officer John Mervolion, driving his police cruiser, was returning from an off-duty job. He spotted Lloyd driving erratically on his motorcycle and began to chase the cycle. When Lozano picked up his radio, he heard about the chase and then heard the roar of Lloyd's motorcycle coming his way. He stepped into the street with his weapon drawn and fired a single shot at the motorcycle. Seconds later it crashed into an oncoming car carrying two passengers. Lozano had fatally shot Lloyd in the head. His passenger, Blanchard, was seriously injured in the crash and died the next day. The two people in the oncoming car were treated and released from Jackson Memorial Hospital.

Soon after the motorcycle crashed, a crowd of about two hundred residents took to the streets throwing rocks and bottles at police officers. At 7:30 P.M., Mayor Xavier Suarez and City Manager Cesar Odio arrived at the scene and were met by the irate crowd. Less than an hour later, the Miami Police Department called in all off-duty officers and all supervisors. Overtown was again slipping into full-scale riot.

121. The January 1989 scene of the Lozano shooting in Overtown. Clement A. Lloyd's body has not yet been removed from the wreckage. Moments after this photograph was taken, Overtown erupted in a full-scale riot. Courtesy *Miami Herald*.

122. The mother of Allan Blanchard (center), one of the men killed in the Lozano incident, reacts to news that her son has died. Due to its sensitive nature, this photograph was not published within fifty miles of Miami. The woman on the right is Blanchard's sister. Courtesy *Miami Herald*/Jon Kral.

At 8:30, Channel 23's news van was set on fire at Northwest Seventeenth Street and Third Avenue. At that time, all media were ordered out of the area. A caravan of police cruisers circled the area, each car carrying several officers with guns pointed out the back doors in an effort to discourage rioters. By 10:00 some of the action had diminished, but there was still sporadic gunfire. Looting had begun at an Amocc Station on the corner of Northwest Twentieth Street and First Avenue. Over the next three hours eleven people were arrested. Fires were set, one at an auto parts store which firefighters drove by without stopping.

Because of the disturbances, portions of Interstate 95 and other major arteries were closed. By midnight, the blocked-off section of Miami was bounded by Miami Avenue on the east, Northwest Seventh Avenue on the west, Northwest Twenty-fifth Street on the north, and Northwest Fifth Street on the south.

Violence spread from Overtown into Liberty City and Coconut Grove as Miami entered its second night of rioting. There were reports of eight people being injured by gunfire, five of whom were unidentified and one of whom died.

123. Four looting suspects under arrest during the Overtown disturbance that followed the 1989 Lozano incident. Courtesy *Miami Herald*/Al Diaz.

Eleven stores were reportedly looted, including two convenience stores, three supermarkets, a Zayre department store, an arts and crafts store, a Kentucky Fried Chicken restaurant, and a fashion store. Most of the establishments involved were located in the northwest section.

Although not confident of their ability to influence the rock-throwing and looting, some of Miami's prominent black citizens tried to use the airwaves to calm the violence. WMBM 1490 AM and WEDR 99.1 FM warned listeners that rioting was illegal and people would be arrested for being on the streets. The radio stations, although raising questions about the fatal shooting of the black motorcyclist, did call upon their audiences to make nonviolent responses and stay away from the rioting areas. "People are pretty much against this thing. I would say in at least nine calls out of ten, people condemn the rioting aspect," said Jerry Rushin, vice-president of WEDR. According to Rushin, "Most of the chaos in the streets was created by a small yet conspicuous segment of the black community. A lot of the youngsters think this is the manly, macho thing to do, to throw a rock at the police."[25]

The violence started to wind down on January 20, 1989. The disturbances left one unidentified man dead, 11 injured, and 372 arrested. At least thirteen buildings were burned, and damages were estimated at $1 million. The Miami City Commission created an independent review board to investigate the shooting, and the United States Attorney's Office and the Dade State Attorney's Office conducted their own investigations.

A solemn and pensive Mayor Xavier Suarez met with some of the rioters in a quiet jail chapel. Most said that they acted out of rage, fear, curiosity, opportunity, and poverty. They also claimed to be influenced by alcohol, friends, and television. They described themselves as victims of violence as well as perpetrators, and they felt wronged as well as wrong. A few admitted that they had stolen items such as perfume, meat, shaving cream, beer, and furniture.

Those caught looting ranged in age from thirteen to fifty-five. They blamed their illegal actions on the rage they felt at being verbally and physically abused by the police, as well as lack of opportunity, poverty, and fear. Richard Keith Davis, twenty-six, justified his looting with, "I was trying to get something out of there; trying to do like everybody else. It was free and a job is hard to find." Davis was unemployed.[26]

The rioting caused the last-minute postponement of the Miami Heat/ Phoenix Suns game at the Miami Arena after the three referees were hurt when an object was thrown through the windshield of their car. Several other cars parked near the arena were vandalized. Ten minutes before it was to begin, the game was canceled and the players were escorted through a back exit and out of the area. Only twice before in the history of the NBA had professional basketball games been canceled: once due to weather and the other when President Kennedy was assassinated.

On January 23, 1989, Officer William Lozano was charged with two counts of manslaughter with a firearm and was released on five thousand dollars bail. He faced a possible sixty years in jail and summoned Roy Black, perhaps the most brilliant criminal defense attorney in Miami, to defend him. The case was prosecuted by two gifted and finely tuned assistant state attorneys, Don Horn, a black man, and John Hogan, white.

On October 23, 1989, jury selection began in one of the most sensational trials in Florida history. The composition of the jury was crucial because the case centered on the officer's judgment rather than his actions: Was it appropriate for Lozano to have fired his weapon? Did he legitimately fear for his life? Should he have retreated rather than fire his weapon?

The choosing of jurors was an ordeal in itself because the case had received such widespread publicity. After three weeks, jury selection was abruptly halted for an emergency appeal to the Third District Court of Appeals by the defense. Roy Black had tried to dismiss a black, middle-aged mail-handler and union activist from Liberty City. Black argued that the man expressed distrust of postal inspectors, that he was forceful and likely to dominate the jury, that he represented union employees accused of drug use, and that he lived in Liberty City. The prosecutor protested that the strike was racially motivated, and the trial judge agreed. He seated the disputed juror and completed jury selection. The judge then halted the proceedings for the appeal process rather than scrap the entire three weeks' work and start over with a new pool of potential jurors. Within days the appellate court refused to hear the case, leaving the jury intact.[27]

The jury consisted of one black man, one black woman, one Hispanic, two Anglo women, and one Anglo man. The alternates included one Hispanic woman, a Hispanic man, and two Anglo women. They would hear a long and complicated case—one based less on facts than feelings, fears, biases, and values. One prominent Miami defense attorney suggested that because the case was so full of emotions, it actually had been won or lost when the jury was picked.

And so it began. At 9:12 A.M. on Wednesday, November 15, 1989, Assistant State Attorney Donald Horn, a young lawyer from Overtown, faced the jury. Horn carefully explained to the jury that what happened in Overtown that night was not a life-or-death situation and the officer did not have to shoot. He sat down to a hushed courtroom.

Roy Black rose to Lozano's defense. He introduced his client as a hard-working policeman with a good record who was defending his life when he pulled the trigger and shot Lloyd, thinking that the motorcycle was going to run him down. Horn told the jury that Lozano stepped out from behind his patrol car, walked into the street, pulled his gun, took a marksman's stance, and pulled the trigger.

A dramatically different version of events came from the defense. Black said Lozano saw the lights of the police car chasing Lloyd and

124. Miami police officer William Lozano demonstrating how he held his gun when he fired the shot that killed cyclist Clement Lloyd. He was found guilty of manslaughter for the December 7, 1989, shooting and was sentenced to seven years in prison. He appealed the conviction, was retried in May 1993, and was acquitted. Courtesy *Miami Herald*/Jon Kral.

moved into the street to see what was happening. Lozano thought the police car was chasing someone on foot, because it approached so slowly. He was looking for a break in traffic to cross the street and join the chase, when all of a sudden, he saw the motorcycle in the southbound lane coming at him. The defense maintained that Lloyd was driving recklessly through pedestrian-filled streets after an afternoon of drug dealing, that he was high on drugs, and that he was going to run down Lozano. Clement Lloyd had marijuana, the equivalent of one alcoholic drink, and a trace of cocaine in his system at the time of his death.

The prosecution insisted, however, that Lozano was trained not to put himself in the path of speeding vehicles and that he was trained not to use deadly force unless absolutely necessary. They contended Lozano was in a safe position behind his patrol car and that he knowingly moved into a dangerous position in the street. Three eyewitnesses claimed to have seen Lozano confront the motorcyclist and fire the shot. They testified that Lozano had time to get out of the way and that he had his weapon drawn when he stepped into the street.[28]

Lozano's partner, Dawn Campbell, claimed to have been standing on the sidewalk beside the police car while Lozano was reaching into the trunk to look for the forms. She said Lozano stepped more than one or two steps away from the trunk, until he was even with the middle of the police car.

Rozina Lewis was climbing the stairs to her apartment when she saw the speeding motorcycle. She claimed it was not endangering Lozano, because the cyclist was in his own lane. She claimed Campbell ducked behind the patrol car.

Eddie Johnson was attempting to report a stolen license tag decal when he heard the racing motorcycle and wondered where was it going in such a hurry. As he watched Lozano take a couple of steps into the street, he wondered how Lozano was going to stop the motorcycle. Johnson admitted not seeing everything, because he ducked before Lozano fired, but he did notice that the motorcycle was in the northbound lane. He claimed the motorcycle never swerved into the southbound lane where Lozano was standing.

Fred Johnson was waiting to turn left onto Northwest Sixteenth Terrace from Third Avenue when Lloyd's motorcycle crashed into him head-on. He told investigators that the motorcycle moved slightly into the southbound lane but did not endanger Lozano.

The defense attacked the witnesses by claiming that one was not wearing her glasses, another had ducked at the critical moment, and that a third was sitting in a car with an ashtray full of marijuana butts. Black built his defense on the idea that Clement Lloyd would have run over Lozano if he had not been shot.

On December 7, 1989, William Lozano was found guilty of manslaughter. The executive director of PULSE (People United to Lead the Struggle for Equality), Aleem Fakir, stated, "I think you see the beginning of the end of riot syndrome in this community. Trust in the judicial system will be restored." In Overtown blacks were openly rejoicing.[29]

Officer William Lozano was sentenced to seven years in prison on January 24, 1990, by Circuit Court Judge Joseph Farina. As a result of Lozano's successful appeal on the change-of-venue issue, he was retried in Orlando in May 1993 and was found not guilty.[30]

In April 1991, the City of Miami agreed to pay $500,000 each to the families of Clement Anthony Lloyd and Allan Blanchard. Under the agreement, the city acknowledged no legal responsibility for the deaths. The structured settlement included a cash payment of $225,000 each, with the balance in an annuity with guaranteed payments for thirty years.[31]

Metro-Dade and Miami police made changes in the early 1980s to deal with the community's perception that the departments were indifferent to claims of brutality, especially against blacks and Hispanics. The percentage of black officers on the Miami police force increased from 10 to 22 percent between 1980 and 1992, and on the Metro-Dade force it increased from 8 to 16 percent. In 1979, Miami officers were disciplined in 8.5 percent of all complaints about excessive use of force; in 1991, 14 percent of the complaints resulted in discipline. In 1984, public complaints of police misconduct did not result in the firing of any officers; in 1990, eight officers were fired.

In a move intended to be symbolic, Metro built a "team police" program of officers to patrol Dade's housing projects, and mini-precincts were built in Liberty City and Overtown. The moves apparently had real impact on the neighborhoods. As the forces became more reflective of the community's diversity, the public complained less about police misconduct.

Meanwhile, the police departments had nearly perfected their riot-control plan, creating mobile field force platoons of fifty to sixty officers deployed in one area to seal it off and immediately begin making arrests. Although effective in some cases, the riot plan did not always work. In December 1990, the heavily Puerto Rican Wynwood section of Miami rioted after a federal jury acquitted six Miami police officers of the beating death of drug dealer Leonardo Mercado. Critics later said that the police were surprised by the disturbance and did not try to quell the violence quickly enough.[32]

PART 4

BLACKS IN CONTEMPORARY DADE COUNTY

The arrival of tens of thousands of immigrants, legal and otherwise, in Dade County since 1960 has greatly impacted south Florida, including blacks in the region. Most people believe that the economic impact on resident blacks has been negative, particularly in terms of job loss. The Cuban influx began in earnest in the 1960s and has been followed by waves of other immigrants and refugees ever since. Most significant of these has been immigration from Haiti and the Caribbean Basin. Black demands for housing, health care, and social services have been negatively impacted by the sudden arrival of tens of thousands of foreigners, many living in residential areas contiguous to their own. The result has been increased competition for those services and other kinds of public support such as small business loans.

Miami's Little Haiti has evolved as a distinct community in the area once called Lemon City. It has its own community-based organizations and leaders, whose activities and agendas have been much influenced by events in their homeland. As a result of immigration the ethnic composition of black Dade County has become much more diverse, and poor blacks have had to compete with foreign-born immigrants for basic services. But given available data about black economic advancement between 1960 and 1990, the much-touted negative economic impact of immigration on resident blacks does not seem to exist.

The Cubans Arrive

Miami's history since the early 1960s has been greatly affected by immigration. In a sense, much that has happened in Dade County since the waves of immigrants started to arrive has been in reaction to, or a result of, immigration. This process has directly affected native-born blacks.

Prior to a revision of the United States immigration policy in 1965 when President Lyndon B. Johnson signed Public Law 89–236, U.S immigration policy was governed by the National Origin Quota Acts of 1920 and 1924. Until 1967, when the new law took effect, the annual immigration quota for various nationalities was set at one-

125. Cuban refugees arriving in Miami in 1980. Starting in 1960, hundreds of thousands of Cubans came to Miami to avoid the Castro regime in their homeland. They arrived just as the civil rights movement in Dade County was getting underway. Many blacks believe that this curtailed black advancement in Dade County. Courtesy *Miami Herald.*

sixth of 1 percent of the number of inhabitants already in the United States attributable to a particular national origin. This law made black immigration to the United States very difficult, although whites were admitted in great numbers. In practice, this meant that the United States allowed only 122 Africans into the United States in 1924. Later, the McCarran-Walter Immigration Act of 1952 put a ceiling on immigrants from the Western Hemisphere at 120,000 and a maximum from any one country at 20,000 per year. For various reasons, they made exceptions for Cubans, Mexicans, and Canadians.

Just as the civil rights movement of the 1960s started to translate into significant gains for blacks in the southern United States, Fidel Castro came to power in Cuba. He effectively took control of the island on New Year's Day 1960. In most southern cities, blacks then occupied center stage in the desegregation process. Their social and economic problems were given space in the press. Public officials seemed concerned about their plight. Their leaders offered solutions, and whites listened. In most cities, blacks received a disproportionate share of federal support for education, health, housing, and economic development. In Miami, attention suddenly turned away from black concerns to the tremendous problems caused by the arrival of hundreds, then thousands, of Cuban exiles fleeing the Castro regime.

Most of the early arrivals came from Cuban upper and middle classes and looked as white as the Anglo population of south Florida. The migration of Cubans to Miami began in earnest in December 1965 with the twice-daily freedom flights from Varadero, Cuba. During the first year of the flights, more than one hundred thousand Cuban refugees arrived in Miami. Eventually more than half a million would come, changing the city forever.

The Cuban influx succeeded not only in diverting attention from Miami blacks during the crucial integration period, but also by virtue of their greater social acceptability and entrepreneurial skills, Cubans began winning the lion's share of public dollars, especially for business development. In 1968, for example, Dade County non-Hispanic whites received $3,356,875 in loans from the Small Business Administration (SBA). Hispanics received $1,078,950, and blacks received $82,600. Considering all SBA loans made in Dade County from 1968 to 1980, Hispanics received 46.9 percent of the funds made available ($47,677,660), non-Hispanic whites received 46.6 percent ($47,361,773), and blacks received 6 percent ($6,458,240).

Even after the catastrophic riot of 1980, blacks in Miami did not fare well in obtaining federal (SBA) funds for rebuilding the riot-impacted areas. The surge of Cuban economic activity should not be surprising considering that the group that had fled Cuba in the 1960s was largely professional and entrepreneurial. Further, the working-class element that had joined in the exodus tended to share the historic willingness of other immigrant groups to take on lower-order jobs which often were spurned by black Americans who felt they deserved something better.

Particularly galling to blacks was the fact that much of the capital Hispanics needed for their business success was provided by the U.S. government. Because Hispanics qualified as a minority group, their businesses got special consideration from contractors who did business with the federal government. The government required those businesses to use a certain proportion of minority-supplied goods and services. For instance, in the construction of Dade County's rapid transit system, the minority contractors' share of the business was $318,105 in fiscal year 1978. Of this, $168,528 (53 percent) went to Hispanic firms and $111,240 (35 percent) went to firms owned by women; only $38,337 (12 percent) went to black-owned businesses.[1]

It should be noted that Dade County has a substantial Puerto Rican population, one that grew from approximately 10,000 in 1950 to 100,000 by the mid-1980s. But by the early 1980s it was the Cubans who were becoming established as the largest Hispanic ethnic group in the county. The 1970 census counted 291,000 Cubans, or 23 percent of the population in Dade County. During the next decade, the number would more than double, rising to 41 percent of the county population. Whites began leaving Miami in great numbers in the 1970s as the city became more Cuban.

With the Cubans and other Hispanics came rapid economic growth for Dade County—growth resulting from more jobs and new businesses. During the 1970s and early 1980s, businesses were established in Dade County at a rate higher than in the United States as a whole. The county's economy also increased in revenues more rapidly than did the national economy. In 1977, Dade County's wholesale trade industry produced sales revenues of $8.68 billion, a 374.6 percent increase from 1963. The corresponding national increase was 251.1 percent. Similarly, receipts for services and retail sales increased faster in Dade County than nationally during the same fourteen-year period, and payrolls for all businesses increased twice as much in Dade County as nationally in the twenty-one years preceding 1977.

Contrary to popular opinion, it appears that blacks generally benefited from this expansion of the Dade economy. Many but not all blacks improved their economic position during the time of great Hispanic immigration. However, racial and ethnic disparity in unemployment rates in Dade County continued during the 1970s. In 1979, with the national unemployment rate at 5.8 percent and an overall Dade unemployment rate of 5 percent, the rate was 15.3 in the community-development areas where 73 percent of Dade County's black population resides. In Overtown, Model Cities, and Coconut Grove, the unemployment rate was even higher—19.4, 17.8, and 16 percent respectively. Although the unemployment rate has always been higher in those areas, some blacks in these communities complained that they were the victims of preferential hiring of Hispanics.

Another wave of Cuban immigration hit Miami in early 1980. In the spring of that year about ten thousand Cubans seeking to leave their homeland occupied the Peruvian Embassy in Havana. The Cuban government dealt with this embarrassing incident by opening the port of Mariel to all who wished to emigrate to the United States. A massive flotilla organized by Cuban Americans ferried Cuban refugees from Mariel to Key West in astonishing numbers. As a result, approximately 125,000 additional Cubans emigrated to the United States in six months, with more than 86,000 arriving in one month alone.[2] Various sources estimated that 60,000 to 80,000 of these new arrivals resided permanently in Miami or Dade County.

The new refugees differed from their predecessors. Earlier Cuban refugees were mostly white and, even though they did not belong to the middle or upper classes themselves, they often had relatives in the United States who did. Many Mariel Cuban refugees were black, unskilled, and without blood ties to American citizens or residents.

This new wave of Cuban immigration sparked resistance from many local residents, who viewed it as the transformation of Dade County into a bilingual, bicultural area of strong Latin political and economic influence. Increasingly, Spanish was being used in business and public transactions of all kinds. The resistance sparked the overwhelming approval of a bitterly contested countywide antibilingualism referendum on November 4, 1980. The ordinance virtually prohibited the expenditure of county funds to utilize any language other than English or promote any culture other than that of the United States. It also infuriated many Hispanics.

Throughout the 1980s, Cubans and other Hispanics consolidated their economic and political gains in south Florida. In Miami, Cubans became a dominant political force during this decade. They began to elect Cuban Americans to various political posts, including Xavier Suarez, a Cuban American, elected as Miami's mayor in 1985. Most Cubans registered as members of the Republican party, and the county's once-unassailable Democratic party became the minority party in the city of Miami. Local political issues often became entwined with international issues because of the Cubans' experiences and their strong hatred of Fidel Castro.

Throughout the 1980s many Hispanics from other regions, particularly from the Caribbean and Central and South America, immigrated to the United States. Many, if not most, settled in Dade County. Like the Mariels before them, most of these immigrants were poor. By the mid–1990s, with over 40 percent of the county being Hispanic, Dade

County itself was well on the way to having a Hispanic majority population.

The Haitians Arrive

The first group of Haitian refugees to arrive in south Florida landed at Pompano Beach on December 12, 1965. Having shot up Haiti's presidential palace, they qualified for and were given political asylum. In December 1972, the second boatload of Haitians arrived, again at Pompano Beach. Through the 1970s and 1980s thousands followed. In the early stages, most Haitians initially were detained and then taken in government buses to the black section of town, where they were dropped off at local churches.

Generally, local blacks were not inclined to help the Haitians assimilate into the larger population as Miami's Cubans were doing for Cuban refugees. In fact, Haitians met outright hostility from some

126. Haitians arriving on a south Florida beach. Starting in 1965 a flood of Haitian boat people began arriving on the shores of south Florida on dangerously overcrowded vessels such as the one shown here. The man lying prone kisses American soil. Most of the Haitians who came to the United States were detained at the Krome Avenue Detention Center run by the U.S. Immigration and Naturalization Service. Courtesy *Miami Herald*.

resident blacks. A small coalition of blacks led by the Reverend James Jenkins of Liberty City's Friendship Missionary Baptist Church and a small group of black ministers called the Black Baptist Alliance helped to provide food, shelter, and clothing for the newcomers. Since the Haitians were not recognized as refugees, they did not receive welfare in its various forms; nor were they given work permits, which would have enabled them to support themselves. Ray Fauntroy, head of Dade's chapter of the Southern Christian Leadership Council, became an early and visible advocate for Haitian refugees. He led demonstrations and organized community support for Haitians when most other black leaders were preoccupied with other priorities.

By the spring of 1974 there were about four hundred Haitians settling into an area in Miami that became known as Little Haiti, located in the old Lemon City area northeast of downtown. With the number of Haitian refugees growing and the U.S. government refusing to provide support, it became increasingly difficult for the Baptist Alliance to carry the burden of assisting the immigrants. In 1974 the National Council of Churches sent a fact-finding team to south Florida to look into the human service needs of Haitians. The end result was the establishment by the National Council of Churches of the Christian Community Service Agency to act as a conduit of church funds to assist Haitian refugees. This organization remained the primary source of support for the Haitians, who continued to arrive in such numbers that by mid–1978 it became clear that Miami had a new refugee problem.[3]

The new immigrants were essentially unskilled poor people from rural Haiti. Their native language was Creole, and few spoke English. Many were sick. They were disoriented, vulnerable, and essentially passive people. Although no one knows how many had come by the late 1970s, numbers have been estimated at more than twenty-five thousand in the south Florida area alone. The vast majority appeared motivated by the desire to escape from the devastating poverty and economic decline that gripped Haiti, the poorest nation in the Western Hemisphere. Some fled the oppressive Duvalier government, which had ruled the island for decades before the Duvalier family was deposed in early 1986.

As the number of refugees grew, the U.S. government moved to a policy of long-term detention for Haitians. Many blacks viewed the detention policy as inherently or intentionally racist. Two federal judges

127. Bodies of Haitian refugees washed up on a south Florida beach. Some Haitians did not make it; unknown numbers of refugees died at sea. Courtesy *Miami Herald*.

in south Florida agreed that the policy was racially flawed and re-leased many Haitian detainees. Nonetheless, some blacks resented the exceptions to the immigration laws: These laws gave favorable treat-ment to Cuban refugees, who were considered to be politically moti-vated to leave their country, while denying entrance to Haitians who were making the same claims. The media focused much public atten-tion on Cubans being reunited with their families; meanwhile media stories regarding immigration from Haiti focused on the hundreds of Haitians being detained in the controversial Krome Avenue facility run by the Immigration and Naturalization Service in isolated west Dade County.

After the Reagan administration took office in 1981, a policy was instituted to interdict fleeing Haitians at sea and use the Coast Guard to escort them back to Haiti. This led to a dramatic drop in the human tide from Haiti. Congressional sanctions against employers who know-ingly hired illegal immigrants appeared to stem the flow even further. In early 1989, however, the Coast Guard noted a dramatic increase in the number of Haitian boats heading for the American shoreline. By the early 1990s, it became apparent that a new flow of Cuban and Haitian refugees was coming to Miami.

The Reagan interdiction policy continued under the Bush administration. During the 1980s an estimated 23,000 Haitians were interdicted at sea and sent back to Haiti. Only 24 Haitians were allowed to
seek political asylum. In the first six months of 1991, 1,030 Haitians
were interdicted, with only 17 being allowed to seek asylum. During
the same six months, the Coast Guard rescued 1,081 Cubans at sea
and brought them to south Florida. Few of the Cubans applied for
asylum, since immigration law allowed them to become permanent
U.S. residents after a year in the country. However, this policy did not
apply to Haitians.

In September 1991 Haiti's first democratically elected president, Jean-
Bertrand Aristide, was toppled by a right-wing military coup. There
was an almost immediate increase in the number of Haitian boat people
trying to enter the United States. The American government was faced
with the unpleasant choice of either returning refugees to a military-
backed regime or allowing them to enter the country and increase the
likelihood of a flood of Haitians from the impoverished and oppressed
nation.

By the mid–1990s nearly fifty thousand Haitians were known to
reside in Dade County, but the actual number was probably much
higher due to the illegal entrants who were not counted.

The most noted expert on Haitians in Miami is Florida International University anthropologist Alex Stepick. In his essay "The Refu-

128. Haitians, in an ironic twist, being forced to return to Haiti on a Cuban-owned
airliner. Local African Americans and Haitians complained that Cubans were given
preferential treatment. Courtesy *Miami Herald*.

gees Nobody Wants: Haitians in Miami," published in *Miami Now: Immigration, Ethnicity, and Social Change,* which he coedited with Guillermo J. Grenier, also of Florida International University, Dr. Stepick reviewed the arrival and status of Haitians in Miami. This discussion relies heavily on his work.

The newly arriving Haitians faced many obstacles in Dade County. One of these was the widespread stereotype that Haitians exposed Americans to a number of communicable diseases. "During the period of greatest influx at the end of the 1970s, a hysterical scare swept through south Florida that tuberculosis was endemic among Haitians and was likely to spread through the general population. Those businesses most likely to employ low-skilled Haitians, the hotels and restaurants, were the most concerned that their employees might harbor a communicable disease."[4] Haitian students were reportedly subjected to verbal abuse and ridicule from their African-American peers at Little Haiti's Miami-Edison Senior High School.

The fear proved unfounded and the hysteria gradually subsided, but the damage had been done. Many Haitians lost their jobs, and negative stereotypes and fears of Haitians became firmly embedded in the general south Florida population. Haitians were perceived to be not only disease-ridden, but also uneducated and unskilled peasants who could prove to be only a burden to the community. Such views were expressed by black as well as white established residents. These negative stereotypes, however, were misleading.

According to Stepick, not all Haitian immigrants who came directly to Miami from Haiti were boat people. A survey compiled in 1983 and 1984 revealed that 20 percent arrived by airplane, reflecting a higher socioeconomic background than the stereotype. This does not include the earlier immigrants from the 1960s who have subsequently resettled in Miami. Even the Haitians who did come by boat were much like immigrants from other countries, slightly better off than their compatriots left behind. The refugees tended to be semiskilled, had some education, and lived in urban areas in Haiti.

Stepick, however, cautions: "Yet, because Haiti is the least developed nation in the Western Hemisphere, to be semiskilled and have some education and urban experience still leaves one at a disadvantage in the United States. The refugees had completed only an average of four to six years of formal education prior to arrival, and fewer than 5 percent had graduated from high school. Although extremely low by U.S. standards, these levels of education still are higher than those of the Haitian adult population, 80 percent of which is estimated to be illiterate."

Nevertheless, the negative stereotypes prevailed. The result proved devastating to Haitians. Indeed, the widespread fear of communicable diseases was the basis of much of the local opposition to Haitian immigration. Even Cubans arriving during the 1980 boat lift from Mariel did not face this particular obstacle. Local political groups goaded national authorities into an unparalleled campaign to repress the flow of Haitians into Miami and to deport those Haitians already in Florida. Members of south Florida's political elite—including Democratic party members, elected officials, and some Cubans—believed that the boat people were a disruptive force, destroying the community and draining public resources. There was some truth to the contention that Haitians were causing a drain on public resources, but so were Cubans and others who immigrated to the country during this time.

In 1973, in concert with local Protestant denominations, the National Council of Churches (NCC) funded what would become the Haitian Refugee Center (HRC). After HRC attained autonomy and a primarily Haitian staff, support from the local black community diminished and was limited to expressions of solidarity and appeals for equal treatment of the black boat people.

The newly arrived Haitians were imprisoned in the Krome detention center, described by some as a concentration camp in the middle of the Everglades. At one point, more than two thousand Haitians were incarcerated at Krome, some for more than a year. Many became profoundly depressed, and a few attempted suicide. Some participated in hunger strikes and other forms of protest. The federal court ultimately ordered the release of the detained Haitians, but the administration still refused to provide a firm immigration status either to the recently released or to Haitians who had arrived earlier and had made claims for political asylum.[5]

At about the same time, the Centers for Disease Control (CDC) announced that Haitians were one of the prime at-risk groups for Acquired Immune Deficiency Syndrome (AIDS), joining homosexuals, intravenous drug abusers, and hemophiliacs in this category. This caused yet another onslaught of criticism and abuse from established residents. The community's response was just as it had been a few years earlier when Haitians had been accused of spreading tuberculosis.

Stepick relates that "many Haitians lost their jobs. The primary employment agency for Haitians suddenly found it impossible to place any of its clients, and the widespread negative stereotypes of Haitians stretched even more broadly and deeply. Subsequently, the CDC removed Haitians from the list of at-risk groups, but again it was too late. The damage had been done. In the public mind, all Haitians were black boat people who were disease-ridden, desperately poor, and pathetic."

After many legal battles and much public pressure, most of the Haitian boat people qualified for legal permanent immigration status under the Immigration Reform and Control Act of 1986, and thousands began the legal adjustment process. Haitian farm workers, like other farm workers, were supposed to be eligible, but the INS District Office suspected massive fraud and rejected the vast majority of farmwork applications. In spite of these difficulties, by the mid–1980s there were approximately eighty thousand Haitians in Florida, about half of whom lived in the Greater Miami area of Dade County. This is less than 1 percent of the total immigration to the United States in the past ten years, and the number in the Miami area is less than one-fifth the number of Haitians in New York.

According to Stepick, local Haitian leaders have emerged to voice the aspirations of their people. Foremost among these, at least in terms of public visibility, has been the Reverend Gérard Jean-Juste, who was executive director of the Haitian Refugee Center, when he arrived in Miami from Boston, until 1990. He left Haiti as a young man and attended a seminary in Puerto Rico. In 1971 an exiled Haitian bishop in New York ordained him. Jean-Juste then taught English to Haitians in Boston. Upon arriving in Miami, he criticized the local archbishop, Edward McCarthy, for his inactivity on behalf of Haitian refugees.

The local Catholic hierarchy ostracized Jean-Juste and barred him from celebrating mass locally. But Stepick notes that Jean-Juste relishes his role as a constant thorn in the side of the local establishment. "His vocal opposition to the status quo eventually resulted in *Combité Liberté* losing its support from the National Council of Churches. The Ford Foundation stepped into the breach for nearly ten years until the implementation of the Immigration Reform and Control Act of 1986 provided legal status to the majority of Haitians in Miami."

The Haitian American Community Agency of Dade (HACAD) is the only Haitian-run organization providing social services to the Haitian community. It was chartered in the fall of 1974 by three Haitian business persons from New York. HACAD's executive director during this period of growth was Roger Biamby. He left Haiti in 1963, lived for a year in the Dominican Republic and then seventeen years in New York, where he obtained a master's degree in political science. Biamby came to Miami in 1981 to assume the directorship of HACAD. Like HRC, HACAD also provides an institutional basis for its director's political activities. Biamby has been somewhat lower-key than Jean-Juste and is not generally considered by outsiders to be the spokesperson for the Haitian refugee community. Nevertheless, his political activities subjected him to considerable attention within the Haitian community, and in 1989 he was ousted as executive director.

One Haitian organization assiduously avoids politics back in Haiti. It has become the most visible organ of political involvement for Haitians in south Florida. "The Haitian American Democratic Club (HADC)," Stepick explains, "is devoted solely to the task of speeding Haitian assimilation into U.S. culture and society. Its founder, Jacques Despinosse, left the Haitian middle class to come to Miami. He became a citizen in 1979 and founded HADC in 1980, after having been involved in the 1980 Democratic presidential race. By the mid–1980s the club had over 400 members, but Despinosse remained the dominant figure."

By far the most visible and important religious institution in Little Haiti is the Haitian Catholic Center, its Sunday masses overflowing with worshipers. Ironically it is headed by a Polish-American priest, Father Tom Wenski, who speaks Haitian Creole fluently and conducts all services in that language. The center is staffed primarily by nuns and priests on loan from Catholic religious orders in Haiti. It is housed in a former girls' Catholic high school and provides room and support for night-school English classes, day care, Catholic community/charity services to Haitians, and numerous organizations and initiatives for the Haitian community. Satellite centers have also been established throughout south Florida wherever there is a significant Haitian community.[6]

129. The Haitian Marketplace, Little Haiti. Most of the newly arriving Haitians settled in an area which once had been Lemon City and now is known as Little Haiti. The marketplace was established to attract tourists to the area, where many Haitian-oriented businesses are found. Notice the African influence in the architecture of the building. Courtesy Sergio Campos.

The Impact of Immigration

As more and more refugees arrived between 1960 and the mid–1980s, competition among immigrants and Dade County's poor for dwindling local human services was intensified. Many of the immigrants and refugees did not arrive rich—they were desperately poor people who came to live with or next to African Americans who were also very poor. The result was inter-group friction and competition for limited resources, particularly with respect to public facilities such as hospitals, health clinics, schools, public housing, emergency relief support and general welfare services. Native blacks, comprising a disproportionate number of the area's poor, were especially affected.[7]

In 1982, more than 60 percent of the County's community-action agency clients in Dade County were Hispanic or Haitian. The most acute child care needs were in those areas of Dade County that were most directly impacted by immigrants: Liberty City, a major black area; Edison-Little River, where most Haitians settled; and Little Havana, where Cuban immigrants established themselves.

Dwindling resources and increased demands for many kinds of services, especially from the rising number of Hispanic poor, resulted in complaints from blacks of longer lines and much longer waits. With the arrival of so many immigrants, between 1980 and 1982 demands by blacks and non-Hispanic whites for short-term emergency assistance showed significant drops (34 percent) while Hispanic demands for assistance increased by more than 100 percent. This index of an area's most economically threatened groups supported other data suggesting that Hispanics, not blacks, were now most at risk in Dade County, and it reflected the significant influence of immigration on the south Florida area.

According to the Dade County Public Health Department, the influx of refugees into the county has negatively impacted both blacks and whites. Since the department's policy is to serve those who are most at risk first, the result was a dramatic increase in public health services to Haitians during this period. Haitian immigrant demands between 1979 and 1982 rose from 12 percent to 30 percent of all clients served in the infant nutrition program, for example. Since the total number of people served had not increased significantly during this period, this meant that the number of clients in other ethnic groups was proportionately diminished. Presumably this resulted not because of a decrease in need among blacks and others, but because of displacement by immigrants and refugees.

The increased shortage of suitable, affordable rental properties as a result of immigration very likely put recent arrivals in direct competition with blacks, who were overrepresented among those living under crowded conditions, as immigrants tended to settle in neighborhoods that were contiguous to the area's black communities. All these factors have increased interethnic tensions in Miami as native residents, black and white alike, appear to resent the necessity to carry the economic burden of providing services to the immigrants. Blacks particularly seem to perceive themselves as squeezed out of these services.

Another impact of immigration policy upon the Miami community has been to initiate and prolong racial and ethnic tensions among various groups of residents who identify to some degree with one or another of the groups of immigrants and refugees. There has always been sufficient ill-will between American citizens and immigrant groups when the number of newcomers has reached a critical mass, and Miami reached that point during this period. Anger and resentment are common as people feel increasingly vulnerable to the vicissitudes of international affairs and policies. The favorable treatment of Cuban refugees, who were considered to be politically motivated to emigrate to this country, and the detention procedures applied to Haitians, who were considered to be motivated by economic considerations, antagonized many blacks, who viewed such a policy as racially discriminatory.

The Mariel boat lift heightened resentment in Florida and around the nation as thousands of dangerous criminals and mentally incompetent people were herded aboard the boats at the insistence of the Cuban government. In any given month, Dade County had 350 to 450 Mariel entrants in jail; in May 1985, 510 Mariel refugees were incarcerated in the Dade County jail, and Dade's residents paid for their care and all costs associated with their trials. As Miami's Cubans celebrated spiritedly the long-awaited reunification of some families and the release of a few political prisoners, anger among the native population was quiet and deep. It remains. The vacillation of the Carter administration didn't help: The administration first tried to enforce the law against illegal entry, next appropriated special funds to assist the refugees, and then impounded the boats being used to bring more refugees.

Regarding job displacement of blacks in Dade County by Cuban and Haitian immigrants, the data suggest that no significant black displacement has taken place except in some low-level jobs in the tourist industry; yet many blacks believe that it has occurred. For example, there is no evidence that the arrival of immigrants made native black residents all the poorer. It may have blunted black advancement, but it did not push more blacks into poverty. In 1969, 31.6 percent of the county's blacks were poor. By 1979 that number had actually decreased to 29.8 percent. Non-Hispanic whites also showed a slight drop in poverty level from 9.5 to 8.3 percent. Hispanics, however, sank even deeper into poverty. Poor Hispanics increased from 14.9 percent to 16.9 percent during this period.[8] With the more recent influx of significantly poorer refugees from the 1980 Freedom Flotilla, as the Mariel boat lift came to be called, this trend is likely to continue.

Even if immigration blunted black economic advancement, it did not stop it. According to the Dade County Planning Department, in Dade County between 1969 and 1979 only blacks as a group increased in median income (by 10.6 percent), whereas both non-Hispanic whites and Hispanics dropped in median income. Non-Hispanic white median income dropped by 6.5 percent, and Hispanic median income dropped by 1.8 percent. Blacks went from $11,855 to $13,108, while Hispanics went from $16,042 to $15,749. Non-Hispanic whites went from $20,943 to $19,585. These data were collected prior to the Mariel influx of substantially poorer Cubans. The figures appear to refute the commonly accepted premise that blacks in Dade County are falling farther and farther behind Hispanics and non-Hispanic whites in income level.[9]

During the 1980s the picture became considerably more complex as blacks from other Caribbean islands also began settling in Miami. Other than the early-arriving Bahamians, most Caribbean blacks who came to the United States before the late 1970s had bypassed Miami and the rest of the South, fearing the legacy of segregation and attracted by the greater opportunities and openness of the Northeast, particularly New York City. Black Cubans, for example, were more visible in New York and New Jersey than in Miami.

Similarly, when the Duvalier-inspired Haitian diaspora began in the late 1950s and 1960s, the primary destination was New York. But the civil rights victories of the 1960s and 1970s made Miami more attractive to Caribbean blacks. Communities of Haitians, Jamaicans, and Dominicans soon became visible, while smaller groups of other Caribbean blacks also established themselves. The percentage of Dade County's black population that was foreign-born was about 20 percent by 1980 and about 30 percent by 1990, and it is projected that by the year 2010 over half of the county's black population will be foreign-born. At that point African Americans will have become a minority within a minority.

By the year 2000 nearly a half-million black people will reside in Dade County. They will be very unlike those who came with the railroad in 1896. Blacks in Dade County today are better educated and hold better jobs than ever before. They are more ethnically diverse than ever before. They live in most sections of the county; and, relative to other racial groups, they have made steady progress on virtually all fronts. There are more black elected and appointed officials than anyone could have imagined in 1896. Even more will ascend to influence in the coming decades. Blacks are making steady gains in education and in income relative to other groups. However, black business development, although supported to some degree by the public sector with contracts and services, remains embryonic in comparison to white and Hispanic business growth.

In spite of significant black progress over the past century on Biscayne Bay, one-third of the black population of Dade County remains mired in poverty with little or no hope of escape. Poor black children in Dade County are worse off than ever; they are the poorest of the poor. Currently, popular social-welfare reforms are ominous to many poor blacks, and for good reason: The proposed reductions in public support will not make their lives better. The future of blacks in Miami, indeed the future of the city itself, depends in no small measure on its success in integrating this alienated segment of the community into the vibrant heart of the city in its second century.

Demographics

The black population of Dade County in 1930 was about 30,000; it had grown to more than 300,000 by the early 1980s and to 397,993 by 1990. The 1990 census shows 1,937,094 residents in Dade County and 358,548 in Miami. Of the Miamians, 98,207 (27 percent) were black. By the early 1980s, greater Miami became one of only sixteen metropolitan areas in the United States with more than 300,000 blacks. Between 1970 and 1980, Dade's black population grew by 47 percent, a growth rate exceeded only by that of Atlanta.[1] For more than thirty years Dade's black population outpaced the growth of the total popu-

Table 10.1. Population of Dade County, Florida, by race and ethnicity

Year	Total population	Black	Hispanic origin	Whites and others
1930	142,955	29,894	n/a	n/a
1940	267,739	49,518	n/a	n/a
1950	495,084	65,392	20,000	409,692
1955	715,000	101,000	35,000	579,000
1960	935,047	137,299	50,000	747,748
1965	1,101,500	163,500	174,500	763,500
1970	1,267,435	189,042	296,820	781,573
1975[a]	1,462,000	237,000	467,000	773,000
1980	1,625,781	280,358	580,340	775,914
1985	1,775,000	367,000	768,000	662,000
1990	1,937,094	397,993	953,407	614,066
1995	2,057,000	440,200	1,134,300	515,900

[a]There is some overlap of blacks and persons of Hispanic origin beginning in 1975.

Source: Metro-Dade Planning Department, "Profile," 4. Estimates for 1955, 1965, 1975, 1985, and 1995 by Metro-Dade Planning Department, Research Division, 1995.

lation. Table 10.1 shows the county's population growth by race and ethnicity since 1930.

The overwhelming majority of the county's blacks live in northwest Dade County, north of Northwest Thirty-fourth Street and east of Red Road (Northwest Fifty-seventh Avenue). Concentrations of blacks in Dade County have mirrored the patterns around the country in which middle- and working-class blacks have escaped the ghettos, leaving behind the black underclass. About one-third of Dade County's blacks are in poverty, and over eighty-two thousand live in the economically depressed areas commonly referred to as the inner city. Most people believe that far more blacks live in poverty than in fact do: Nearly two-thirds of Dade's black population lives in neighborhoods that can be described as working class or better.

The black population of Dade County accounted for 22.6 percent of Florida's black population in 1990. This was a disproportionately high share. Dade accounted for 15 percent of the state's total population in 1990. Each of the decennial censuses between 1940 and 1990 recorded an increase in the proportion of black Floridians living in Dade County. Part of the shift was accounted for by Dade's rapid

Table 10.2. Country of birth, Caribbean-born blacks in Dade County, 1980, 1990

	1990	*1980*	*Change*
Haiti	45,339	12,860	32,479
Jamaica	27,204	9,200	18,004
Bahamas	7,485	5,040	2,445
Cuba	6,382	2,620	3,762
Dominican Republic	4,271	1,000	3,271
Trinidad and Tobago	2,404	1,000	1,404
Puerto Rico	1,422	460	962
Other Caribbean	4,309	1,480	2,829
Total	98,816	33,660	65,156

Source: Metro-Dade County Planning Department, "Profile," 19.

growth rate, which outpaced Florida's prior to the 1970s. But it was also due to a gradual change in the racial profiles of the state and county: The state gradually became less black, while Dade became more black. It should be noted that the increase in Dade's black population occurred as a result of black immigration from abroad, primarily from the Caribbean, rather than as a result of American-born blacks moving to Dade County. This pattern is likely to continue.

From which countries do Dade's black immigrants come? The census does not specify the country of origin of immigrants, but it does identify the country of birth and the ancestry of the population. These data show that Dade's black population is diverse in terms of national origin and ancestry. The 1980 data indicate that one in every six black residents of Dade County was born abroad, the vast majority in Caribbean countries.[2] Table 10.2 reflects the country of birth of Caribbean-born blacks in 1980 and 1990.

By 1990 one in four Dade blacks was born in the Caribbean, primarily in Haiti and the West Indies. There were 117,000 foreign-born blacks in Dade County in 1990, about 30 percent of the total. The bulk of these, about 99,000 persons or 25 percent of all blacks, were born in the Caribbean, including Puerto Rico. Of these, the largest ancestry groups indicated were Haitian and West Indian, followed by those of Hispanic or Spanish origin. Of those who reported being born in a Central American country, most were from Nicaragua, Hondu-

Table 10.3. Place of birth, by ancestry, black population, Dade County, 1990

Place of birth	Afro-American	Haitian	West Indian	Hispanic	Other	Uncoded	Total
U.S.	199,139	14,223	9,459	4,440	5,974	48,386	281,621
Caribbean	4,399	40,118	32,946	10,684	3,045	7,624	98,816
Central America	417	0	556	3,030	105	282	4,390
Other	657	162	730	717	3,217	611	6,094
Unspecified Abroad	114	687	560	365	84	6,240	8,050
Total	204,726	55,190	44,251	19,236	12,425	63,143	398,971

Source: Metro-Dade Planning Department, "Profile," 18.

ras, and Panama.[3] Table 10.3 reflects these statistics from the 1990 census.

The Dade County Planning Department reports:

> In the future Black population expansion may be more evenly balanced between natural increase and net migration. In summary the population growth of Dade County in the 1980s has consisted of about one-third natural increase and two-thirds immigration. Blacks were responsible for about 70 percent of the natural increase but far less of the immigration, just under 30 percent. Of the Black immigrants more than 80 percent were from various Caribbean countries, primarily Haiti and Jamaica. This same general pattern will most likely prevail throughout the 1990s except that the Black shares will decline relative to the Hispanics. The latter will constitute the bulk of the immigration and their contribution to natural increase is growing.[4]

Current Residential Patterns

In the 1980s, the crack cocaine epidemic hit Overtown and other low-income areas of black Dade County. Predictably, the crime rate soared, adding to the decline of old black neighborhoods. Black businesses were crushed by the violence, as many of their customers moved to other areas or were frightened away. Business-insurance rates in the low-income black areas skyrocketed, in part resulting from racial disturbances in those communities. Those left behind were the least able to resist the crime and violence that swirled about them.

Table 10.4. Deaths of Dade teens by gunshot, 1987–1991

Group	1991	1990	1989	1988	1987
Black males	20	27	25	23	20
White males	11	5	9	8	4
Black females	3	2	3	4	4
White females	1	1	1	2	0

According to a 1989 study by a group of local black leaders, "The absence of traditional avenues of success has allowed the drug trade to serve as the jobs program as well as the entrepreneurial development program in certain underclass sections of the black community. The dearth of successful entrepreneurs and other successful blacks provides limited visible competition with the drug dealer as the neighborhood role model and mentor."[5] In their report, the leaders sounded themes that are becoming more and more popular in urban black America: the need to stop crime in the inner city and the urgency to deal with welfare dependency, especially single black women with children.

A committee of the Dade County Criminal Justice Council studied the problem of black-on-black crime and found that for every violent white-on-white crime, there were 4.3 violent black-on-black crimes. In 1985, 37 percent of all homicides, 56 percent of all rapes, and 46 percent of all aggravated assaults were perpetrated in black residential areas of Liberty City, Little River, Overtown, and Coconut Grove. According to a study prepared for the Metro-Miami Action Plan, a highly touted community improvement group, 57 percent of the 5,340 inmates in the Dade County Detention Centers in 1985 were black, 11 percent were white, and 31 percent were Hispanic.

The Dade Medical Examiner's office keeps its own figures on violent deaths in the county. Table 10.4 shows how racial groups compare in terms of teen deaths by gunshot. In Dade, 68 of 51,060 black male teenage residents died from gunshots between 1987 and 1989. In Broward, 33 of 23,057 black male teens were shot to death during the same period.[6]

By the 1960s the decline of historically black neighborhoods was apparent. In addition to the increase in crime in poor areas, many other factors account for the change. Among them are the movement of upwardly mobile blacks into newer black areas, such as Richmond

Heights and Carol City, and into traditionally white sections. Primarily as a result of the elimination of laws and practices limiting housing opportunities for blacks, but also as a result of the relocation of large numbers of blacks by expressway construction in the early sixties, the black population of Miami spread across Northwest Seventy-ninth Street and into previously all-white areas. West Little River changed from an all-white area in 1960 to a population more than 50 percent black within two decades.

As the black population continued its growth to the northwest in the 1970s, North County was established north of Opa-Locka. It consists of two contiguous communities, Lake Lucerne (east of Northwest Twenty-seventh Avenue) and New Liberty City (west of Twenty-seventh Avenue). Lake Lucerne began as a development primarily for white residents, but it later began a transformation to a tri-ethnic community including non-Latin white, Latin, and black residents.

Overtown today is but a shadow of the bustling community it was less than a generation ago. Although a few scattered middle- and upper-income families still choose to live in Overtown, and in spite of recent plans for the revitalization of the area, there is little question that the community is in a continuous state of social and economic decline.

Comparatively speaking, the Black Grove has not experienced as much decline in the quality of life as other old sections of black Miami. Still, things are hardly as they were. There is a thriving drug trade with all its associated problems. There are low-income properties in decline, and the businesses serving the Black Grove struggle to exist. Nonetheless, the Black Grove is a viable and stable community with a substantial black middle- and upper-class segment living in well-kept, neatly trimmed neighborhoods.

Relatively few black residents from the Grove migrated to other areas of Dade County. Socially, the Grove's black population is a tightly knit group. Nearly 80 percent of black residents own their homes; the others rent primarily from black owners. In the 1950s, the renting population increased when two- and three-story apartment buildings were erected between U.S. 1 and the Florida East Coast Railroad tracks and when single-family homes along LeJeune Road were replaced with federally subsidized houses. The federal government, working with local government and residents, also made improvements in the area's sewer system, sidewalks, and streets.

130. Second Avenue as it appears today. The view is looking north from the top of the Miami police station at Fifth Street. Notice the Lyric Theater at top center with cupola. Courtesy Sergio Campos.

To the north, Liberty City was a bulging community by 1950 with a large proportion of middle-income blacks, including many homeowners who had moved north from Overtown to the new development. As both Liberty City and Brown's Subdivision expanded and merged into an area now known as Model City, the population became predominantly black and poorer. Within three decades, Liberty City's pattern of development had shifted from private ownership to rentals as a result of a significant increase in population, due primarily to the intentional displacement of thousands of blacks from Overtown by the I–95 expressway system in the early 1960s. The demand for housing in the area was met in part by white developers, who built tracts of cheap two- and three-story apartment buildings that are known today as concrete monsters and are badly deteriorated.

In 1950 there were less than 11,000 residents in Liberty City, compared to nearly 30,000 in 1980. By 1990 there were 55,038 blacks living in the Model City area. During the 1980 riot, although there was some destruction within Liberty City's original boundaries, most of the damage occurred in adjacent communities. Because of the media's unfamiliarity with the names and boundaries of the various communities, the 1980 riots made Liberty City a household name throughout the nation.

It must be noted that despite their advance to the northern section of the county, blacks have remained in highly segregated neighborhoods. Some census tracts have few or no blacks, while other tracts show a black population of greater than 95 percent. By 1990 areas of very high concentration of blacks expanded substantially in the northern half of the county, and areas of moderately high concentrations expanded east of I–95 into North Miami and North Miami Beach. In the southern half of Dade County, change was more moderate, with some continued expansion of moderately high densities near the existing black areas.

Two attempts to create new cities in predominantly black areas failed. New City, in central northwest Dade, was turned down by the county commission in the 1980s in the face of strong local opposition, primarily from blacks who would have lived in New City. In 1995 the proposed City of Destiny, in far north Dade, also failed to capture the support of voters.[7]

The past decade appears to have been marked by two contrasting but not contradictory movements of the black population. On one hand, there has been an expansion of the population and size of majority-black areas; on the other hand, there was a more widespread movement of blacks into formerly all-white areas. While there were more areas of very high concentration of blacks, they accommodated a smaller proportion of Dade's black population. One-third of all blacks now live outside predominately black areas.[8]

There is no visible trend away from this pattern of racially segregated neighborhoods, as table 10.5 reflects. Eighty percent of the county's blacks live in the area reaching from Overtown through the Allapattah, Liberty City, and Brownsville areas to West Little River

Table 10.5. Population of black neighborhoods in Dade County, 1960–1990

Neighborhood	1960	1970	1980	1990
Carol City	222	7,384	27,564	29,213
Washington Park	640	965	1,477	6,630
West Little River	10	12,121	21,648	22,887
Edison Park	90	8,922	24,081	34,851
Model City	49,025	73,799	61,561	55,038
Seminola	842	970	955	314
Overtown	38,581	20,899	13,386	12,510
Coconut Grove	9,463	9,281	5,961	5,701
Richmond Heights	4,400	7,469	6,036	7,485
Perrine	5,057	5,502	4,485	7,667
Goulds	3,900	6,165	6,024	6,004
Naranja	726	711	1,426	1,556
Total neighborhoods	112,956	154,188	174,604	189,856
Blacks, Dade County	137,299	189,042	280,358	397,993

Source: Metro-Dade County Planning Department, "Profile."

and the City of Opa-Locka. Table 10.6 shows Dade's black population according to municipalities.

Population projections suggest increasing concentrations of the black population north of the Miami River and east as well as northeast of the city of Hialeah. If historical patterns continue and if the growth of black communities occurs in contiguous tracts to already heavily black areas, Dade County blacks are projected to live in increasingly segregated conditions well into the next century.

Socioeconomic Status of Blacks

In the 1980s, despite Dade County's relatively large low-income black population, the average income of a black family in Dade County was higher than the average income for black families in Florida and in the nation. The mean family income for blacks in Dade County in 1979 was 68 percent of the average for all families in the county, while for the United States as a whole in the same year, mean family income for blacks was 59 percent of average income for all families.

In 1989 the median family income for U.S. blacks was 66 percent of the median for all families. In Dade County, however, the black me-

Table 10.6. Black population and percent of population, selected cities, Dade County, 1950–1990

City	1950 No.	%[a]	1960 No.	%	1970 No.	%	1980 No.	%	1990 No.	%
Miami	40,265	16	65,213	22	76,156	23	87,110	25	98,207	27
N. Miami	17	0	51	0	69	0	1,597	4	15,941	32
Opa-Locka	1,681	32	3,544	36	3,503	29	9,182	63	10,603	69
N. Miami Beach	n/a	0	719	3	1,010	3	93	0	7,707	22
Homestead	1,691	37	3,178	35	3,871	28	5,278	26	6,178	23
Miami Beach	640	1	568	1	319	0	894	1	4,798	5
Florida City	1,547	100	2,403	58	3,040	59	3,678	60	3,540	61
South Miami	1,599	33	2,403	24	2,842	24	3,282	30	3,078	30
Miami Shores	n/a	0	n/a	0	n/a	0	123	1	2,056	20
El Portal	n/a	0	n/a	0	n/a	0	314	15	1,312	53
Other Dade	18,147	8	59,788	11	99,174	12	170,214	15	252,739	18
Dade County	64,947	13	137,299	15	189,666	15	280,434	17	397,993	21

[a]Percentage is of city population.

Source: Metro-Dade Planning Department, "Profile," 26.

Table 10.7. Dade County black families, by income, 1980,
1989, 1990 (percentages)

Income group	1980	1989	1990
Less than $5,000	14.4	14.1	14.7
$5,000–$9,000	18.9	17.2	12.2
$10,000–$14,900	13.8	11.9	11.2
$15,000–$24,999	20.8	19.6	20.0
$25,000–$34,999	13.9	13.8	15.1
$35,000–$49,999	11.1	12.0	14.1
$50,000–$74,999	5.8	8.5	9.3
$75,000–$99,999	1.0	2.2	2.3
Over $100,000	0.3	0.8	1.0

Source: U.S. Census, 1990.

dian income had risen to 72 percent of the income of Dade's total
population. Thus, blacks in Dade were narrowing the income gap more
effectively than blacks in the United States as a whole. It is notable
that the county's black income went up in real terms between 1979
and 1989 while the income for the total Dade population and Hispanics declined. Table 10.7 reflects the income of Dade County's black
families.

Despite the economic stagnation of the 1970s and the decline in the
real income of black families nationwide, Dade's black families succeeded in posting an increase in income of 7 percent between 1970
and 1980. This is especially important since this was the period in
which large numbers of immigrants were establishing themselves in
Dade County. It has been assumed that the Latinization of the county
occurred at the economic expense of local blacks, but in fact, no other
group in Dade did as well as blacks in terms of improving its income
level during the immigration tumult of the 1970s and 1980s.

Table 10.8, based on census data released in 1990, suggests that the
trend in gradual economic advancement for blacks continued through
1989. The table shows that black income in Dade County remained
stable in the lower income brackets and increased slightly in the higher
income levels.

One reason for the gradual narrowing of the black–white income
gap was the emergence of a small but growing class of affluent black
families, a trend that continued through the 1980s and mid–1990s. To

Table 10.8. Income distribution by total, black, and Hispanic households, Dade County, 1989

	Total		Black		Hispanic	
	No.	%	No.	%	No.	%
LT $10,000	133,212	19.2	32,259	26.9	68,024	21.4
$10,000–$19,999	129,830	18.8	26,260	21.9	66,269	20.9
$20,000–$29,999	114,327	16.5	20,929	17.4	55,136	17.3
$30,000–$39,999	90,203	13.0	15,588	13.0	41,197	13.0
$40,000–$49,999	67,927	9.8	9,780	8.1	30,574	9.6
$50,000–$59,000	47,243	6.8	6,163	5.1	19,218	6.0
GT $60,000	109,495	15.8	9,098	7.6	37,412	11.8
Total	692,237	100	120,077	100	317,830	100

Source: Metro-Dade Planning Department, "Profile," 86.

a significant degree, this group represented blacks who were the direct beneficiaries of the civil rights and affirmative action movements in Dade County. Black economic progress is also the result of black access to a wider array of career options through improved educational opportunities in the county. The 1990 census counted about seventeen thousand black families with incomes of more than thirty-five thousand dollars, compared with forty-six hundred families in 1980. Eleven thousand blacks in this group in 1990 had incomes of more than fifty thousand dollars, compared to fourteen hundred such families in 1980.

An increasing proportion of the county's households are headed by a Caribbean householder. In terms of income, Jamaicans can be identified as being above average, with black Cubans and Dominicans being worse off, even more so than Haitians. Approximately 49 percent of all black households had incomes of less than twenty thousand dollars in 1989. This low-income category included only 38 percent of Jamaicans but 70 percent of Dominicans. Jamaican households represented the highest proportion of incomes over fifty thousand dollars in 1989: 19 percent versus 13 percent for all black households. Ten percent of Dominican and Bahamian households reported fifty thousand dollars or more in 1989, while 7 and 5 percent of Haitians and Cuban households, respectively, received fifty thousand dollars or more.[9] Table 10.9 shows family income data for Dade blacks of Caribbean descent.

Table 10.9. Family income distribution, by black householder's Caribbean country of birth, Dade County, 1989

Income	Total black	%	Bahamas	%	Cuba	%	Dom. Rep.	%	Haiti	%	Jamaica	%	Other	%
LT $10,000	20,837	(23.2)	408	(24.5)	460	(26.4)	581	(44.3)	4,159	(29.4)	799	(9.9)	273	(13.1)
$10,000–$19,999	19,572	(21.8)	346	(20.8)	499	(28.7)	357	(27.2)	3,391	(24.0)	2,025	(25.1)	353	(16.9)
$20,000–$29,999	16,336	(18.2)	339	(20.4)	357	(20.5)	156	(11.9)	3,030	(21.4)	1,328	(16.5)	422	(20.2)
$30,000–$39,999	12,171	(13.6)	286	(17.2)	122	(7.0)	93	(7.1)	1,915	(13.5)	1,113	(13.8)	346	(16.5)
$40,000–$49,999	7,753	(8.6)	104	(6.3)	142	(8.2)	38	(2.9)	777	(5.5)	976	(12.1)	339	(16.2)
$50,000–$59,000	5,178	(5.8)	91	(5.5)	72	(4.1)	38	(2.9)	466	(3.3)	613	(7.6)	130	(6.2)
GT $60,000	7,911	(8.8)	89	(5.4)	88	(5.1)	48	(3.7)	423	(3.0)	1,208	(15.0)	229	(11.0)
Total	89,758	(100)	1,663	(100)	1,740	(100)	1,311	(100)	14,161	(100)	8,062	(100)	2,092	(100)

Source: Metro-Dade Planning Department, "Profile," 91.

Despite these gains blacks continue to complain about being economically isolated because business opportunities for blacks outside their own communities remain limited. According to Milton Vickers, Director of the Dade County Office of Minority Business Development, in the early 1990s, many of those blacks who have risen into the more affluent class have done so through jobs with the school system or other government agencies. In Vickers's view, set-aside programs (which reserve a share of local government contracts for minority-owned businesses) have been a road to prosperity and even wealth for some Dade blacks in the past twenty years.[10]

Still, black participation in some sectors of the economy is less impressive than in others. According to the U.S. Equal Employment Opportunity Commission, Miami's tourism industry lags behind almost every major convention area in the nation in employing black professionals. The low number of black professionals working in major Dade hotels mirrors the overall employment picture in the county. Blacks, who make up 18 percent of the Dade work force, are overrepresented in low-skilled, low-paying jobs in the tourist industry, and despite some progress, are still underrepresented in upper-level positions. In spite of recent gains by blacks moving into managerial positions in other sectors of the Dade economy (including the public sector), few blacks in tourism hold executive or managerial positions.[11]

Increasing black employment in tourism was a key demand of the black convention boycott of 1990, which started after anti-apartheid leader Nelson Mandela visited Miami on June 28, 1989, and received no official welcome. Miami attorney H. T. Smith and other black leaders demanded an apology from Dade political leaders and targeted the convention industry for a boycott. Several major black organizations canceled national conventions in Miami, resulting in an estimated loss of over $10 million to the local economy within the first few months of the boycott.

In response, Visitors Bureau president Merrett Stierheim pledged to push the industry to hire more blacks in high-ranking positions. He also argued that the boycott hurt the black community because of the number of blacks who already worked in tourism. Stierheim ordered a survey of the twenty-four largest hotels in Dade County to determine black employment rates. It revealed that more than 25 percent of all hotel employees in Dade County in 1990 were American blacks. The EEOC statistics from 1988 show 22.2 percent black employment

131. Miami attorney H. T. Smith, who led the black boycott of tourism in Dade County following a visit to Miami by South Africa's Nelson Mandela in the early 1990s. Smith and many blacks believed Mandela was snubbed by local politicians. The tactic cost local tourism millions in lost income from black conventions. Ultimately, the boycott succeeded in several gains for blacks. Courtesy H. T. Smith.

in tourism in Miami, but only 5.1 percent in jobs requiring a college degree.

Area hoteliers argued that few blacks are employed in jobs requiring a college education because they lack interest, they lack qualifications, or they do not apply. Of 821 students enrolled in 1989 in Florida International University's nationally renowned School of Hospitality, only 33 were black. "One of the things we could do in this community is create a fund to go to the high schools, find people interested, and help them get the education," said Leo Salom, general manager of the twelve-hundred-room Fontainebleau Hilton Hotel on Miami Beach.[12]

The black employment issue is not confined to tourism. According to the most recent figures of the U.S. Bureau of Labor Statistics, in all areas of employment in Dade County, in 1987 blacks held 5.8 percent of the executive, administrative, or managerial positions; they held 14.2 percent of the specialty jobs such as engineers, doctors, lawyers, accountants, or psychologists. Comparatively, Anglos (31 percent of the work force) held 47 percent of executive or managerial jobs and 53 percent of specialty professions. Hispanics (52 percent of the work force in 1987) had 47 percent of the executive jobs and 31 percent of the specialty occupations. Of labor, service, and transportation jobs, blacks held 30 percent, Hispanics about 50 percent, and whites only about 19 percent.[13]

Unemployment among black teens remained inordinately high in the early 1990s. A statewide survey taken in April 1992 found that black males in Dade County had an unemployment rate of 14.3 percent, compared to 7.3 percent for white males. For black females, unemployment was 13.8 percent, compared to 10.4 percent for white females. The study did not consider Hispanics a distinct racial category; they could fall into either racial designation. Teens of all groups had higher unemployment in Dade, with black unemployment rates much higher. The overall unemployment rate for people sixteen to nineteen years old was 23.1 percent in Dade, up from 18.8 percent a year earlier. Whites ages sixteen to nineteen had an unemployment rate of 17.7 percent. The unemployment rate was 18 percent for males and 17.3 percent for females. Blacks in the same age category had an unemployment rate of 38.3 percent, or more than twice as high. The rate was 34.6 percent for black teen males and 42.5 percent for black teen females.[14]

According to the 1990 census report, the tens of thousands of white non-Hispanics who fled Dade County in the 1980s were poorer and less educated than those who stayed, leaving behind an area deeply divided by ethnicity and class. That exodus and a stunning influx of immigrants widened the economic chasm in Dade. The rate of increase for blacks slowed, while that of Hispanics lagged as immigration swelled their numbers. By contrast, many of the white non-Hispanics who stayed in Dade became a well-educated affluent elite. Eighty-five percent had high school diplomas, up from 69 percent a decade earlier; one-third had college degrees, up from 18 percent. Though white non-Hispanics constituted just one-third of the Dade County population in 1992, they controlled half the income.

The 1990 census found striking differences among ethnic groups in a variety of standard-of-living indicators. Table 10.10 reflects those differences.

The arrival of thousands of poor Hispanic and Haitian immigrants, the continuing misery of the black inner city, and the transformation of the white non-Hispanic population were all part of the dramatic picture provided by social data from the 1990 census. The *Miami Herald* analyzed the subject in 1992 and concluded that the incomes of white non-Hispanics in Dade grew twice as fast as those of blacks and outpaced Hispanics even more—at least partly because many of

Table 10.10. Ethnic disparities in income, adults age twenty-five and over
(percentages)

Group	Living in poverty	H.S. diploma	College degree	Owning house
Broward County				
Blacks	27	56	10	45
Hispanic	14	68	16	54
White Non-Hispanic	6	81	20	72
Dade County				
Blacks	30	56	10	44
Hispanic	20	55	14	48
White Non-Hispanic	6	85	30	67
Monroe County				
Blacks	27	59	8	34
Hispanics	23	48	7	54
White Non-Hispanic	8	85	23	65
Palm Beach County				
Blacks	30	50	9	41
Hispanics	18	54	14	52
White Non-Hispanic	5	84	24	76
Florida				
Blacks	32	56	10	47
Hispanics	20	57	14	50
White Non-Hispanic	8	80	20	72

Source: Miami Herald, May 3, 1992, 1A.

those who left were on the lower end of the economic scale. Also, as
thousands of poor and unskilled immigrants poured into Dade, the
average income of Hispanic families fell slightly after adjustment for
inflation. Finally, income for black households in Dade grew 10 percent over the decade. But incomes for the shrinking number of white
non-Hispanic households grew 17 percent, so the typical black family
actually fell further behind the typical white family.

Blacks who lived in poor inner-city areas like Liberty City and Overtown suffered income declines while the size of the typical inner-city
family grew, leaving poor blacks worse off than before. However, as
noted earlier, some blacks prospered in the 1980s, moving up from
the ghetto and into walled suburban communities. This split between
wealthy and poor blacks grew. In 1992 the most affluent quarter of

Dade blacks had incomes above thirty-seven thousand dollars, while the poorest quarter earned less than nine thousand dollars.[15]

According to the county planning department:

Historically, a significant proportion of the County's Black households have resided within the city limits of Miami. In 1990, 31,300, or 26 percent of total Black households lived in the city of Miami. A large number of these households in Miami, 56 percent, were receiving less than $15,000 in 1989. At the higher income level, only 5 percent of Black households in the City were reporting $50,000 or higher in 1989.

A disproportionate income distribution was also evident in the City of Opa-Locka. About 50 percent of the city's 3,500 Black households had an income of less than $15,000 in 1989 and a low 5 percent had income of $50,000 or greater. Although they had fairly small numbers of Black households, the cities of Florida City, Homestead, and Miami Beach all surpassed the 50 percent mark for the below $15,000 level with a corresponding low number of households at the high end.

In the cities of Miami Shores and South Miami, a larger-than-average percent of the Black households had incomes of $50,000 or greater. Approximately one out of five of Miami Shores' 510 Black households had incomes surpassing $49,999. In South Miami 16 percent of its 850 Black households were in the $50,000 or more bracket in 1989.[16]

Black Poverty in Dade County

Although many blacks are moving into the economic mainstream of the community, a large number remain bottled up at the very bottom of the economic scale. The proportion of Dade County blacks in this class has remained relatively stable over recent decades. However, the problems facing the county's very poor people in the 1990s are far more compelling than those facing the very poor in past decades.

The 1990 census brought good news and bad news about Dade County blacks in poverty. The bad news was that blacks still accounted for about one-third of Dade's poor, a share largely unchanged over the previous decade. This was a high percentage, almost twice as high as the black share of the total population, but not much different from the national average for blacks.

Table 10.11. Persons below poverty level, by race and
Hispanic origin, U.S. and Dade County, 1969, 1979, 1989

| | 1969 | | | |
	U.S.	%	Dade	%
Total	27,124,985	(13.7)	177,886	(14.2)
Black	7,680,105	(35.0)	59,922	(30.7)
Hispanic	2,153,834	(23.5)	44,530	(14.9)

Source: "Profile of the Black Population 1990," Metro-Dade County
Planning Department, Miami (1995), 98.

The U.S. poverty rate was virtually unchanged between 1969 and
1989, declining only from 13.7 percent in 1969 to 13.1 percent in
1989. The black poverty rate was more than double the overall rate
and remained so in 1989. Approximately 35 percent of black persons
lived in poverty in 1969, and the level remained near 30 percent in
1979 and 1989. Table 10.11 reflects the foregoing figures.

The multiethnic immigration waves into Dade County, particularly
those in the last decade, resulted in a more pronounced increase in
poor persons locally than nationally. "Since 1969 the total number of
poor persons grew by 92 percent, from 177,900 to 341,300 in 1989,
and the number of poor Black persons almost doubled from 59,900 to
117,400 in 1989. Hispanic poor increased fourfold, from 44,500 to
183,200 in just two decades. Poverty rates for Black Caribbean na-
tives were as high as 34 percent (Bahamians) and as low as 14 percent
(Jamaicans) but overall were lower than the rate for all Blacks (25
percent versus 30 percent). Those Black persons from the Bahamas,
Cuba, Dominican Republic and Haiti have the highest poverty rates."[17]

Primarily as a result of the influx of poor immigrants and the stagnation of one-third of Miami blacks at the bottom of the socioeconomic ladder, by 1992 Miami had attained the status of being one of
the poorest cities in the nation. The city had a higher percentage of
residents in poverty than all but three large cities in the United States.
Laredo, Texas, which borders Mexico, topped the list with 37.3 percent of its residents falling below the federal poverty line. Next among
cities with more than one hundred thousand people came Detroit, New
Orleans, and Miami, where 31.2 percent of the people were living in
poverty according to Census Bureau data. Poverty was so pervasive

		1979				1989		
U.S.	%	Dade	%	U.S.	%	Dade	%
27,392,580	(12.4)	240,892	(15.0)	31,742,864	(13.1)	341,261	(17.9)
7,648,604	(29.9)	81,936	(29.6)	8,441,429	(29.5)	117,357	(30.3)
3,371,134	(23.5)	97,306	(16.8)	5,403,492	(25.3)	183,207	(19.5)

inside Miami's city limits that the rate for the entire city approached the poverty rate in some of the most infamous districts of other American cities, including South Los Angeles where riots erupted in 1992. In parts of Miami, the poverty rate reached staggering proportions. In one area of Liberty City, 68 percent of all families were living in poverty. In an adjoining neighborhood, the median household income plummeted from $11,500 in 1980 to $6,221 in 1990.[18]

Table 10.12 lists the ten poorest cities in the United States with a population of one hundred thousand or more in 1990.

Poverty among American blacks in Dade is a more severe type of poverty than one finds among the poor of other ethnic groups in the county: Dade's poor African Americans are the poorest of the poor and the most dependent. In this class there is a concentration of unmarried black women with dependent children.

While the poverty rate for black children improved during the 1970s, the incidence of poverty among other children worsened in Dade County. The county had sixteen thousand more poor children in 1980 than in 1970. The child poverty rate worsened markedly, swelling from 16 percent in 1970 to nearly 20 percent in 1980. In 1990 that figure had risen to 24.9 percent. The impact of immigration and the increase in the Hispanic poor, in part, account for this change in Dade County, but the deterioration in poverty rates mirrored the national trend. For children in Dade, the odds of being poor depended more on the presence of two parents than on skin color or ethnicity. Children in single-parent families, particularly female-householder families, had a fifty-fifty chance of being in poverty. The chances were somewhat higher for blacks than for whites or children of Hispanic origin.

Fatherless black families constituted about 39 percent of all black families in Dade County in 1980, up from 23 percent in 1970; by

Table 10.12. The nation's poorest cities, 1990

City	Population	Poverty rate[a]
Laredo	122,899	37.29
Detroit	1,027,974	32.41
New Orleans	488,518	31.63
Miami	358,548	31.17
Flint	140,761	30.58
Gary	116,646	29.43
Waco	103,590	28.68
Cleveland	505,616	28.67
Hartford	139,739	27.51
Atlanta	394,017	27.29
Elsewhere in Florida		
Tampa	280,015	19.44
Hialeah	188,004	18.20
Fort Lauderdale	149,377	17.11
Orlando	164,693	15.76
St. Petersburg	238,629	13.55
Jacksonville	635,230	12.97
Hollywood	121,697	11.01
Tallahassee	124,682	10.17

[a]Rate is for persons not families.
Source: U.S. Census Bureau.

1990 the percentage had jumped to 46.9. Blacks accounted for 42 percent of all Dade County fatherless families in 1980, a level almost three times higher than the black share of all families in the county. By 1990 blacks accounted for 55 percent of all fatherless families in Dade County.

Why are women increasingly living alone, particularly black women with children? A number of factors have contributed to this phenomenon. First, more women have been able to land good jobs and establish economic independence. Other contributing factors include increased Social Security benefits which provide many older women with the financial resources needed to establish independent households, increasing divorce rates, and postponement of the first marriage.

In 1980 most mothers with children and no husband present were divorced (45 percent) or separated (24 percent). About 16 percent, however, had never married. The marital status patterns were quite different for blacks, whites, and Hispanics. For blacks, about 29 percent were never married, 29 percent were separated, and 27 percent were divorced. For whites, only 6 percent were never married and 59 percent were divorced or separated.

In 1983, there were 8,100 births to Dade County residents who were not married. This represented 30 percent of all births, a proportion that has been increasing. About three-fourths of these births were to black mothers; this was a very high percentage, considering that only one-third of all births were to black mothers. In 1990 close to 60 percent of all births to black mothers in Dade were to unwed mothers. This proportion has been steadily increasing and is now about five times the comparable rates for white mothers.

Half of the children born out of wedlock in 1983 were not first-born children. This percentage has been increasing and suggests that the social stigma traditionally associated with bearing a child out of wedlock may no longer be an important factor in the decision to have a child. By the early 1990s, 74.5 percent of all black infants born in Dade County were born to unwed mothers, half of them to teenagers. Although the teenage pregnancy problem is most acute for black teens, this is not just a minority problem. For the past twenty years, there have been about eighty babies for every one thousand unmarried African-American teenagers. At the same time, the rate for white unmarried teenagers grew from eight babies per one thousand in 1970 to twenty babies in 1990. However, contrary to popular perception, about 62 percent of single parents in 1990 were high school graduates and worked at least part-time. Over 50 percent of the welfare expenditures in the county go to families in which the mother became a parent in her teens.

Poor black families were larger than poor white families or those of Hispanic origin. The average size of a poor black family was 4.1 persons compared with an average of 3.1 for whites and 3.3 for families of Hispanic origin. Moreover, black families had a higher proportion (30 percent) of children under five in need of day care if the mother was working.

In 1980 the chance that a Dade County child would live in poverty was 36 percent for a black child and 19 percent for a child of Hispanic origin. But a child in a family maintained by a woman alone, regardless of her ethnicity, had a 46 percent chance of being poor. Black children in female-householder families had a better-than-even chance (58 percent probability) of being poor. For children of single Hispanic women, the odds of being poor were close to fifty-fifty (46 percent probability). Clearly, the absence of a man in the house was a major factor in determining the poverty status of children and families in Dade County.[19]

According to the Dade County Planning Department, families maintained by a woman with no husband present increased at about four times the rate of increase for two-parent families (77 percent versus 19 percent). In 1970, one in every eight Dade County families was managed by a woman alone; in 1980 the ratio was one in every six; by 1990 it was one in five. The rate of increase in female-householder families was even more rapid for black families and for families of Hispanic origin. Numbers of black female-householder families doubled. Those of Hispanic origin tripled, but this increase must be viewed in the context of the rapid growth of all Hispanic-origin families and the relatively small number of Hispanic female-householder families in 1970 (eight thousand). By 1980, despite the high rate of growth, the proportion of Hispanic-origin families that were maintained by a woman with no husband present (16 percent) was still lower than the average for all families (17 percent). By 1990, 19 percent of Hispanic families were managed by a woman with no husband present, compared to 21.5 percent of all families in Dade County.

It must be acknowledged that the problems faced by women in low-paying, full-time jobs with young children at home are enormous. These problems are reflected in the poverty rate for these families. The already-high poverty rates of female-householder families become much higher when these families have children under eighteen, and higher still when the children are under six. With or without children, the poverty rates for black female-householder families were much higher than the rates for white householders, and somewhat higher than the rates for female-householder families of Hispanic origin.

The high incidence of poverty among female-headed families might lead one to assume that most of these poor mothers are unable (or unwilling) to work and prefer to subsist on welfare payments and various family-assistance programs. But such is not the case. Three out of four mothers with no husband present in Dade County in 1980 were in the labor force. Most female-headed families in Dade County are surviving on their own, and increasing numbers of these women, including blacks, are becoming well entrenched in the county's middle and upper income levels. The labor-force participation rates of single women with children exceeded those of single women without children. Many of the latter were older women, widowed and retired. Female-headed households with school-aged children had a labor-force participation rate as high as householders in married-couple families.

The improvement trend in the employment status of black women continued during the 1980s. In 1970 almost 56 percent of black females were in service occupations (half as private household workers). Less than 9 percent were employed in professional, specialty, and technical occupations. By 1990 the percentage in service jobs was down to 29.4 and less than three thousand were in private household occupations, compared to almost ten thousand twenty years earlier. In contrast, black women's share of professional and technical jobs had doubled to just over 18 percent, with six times as many black women in these occupations as in 1970.[20]

The majority of the low-income black families (21,600 families, or 85 percent of the countywide total) resided in the northern half of Dade County in an area stretching from downtown Miami through Allapattah and Liberty City to Opa-Locka and Bunche Park, and on to the Broward County line. Only one in six of Dade's low-income black families (3,900 families) resided in the southern half of the county. These were clustered in the Homestead/Florida City area (more than 1,000 families), the Goulds area (about 750 families), the Perrine neighborhood (about 580 families), the Richmond Heights area (more than 500 families), the Coconut Grove neighborhood (460 families), and the South Miami neighborhood (about 300 families).[21]

It is widely believed that blacks receive most of the welfare money spent in the United States. This is generally assumed to be the case in Dade County, also. But if we examine the actual numbers of blacks involved in welfare programs, a more realistic picture of facts and trends emerges. This discussion considers the various economic services offered by the Department of Health and Rehabilitative Services (HRS) in Dade County. HRS is the arm of state government responsible for implementing programs to help the poor.

There are several programs, each with specific requirements for eligibility; these include food stamps, Aid for Families with Dependent Children (AFDC), Emergency Financial Assistance for Housing, Low-income Home Energy Assistance, Project Independence (aimed at help-

Table 10.13. Food stamp and/or AFDC households, Dade and Monroe
Counties, 1987, 1990

Ethnic group	Feb. 1987		April 1990	
	No.	%	No.	%
Black	16,595	23.4	21,793	24.3
Hispanic	45,535	64.3	56,219	62.7
White	3,785	5.3	4,787	5.3
Other	169	.2	2,157	2.4
Refugee	4,804	6.8	4,665	5.2
Total	70,888	100.0	85,407	99.9

Source: Florida Department of Health and Rehabilitative Services.

ing those on welfare escape the cycle of dependency), individual and
family grants, and Medicaid. An examination of food stamp distribution in the Dade-Monroe district in April 1990 revealed that Hispanics receive the largest amount of support. Table 10.13 shows that Hispanic households received 62.7 percent of the food stamps distributed
in April 1990. This does not count the aid dispersed to Hispanic refugees. Black households made up 24.3 percent of those receiving food
stamps, and white households constituted 5.3 percent.

HRS officials add that these statistics must be interpreted with care.
Table 10.13 reflects the aid according to household, not individuals.
Black households tend to contain more members than the average Hispanic or white household, therefore their participation in the program
is probably somewhat higher than the figures suggest. HRS figures
show that 48.4 percent of the persons receiving food stamps in June
1995 were Hispanic and 33.0 percent were black. By October 1995,
54.9 percent were Hispanic and 35.8 percent were black.

How much do these families receive? Table 10.14 outlines the pa-
rameters used for the distribution of food stamps for selected years
between 1983 and October 1995.

Of those receiving Medicaid in Dade County during the late 1980s,
36.7 percent were black, 32.9 percent were white, and most of the
others were Hispanics. This reflects nearly equal enrollment by each
of the three segments of the population.

It is popularly believed that programs such as Medicaid and food
stamps, coupled with the availability and increase in federal and state
transfer payments, are to blame for the rise in marital dissolution,

Table 10.14. Maximum monthly allotment, food stamp program, 1983–1995

Family size[a]	1995	1989	1988	1987	1985	1983
1	$119	$99	$90	$81	$80	$76
2	218	182	165	149	147	139
3	313	260	236	214	211	199
4	397	381	300	271	268	253
5	472	390	356	322	318	301
6	566	472	427	387	382	361
7	626	521	472	428	422	399
8	716	596	540	489	483	457
9	806	671	608	550	543	514
10	896	746	711	676	603	571
Each additional	+90	+75	+68	+61	+60	+57

[a]Number in household.

Source: Florida Department of Health and Rehabilitative Services.

female-headed households, out-of-wedlock births, and other changes in black family structure. Investigators propounding this theory claim that liberal welfare policies allow unmarried pregnant women to forgo marriage but keep their children, encourage unhappy married parents to break up, and enable young unmarried mothers to maintain separate households rather than live with their parents.

A 1994 compilation of studies on minority families in the United States reported:

> A number of studies have sought to assess the impact of welfare benefits on the structure and stability of families. These studies have yielded inconclusive, largely negative results. In assessing the effects of public assistance on out-of-wedlock births, a number of studies have compared illegitimacy rates or ratios across states with varying welfare benefit levels. Overall, such studies have found no relationship between the level of welfare benefits and births to unmarried women, or more precisely, that the availability of welfare benefits does not lead women to bear more children. In fact, the percentage of black children living in female-headed households increased sharply during the 1970s, while benefit levels and the number of households receiving such benefits declined.[22]

A similar conclusion was reported by the *Miami Herald* in 1995 in an exhaustive article highlighting the issue.[23]

The Black Elderly in Dade County

In a survey of Dade County's elderly population, Florida International University's Elders Institute reported that in 1995 approximately 9 percent of the county's seniors were black non-Hispanic; they were somewhat younger than average, with a mean age of 69.30 years. Marital status of black elderly persons was comparable to the county's overall rates: 39.1 percent married and 40 percent widowed. Nearly three-fifths had less than a high school education, and 21.3 percent had some high school education. Of those reporting their household income, 60.4 percent received less than ten thousand dollars. The mean household size was 2.6 persons per household, with 25 percent living alone.

The aging of the black population brings the promise of both good news and bad news. By the year 2000, the large cadre of black baby boomers will be thirty-five to fifty-four years old, an age when earning levels are highest and when home ownership is at a peak. Elderly blacks will remain relatively few in number, accounting for about one in every twenty Dade County residents.

The problems that elderly black non-Hispanic survey respondents most frequently listed as serious were the same as those reported by county residents at large: crime, health, money, and personal or family stress. However, the order was slightly different. For example, more black non-Hispanics reported that money was a serious or somewhat serious problem, while in the county as a whole it was the second-most-frequently mentioned problem.

With respect to the future, the two concerns for the future most frequently cited by black non-Hispanics and elders in general were the same: loss of independence due to physical deterioration and becoming a victim of crime. Becoming a financial burden was third for black non-Hispanics, compared to fifth among all county seniors. Becoming a victim of fraud was the fourth-most-frequently mentioned concern among black non-Hispanic respondents. Concern for loss of independence due to mental deterioration was the fifth-most-frequently mentioned problem among black seniors, compared to a third-place mention countywide. Going to a nursing home did not make the top five most frequently mentioned concerns among blacks.

Table 10.15. Persons aged sixty-five and older living alone, Dade County, 1990

	Total	%	Black	%	White	%	Hispanic	%
Male	17,366	25	1,821	32	15,162	24	5,937	26
Female	52,059	75	3,834	68	47,369	76	16,967	74
Total	69,425	100	5,655	100	62,531	100	22,904	100

Source: Metro-Dade County Planning Department, "Profile," 44.

More than half of respondents reported excellent or good physical health (55.4 percent), and over two-thirds reported excellent or good emotional well-being (68.5 percent). Over 87 percent of the respondents reported being very or somewhat satisfied with their lives in the last six months.

Slightly less than one-third (31.2 percent) of the elders overall reported that they had no one available as a potential care giver. The other two-thirds of the respondents most frequently cited children and, in particular, daughters as potential care givers. Spouses were the second-most-frequently mentioned as potential care givers. Over half of potential care givers lived in the household (54.6 percent), and 26.6 percent lived less than ten minutes away. However, of all racial/ethnic groups, black non-Hispanic seniors reported the highest frequency of potential care givers living more than one day away.[24]

A profile of Dade County's elders living alone is contained in Table 10.15.

Education

Today the Dade County Public School System is one of the largest in the country, ranking fourth behind New York, Los Angeles, and Chicago in student enrollment. It faces the challenge of educating a culturally and linguistically diverse student population. In the 1994–1995 school year there were 321,955 students in the Dade County Public School System: 159,145 Hispanics, 109,968 blacks, 48,528 whites, and 4,131 listed as Asian or other racial groups. Table 10.16 shows the Dade County public school population by grade and race/ethnicity.

Great strides in black education in Dade County became apparent in the 1970s. According to the U.S. census data and Greater Miami United, an organization established in the 1980s to improve race and ethnic relations in the county, blacks have made dramatic progress in

Table 10.16. Dade County public schools student membership by race, 1995–96

Grade	White non-Hispanic		Black non-Hispanic		Hispanic		Asian/Indian multiracial		Total
	No.	%	No.	%	No.	%	No.	%	No.
PK–5	23,648	14	57,617	34	85,639	51	2,254	1	169,158
6–8	11,010	14	26,645	34	39,572	51	1,055	1	78,282
9–12	12,667	15	28,550	33	43,485	51	1,302	2	86,004
Total	47,325	14	112,812	34	168,696	51	4,611	1	333,444

Source: Dade County Public School System, Districtwide Summary, 1995–96.

education in Dade County since the 1970s. The median years of schooling for blacks had gone from 9.5 in 1970 to 11.9 years in 1980, leaving blacks only six months behind whites in years of schooling completed. The percentage of black high school graduates was up from 31 in 1970 to 50 in 1980. In 1990 about 61 percent of black adults aged twenty-five and older had graduated from high school, a remarkable improvement.

Table 10.17 shows the number of high school graduates in Dade County since the 1989–1990 school year. Table 10.18 shows the educational attainment of the Dade population aged twenty-five and over.

The number of blacks with one or more years of college more than doubled from 9 to 20 percent between 1970 and 1980. The percent-

Table 10.17. Number of high school graduates by race/ethnicity, Dade County, 1989–1994

	1989–90 %[a]		1990–91 %		1991–92 %		1992–93 %		1993–94 %	
White, non-Hispanic	3255	88.5	2946	88.4	3014	88.3	2719	87.3	2549	87.1
Black, non-Hispanic	4330	92.3	4154	88.7	4238	83.2	4262	84.7	4464	84.0
Hispanic	5772	87.7	5925	85.4	6613	62.4	7078	84.1	7297	88.4
Asian/American Indian	214	92.6	282	97.6	278	93.0	236	91.6	247	92.6
District	13,571	89.4	13,317	86.3	14,143	83.7	14,295	85.0	14,557	86.8

[a]Percentage of twelfth-grade students. Graduates include regular and exceptional student diplomas but exclude certificates of completion.

Source: Dade County Public Schools Statistical Abstract, 1994–95.

Table 10.18. Educational attainment, persons aged twenty-five and older, Dade County, 1970–1990

	1970		1980		1990	
	No.	%	No.	%	No.	%
Total						
Jr. High or less[a]	217,742	29.0	244,258	23.0	228,426	17.8
Some high school	133,541	17.8	133,329	12.7	219,856	17.2
H.S. graduate	226,859	30.2	319,136	30.4	296,444	23.0
Some college	89,693	11.9	176,133	16.8	296,109	23.1
B.A. or more	83,025	11.1	175,795	16.8	240,460	18.8
Total	750,860	100.0	1,048,651	100.0	1,281,295	100.0
Black						
Jr. High or less	39,476	46.7	40,704	29.4	39,036	18.0
Some high school	21,042	24.9	29,391	21.2	56,355	26.0
H.S. graduate	16,680	19.7	37,765	27.3	54,160	25.0
Some college	3,804	4.5	19,026	13.7	45,598	21.1
B.A. or more	3,459	4.1	11,519	8.3	21,409	9.9
Total	84,461	100.0	138,405	100.0	216,558	100.0
Hispanic origin						
Jr. High or less	73,930	43.1	141,853	38.3	171,156	26.6
Some high school	19,901	11.6	37,162	10.0	118,069	18.3
H.S. graduate	43,514	25.3	95,303	25.7	130,078	20.2
Some college	17,146	10.0	46,072	12.4	133,747	20.8
B.A. or more	17,211	10.0	50,407	13.6	91,081	14.1
Total	171,702	100.0	370,797	100.0	644,131	100.0

[a]Junior high or less equals less than ninth grade.

Source: Metro-Dade Planning Department, "Profile," 49.

age of black people from twenty-five to thirty-four years old enrolled in adult education programs doubled from 5 to 10 percent. The sharp rise in educational attainment was due in part to the replacement of older, less-educated age groups with younger, better-educated groups. Among younger groups, the disparity in black and white educational attainment appeared to be diminishing rapidly.

The linkage between educational attainment and future earnings suggested a brighter economic future for blacks in Dade County. Nowhere was the improvement more evident than in postsecondary rolls. In 1980, 22 percent of Dade's adult black population had completed one or more years of college. Again, this was lower than the comparable rate for the entire population (34 percent), but it was a striking improvement from the 16 percent level reported in 1970. The number and the percentage of the total Dade County population enrolled in college doubled between 1970 and 1980, but quadrupled among blacks and Hispanics. For blacks, enrollment increased from thirty-five hundred students in 1970 to fourteen thousand in 1980. More importantly, black college students as a percentage of all college students increased from 9 percent in 1970 to 15 percent in 1980.

In the 1980s, as a result of available assistance to poor minority students, the proportion of blacks enrolled in higher education began to approach the black share of Dade's total population. But by the 1990s public support for government-funded aid to poor students had slackened and the trend toward black inclusion in higher education had slowed. By 1990 only 19.6 percent of adult blacks had completed one or more years of college, down from 22 percent in 1980.

At the community-college level, in 1992 about 10 percent of the students were black and 10 percent Hispanic. Community-college faculties were 9.3 percent black and 4.8 percent Hispanic, and of professional employees 14.9 percent black and 4.2 percent Hispanic. Most of the minority enrollment in Florida community colleges was at Miami-Dade Community College, which was 54.4 percent Hispanic and 17.8 percent black.[25]

The educational attainment of Caribbean-born blacks from selected countries is compared in Table 10.19 to Dade County's total black population. There are notable differences in educational attainment among Dade's foreign-born blacks. The five island nations listed were the most heavily represented in the county's population in 1990. (Puerto Rico and the Virgin Islands are U.S. possessions and are not included.)

Jamaicans were most likely to be high school graduates. Almost 70 percent of Jamaican-born persons in Dade County had a high school diploma. About 55 percent of black Bahamian-born persons twenty-five years or older had at least graduated from high school, almost the same as the 56 percent graduation rate among all blacks. Black Cubans, Dominicans, and Haitians were less likely to have graduated from high school.[26]

In spite of these gains a large number of blacks continued to fail to complete high school. The 1980 census reported that 21 percent of the adult black population had failed to complete high school. This was

Table 10.19. Educational attainment of black Caribbean-born persons aged twenty-five and older, Dade County, 1990

	Total black	%	Bahamas	%	Cuba	%	Dom. Rep.	%	Haiti	%	Jamaica	%	Other	%
Jr. High or less	39,274	18.0	595	17.5	2,052	35.7	1,367	42.1	10,447	30.6	2,376	11.8	794	15.5
Some H.S.	5,830	25.6	955	28.0	1,574	27.4	468	14.4	9,990	29.3	3,981	19.7	888	17.3
H.S. graduate	55,829	25.6	770	22.6	1,048	18.2	607	18.7	5,828	17.1	5,574	27.6	1,717	33.4
Some college	45,220	20.8	772	22.6	793	13.8	381	11.7	5,966	17.5	5,369	26.6	1,114	21.7
B.A. or more	21,695	10.0	318	9.3	286	5.0	422	13.0	1,888	5.5	2,925	14.5	623	12.1
Total	217,848	100	3,410	100	5,753	100	3,245	100	34,119	100	20,225	100	5,136	100

Source: Metro-Dade Planning Department, "Profile," 51 (excludes Puerto Rico and U.S. Virgin Islands). Total black numbers may differ from other tables due to sampling size.

Table 10.20. School enrollment by race/Hispanic origin, persons aged fifteen to seventeen, Dade County, 1990

	Total		Black		Hispanic origin	
	No.	%	No.	%	No.	%
Enrolled	69,512	90.5	19,118	90.0	34,591	90.2
Not enrolled	7,279	9.5	2,122	10.0	3,755	9.8
Total	76,791	100	21,240	100	38,346	100

Source: Metro-Dade County Planning Department, "Profile," 55.

only a modest improvement from the 1970 level of 25 percent, and was still substantially higher than the 12 percent dropout rate reported for whites. But by 1990 the black high school dropout rate was again up to 24.5, about equal to its level in 1970.

Another measure of the failure to retain high school students is the percentage of the population aged sixteen to seventeen years actually enrolled in school. Enrollment rates for the younger population (fifteen and under) are typically close to 100 percent, but at age sixteen the percentages begin to drop. In 1980, 82 percent of the black population, 87 percent of the white population, and 86 percent of the Hispanic population aged sixteen to seventeen years were enrolled in school in Dade County. These levels were virtually unchanged from the levels reported in 1970. By 1990, 90.5 percent of the population between fifteen and seventeen years old was enrolled in school. For blacks and Hispanics, the school enrollment rate for this age group was also 90 percent, as shown in Table 10.20. Table 10.21 reflects the enrollment rates in public and private schools in Dade County.

Levels of education vary between different racial and ethnic groups and between the sexes, as detailed in Table 10.22. Black males had the

Table 10.21. Public and private school enrollment rates, elementary to high school, Dade County, 1990

	Total		Black		Hispanic origin	
	No.	%	No.	%	No.	%
Public school	281,730	86.5	93,409	95.0	132,409	85.4
Private school	44,139	13.5	4,922	5.0	22,582	14.6
Total	325,869	100.0	98,331	100.0	154,991	100.0

Source: Metro-Dade County Planning Department, "Profile," 59.

Table 10.22. School enrollment, by sex, race, and Hispanic origin, persons aged eighteen to twenty-four, Dade County, 1990

	Total		Black		Hispanic origin	
Males	No.	%	No.	%	No.	%
Enrolled	43,419	46.5	8,613	41.7	21,824	45.4
Not Enrolled	49,986	53.5	12,022	58.3	26,267	54.6
Total	93,405	100	20,635	100	48,091	100
Females						
Enrolled	42,255	48.1	11,221	47.0	22,164	47.4
Not Enrolled	48,908	51.9	12,633	53.0	24,552	52.6
Total	94,163	100	23,854	100	46,716	100

Source: Metro-Dade County Planning Department, "Profile," 56.

highest proportion without a high school diploma in Dade County (58.3 percent) in 1990. Among Hispanics and all other racial/ethnic groups, females had the highest proportion without a high school diploma. Similarly, there were fewer black males than females with some college education or a degree (29 versus 33 percent). Again this was the reverse of the pattern for Hispanics and others.[27]

Underrepresentation of minority children in the system's gifted program is another disturbing problem for some blacks. According to data from a survey conducted by the state of Florida in October 1987, blacks and Hispanics jointly made up 76 percent of students in the Dade school system, but only 36 percent of students enrolled in the gifted program were black or Hispanic. Non-Hispanic white students, in contrast, made up 23 percent of all students but almost 62 percent of students in the gifted program. Only 15.2 percent of the participants in the school system's gifted program were black, compared with 33.2 percent black representation of the entire school enrollment. These figures nonetheless show substantial improvement in black and Hispanic representation compared to the previous five years, when 75 percent of all students in the gifted program were non-Hispanic whites.

The magnet school program has been used as the primary method of desegregation in the Dade County schools. During the 1994–1995 school year 39 percent of all students enrolled in that program were black, 30 percent were Hispanic, and 31 percent were white.

The issue of discipline and black students is another major one in education today, including in the schools of Dade County. In Dade

County, as in the nation as a whole, blacks are punished more frequently and more severely than their white and Hispanic counterparts.
This includes corporal punishment, suspensions, and expulsions.[28] The
question of whether this pattern reflects discrimination is hotly debated.

Black Business Development

An expansive 1989 study by a group of Dade business and professional leaders reported that there were relatively few black business
success stories in Dade County in the late 1980s.[29] "Not surprisingly
at the end of the 1980s, there were still few black businesses in Dade
County. Only 1.4 percent of Dade's black population owned businesses in 1988, and only one black Miami business was among 300
firms on six separate lists of top firms in *Black Enterprise* magazine in
June 1988. In 1991 black businesses in Dade County numbered about
fifty-four hundred, with an average revenue of $248,000 per firm.
The total of all persons employed in those businesses (including the
entrepreneurs) was 6,208, or 4 percent of the black population."[30]

The study cited crime and racial violence in poor black sections of
Miami as an obstacle to black businesses. Another hindrance has been
unrealistically expensive liability insurance and the reluctance of banking institutions to accept area real estate as loan collateral at loan-to-
value ratios comparable with other areas. Invigorating the county's
stagnant black business community became a major issue among blacks
in the early 1990s, because many blacks believed that increasing the
number of black businesses could do more than create jobs: It could
increase the circulation of income within the black community, create
successful role models, expand the support base for community institutions and charitable causes, and provide candidates for revitalized
commercial areas of the black community.

According to the report, there is a widely held perception that
capital is unavailable to Dade's black businesses. An analysis of the
data revealed that debt capital for black entrepreneurs with relatively
good packages, although very difficult to obtain, is often accessible.
Reportedly, however, institutionalized risk capital (*e.g.*, equity from
MESBIC or venture capital firms) is virtually unavailable to blacks
within Dade County. Without adequate leverage from risk capital, the
debt capital becomes inaccessible. Because very few blacks have inher-

ited wealth, few sizeable black deals are completed. Many of the components of the support services needed by Dade County's black businesses are not present. Business "incubators" (small-business consultant and support organizations) have been successful in comprehensively shoring up the administrative requirements of small firms in many cities, but few such support systems or business incubators exist in Dade County.

In addition to the absence of targeted risk capital and incubators, the quality of business packages by black entrepreneurs often fails to meet lender criteria. According to the study, "There are few true entrepreneurial development avenues, and local higher-education alternatives are limited, creating a 'brain drain' of emerging black entrepreneurial and management talent. There is no mechanism for focusing the activities of the many organizations that are currently addressing the problem. In short, Miami has yet to establish the tools required in a positive, proactive black business development climate."[31]

As noted earlier, black businesses in Dade County number about fifty-four hundred, with an average revenue of $248,000 per firm. These figures do not include, however, the myriad of informal business operations conducted by blacks on the streets of Dade County, especially in the various black communities. These include car washes, lawn maintenance services, food stands, and many others. Although such operations represent a substantial chunk of Dade's black economy, they tend to remain relatively stagnant, one-person operations. By far the largest number of recognized black-owned businesses appear to be in the franchise industry, followed by the retail trade. The smallest number of black-owned businesses are in the manufacturing and wholesale trade.

Following the Miami riots of 1980, city leaders looked for ways to include more black participation in city and county expenditures, thus providing more employment opportunities for blacks. In 1982 the county embarked on an ambitious plan to include minority firms in its expenditure of funds. The subsequent minority participation program in 1982 allocated 3.8 percent of the county's work to black firms. This represented some $44 million. The Florida Contractors Association, a white group, unsuccessfully sued the county in 1984 to abandon the set-aside programs. Despite the challenges, minority participation grew. The City of Miami's Minority and Women Business Affairs and Procurement Program took effect in January of 1986. It gave 5.4 percent of its expenditures to black firms in 1988.

The county's black business participation level dropped precipitously in 1985. To explain the drop, the county pointed out that the construction industry plummeted 6.9 percent in 1985 and another 1.5 percent by 1988. The county also cited the black contractors' inability to secure the required bond and adequate insurance coverage for their projects. The mountain of paperwork required for participation with the county was also a negative factor, as many blacks were unable to keep up with the office work.[32]

A severe blow to black participation occurred in 1988 when the U.S. Supreme Court ruled that local governments must show identified discrimination in establishing narrowly tailored minority set-aside and preference programs. In April 1990, Dade County abandoned its set-aside program until the need for the program could be better proved in court. In 1995 the U.S. Supreme Court virtually eliminated minority set-asides by requiring strict scrutiny of the process, making them much more difficult to justify within the bounds of the Constitution.[33]

In September 1996 U.S. District Judge Kenneth Ryskamp ruled in a suit filed by white-owned construction companies that Metro-Dade County's minority set-aside program was unconstitutional. The judge ordered the county to halt the program immediately. Black contractors decried the decision. Under the minority set-aside program in fiscal year 1994–1995, $24.3 million, or 6.4 percent of the county's $378.6 million construction budget, went to minority firms. Black-owned firms received $19.9 million, while Hispanic-owned firms received $4.3 million. In subcontracts during this period, the county's prime contractors spent $39.6 million, or 10.5 percent of the county's subcontracting dollars, with minority- and female-owned firms. Of that money $33.1 million went to black-owned firms, $5.6 million to Hispanic-owned firms, and $914,000 to female-owned firms.[34]

EPILOGUE

It is a very long way from Black Caesar to Carrie Meek, the first black person elected to the U.S. Congress from Dade County. What has happened to blacks in Dade County since the fearsome pirate buried his treasures and blacks elected one of their own to the U.S. House of Representatives? First, blacks seem to be moving both forward and backward at the same time. For most blacks this first century in Dade County has yielded many gains, albeit at great costs. Two-thirds of the black population is doing well and will continue to do so into the next century. But for the one-third of the black population at the bottom of the economic heap, the next century does not hold much promise. Matters likely will get worse for them as we move into a period in America's and Miami's history in which social class and eth-nicity mean more than skin color.

Blacks who are successful did not make it this far entirely on their own. If the history of black people in Miami is to be accurately and fairly told, recognition must be given to those whites who knew that racism, segregation, and oppression were wrong and who were willing to do something about it. John E. Culmer might never have become a clergyman, much less a great leader, had not a white woman stopped to bind his mangled foot. Even more blacks might have been killed or maimed in the Miami Police Department's torture chamber had not an all-white Dade grand jury insisted that enough was enough. Howard Dixon, the white civil rights attorney, would not have represented arrested black and white civil rights protesters had he not been a man of conscience, and he was not alone. Liberal northern Jews like Herbert and Marilyn Bloom of Miami Beach gave time, money, and energy to the movement. Blacks would not have achieved political prominence when they did had Puerto Rican-born Miami mayor Maurice Ferre and Cuban-born mayor Xavier Suarez cared less than they did. Miami institutions such as the *Miami News* and the *Miami Herald,* once enlightened, spread the news and the opinion that change was necessary and morally compelling. We must not dismiss the fact that although the early white Miami newspapers were decidedly racist in tone and substance, the *Miami Herald* and the *Miami News* (particularly under white liberal editor Bill Baggs) eventually came to champion the aspirations of Miami blacks. This, too, made a difference.

Nonetheless, blacks in the next century must accept the realities of the times and become even more self-reliant in finding solutions to their problems. To do so, they must draw upon their history. Black pioneers were survivors. While it is not exactly accurate to say that blacks built the railroad and Miami, it is very close to the truth. The black pioneers did not have civil rights or affirmative action. They did not have even basic human rights. They could not do business with white people or live close to them or send their children to school with white children. They could not vote in a meaningful sense. But they survived and they endured. They worked hard and overcame tremendous obstacles in order to create a better Dade County for themselves and for their progeny. Their legacy and dreams must not be denied.

It can also be said that much of what is believed to be true about Dade County blacks simply is not true. Those who say that black people have gotten nowhere in a hundred years in Dade County are wrong. Congresswoman Carrie Meek and Dade School Board chairman Solomon Stinson, a black, are not to be dismissed as mere figureheads. Their power is very real indeed. Those who believe that most blacks are poor and live in crime-infested ghettos are wrong. Although black income still lags behind white and Hispanic income, blacks continue to hold their own economically and even surpass other groups in terms of relative progress in earnings. Old black neighborhoods like Coconut Grove and South Miami remain stable and strong. Those communities defy the very notion of ghettos.

Those who believe that black people receive most of the welfare money spent in Dade County (and in the United States) are wrong, too. Most welfare money spent in Dade County goes to Hispanics; most welfare money spent nationally goes to white people. Those who believe that blacks have had too much given to them in their first century in Dade County are wrong. Despite black progress, disparities in income between blacks and other groups say otherwise.

Those who believe that blacks have been ruined by Cuban and Haitian immigration are wrong. The Latinization of the south Florida economy did not hurt most blacks, as census data have shown in many ways. And those who believe that blacks in Miami have rioted because of the lack of jobs and economic opportunities are wrong. Economic development in response to social disorder is a businessman's answer to a complicated and multifaceted social problem. The riots were never about jobs or immigration. They were about injustice, real or perceived, and about police abuse of power.

This book addresses these and other questions about the black presence in south Florida during this the first century of Miami's existence. As a result of this examination, it should be clear that blacks are not likely to move ahead by great leaps and bounds in the next century. If history is to be our teacher, blacks will continue to make gains, but it will be a gradual process punctuated by great events and individuals who will shape the future in ways we cannot yet imagine. By the year 2096 most black Dade residents probably will be foreign-born, or at least of foreign-born ancestry, and the influence of the Caribbean will carry the day. African Americans may find themselves an ethnic minority among other black people.

As the next century unfolds, blacks must look inward and examine their own shortcomings and internal problems. Although many of today's problems are rooted in racism, whites are not to blame for all of the difficulties blacks face as the new century begins. For example, if the problem of black-on-black crime is to be solved, blacks must solve it. If the problem of teen pregnancy among blacks is to be solved, blacks must solve it. Blacks must also look closely at relations among themselves as they become a more ethnically diverse group in the next century. Rampant intraracial and interethnic conflict between American-born blacks and Haitians is one example. This became very apparent as Haitians moved into the Edison area adjacent to Liberty City. Although the problem has been somewhat eased, in part because of the sheer number of Haitians who have moved into this area, Haitians in Miami today continue to be subject to disdain by many African Americans.

Will there be more riots? Probably. Dade County in many ways is still an unjust society, and, after all, the riots have almost always been about justice or the lack thereof. The circumstances that gave rise to the killing of Kier in 1928 and McDuffie in 1979 are strikingly similar, although nearly a half-century separated the two events. The problems within police organizations in south Florida that give rise to unprofessionalism and abuse by some police officers still have not been fully addressed. Of course most white and Hispanic police officers treat blacks with due respect. But some officers in Dade County today are just as dangerous to black people as were Tibbits and Quigg.

Blacks continue to call for community policing, but the response from local law enforcement has been tepid. As long as the basic approach to policing black areas is cruising in air-conditioned police cars with dogs in the back seat and shotguns in the trunk, the potential for abuse and misunderstanding will be great and the potential for racial violence all the more real. Advances have been made in improving the status of blacks in local police organizations. In January 1985 Clarence Dickson became Miami's first black police chief. Moreover, Howard Gary became the city's first black city manager in 1979.

The future of black business growth in the next century is questionable. In 1896 there were no black businesses operating on what would become Flagler Street and Miami Avenue. A century later black businesses are still virtually absent from those streets. A number of initiatives may hold promise. Tools for Change, an organization of business executives concerned about this problem, continues to support and stimulate black business growth, and some white business leaders are trying seriously to address this problem. In December 1995 Republic National Bank opened a branch office in Overtown, bringing long-absent banking services to that community. But as we have seen, recent court decisions have stunted set-aside programs for black businesses. In the future, this avenue of access will likely be closed to aspiring black business operators. The private business sector will have to assume more responsibility for addressing the problem.

Local black leaders have been criticized by some people for being ineffectual in bringing about change. In many instances those criticisms have been unfair. Had it not been for John E. Culmer, Sam Solomon, Elmer Ward, Theodore Gibson, G. E. Graves, Dr. John O. Brown, Athalie Range, and many others, the likes of Carrie Meek would not have ascended to power.

In the next century a new generation of black leaders, their names unknown to us today, will emerge and assume the mantle of leadership. Theirs will be a daunting task. But the next century will belong to them, and if they in their time can accomplish as much as those who led in this first century, Dade blacks in 2097 will have reached the golden shore sought by so many after the Great Freeze more than one hundred years ago.

NOTES

Chapter One: Blacks in Early South Florida (1646–1895)

1. Woodman, *Key Biscayne,* 16–18. Information regarding Black Caesar in the paragraphs that follow is drawn from this source.
2. Munroe, *Commodore's Story,* 77.
3. Woodman, *Key Biscayne,* 42–43.
4. Blank, *Key Biscayne,* 42.
5. Glassman, "Miami Black Families," 1:117.
6. Smith, Basil, "Goombay."
7. Crahan and Knight, *Africa and the Caribbean,* 91.
8. Johnson, Rebecca, interviewed by the author, Miami, 1991.
9. Laumer, *Massacre,* 149.
10. Ibid., 162.
11. Jumper, Mabel, interviewed by the author, Seminole Indian Reservation, Dade County, 1990.
12. Laumer, *Dade's Last Command,* 156.
13. Black, "Fitzpatrick's South Florida," 68–71.
14. Tebeau, *A History of Florida,* 260.
15. Peters, *Biscayne Country,* 26.
16. Peters, *Lemon City Pioneering,* 236.
17. Ibid., 230.
18. Ibid., 232.
19. Merrick, "Pre-Flagler Influences," 5.
20. Peters, *Lemon City,* 230.
21. Davis, Louise Stirrup, interviewed by the author, Miami, 1990.
22. Rodriguez, "The Stirrup Family," 1:217.
23. Ibid., 221.
24. Davis, Louise Stirrup, interviewed by the author, Miami, 1990.
25. Johnson, Rebecca, interviewed by the author, Miami, 1991.
26. Smith, Lourena, interviewed by the author, Miami, 1992.
27. Johnson, Rebecca, interviewed by the author, Miami, 1991.
28. Smith, Lourena, interviewed by the author, Miami, 1992.
29. *Daily Florida Citizen,* December 28, 1894.
30. *Florida Times-Union,* January 13, 1895.
31. Wolfe, *Citrus Growing in Florida,* 86.
32. DeLand, *Story of DeLand.*
33. Peters, ed., *Memoirs of Zumwalt,* 1.

Chapter Two: Blacks in Early Miami (1896–1926)

1. Sewell, *Memoirs,* 57.
2. Ibid., 46.
3. Ibid., 42.
4. Ibid., 44.
5. Cohen, *Historical Sketches,* 14.
6. Sewell, *Memoirs,* 131.
7. Fleischmann, "Black Miamians," 28.
8. *Miami Herald,* November 6, 1990, 19A.
9. Fleischmann, "Black Miamians," 29.
10. Jimenez, "A Statistical Analysis," 3:40.
11. Hines, "Dr. Samuel Hensdale Johnson."
12. Marks, "Labor Problems," 32.
13. Fleischmann, "Black Miamians," 21–25.
14. Ibid., 22; *Miami Metropolis*, July 2, 1897.
15. Ibid.
16. Ibid., 23.
17. Ibid., 24.
18. Ibid., 25.
19. George, "Criminal Justice in Miami," 159.
20. *Miami Metropolis,* December 11, 1903.
21. Peters, *Lemon City,* 231.
22. Ibid., 232.
23. *Miami News,* December 15, 1980.
24. Peters, *Lemon City,* 236.
25. *Miami News,* December 15, 1980.
26. Taylor, Jean, *Villages of South Dade,* 37.
27. Ibid., 97.
28. Tully, "Race Relations," 2:220.
29. Ibid., 2:221.
30. *Miami Metropolis,* January 23, 1903, 4.
31. *Miami Herald,* October 5, 1911, 1A.
32. George, "Colored Town," 441; "Policing," 440.
33. George, "Policing," 443.
34. Ibid., 438.
35. Kleinberg, *Miami the Way We Were,* 87.
36. Johnson, Ellen, interviewed by the author, Miami, 1990.
37. McCarthy, *Black Florida,* 192.
38. Ibid., 193.
39. Johnson, Ellen, interviewed by the author, Miami, 1990.
40. Peters, ed., *Memoirs of Zumwalt,* 34.
41. McCarthy, *Black Florida,* 187.

42. Sawyer, William B., Jr., and Bernice Sawyer, interviewed by Heidi Alles-pach-Stanley, Miami, 1991.

43. *Miami Herald,* December 1, 1915, 5A; March 25, 1917, 8A.

44. *Miami Herald,* February 28, 1915, 5A.

45. *Miami Herald,* January 14, 1917, 1A.

46. Nimmo, James E., interviewed by the author, Miami, 1990.

47. Hafter, "1900 Dade County," 2:23–24.

48. Mohl, "Shadows in the Sunshine," 67–68.

49. *Miami Herald,* August 6, 1987, Neighbors section.

50. Kleinberg, *Miami the Way We Were,* 97.

51. *Miami Herald,* November 17, 1914, 8.

Chapter Three: Blacks in Early Dade County (1896–1926)

1. McCarthy, *Black Florida,* 189.

2. Peters, *Lemon City,* 233.

3. *Miami Herald,* October 2, 1916, 3.

4. Culmer, *Homecoming Celebration,* 17.

5. Overtown Advisory Committee, *Revival,* 9.

6. Walker, Lydia Everett, interviewed by the author, Miami, 1990; Wise, James, interviewed by the author, Miami, 1990.

7. *Miami Herald,* June 30, 1920, 8.

8. *Miami Herald,* July 2, 1921, 1.

9. Smith, Lourena, interviewed by the author, Miami, 1992.

10. Tully, "Race Relations," 2:220.

11. *Miami Herald,* July 18, 1921, 1A.

12. *Miami Herald,* July 26, 1921; August 26, 1921, 1A.

13. *Miami Herald,* January 26, 1922, 8A.

14. *Miami Herald,* June 16, 1923, 1A.

15. Taylor, Jean, *Villages of South Dade,* 186.

16. Wilbanks, *Forgotten Heroes.*

17. Nimmo, James E., interviewed by the author, Miami, 1990.

18. Adker, Ann Marie, interviewed by Heidi Allespach-Stanley, Miami, 1991.

19. Fleitas, "Impact of the Hurricane," 3–4.

20. Johnson, Rebecca Gibson, interviewed by the author, Miami, 1991.

21. Smith, Lourena, interviewed by the author, Miami, 1992.

22. Davis, Louise Stirrup, interviewed by the author, Miami, 1990.

23. *Miami Herald,* August 6, 1987, Neighbors section.

24. Fleitas, "Impact of the Hurricane."

25. *Miami Daily News and Metropolis,* September 30, 1926.

26. *Miami Metropolis,* September 2, 1904; George, "Policing," 436.

27. George, "Colored Town," 443.

28. Dade County Grand Jury Final Report of the Spring Term, 1926.

29. Dade County Grand Jury Report, March 23, 1928.

30. *Miami Herald,* "Grand Jury Report," March 24, 1928, 2.

31. *Miami Herald,* July 16, 1925.

32. *Miami Herald,* March 2, 1928; March 7, 1928; "Quigg Held for Murder," March 24, 1928. *New York Times,* March 27, 1928.

33. Dade County Grand Jury Report, March 23, 1928.

34. Kennedy, Stetson, interviewed by the author, Miami, 1990.

35. *Miami Herald,* April 7, 1946, 1C.

Chapter Four: The Pre–Civil Rights Period (1926–1945)

1. Sawyer, William B., Jr., and Bernice Sawyer, interviewed by Heidi Allespach-Stanley, Miami, 1991.

2. Reeves, Garth, interviewed by Heidi Allespach-Stanley, Miami, 1991.

3. Dunn, James C., interviewed by the author, Miami, 1995.

4. Adker, Ann Marie, interviewed by Heidi Allespach-Stanley, Miami, 1991.

5. Parks, *Miami the Magic City,* 141.

6. Sawyer, William B., Jr., and Bernice Sawyer, interviewed by Heidi Allespach-Stanley, Miami, 1991.

7. Mohl, "Shadows in the Sunshine," 75.

8. Ibid.

9. Adker, Ann Marie, interviewed by Heidi Allespach-Stanley, Miami, 1991.

10. *Miami Daily News,* February 8, 1942, 9A.

11. *Miami Herald,* May 10, 1945, 1B.

12. *Miami Herald,* August 25, 1989, 1B.

13. Powell, Richard, interviewed by the author, Miami, 1996.

14. George and Petersen, "Liberty Square."

15. Brown, John O., M.D., interviewed by the author, Miami, 1996.

Chapter Five: The Dade County Civil Rights Movement (1944–1970)

1. Dunn, Corine E., interviewed by the author, Miami, 1995.

2. Liberty, Eunice, interviewed by Heidi Allespach-Stanley, Miami, 1991.

3. *Miami Herald,* October 19, 1920, 1A.

4. White, Ralph, interviewed by the author, Miami, 1990.

5. *Miami Herald,* November 2, 1946, 1A.

6. *Miami Herald,* April 2, 1990, 1A.

7. *Miami Herald,* September 12, 1991, 1B.

8. Culmer, Mrs. John E., interviewed by the author, Miami, 1991.

9. Brown, John O., M.D., interviewed by the author, Miami, 1996.

10. Range, M. Athalie, interviewed by the author, Miami, 1991.

11. *Miami Herald,* May 3, 1939, 1.

12. *Miami Herald,* April 27, 1945, 2A.

13. *Miami Herald,* January 23, 1946, 6A.

14. Range, M. Athalie, interviewed by the author, Miami, 1991.

15. *Miami Daily News,* June 12, 1941, 1B; June 17, 1941, 1B.

16. *Miami Daily News,* January 27, 1941, 1B.

17. *Miami Daily News,* June 23, 1944, 1B; June 20, 1944, 1B.

18. *Miami Herald,* May 16, 1946, 1B; May 21, 1946, 1B.

19. *Miami Herald,* May 1, 1946, 1B.

20. *Miami Herald,* May 7, 1946, 6A.

21. *Miami Herald,* July 8, 1946, 4A.

22. Graves, interview.

23. Dunn, Marvin, "Blacks in Miami," 51.

24. Brown, John O., M.D., interviewed by the author, Miami, 1996.

25. *Miami Times,* April 1, 1961.

26. Brown, John O., M.D., interviewed by the author, Miami, 1996.

27. *Miami Times,* September 9, 1959, 1A.

28. *Miami Times,* March 12, 1960, 1A.

29. Brown, John O., M.D., interviewed by the author, Miami, 1996.

30. Dixon, Howard, interviewed by the author, Miami, 1991.

31. Quotations from Gibson in the following paragraphs are from *Miami News,* December 13, 1959, 2B.

32. *Miami Times,* September 15, 1963.

33. *Miami Herald,* February 26, 1963, 1C.

34. Ibid.

Chapter Six: School Desegregation

1. *Miami Herald,* May 18, 1954, 6A.

2. Tebeau, *A History of Florida,* 284.

3. Ibid., 441.

4. Kleinberg, "A Patriot for All People," 15A.

5. Ibid.

6. Porter, Gilbert, interviewed by the author, Miami, 1990.

7. *Miami Herald,* June 13, 1956, 1A.

8. *Miami News,* September 24, 1958, 1C.

9. *Miami News,* July 7, 1956; *Miami Herald,* 18 June 1958, 2A.

10. Dumenigo, "Dade School Desegregation," 6.

11. *Miami Herald,* June 13, 1987, 22A.

12. *Miami News,* February 14, 1979, 7A.

13. *Miami Herald,* January 20, 1983, 1D.

14. *Miami News,* March 31, 1983, 5A.

15. *Miami News,* April 25, 1985, 5A.

16. *Miami Herald,* December 11, 1984, 1B; *Miami Herald,* December 13, 1984, 2D.

17. *Miami Herald,* February 21, 1985, 1C.

18. *Miami Herald,* August 4, 1989, 1B; November 29, 1989, 21A; Novem-

ber 30, 1989, 1B.

19. *Miami Herald,* July 24, 1970, 4A.

20. *Miami Herald,* November 1, 1987, 6B; October 10, 1984, 20A; October 6, 1984, 1A.

21. Sands, Portia, interviewed by the author, Miami, 1991; Rogers, Barbara, interviewed by the author, Miami, 1991.

22. Smith, Shauna, *Historical Black High Schools.*

23. McCarthy, *Black Florida,* 191.

24. *Miami Herald,* December 6, 1987, 14B.

25. *Miami Herald,* June 6, 1992.

26. *Miami News,* February 10, 1988, 1A.

Chapter Seven: Prelude to the 1980 Riot

1. Tscheschlok, "Long Time Coming," 444.

2. Porter and Dunn, *Miami Riot,* 17; Tscheschlok, "Long Time Coming."

3. *Miami Herald,* June 21, 1970, 27A.

4. Porter and Dunn, *Miami Riot.*

5. *Miami Herald,* March 23, 1971, 1B.

6. *Miami Herald,* January 25, 1979, 3C.

7. Powell, Richard, interviewed by the author, Miami, 1996.

8. *Miami Herald,* May 4, 1980; June 18, 1982; December 26, 1982; September 23, 1984; February 27, 1985; February 28, 1985; August 10, 1985; October 24, 1985; December 4, 1985; December 7, 1985; July 4, 1986.

9. *Miami Herald,* January 21, 1980, 1A, 16A.

10. *Miami Herald,* February 14, 1979, 1A.

Chapter Eight: Riots of the 1980s

1. *CBS Reports,* "Miami: The Trial," August 27, 1980.

2. Ibid.

3. Porter and Dunn, *Miami Riot,* 35.

4. *Miami Herald,* December 27, 1979, 1B.

5. Dunn, Marvin, "The McDuffie Killing."

6. Porter and Dunn, *Miami Riot,* 37.

7. *Miami Herald,* March 3, 1980, 1B.

8. *CBS Reports,* "Miami: The Trial," August 27, 1980. Quotations regarding the trial in the paragraphs that follow are drawn from this source.

9. Porter and Dunn, *Miami Riot,* 43.

10. *Miami Herald,* May 18, 1980, 32A.

11. Porter and Dunn, *Miami Riot,* 47–50. Quotations in the following paragraphs regarding early reactions to the verdicts are drawn from this source.

12. Ibid., 51.

13. Ibid., 53.

14. Ibid., 61.

15. Ibid., 62–63.

16. Ibid., 65.

17. Ibid., 73.

18. Ibid., 167.

19. Ibid., 168.

20. *Miami Herald,* May 17, 1990.

21. *Miami Herald,* December 29, 1982.

22. *Miami Herald,* December 30, 1982.

23. *Miami Herald,* December 29, 1982, 1A.

24. *Miami Herald,* January 12, 1983, 1A.

25. *Miami Herald,* January 19, 1989, 2C.

26. *Miami Herald,* January 29, 1989, 1A.

27. *Miami Herald,* November 14, 1989.

28. *Miami Herald,* November 15, 1989.

29. *Miami Herald,* December 8, 1989.

30. Captain, "Lozano Retrial"; Dunn, Marvin, "Trial Should Be Moved."

31. *Miami Herald,* April 6, 1991.

32. *Miami Herald,* May 5, 1992.

Chapter Nine: Blacks and Immigration in South Florida

1. Stepick, Castro, Dunn, and Grenier, "Changing Relations," 36.

2. Perez, "Cuban Miami," 86.

3. Stepick, Castro, Dunn, and Grenier, "Changing Relations," 26.

4. Stepick, "Refugees Nobody Wants," 58–60.

5. Ibid., 64–65.

6. Ibid., 71–74.

7. Stepick, Castro, Dunn, and Grenier, "Changing Relations," 27.

8. Dunn, Marvin, "Blacks in Miami," 46–47.

9. Stepick, Castro, Dunn, and Grenier, "Changing Relations," 38–42.

Chapter Ten: Current Status of Blacks in Dade County: An Overview

1. Stepick, Castro, Dunn, and Grenier, "Changing Relations," 27.

2. Metro-Dade County Planning Department, *Demographics.*

3. Metro-Dade County Planning Department, "Profile," 18.

4. Ibid., 6–8, 16.

5. Miami-Dade Chamber of Commerce, *Tools for Change,* 14.

6. *Miami Herald,* "Gun Epidemic," June 10, 1992.

7. Metro-Dade County Planning Department, "Profile," 25.

8. Ibid., 29.

9. Ibid., 87.

10. Vickers, Milton, interviewed by the author, Miami, 1990.
11. *Miami Herald,* September 30, 1990, 16A.
12. Ibid.
13. Ibid.
14. *Miami Herald,* "Job Outlook," June 10, 1992, 1C.
15. *Miami Herald,* May 3, 1992, 1A.
16. Metro-Dade County Planning Department, "Profile," 97.
17. Ibid., 98–99.
18. *Miami Herald,* June 25, 1992, 1B.
19. Metro-Dade County Planning Department, *Demographics.*
20. Metro-Dade County Planning Department, "Profile," 79.
21. Metro-Dade County Planning Department, *Demographics.*
22. Taylor, Ronald, *Minority Families,* 39.
23. Offner, "Welfare Didn't Do It," 1C.
24. Rothman, Dunlop, and Condon, *The Elders of Dade County.*
25. *Miami Herald,* June 6, 1992.
26. Metro-Dade County Planning Department, "Profile," 51.
27. Ibid., 52.
28. Greater Miami United, "Ethnic Audit"; Dade County Planning Department, *Demographics.*
29. Miami-Dade Chamber of Commerce, *Tools for Change,* 7.
30. Dunn, Marvin, "Blacks in Miami," 53.
31. Miami-Dade Chamber of Commerce, *Tools for Change,* 9.
32. Hartley and Martinez, *Black Businesses.*
33. *City of Richmond vs. J. A. Croson Co.,* 488 U.S. 469 (1988); *Adarand Constructors, Inc. vs. Peña,* 115 S.Ct. 2097 (1995).
34. *Miami Herald,* September 20, 1996.

BIBLIOGRAPHY

INTERVIEWS

Adker, Ann Marie. Miami, 1991.

Baker, Dorothy. Miami, 1991.

Blue, Isabelle Sharpe. Miami, 1996.

Brown, John O., M.D. Miami, 1996.

Burke, James C. Miami, 1990.

Culmer, Mrs. John E. Miami, 1991.

Daughtery, Newall. Miami, 1990.

Davis, Louise Stirrup. Miami, 1990.

Dixon, Howard. Miami, 1991.

Dunn, Corine E. Miami, 1995.

Dunn, James C. Miami, 1995.

Edwards, Clarence. Miami, 1996.

Fair, T. Willard. Miami, 1990.

Ferguson, Wilke D., Jr. Miami, 1989.

Ferre, Maurice. Miami, 1992.

Foster, Gordon. Miami, 1990.

Graves, G. E. Miami, 1990.

Greer, Tee S. Miami, 1990.

Ingram, Robert. Miami, 1990.

Jennings, Wilhelmenia Franks. Miami, 1996.

Johnson, Ellen. Miami, 1990.

Johnson, Enid. Miami, 1996.

Johnson, Rebecca Gibson. Miami, 1991.

Johnson, William. Miami, 1990.

Jumper, Mabel. Seminole Indian Reservation, Dade County, 1990.

Kennedy, Stetson. Miami, 1990.

Laumer, Frank. Dade City, 1996.

Liberty, Eunice. Miami, 1991.

Macky, D. Miami, 1990.

McCrary, Jesse. Miami, 1996.

Miller, Helen. Miami, 1990.

Nimmo, James E. Miami, 1990.

Parrish, Sidney. Miami, 1990.

Phillips, Roy. Miami, 1990.

Porter, Gilbert. Miami, 1990.

Powell, Richard. Miami, 1996.

Range, M. Athalie. Miami, 1991.

Reeves, Garth. Miami, 1991.

Rogers, Barbara. Miami, 1991.

Sands, Portia. Miami, 1991.

Sawyer, William B., Jr., and Bernice Sawyer. Miami, 1991.

Smith, Lourena. Miami, 1992.

Stirrup, Franklin. Miami, 1990.

Trice, Jessie. Miami, 1989.

Turner, William "Bill." Miami, 1990.

Vickers, Milton. Miami, 1990.

Walker, Lydia Everett. Miami, 1990.

Wallace, Otis T. Miami, 1990.

Warren, Roscoe. Miami, 1990.

Wenski, Father Tom. Miami, 1990.

White, Ralph. Miami, 1990.

Williams, Eldridge F. Miami, 1990.

Wise, James. Miami, 1990.

Wright, Sonny. Miami, 1990.

BOOKS AND JOURNAL ARTICLES

Black, Hugo L., III. "Richard Fitzpatrick's South Florida, 1822–1840, Part I, Key West Phase." *Tequesta: The Journal of the Historical Association of Southern Florida* 40 (1980): 47–73.

Blank, Joan Gill. *Key Biscayne: A History of Miami's Tropical Island and the Cape Florida Lighthouse*. Sarasota: Pineapple Press, 1996.

Captain, Catherine. "The William Lozano Retrial." Miami: Florida International University, Psychology Department, 1993.

Carney, James J. "Population Growth in Miami and Dade County, Florida." *Tequesta: The Journal of the Historical Association of Southern Florida* 2, no. 6 (1946): 53.

CBS Reports. "Miami: The Trial That Sparked City Riots." August 27, 1980.

Cohen, Isidor. *Historical Sketches and Sidelights of Miami, Florida*. Cambridge: Cambridge University Press, 1925.

Crahan, Margaret E., and Franklin W. Knight. *Africa and the Caribbean: The Legacies of a Link*. Baltimore: Johns Hopkins University Press, 1979.

Culmer, Mrs. John E. *Homecoming Celebration*. Miami: St. Agnes Episcopal Church, 1981.

Dade County Grand Jury. "Final Report of the Spring Term, 1926."

———. "Report, March 23, 1928."

DeLand, Helen Parce. *Story of DeLand and Lake Helen Florida*. DeLeon Springs, Fla.: West Volusia Historical Society, 1990.

Dumenigo, Mite, and Josefina C. Gonzalez. *Dade School Desegregation.* Miami: Florida International University, Psychology Department, 1990.

Dunn, Marvin. "Blacks in Miami." In *Miami Now: Immigration, Ethnicity and Social Change,* edited by Guillermo J. Grenier and Alex Stepick III, 41–56. Gainesville: University Press of Florida, 1992.

———. *Specific Impact of Immigration upon the States; Demographic Consequences of Immigration.* U.S. Congress, Joint Economic Committee, Subcommittee on Economic Resources, Competitiveness and Security. 99th Cong., 1st sess., 1986.

Fernandez, Alfonzo. "Dade Blacks in Sports." Miami: Florida International University, Psychology Department, 1990.

Fleischmann, Thomas F. "Black Miamians in *The Miami Metropolis,* 1896–1900." *Tequesta: The Journal of the Historical Association of Southern Florida* 52 (1992): 21–38.

Fleitas, Iris. "The Impact of the 1926 Hurricane upon Blacks." In *Blacks in Miami, 1896–1990,* edited by Brian Peterson. Miami: Florida International University, History Department, 1990.

George, Paul S. "Colored Town: Miami's Black Community, 1896–1930." *Florida Historical Quarterly* 56, no. 4 (April 1978): 432–47.

———. "Criminal Justice in Miami, 1896–1930." Ph.D. diss., Florida State University, 1975.

———. "Policing Miami's Black Community, 1896–1930." *Florida Historical Quarterly* 57, no. 4 (April 1979): 434–50.

George, Paul S., and Thomas K. Petersen. "Liberty Square, 1933–1987: The Origin and Evolution of a Public Housing Project." *Tequesta: The Journal of the Historical Association of Southern Florida* 48 (1988): 53–68.

Glassman, Todd. "Miami Black Families vs. Bahamian Black Families: Range 1900–1910." In *Blacks in Miami, 1896–1990,* edited by Brian Peterson. Miami: Florida International University, History Department, 1990.

Greater Miami United. *Ethnic Audit: Documenting Dade's Diversity.* Miami, 1989.

Grenier, Guillermo J., and Alex Stepick III, eds. *Miami Now: Immigration, Ethnicity, and Social Change.* Gainesville: University Press of Florida, 1992.

Hafter, Eric. "The 1900 Dade County, Florida, African-American Community: A Cliometric Study." In *Blacks in Miami, 1896–1990,* edited by Brian Peterson. Miami: Florida International University, History Department, 1990.

Hartley, Kenny R., and Marilyn Martinez. *Black Businesses in Dade County.* Miami: Florida International University, Psychology Department, 1990.

Jimenez, Ricardo. "A Statistical Analysis of the Black American Population during 1900." In *Blacks in Miami, 1896–1990,* edited by Brian Peterson. Miami: Florida International University, History Department, 1990.

Kleinberg, Howard. *Miami Beach*. Miami: Centennial Press, 1994.

———. *Miami the Way We Were*. Tampa: Surfside Publishing, 1989.

Laumer, Frank. *Dade's Last Command*. Gainesville: University Press of Florida, 1995.

———. *Massacre*. Gainesville: University Press of Florida, 1968.

Marks, Henry S. "Labor Problems of the Florida East Coast Railway Extension from Homestead to Key West: 1905–1907." *Tequesta: The Journal of the Historical Association of Southern Florida* 32 (1972): 28–33.

McCarthy, Kevin M. *Black Florida*. New York: Hippocrene Books, 1995.

Merrick, George E. "Pre-Flagler Influences of the Lower Florida East Coast." *Tequesta: The Journal of the Historical Association of Southern Florida* 1 (March 1941): 1.

Metro-Dade County Planning Department. *Demographics of Black Americans in Dade County, 1989, Based on 1990 U.S. Census Report*. Metro-Dade County Planning Department.

———. "Profile of the Black Population 1990." In *An Analysis of Income Circulation in Black Dade County*. Miami, 1995.

Miami-Dade Chamber of Commerce. *Tools for Change: The Planned Process to Stimulate Black Economic Development in Dade County*. Miami, 1989.

Mohl, Raymond A. "The Pattern of Race Relations in Miami since the 1920s." In *The African American Heritage of Florida*, edited by David R. Colburn and Jane L. Landers, 326–56. Gainesville: University Press of Florida, 1995.

———. "Race and Space in the Modern City: Interstate–95 and the Black Community in Miami." In *Urban Policy in Twentieth-Century America*, edited by Arnold R. Hirsch and Raymond A. Mohl, 100–158. New Brunswick, N.J.: Rutgers University Press, 1993.

———. "Shadows in the Sunshine: Race and Ethnicity in Miami." *Tequesta: The Journal of the Historical Association of Southern Florida* 49 (1989): 63–80.

Munroe, Ralph Middleton, and Vincent Bilpin. *The Commodore's Story*. New York: Ives Washburn, 1930.

Overtown Advisory Committee. *Revival: An Overtown Resource Directory*. Miami, 1995.

Parks, Arva. *Miami the Magic City*. Tulsa: Continental Heritage Press, Inc., 1981.

Perez, Lisandro. "Cuban Miami." In *Miami Now: Immigration, Ethnicity and Social Change*, edited by Guillermo J. Grenier and Alex Stepick III, 83–108. Gainesville: University Press of Florida, 1992.

Peters, Thelma. *Biscayne Country: 1870–1926*. Miami: Banyan Books, 1981.

———. *Lemon City Pioneering on Biscayne Bay 1850–1925*. Miami: Banyan Books, 1976.

Peterson, Brian, ed. *Blacks in Miami, 1896–1990*. Miami: Florida International University, History Department, 1990.

Porter, Bruce, and Marvin Dunn. *The Miami Riot of 1980: Crossing the Bounds*. Lexington, Mass.: Lexington Books, 1984.

Rodriguez, Alma I., Mayra Casanova, Carlos Arias, and Luis Duran. "History of Miami: The Stirrup Family in Coconut Grove." In *Blacks in Miami, 1896–1990*, edited by Brian Peterson. Miami: Florida International University, History Department, 1990.

Rothman, Max B., Burton D. Dunlop, and Katherine M. Condon. *The Elders of Dade County: A Needs Assessment of Persons 60 and Over*. Miami: Florida International University, 1994.

Sewell, John. *John Sewell's Memoirs and History of Miami, Florida*. Vol. 1. Miami: Franklin Press, 1933.

Smith, Basil, and Gene Tinnie. "Goombay." In *Goombay Festival*. Miami: Jamye Associates, 1988.

Smith, Shauna. *Historical Black High Schools*. Miami: Florida International University, Psychology Department, 1990.

Stepick, Alex. "The Refugees Nobody Wants: Haitians in Miami." In *Miami Now: Immigration, Ethnicity and Social Change*, edited by Guillermo J. Grenier and Alex Stepick III, 57–82. Gainesville: University Press of Florida, 1992.

Stepick, Alex, Max Castro, Marvin Dunn, and Guillermo Grenier. "Changing Relations among Newcomers and Established Residents: The Case of Miami." Report to the Ford Foundation, 1990.

Taylor, Jean. *The Villages of South Dade*. St. Petersburg, Fla.: Byron Kennedy, 1985.

Taylor, Ronald L., ed. *Minority Families in the United States: A Multicultural Perspective*. Englewood Cliffs, N.J.: Prentice-Hall, 1994.

Tebeau, Charlton W. *A History of Florida*. Miami: University of Miami Press, 1971.

Tscheschlok, Eric. "Long Time Coming: Miami's Liberty City Riot of 1968." *Florida Historical Quarterly* 74, no. 4 (Spring 1996): 440–60.

Tully, Chris. "Race Relations and Segregation in Miami 1896–1920." In *Blacks in Miami, 1896–1990*, edited by Brian Peterson. Miami: Florida International University, History Department, 1990.

Wilbanks, William. *Forgotten Heroes: Police Officers Killed in Dade County, 1895–1995*. Paducah, Ky.: Turner Publications, 1996.

Wolfe, Herbert S., and Louis W. Ziegler. *Citrus Growing in Florida*. Gainesville: University Press of Florida, 1961.

Woodman, Jim. *Key Biscayne: The Romance of Cape Florida*. Miami: Miami Post Publishing Co., 1961.

Zumwalt, Estelle DesRocher. *Memoirs of Estelle DesRocher Zumwalt, a Miami Pioneer*. Edited by Thelma Peterson Peters. Miami: 1973.

NEWSPAPER ARTICLES

Daily Florida Citizen

"This Year's Orange Crop," December 28, 1894.

Florida Times-Union

"The Great Freeze of '94," January 13, 1895.

Miami Daily News

"Housing Project Site Turned Down," January 27, 1941, 1B.
"Coconut Grove Citizens Fight Negro Zone Change," June 12, 1941, 1B.
"Coconut Grove Citizens Win in Fight on Zoning," June 17, 1941, 1B.
"Navy Seeks Negroes for Steward Posts," February 8, 1942, 9A.
"Grove Residents Meet Tonight in Zone War," June 20, 1944, 1B.
"Negro Housing Plan in Grove Withdrawn," June 23, 1944.

Miami Daily News and Metropolis

"Florida Relief Fund Goes over 2 Million Mark," September 30, 1926.

Miami Herald

"Disfigures the City," October 5, 1911, 1A.
"Nassau Negro Laborers Are Coming Strong," September 26, 1912, 1A.
"Investigate Nassau Negroes Coming to Miami," November 17, 1914, 8.
"The Trials of a Negro Chauffeur," February 28, 1915, 5A.
"Again Negro Chauffeurs," December 1, 1915, 5A.
"Industrial School for Colored Pupils Will Resume Today," October 2, 1916, 3.
"Negro Chauffeur Was Given Protection," January 14, 1917, 1A.
"Negro Chauffeurs Replaced by White," March 25, 1917, 8A.
"300 Armed Men Rushed to Colored Town Following Explosion of Dynamite Bombs," June 30, 1920, 8.
"Colored Board of Trade Asked Strict Enforcement of Law and Prison Walls Bulge as Result," October 19, 1920, 1A.
"Kidnaped Negro Preacher Causes Race Riot Alarm; Bridge Guard Shoots Two," July 2, 1921, 1.
"Tar and Feather White Pastor of Negro Church," July 18, 1921, 1A.
"Auto Band Gets the Wrong One," July 26, 1921.
"Negro Beaten for Klan Talk," August 26, 1921, 1A.
"Flogged Negroes Hasten Departure," January 26, 1922, 8A.
"Negro Lynched Near Homestead; Killed Marshal," June 16, 1923, 1A.
"Police Sergeant Shot," July 16, 1925.
"Miami Police 'Terrorism' Is Revealed in Negro Death Probe Involving Quigg," March 2, 1928.

"Quigg Accused as Instigator of Death Ride," March 7, 1928.

"Grand Jury Report Reflects on Police," March 24, 1928, 2.

"Quigg Is Held for Murder in First Degree," March 24, 1928.

"Condemned Houses Will Be Torn Down," September 14, 1934, 11.

"Klan Parades, Burns Crosses to Frighten Off Negro Voters," May 3, 1939, 1.

"Twelve Candidates Bid for Miami Negroes' Vote," April 27, 1945, 2A.

"Negroes Test Beach Rights at Haulover," May 10, 1945, 1B.

"The Negro Vote," January 23, 1946, 6A.

"Pat Cannon, Smathers Assail Klan," April 7, 1946, 1C.

"State Supreme Court Rules County Can't Zone Negro Residence Areas: Segregation Powers Are Denied," May 1, 1946, 1B.

"Negro Housing Problem Awaits Solution by Committee," May 7, 1946, 6A.

"Negro Project Rejected," May 16, 1946, 1B.

"White Owners Fight Negro Housing Plan," May 21, 1946, 1B.

"Every Argument for Negro Housing," July 8, 1946, 4A.

"First Negro Officer Slain Outside Park," November 2, 1946, 1A.

"U.S. Allocation Approved, $90,000 Okayed for Slum Clearance," November 17, 1949, 1A.

"Florida Will Take High Court Ruling in Stride," May 18, 1954, 6A.

"Six Students' Fathers Also Sue," June 13, 1956, 1A.

"Integration Appearing Imminent: Final Decision Near in Two Suits," June 18, 1958, 2A.

"Supreme Court Voids Sentence-Fine," February 26, 1963, 1C.

"Grocery Store Owner Ponders What Went Wrong in Ten Years," June 21, 1970, 27A.

"Five Schools Granted Tax Breaks Will Be All White This Fall," July 24, 1970, 4A.

"Man Slain, Officer Shot," March 23, 1971, 1B.

"Blacks Stone Passersby after Arrest," January 25, 1979, 3C.

"His Skull Cracked as Police Raid Wrong House," February 14, 1979, 1A.

"Opa-Locka Disturbance Quelled," July 9, 1979, 1B.

"Cyclist's Death Termed a Murder," December 27, 1979, 1B.

"Florida Highway Patrol Trooper Molested Girl; He's Cured before His Victim," January 21, 1980, 1A, 16A.

"Trial Moved to Tampa," March 3, 1980, 1B.

"How Lawyers Judge the Jones Trial," May 4, 1980.

Dunn, Marvin. "The McDuffie Killing: A Black Leader Cries Out: What's Next?" June 6, 1980, Viewpoint.

"Rage at Verdict," May 18, 1980, 32A.

"Johnny Jones Takes the Heat—as Chief," June 18, 1982.

"Ex-School Chief Jones Seeks Reversal of Theft Conviction," December 26, 1982, 13D.

"Shooting by Cop Starts Overtown Disturbance," December 29, 1982, 1A.

"Was Victim Armed? Police Chief, Witness Disagree," December 29, 1982.

"Blacks Save White Judge from Overtown Attackers," December 30, 1982.

"Panel: Miami Blacks Still Isolated," January 12, 1983, 1A.

"End Busing, Black, White Parents Urge," January 20, 1983, 1D.

"Johnny Jones' Car Hits House, Kills Child," September 23, 1984.

"Segregated American Cities Slowly Blending," October 6, 1984, 1A.

"Suburban Equality," October 10, 1984, 20A.

"Board Action Urged to Ease Overcrowding," December 11, 1984, 1B.

"Board Gives Go-Ahead to Set Up New Transfer Rules," December 13, 1984, 2D.

"Schools Limit Transfers for Racial Balance," February 21, 1985, 1C.

Hines, Bea L. "Dr. Samuel Hensdale Johnson, the 85-year-old Patriarch of a Pioneer South Florida Family, Remembers Life on the Black Side of Town," February 25, 1985, 1C.

"Jones' 'Gold Plumbing' Conviction Reversed," February 27, 1985.

"Johnny Jones . . . Again," February 28, 1985.

"Johnny Jones Cleared in Fatal Wreck," August 10, 1985.

"Johnny Jones, IRS Settle Tax Case," October 24, 1985.

"Contrite Jones Seeks Reduction in Jail Sentence," December 4, 1985.

"Ex-Dade School Chief Released from Jail Term," December 7, 1985.

"State Won't Retry Jones Case," July 4, 1986.

"Integrate Teachers," June 13, 1987, 22A.

"Bitter Sweet Looks at the Old Grove," August 6, 1987, Neighbors section.

"Segregated Schools Blamed on Housing Patterns," November 1, 1987, 6B.

"Black Recruitment Erodes at Universities," December 6, 1987, 14B.

"Black-oriented Radio Stations Try to Calm Listeners," January 19, 1989, 2C.

"Violence a Shame, Say Miamians Held in Disorder," January 29, 1989, 1A.

"Firms Invest in High School Students' Future," August 4, 1989, 1B.

"Ousted Homesteaders Remember Indignity," August 25, 1989, 1B.

Dunn, Marvin. "Why the Lozano Trial Should Be Moved," October 29, 1989, Viewpoint.

"Lozano Trial Is Back on Track," November 14, 1989.

"For Lozano, Day in Court Is Here," November 15, 1989.

"A Sneak Preview of Education's Future," November 29, 1989, 21A.

"First Magnet School Expo Opens Recruiting Drive," November 30, 1989, 1B.

"Jury Finds Lozano Guilty," December 8, 1989.

"Cop-Killer Suspect Prays in 'Tombs,'" April 2, 1990, 1A.

"Less Needy Areas Are Getting Funds," May 17, 1990.

"Few Blacks at the Top in Tourism," September 30, 1990, 16A.

"Artson? Austin? Dorothy Fields Wants You," November 6, 1990, 19A.

"City Seeks Settlement in Two Deaths," April 6, 1991.

"Cop Killer 'Makes Peace with Everybody' Goes Free," September 12, 1991, 1B.

"Dade's Ethnic, Economic Gaps Broadened in 1980s," May 3, 1992, 1A.

"Police Learn Lessons from '80s Unrest," May 5, 1992.

"Race Gaps Persist in Home Loans: Black Buyers Face Subtle Barriers," May 10, 1992.

"College Board Member: Racism Hinders Blacks," June 6, 1992.

"Gun 'Epidemic' Killing Black Youths," June 10, 1992.

"Job Outlook Worsens for Black Teens," June 10, 1992, 1C.

"Miami Poverty Rate Is Number 4 in Country," June 25, 1992, 1B.

Offner, Paul. "Welfare Didn't Do It," March 19, 1995, Viewpoint.

Kleinberg, Howard. "A Patriot for All People," July 4, 1995, 15A.

"Minority Contractors Dealt Blow," September 20, 1996, 1.

Miami Metropolis

"A Military Company Needed," July 2, 1897.

"Riot at Key West," July 2, 1897.

"Fiendish Black Brute Brings Home to Us the Question: What Shall Be Done with These Black Sons of Hell?" January 23, 1903, 4.

Miami News

"They Number Few and Battle Hard," December 13, 1959, 2B.

"Dade School Chief Admits Blacks Bear Brunt of Busing," February 14, 1979, 7A.

"History Lives with the Naz'ree Eight," December 15, 1980, 1C.

"School Board Ponders Possible Busing Changes," March 31, 1983, 5A.

"Board Delays Transferring 225 Students," April 25, 1985, 5A.

"U.S. Desegregation Standards Threaten Florida College Aid," February 10, 1988, 1A.

Miami Times

"Dade Has Five Plans on Desegregation Integration Picture Here," July 7, 1956.

"Priest, Wife Beaten on Bus by Perry Police," August 18, 1956, 1A.

"Bi-Racial Effort Suggested Here," September 24, 1958, 1C.

"Alabama Boycott Leader Speaks Here Thursday," September 9, 1959, 1A.

"Burdines Blocks Ministers Sit-In," March 12, 1960, 1A.

"Protest Dance Bias," April 1, 1961, 1A.

New York Times

"Say Miami Police Shot Man to Death," March 27, 1928.

INDEX

Page numbers in italics refer to illustrations.